Silent Skies

Silent Skies

The Glider War
1939–1945

Tim Lynch

Pen & Sword
MILITARY

First published in Great Britain in 2008 by
Pen & Sword Military
an imprint of
Pen & Sword Books Ltd
47 Church Street
Barnsley
South Yorkshire
S70 2AS

ISBN 978 1 84415 736 5

A CIP catalogue record for this book is available from the British Library.

Typeset in Ehrhardt by Phoenix Typesetting, Auldgirth, Dumfriesshire

Printed and bound in England by Biddles Ltd, King's Lynn

Pen & Sword Books Ltd incorporates the Imprints of Pen & Sword Aviation,
Pen & Sword Maritime, Pen & Sword Military, Wharncliffe Local History,
Pen & Sword Select, Pen & Sword Military Classics and Leo Cooper.

For a complete list of Pen & Sword titles please contact
PEN & SWORD BOOKS LIMITED
47 Church Street, Barnsley, South Yorkshire, S70 2AS, England
E-mail: enquiries@pen-and-sword.co.uk
Website: www.pen-and-sword.co.uk

Contents

List of plates   vi

Acknowledgements   viii

Abbreviations   ix

Introduction   1

1. **The fourth flank**   3

2. **'Here are the Germans!':** Eben-Emael, 10 May 1940   8

3. **'Nothing is impossible':** the Glider Pilot Regiment   30

4. **'The graveyard of the paratroopers':** Mediterranean operations   37

5. **'Hitler's best friend in America':** the US glider programme   74

6. **'Any place, any time, anywhere':** operations in the Far East   81

7. **Over the west wall:** the invasion of Europe 1944–1945   101

8. **War behind the lines:** Russian glider operations 1941–1945   143

9. **Into the cauldron:** German operations on the Eastern Front   151

Epilogue   186

Notes   188

Appendices

    A Flying the Horsa   196

    B Towing techniqies   201

    C Technical details   203

Index   208

List of plates

German gliding enthusiasts after the First World War
Condor II glider in flight over the Wasserkuppe
Artist's impression of how gliders might be used against Britain
How the British press reported the attack on Eben-Emael
The victors of Eben-Emael
German airborne machine gun team ion action
German infantry at Eben-Emael after the attack
A Kirby Kite prepares for takeoff
The King inspects the newly formed airborne force
A Hotspur training glider prepares for launch
British troops in training with the Horsa glider
The Airspeed Horsa coming in to land
Crete: a crashed DFS 230 and its crew
General Kurt Student
Crete's Maleme airfield after the invasion
General Henry H 'Hap' Arnold with a CG-4A glider
Loading the Waco
A glider 'snatch' pickup demonstration in the US
A wrecked German Go242 glider in the North African desert
An Me323 comes under attack
Skorzeny's men prepare for their mission
Skorzeny escorts Mussolini to safety
Burma: a casualty evacuation flight
Burma invasion: Colonel Alison with Wingate and staff on 'Broadway'
A bulldozer being loaded into a Waco
Russian paratroops prepare for operations
Colonel Philip C Cochran
A pilot's eye view of 'Rommel's Asparagus'
A high altitude shot of British landing zones after D-Day
British Hamilcar gliders prepare for D-Day resupply mission
A crashed Hamilcar in Normandy
A contemporary advert for the Hamilcar glider
A Hamilcar on 'high tow' behind a Halifax bomber
British glider pilots after receiving awards at Buckingham Palace
Glider pilot and his tug captain
A Normandy landing zone: a safe landing could be difficult
A Go242 prepares to cast off over Russia
A DFS 230 and its passengers
Allied glider fleet during Operation Overlord
A bust of Colonel Otway
Pilot's eye view of a Horsa on tow
A roadside marker overlooks the LZ of the 6th Airborne north of Ranville
A CG10 'Trojan Horse' on exercise in the US
Artist's impression of the Hamilcar on tow behind a Stirling bomber

Acknowledgements

The story of the glider war is drawn from a number of sources, mainly from the stories left behind by the men of both sides who flew to war in circumstances the rest of us can only try to imagine. I hope this book does justice to their courage.

My thanks go to David Brook of the Glider Pilot Regimental Association for his polite and speedy responses to my requests for help. Anyone interested in British glider operations would do well to subscribe to the association's journal *The Eagle* for its fascinating accounts and profiles of the pilots themselves (c/o David Brook, Birds Hill, Great Bealings, Woodbridge, Suffolk, IP13 6NR). Ray Cunningham and the staff of the Assault Glider Trust were generous in allowing me to visit their project and sparking my interest in the Horsa. Thanks, too, to Joe Larkin for permission to use the photograph taken by his father, Philip M Larkin, Sgt/Photographer 30th Photographic Reconnaissance Squadron, United States Army 9th Air Force, on 7 June 1944. Thanks also to Denis Edwards, one of the first to land at Pegasus Bridge, for his generosity in allowing me to quote from his description of the landing. Further help came from Martin Mace who supplied some of the photos used. At Pen & Sword, Rupert Harding championed the idea for the book and has been a source of encouragement throughout.

Several personal accounts proved invaluable in gaining an insight into the life of a glider pilot. Ronald Seth's *The Lion with Blue Wings* (Panther 1959) is a highly readable account of the GPR whilst John L. Lowden's *Silent Wings at War* (Smithsonian 1992) describes the American point of view. Gerard Devlin's *Silent Wings* (St Martin's Press 1985) tells the story of glider warfare from a primarily US perspective and Alan Wood's *History of the World's Glider Forces* (Patrick Stephens 1990) is just that, a wide-ranging account of the aircraft and operations of all nations. Kevin Shannon and Stephen Wright's *One Night in June* (Airlife 1994) is a must for anyone interested in the 6th Airborne's landing in Normandy. The Allied effort is well documented but I owe a huge debt to Georg Schlaug, whose *Die deutschen Lastensegler Verbände 1937–1945* (Motorbuch Verlag Stuttgart 1985) is the only account available of German glider operations.

Finally, my wife Jacqueline and children Bethany and Josh are all owed thanks for accepting that there comes a point in a man's life when he feels the need to lock himself away and look at pictures of things. It could have been worse guys!

The photographs in this book are taken from a variety of sources. Where possible, they are accredited but some are taken from contemporary publications where the source is either unaccredited or has been impossible to trace. No breach of copyright is intended and anyone affected is invited to contact the author.

Abbreviations

AAC Army Air Corps, formed in 1941, comprising the Parachute Regiment, the Glider Pilot Regiment and attached arms. Technically it also covered the Special Air Service although they remained independent. In 1957, the modern AAC was formed by the amalgamation of the Glider Pilot Regiment with the Air Observation Post Squadrons who acted as spotter planes for the artillery.

CG Cargo glider. The US Air Force categorizes all aircraft by function and gives a number to each design. The most widely used glider was the CG-4, also known as the Waco after its designers but often built by other aircraft companies.

CLE Central Landing Establishment: the British airborne training centre at Manchester's Ringway airfield (now Manchester Airport). Once confused with the Central Laundry Establishment!

DFS Deutsche Forschungsanhalt für Segelflug. The German sail plane research centre, a subsidiary of the Rohen Research Institute originally developing flying observatories for meteorological experiments. The design became the basis of the widely used DFS 230 glider.

DZ Drop zone: an area designated for the landing of parachute troops and supplies.

FO Flight officer: US rank for glider pilots. Commissioned by warrant, they were sometimes referred to as Third Lieutenants – somewhere between enlisted ranks and 'real' officers but enjoying the perks of both.

GAL General Aircraft Ltd, builders of the British Hotspur and Hamilcar gliders.

GO Gotha 242 glider (German).

GPR Glider Pilot Regiment (British).

LLG Luftlande Gruppe: German equivalent of an air landing unit.

LS *Lastensegler*: German term for a glider.

LZ   Landing zone: an area designated for the landing of aircraft including gliders.

RAF   Royal Air Force. Although glider pilots were, for the most part, army personnel, their training was carried out by the RAF, who supplied the tug aircraft to tow the gliders to their destination.

RV   Rendezvous: the meeting point for troops after landing.

SDP   Supply Dropping Point.

TCC   Troop Carrier Command: the US Air Force units tasked with the delivery of airborne troops and supplies.

Introduction

For thousands of years, men dreamed of flight and the power it would bring. Legends of flying warriors bringing death from the skies inspired attempts by the learned, the brave and the foolish to leap from high places in the hopes of finding the secret of flight, knowing that, as Friar Joseph Galien (1699–1762) had speculated, once controlled flight had been achieved it should be possible 'to transport a whole army and all their munitions of war from place to place as desired'. In 1784, shortly after witnessing the ascent of the Charles hydrogen balloon in Paris, Benjamin Franklin wrote that

> five thousand balloons, capable of raising two men each, could not cost more than five ships of the line; and where is the prince who can afford so to cover his country with troops for its defence, as that ten thousand men descending from the clouds might not in many places do an infinite deal of mischief before a force could be brought together to repel them?[1]

Throughout the Napoleonic wars fanciful engravings of French troops descending from the heavens by balloon as others tunnelled under the Channel appeared in British newspapers and propaganda pamphlets but balloons, so dependent on wind direction, remained too unreliable to use as a weapon of war.

It would not be until the mid-nineteenth century when Sir George Cayley sent his coachman by glider across a valley near his Yorkshire home that the dream appeared to be finally within reach. The race now was on to attain the next step – powered flight. Fifty years later, Orville and Wilbur Wright, using a design inspired by Cayley's glider, finally crawled into the sky. Within a single lifetime, men would reach the moon.

In the race to find the secret of powered flight, the glider was all but forgotten but in April 1905, shortly after the Wright brothers made their famous flight, the *Santa Clara*, a tandem winged glider made a high altitude flight watched by over 15,000 people in Santa Clara, California. Designed by Professor John Montgomery of the nearby Jesuit College and piloted by a circus acrobat, Daniel Maloney, the *Santa Clara* was lifted to a height of 4,000 feet by a hot air balloon and released. Maloney took the glider through a series of gentle turns before making a perfect landing less than a mile from the launch site. Four more aircraft were built and taken to shows around California until, on 18 July 1905, a tail brace broke as the glider left the balloon and Maloney plunged to his death just feet from the horrified spectators. Six years later, Montgomery himself would die in a fall of just twenty feet. Yet despite these deaths and the attention given to powered flight, glider manufacturers sprang up across America and by 1910 enthusiasts were experimenting with launching themselves by being towed behind cars.

In the aftermath of the First World War, gliding again began to gain popularity as a sport and aircraft design and flying techniques developed rapidly. German flyers, frustrated by the limitations of the catapult launches available to them, had introduced the concept of towing gliders behind a powered aircraft to gain much greater height and longer flights. The system was introduced to Britain by the unlikeliest of aviation pioneers, romantic novelist Barbara Cartland. Together with two RAF officer friends, Cartland undertook experiments with a 200-mile tow of an aircraft named in her honour and proposed the setting up of an airmail service by glider.[2] Across the world, the ease with which a glider could be towed by a light aircraft made it possible for cargo, especially mail, to be 'snatched' off the ground by lifting its tow rope between two poles where a hook on a low flying powered plane could catch it and raise the glider without ever having to land, making it possible for gliders to operate out of very small airfields. Other experiments showed that several gliders could be towed at one time in what would become known as 'skytrains' and some of these operated in Central Europe for several years. Despite these experiments, though, few countries felt the need to develop cargo gliders for more general use. They may be a nice gimmick, but for the most part, what could they accomplish that ordinary aircraft could not?

The answer came on 10 May 1940, when German DFS 230 gliders delivered an attacking force inside the perimeter of Belgium's Fort Eben-Emael in a stunning coup de main. Within a year, British and American glider projects would be racing to catch up. Within five years, gliders would be the most numerous aircraft of the Second World War. Within ten years the concept would be obsolete.

In those ten years, tens of thousands of gliders would be developed across the world – nearly ninety different types produced in sixteen countries. Around 14,000 of a single type, the US CG-4A Waco (known to the British as the 'Hadrian'), would make it the most widely used aircraft of the war. Their use would range from assault gliders delivering troops to specific targets to the development of the armed Blohm and Voss BV40 Fighter Glider, designed to be towed by a powered fighter and then released to dive onto Allied bomber formations, twin 30 mm cannons blazing. Transport gliders would carry tanks and troops into battle in aircraft so large that it would not be for another thirty years that the Boeing 747 Jumbo Jet would match their wingspan, whilst at the other extreme, the tale of Daedalus and his escape would inspire the building of a glider by prisoners under the very noses of guards at the notorious Colditz Castle.

What follows is the story of the glider years.

Chapter One

The fourth flank

Even as gliding as a sport was becoming an established pastime in the early years of the twentieth century, war clouds were gathering over Europe and attention turned to developing faster, stronger and more powerful aircraft and new uses for them. During the First World War, the use of airborne operations became possible and small teams of special agents jumped by parachute or were landed behind enemy lines on all fronts – the Italians being especially active – but no large-scale actions could yet be undertaken from the aircraft available. Aerial resupply had been used as early as March 1916 to drop supplies to British troops besieged at Kut-el-Amara in Mesopotamia and more than 7 tons were eventually delivered this way. Italian aircraft were especially successful in dropping ammunition to its advancing troops in October 1918 and imaginative leaders began to explore ways in which this new mobility could be exploited. At one point Winston Churchill proposed dropping troops behind enemy lines to destroy key bridges but the plan was shelved, although similar French teams did operate in the Ardennes.

By September 1918, US General William 'Billy' Mitchell commanded a joint Franco-American force of almost 1,500 aircraft and frequently used 200 or more aircraft at a time for the mass bombing of enemy targets, sharing his British counterpart Major-General Hugh Trenchard's view that air power was a vital element of land warfare. As the US First Army fought its way slowly through the Argonne Valley, losing 117,000 men in an advance of less than thirty-two miles, a young officer named Lewis H Brereton proposed an audacious scheme to drop the US 1st Division by parachute from a force of Handley-Page 0/400 bombers to capture the fortified city of Metz. This, he believed, would allow them to leapfrog the fierce German resistance, capture a major defensive position and cut off rail supply to the Germans through the important rail junction in the city. Suitable parachutes were available, having been developed first as a fairground stunt but now adapted for use by the crews of observation balloons who were, quite literally, sitting targets for fighter planes. Although the British Air Board had refused their use by combat pilots, arguing that the provision of an escape mechanism 'invited cowardice in action' (an attitude that would cost around 6,000 lives before the order was overturned in September 1918), no barriers to their use by infantrymen could be found. Mitchell championed the idea but it was halted by the American Expeditionary Force's commander,

General 'Black Jack' Pershing. It would be almost exactly twenty-six years before Brereton saw his plan in action – as commander of the First Allied Airborne Army during Operation Market-Garden in September 1944 and in the years after the war, 'Billy' Mitchell's maverick ideas about the use of air power and 'vertical envelopment' by parachute troops would lead to his eventual court-martial and resignation from the army. He died in 1935 but was posthumously reinstated as a general in the United States Army in 1946 after many of his theories had been proved effective in action.[1]

After the First World War, neither Britain nor America saw any real use for parachute troops but set up training centres purely for the use of air crews. Britain made a few tentative steps towards developing air landing forces by taking delivery of the new twin-engined Vickers Vernon troop carrier in 1922 and using it to rapidly move troops into Iraq to capture dissident tribesmen. Ten years later, infantrymen of the 1st Northamptons were again airlifted into Iraq to quell another anti-British revolt. The American military considered para-chuting to be little more than an entertaining stunt but airlifted US Marines into Central and South America for small-scale policing missions. Some experiments were conducted in the use of parachutes for infantry use but, to use Andre Beaufre's memorable phrase, the allies 'suffered from victory'. Defence spending was low and public opinion strongly anti-military as nations struggled to cope with the massive losses incurred by 1918. Year upon year defence spending was cut to the point that, by 1940, General Bernard Montgomery, then a divisional commander of the British Expeditionary Force in France, complained that some units were unfit to take part in even a realistic exercise, let alone a real war. Sending them into combat, he claimed 'would be sheer massacre'. Faced with financial constraints that prevented even large-scale exer-cises in the late 1930s, the development of new aggressive units took a very low priority.

Elsewhere, though, other armies took a different approach. The Italians, having gained enormously from their use of special teams operating behind Austrian lines, began experiments with parachute troops near Milan in 1927 and opened a second school near Tripoli in 1938 for Italian officers and colonial volunteers. Russia, too, had made good use of airdropped agents during the First World War and by the 1930s parachuting had become a national sport. A 1931 drop of fifteen paratroopers in an operation against bandits at Basmach in Central Asia had demonstrated the potential of such forces and by 1932 four airborne motorized units were formed along with, by 1936, thirty battalions of trained parachute infantry. In the autumn of 1935, Red Army manoeuvres were carried out to demonstrate the new air landing capability to an international audience of military observers. Archibald Wavell, a highly decorated and experienced British officer, watched in amazement as 1,000 paratroops dropped from the skies to be joined by another 2,500 fully equipped soldiers and heavy equipment landed by aircraft and together carried out infantry assaults on nearby targets. 'If I had not seen it for myself' he later wrote, 'I should not have believed it possible'. Impressive as it was, the British War Office chose not to take the matter further. Other observers, however, did.

In 1920, the humiliating Treaty of Versailles formally disbanded the German air force and no fewer than 14,000 aircraft and 25,000 engines were lost as a result. Thousands of former fighter and bomber pilots found themselves grounded. At the same time, the Reichsheer (the German army) had been reduced from six million men to a mere 100,000 and the Reichsmarine (German navy) to 15,000 including 1,500 officers. The Treaty had ensured that the German military would be a toothless force for defence only.

The years immediately following the end of the First World War were chaotic for Germany. The Russian Revolution had inspired communists in Germany to form the Spartakusbund (named after the leader of the slaves' revolt in ancient Rome) and when, in October 1918, the German navy was ordered to sea for one last glorious battle, its ships became afflicted with an epidemic of mechanical trouble. Red flags even appeared on the masts of some battleships and by 6 November the whole coastal region was controlled by the mutineers. Troops ordered to suppress the mutineers joined them instead. Eventually, army units with artillery support were brought in and thirty mutineers died in the ensuing fighting.

The mutiny and other civil disturbances, together with near economic collapse, made restoring order a priority not only for the German government but for the Allied occupation forces too and so a volunteer force of seasoned combat veterans was recruited to act as a peace-keeping force with 4,000 men deployed in a series of bloody clashes against the Spartacus rebels in the streets of Berlin. With Allied approval, fighting against the Russians continued along Germany's eastern borders and fear of communist takeover was used to recruit still more volunteers for the so-called Freikorps. Nearly a quarter of a million volunteers eventually came forward and the fluid nature of guerrilla warfare within Germany would prove to be the ideal training for the emerging tactics of *blitzkrieg*.

Elsewhere, cadres of experienced NCOs were hidden within the ranks of the Prussian police – a force that, armed with armoured cars, machine guns, rifles and pistols would eventually reach a strength of 85,000 men. Among them, the fourteen officers and 400 men of Police Group Wenke had been raised in 1933 by Goering in his capacity as Chief of Prussian police as an anti-terrorist unit to break up revolutionary political meetings and cells. In January 1936, these men were chosen to become the core of the newly emerging Luftwaffe's parachute force. Aware of the Russian advances in airborne warfare, Goering, now Supreme Commander of the Luftwaffe, brought his pet project under the command of the armed forces and thus formed the nucleus of a force that would eventually become eleven divisions strong and would, in a series of devastating attacks, change the face of land warfare forever.[2]

The Treaty of Versailles was specific about military aircraft but failed to make any reference to gliders so that, as early as 1919, former air force pilots began to form gliding clubs to enable them to fly again. By 1920, Oskur Ursinius, editor of *Flugsport* (Sport Flying) was able to announce the first national flying competition to be held that summer at Mount Wasserkuppe, soon to become the mecca of glider pilots everywhere. The following year, Frederic Harth, flying a glider built with the assistance of a young man whose name would become a byword for later aircraft design – Willi Messerschmitt – effortlessly rode the thermals rising up the mountains. Previously, gliding had simply been a matter of flying in a straight line down a slope but Harth proved that soaring flight opened up all kinds of possibilities.

Among those watching the rise in popularity of gliding was Kurt Student, himself a keen glider pilot who would sustain a fractured skull in an accident in 1921. Student had been a cadet at the Imperial Military College at the age of 11 and had, in 1913, volunteered for flying duties fully expecting (and, indeed, hoping) to be rejected. Instead he found he was an able pilot and flew fighters throughout the war. Student and his wife took a paternalistic interest in the young flyers they encountered at gliding competitions across Germany in the 1920s, providing encouragement and financial help to promising pilots. Student was more than a rich enthusiast, though. Since 1920, he had been working in the Fliegerzentrale (Central Flying Office), tasked with the seemingly impossible job of equipping the non-existent German Air Force for future operations. Gliding, he believed, provided the perfect cover for the basic training of Germany's future pilots. Sport flying in Germany had become extraordinarily popular and by 1932 the German glider-flying association had over 60,000 active members. Seven years later, as Germany equipped for war, Goering had 300,000 glider enthusiasts from whom he could pick potential military pilots.

Russia, meanwhile, had not been a signatory to the Treaty of Versailles, nor had it been invited to join the League of Nations. Like Germany, Russia had a Socialist government and was treated as an outcast by the rest of the world and the two countries had much in common. In 1921, Lenin requested German help in training the new Red Army in return for which Germany would be allowed access to factory sites and training grounds far from prying western eyes.

In 1928, Student reverted to command of a battalion of an infantry regiment but took with him his ideas about the use and value of airborne troops. By 1938, his ideas had gained favour with Hitler and he was appointed as major-general in command of the 7th Air Division and given a free hand to build up the formation. Among the equipment available to him was a new development of an old friend.

In 1932, an experimental glider had been developed by the Rhoen-Rossiten-Gesellschaft Research Institute in Munich to act as a 'flying observatory' to allow meteorological readings to be taken at high altitudes without vibration or noise interference. Hitler himself took an interest in the project and raised the question of whether large gliders could be developed for military purposes. As early as 1933, Russian pilots had begun testing cargo-carrying gliders and reports from Student and others who had been involved in glider training in both Germany and Russia had recognized the potential of such aircraft in supporting infantry on the ground. Student believed that Germany should go a step further. Gliders could be used, he argued, not only for supply missions, but as a weapon in itself, capable of delivering assault troops directly on to their objective. Classified 'secret', the project was turned over to the Deutsche Forschungsantalt für Segelflug (DFS or German Gliding Research Institute) and testing of the DFS 230 commenced in 1937.[3]

In June, 1939, senior airborne commanders had discussed the use of special teams of assault troops within the paratroop division and concluded that new tactics were needed to allow these elite groups to fulfill their mission. The design of both parachute and transport aircraft meant that, in order to jump successfully, both hands were needed to push the jumper out of the door in a horizontal dive, otherwise the tremendous force of the static line used to open the parachute could break ribs. This in turn meant that parachutists could not carry equipment or even a rifle so the *Fallschirmjaeger* jumped into action armed only with a pistol, collecting their weapons from canisters dropped from bomb racks at the same time as each 'stick' jumped. Worse, the Junkers Ju52 transport aircraft could only carry twelve men and a typical parachute drop spread the jumpers across at the very least a 300m area even in ideal conditions. Regrouping would take time and they would then have to locate and retrieve their equipment before the mission could start. (Even today, planners assume that in ideal conditions a large-scale parachute drop will require around fifteen minutes to become effective.) In contrast, the new DFS 230 glider, able to carry ten men and a sizeable equipment load, could land silently within 60 feet of a target and deliver a combat-ready force in a fraction of the time. Trials began immediately.

Chapter Two

'Here are the Germans!':
Eben-Emael, 10 May 1940

At noon on 27 October 1939, General Kurt Student, Commander of Germany's 7th Flieger (Airborne) Division received orders to visit the Fuhrer 'alone and without delay'. From his headquarters at Templehof airfield a limousine whisked him to the Chancellery where the puzzled general was immediately led in to see Hitler. Beckoning him to over to his desk, Hitler laid out a set of maps and aerial photographs of the most modern fortifications in the world – the Belgian Fort of Eben-Emael. 'For the war in the West' – Hitler hesitated, seeming unsure how to ask the question,

> . . . I know you have made some tests with gliders. You have some in your Division. I have a job for you and I want to know if you can do it. The Belgians have a fort here . . . The top is like a grassy meadow. They have heavy artillery in cupolas and casemates. I think some of our silent gliders could land on top of the fort and your men storm the works. Is that possible?[1]

It was a formidable task. First proposed in 1887 in the wake of the Franco-Prussian War by the Belgian fort designer General Henri Brialmont, Eben-Emael was the latest of a string of powerful fortifications built along the line of the Albert Canal to defend Belgium's border with Germany around the 'Vise Gap', an area whose loss, Brialmont warned, would cause Belgium to 'weep tears of blood'. In 1914, four of the twelve forts built in the late nineteenth century around the city of Liège to defend Belgium's command centre had been completely destroyed by the siege artillery of General von Kluck's 1st German Army as it crossed the Maas River not far from where Fort Eben-Emael now stood. The construction of the Albert Canal had created a formidable moat and, where it cut through the Caster hill near the towns of Eben and Emael, produced near-vertical 60 metre high cliffs which, coupled with an existing cliff along the Meuse River, provided protection for two flanks and an ideal location for a fortification. Construction began in April 1932 and continued at a relentless pace until completion in 1935 to create a diamond-shaped, two-storey reinforced artillery position 900 m long and 700 m wide with a commanding view of the surrounding area. Its mission was to protect the Vise Gap to the south, the road and bridge network in the north, the Albert Canal due east, and lastly, if required, Belgium to the west. Fully manned, the fort held a garrison of 1,322 men roughly separated into two groups of around 500 artillery men and the rest technical and administrative staff. Garrison commander Major Jean Fritz Lucien Jottrand was, in turn, under the direction of the Regiment of the Fortress of Liège as the regional headquarters.

The fort's weapons systems were separated into two batteries. Battery 1 was composed of the artillery cupolas such as Cupola 120, a fixed non-retractable

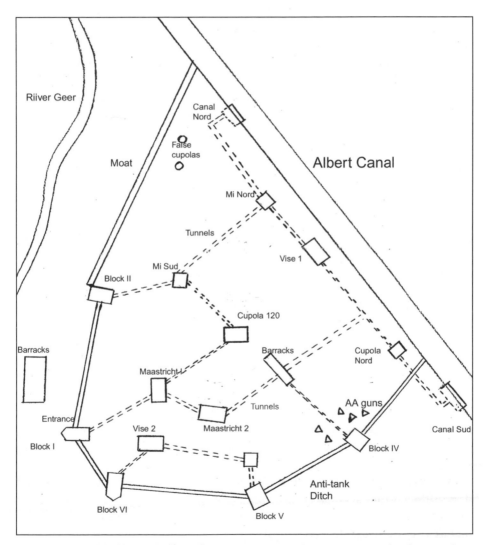

Sketch map of layout of surface of the fort showing German targets for the attack.

cupola that held two 120 mm guns capable of revolving through 360 degrees and with a range of eleven miles; two more 75 mm cupolas named 'Nord' and 'Sud', which could be retracted into the underground fort, could also revolve their guns through 360 degrees and had a range of seven miles, and finally four casements with three 75mm guns each capable of firing five miles through a more limited arc of 70 degrees ('Maastricht 1' and 'Maastricht 2' oriented to the north, with 'Vise 1' and 'Vise 2' to the south).

Battery 2, responsible for local defence, could call upon ten bunkers (usually referred to as 'blocks'), eight of them armed with one or two 60 mm anti-tank guns, five 60 mm anti-aircraft guns and eleven machine-gun positions with 30-calibre machine guns, searchlights and a small observation cupola covering the approaches. On the top of the fort were seven anti-aircraft machine guns, three false cupolas and three more large observation platforms for the forts in Liège sited in cupolas named Eben 1, 2 and 3. Six further observation cupolas were spread throughout the neighbouring countryside overlooking the Albert Canal and its bridges. Inside, seven miles of tunnels were divided into two levels with the ground floor containing barracks, machinery, generators for the heating, air conditioning, decontamination system, water purification from its internal well and a hospital. The intermediate level directly supported the batteries with fire direction control, command and control and ammunition storage. Little wonder that Fort Eben-Emael was widely regarded as virtually impregnable.

In itself, the fort was never really expected to stop an invasion, merely to delay it for as long as possible. Its artillery was tasked with covering three crucial bridges crossing the Albert Canal at the towns of Vroenhoven, Veltwezelt and Canne where von Kluck's army had advanced a quarter of a century before. Control of these bridges could facilitate or deny any invasion so, as historian James E. Mrazek put it, 'The artillery had to support the Belgian infantry which protected these bridges by preventing the enemy from getting close to or taking them. If the bridges fell to the enemy, the fort's artillery had to fire on and destroy the bridges.'[2] Stores for two months were kept stockpiled inside the fort but opinion differed on its likely effectiveness in the event of invasion with the French commander Gamelin confidently predicting it would hold out for five days at best. German estimates, however, suggested at least two weeks and that a direct ground assault could take anything up to six months and cost over 6,000 casualties. In any case, neither timescale suited the German plans for Western Europe.

One month before his meeting with Student, on 27 September 1939, Hitler had informed his General Staff of his decision to invade France and ordered plans made ready. Within weeks, General Walther von Brauchitsch, Commander in Chief, and his Chief of Staff General Franz Halder briefed Hitler on their proposed attack, codenamed *Fall Gelb* (Plan Yellow). As first presented, the plan was simply an enlarged version of the 1914 Schlieffen Plan intended to outflank the Maginot Line to the north with the bulk of the Army attacking through the Netherlands and Belgium. A smaller force would then push through the lightly defended Ardennes and attack into Eastern France. General Erich von Manstein, Chief of Staff for Army Group A, and General Heinz Guderian, XIX Panzer Corps Commander, were both highly critical. In fact, when von Manstein obtained a copy the plan from Berlin in October 1939, he was dismayed. 'I found it humiliating, to say the least,' he later wrote, 'that our generation could do nothing better than repeat an old recipe.' The plan he was presented with anticipated only 'partial victory', not defeating France but only seeking to gain control of large parts of it as a base of operations and he quickly set about revising it to maximize the effects of the *blitzkrieg* ('lightning war') tactics developed by General Heinz Guderian.

When, in January 1940, plans for the attack fell into Allied hands following a plane crash, Hitler was forced to seek alternatives and General von Manstein was able to argue forcefully for his proposal that the attack into the Netherlands and Belgium would be a supporting attack, with the main effort going through the Ardennes near Sedan. On 24 February 1940 the fifth and final version of Plan Yellow was issued, calling for Army Group A, under General Gerd von Rundstedt, to break through the Allied centre and attack through the Ardennes with a total of forty-five divisions, including seven panzer formations, to thrust towards the French coast at Abbeville. Army Group B, commanded by General

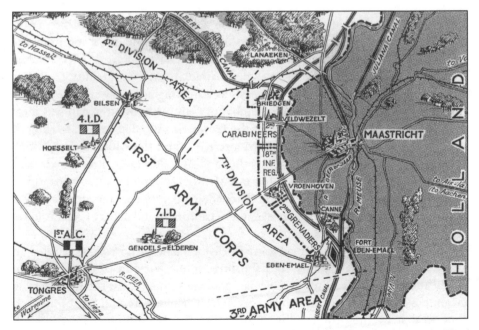

Contemporary map of the area around Eben-Emael with the fort, bridges and Allied units marked.

Kurt Arthur Benno Student

In 1945, Student surrendered to the British and was held at the Island Farm camp at Bridgend in south Wales where he was interrogated about allegations of the mistreatment and murder of prisoners of war and was indicted for war crimes committed in Crete at the Nuremburg trials. Goering had ordered the deportation of male Cretan civilians over the age of 14 in reprisal for a series of horrific partisan attacks on German troops in which captured soldiers were reported to have been crucified and mutilated. During the trial it emerged that Student had been able to undermine the order and New Zealander General Inglis testified that Student had opposed the activities of the SS in the island. In May 1947, the charges were reduced to having failed to prevent war crimes and Student was found guilty of three of the eight counts and sentenced to five years in prison, but the verdict was never confirmed. In September 1947, the Greeks asked to have Student turned over to them, but this request was refused. Later Student was given a medical discharge and was released from prison in 1948. Student was married and had one son, who died on military service. He was known for his energy, intelligence, precision and drive but had few interests outside of his career and hunting. He died aged 88 in Lemgo, West Germany, on 1 July 1978.

Fedor von Bock, would attack into Belgium and the Netherlands with twenty-nine divisions including the remaining three divisions of panzers and draw the French and British to the Dyle Line. If the diversion was to be successful in drawing the allies and preventing a flank attack on the vulnerably stretched supply lines of Army Group A, the slower moving infantry units of Army Group B would need to reach the Gembloux Gap. Although the gap was ideal for the type of highly mobile warfare the Germans intended to use, to reach it they first needed a way to cross the Meuse River and the Albert Canal, which ran parallel to it. Three bridges across the canal at Veldwezelt, Vroenhoven and Canne and three more across the Meuse at Maastricht would need to be captured intact prior to any German advance. The whole operational concept hinged on the destruction of Fort Eben-Emael and the capture of the Albert Canal bridges at the very beginning of the campaign.

Student considered the problem. Both men knew the risks involved in attacking strong fortifications. The fighting around Verdun in 1916 had been costly and inconclusive and the German plan could not afford the time to try a ground assault. For this mission to succeed, the Belgians could not be allowed time to destroy the bridges already prepared for demolition. The DFS 230 glider, carrying ten men and equipment weighing no more than 4,608 lb, could land alongside its target silently and deliver a combat-ready force in a fraction of the time it would take to land an effective parachute unit and seemed the ideal choice for the mission, with the initial attack by glider supported by parachuted reinforcements later. Suitable drop and landing zones existed near the bridges, allowing the reinforcements to be dropped once the Belgian defenders had been overwhelmed. The real problem would be the guns at Eben-Emael and their ability to destroy the bridges from the safety of the fort itself. Student thought the idea sounded both incredible and brilliant but he was unsure and told the Fuhrer he would need to think it over.

During the night, Student wargamed the scenarios and concluded that such a precision assault could not be carried out in a night attack but he told Hitler that the plan 'may be possible under very special circumstances: the landing must be made in daylight, or at least morning twilight and not before; and I am uncertain about the amount and type of explosives needed to be used against the forti- -fications'.[3] With great enthusiasm, Hitler then described a newly developed type of explosive charge, the *Hohlladung* or 'hollow charge'. The principles of a hollow charge had first been described in 1888 by Charles Munroe. It works by allowing a conventional explosion to create a jet of high pressure which gener- ates a tremendous penetrating capability using a relatively small charge. The force of the explosion melts a steel liner and sends a molten metal stream of hot gases and metal splinters through a narrow hole into the target so that, used against armour, 'the explosion would generally blow a one foot hole in the objec- tive and kill everyone inside'. German munitions scientists had perfected the technique and developed a weapon capable of blowing a hole in any known type of steel or concrete. Used properly, Hitler enthused, nothing could withstand it. The large 50 kg charge, capable of penetrating up to ten inches, was divided into two spheres and needed a team of two or three men to assemble the two halves, put it into place as a demolition charge, fuse and detonate it. A smaller single sphere 12.5 kg charge was also available and capable of penetrating up to six inches. Student listened, amazed. Such a weapon made the whole thing not only possible, but almost certain to succeed. Forty-eight hours after their first meeting, Hitler told Student: 'I order you to take Fort Eben-Emael. All aspects of the operation must remain absolutely secret. The code name for this operation will be GRANIT.'

A week later, on 2 November 1939, Hauptmann Walter Koch, a 30-year-old former member of the Prussian Police's Herman Goering Regiment, was notified of a move for himself and men of the 1st Company, 1st Battalion Fallschirmjaeger-Regiment 1 (FJR-1 or 1st Parachute Regiment) to Hildesheim, where they would form part of 'Test Section Friedrichshafen'. There he would be joined by Leutnant Rudolf Witzig and men of the Pioneer Platoon of the 2nd Battalion FJR-1 and by Leutnant Kiess from the division's glider group – supplemented by a number of gliding champions with proven ability to perform precision landings who had been 'invited' to join the group. The unit was soon retitled *Sturmabteilung* (Assault Group) Koch and his comrades began what would become six months of intensive training in the utmost secrecy for their mission.

Koch was ordered to seize and prevent the destruction of the three bridges and silence the artillery positions at Fort Eben-Emael so divided his forces into four assault elements. Each assault element's objective was named for the primary building material used in each structure's construction. The bridges at Veldwezelt, Vroenhoven, and Cannes were named respectively Objectives *Stahl*, *Beton* and *Eisen* (Steel, Concrete and Iron). The fort itself was named Objective *Granit* (Granite). An independent, but connected mission would be undertaken by Battaillon zur besondern Verwendung 100, an undercover *Abwehr* (Intelligence) unit. In civilian clothes they would infiltrate into Maastricht on bicycles to sabotage attempts to blow the three Meuse bridges. They would be supported by motorcycle troops of Sonderverband Hocke disguised in Dutch police uniforms and expected to link with elements of the 4th Armoured Division by 1000hrs on D-Day.

Oberleutnant Altman, with around ninety soldiers and ten gliders, would seize the bridge at Veldwezelt ('Steel'). The bridge at Vroenhoven ('Concrete') would be taken by Oberleutnant Schacht and his assault team of one hundred soldiers and eleven gliders. Hauptman Koch decided that command and control of the whole operation would be best coordinated near this strongly built bridge because of its central location and its being most likely to survive attempts to destroy it. Objective Iron, the operation to seize the bridge at Canne, was commanded by Leutnant Schaechter with eighty men in nine gliders. Oberleutnant Kiess would be responsible for training the pilots and maintaining the gliders and the final, crucial task of silencing Fort Eben-Emael, 'Objective Granite', fell to Oberleutnant Rudolf Witzig and his eighty-six-man engineer platoon.

Witzig was a strict disciplinarian and a meticulous planner. Like many of the new breed of officers emerging within the German military, he had already recognized what the modern German army calls *Auftragstaktik* and describes as

> the pre-eminent command and control principle in the Army. It is based on mutual trust and requires each soldier's unwavering commitment to perform his duty . . . the military leader informs what his intention is, sets clear achievable objectives, and provides the required forces and resources. He will only order details regarding execution if measures which serve the same objective have to be harmonized, if political or military constraints require it.[4]

Believing that realistic training was the only way to rehearse for any operation, Witzig's greatest strength was, as one of his men put it, 'his regard for the enlisted man and his squad leaders, giving them the necessary freedom and responsibility for their own plans'. He had identified three tasks: first, destroy any weapons on top of the fort that could impede the landing of the gliders and movement across the roof area; secondly, put the gun batteries threatening the bridges out of action; and last, prevent a counterattack by the garrison by destroying entrance and exit points from the underground defences. The mission's success relied on speed, with Witzig reckoning that he would have perhaps an hour before what Student later called his 'Lilliputian force' would be overrun by a Belgian counterattack. Recognizing the need for rapid support, a Luftwaffe liaison officer, Leutnant Egon Delica, was assigned to the platoon to act as forward air controller and communications officer responsible for calling in air support from Luftwaffe bombers and fighters and for the planned resupply drop of ammunition. The plan also contained a linkup with lead elements of the 4th Panzer Division after it crossed the Albert Canal. The 51st Engineer Battalion, part of the 151st Infantry Regiment Group, would cross the Canne Bridge to relieve and support Witzig's force.

For the next six months, Sturmabteilung Koch trained in total seclusion at Hildesheim and in Poland and Czechoslovakia where scale model rehearsal sites were set up using aerial photographs and where fortifications of a similar design to Eben-Emael had been found. During glider insertion training, it became clear that the gliders would have difficulty landing on the confined space on top of the fort where there simply was not enough room for all the aircraft. Makeshift efforts, such as wrapping barbed wire around the landing gear, helped shorten the landing whilst DFS worked on the design of a new hand brake (effectively a plywood frame that dug into the ground on landing). The pilots continued to train hard so that, by March 1940, they were able to take off at night in small two to three glider formations and land at airfields they had not seen before, bringing their craft to within 15–30 feet of their target. Witzig took glider training one step further and incorporated the pilots into the assault sections, ensuring that they were soon capable of using every weapon carried by the platoon. Platoon members went to demolition schools, studied fort design by conducting interviews with engineers and contractors (parts of the work building Eben-Emael had been subcontracted to German firms but, contrary to later reports, these contracts were limited to outside walls and had very little to do with the fort's weapons and internal layout) and underwent endless 'Battle Focused' physical training, emphasizing climbing and running with full equipment. By March, Assault Force Granite had completed two full dress rehearsals, including glider takeoff and landings and attacking scale model objectives. Only two aspects of the operation were not rehearsed: a full glider takeoff by the entire Sturmabteilung and the deployment of the hollow charge, which was also being developed for use as a detonator for German atomic bomb research and too secret to risk being compromised during training. Witzig was the only member of the assault group to see it detonated before the mission.

Throughout, operational security was the most critical component of mission success. Even the slightest warning of what was to come could have led to the Belgians placing more machine guns on the roof of Eben-Emael and wiping out the assault force as it landed. General Student later wrote that the 'whole premise behind the operation was that no leak in security could compromise the mission, and the only way for this mission to be successful was to achieve total surprise'.[5] As a result, from the time Student first received his orders from the Fuhrer, only five officers knew the exact location and name of the target. Sturmabteilung Koch changed its name every time it moved to a new location, at times becoming Experimental Section Freidichshafen, at others Airport Construction Platoon. No insignia was worn, even the names of team members were kept secret. Each move saw the gliders dismantled and driven to new sites in furniture removal vans before being locked and guarded in hangers where a perimeter fence covered with straw mats shielded them from prying eyes. Letters to families were censored by Witzig, Koch or Kiess and soldiers remained shut away from either civilian or military contact. Sergeant Helmut Wenzl, the senior enlisted man in Witzig's platoon, later recalled that 'we couldn't go into bars but we could go to the movies. However, we had to have guards. Also, we didn't wear insignia, and we had no names. Once we ran into some girls we knew [and] the whole unit had to be transferred.'[6] In addition, every man in the company signed a statement that: 'I am aware that I shall risk sentence of death should I, by intent or care-lessness, make known to another person by spoken word or illustration anything concerning the base at which I am serving.'[7] Two members of the team, seen talking to men of another unit near the hangar, were even sentenced to death but reprieved to take part in the operation and, on the day before the assault, two Luftwaffe men who strayed too close to hangar found themselves arrested and held until the operation was over.

As May 1940 approached the men were anxiously awaiting the assault order, code name 'Danzig'. Finally, at 1930hrs on 9 May 1940, the call came and the teams made their way to two airfields near Cologne, Germany, happy to be finally on their way after months of virtual captivity. The glider takeoff had been sched-uled for 0430hrs on 10 May, to allow for all four objective groups to land simultaneously at 0525hrs, just five minutes before the main German attack west began. In the pre-dawn gloom, the men sang as they bumped across the airfield, drowning out the rattling noises until silence descended as they rose behind their Ju52 towplanes. By 0450hrs, forty-two unmarked gliders were airborne and under strict radio silence followed a route marked with light beacons until they reached the border.

Inside Fort Eben-Emael, an alert warning had been received from the Liège Headquarters at 0130hrs detailing German troop movements near the border but already there had been three similar alerts that month alone and the message was treated as just another drill. The fort's commander, Major Jottrand, was sleeping in his villa when the report was received and he was woken to be informed of the situation.[8] He immediately contacted Liège for more information and ordered the garrison to go through the standing alert drill which required gun crews to fire twenty blank rounds from the 75mm gun at Cupola 31 at 90 second intervals to alert the canal bridge section of a possible attack and summoned any remaining gun crews garrisoned in the local area. Fort Eben-Emael, largely underground, was not a healthy place to work. Of the 1,322 men garrisoned there, only 1,198 were fit for duty that night.

By 0415hrs, Lieutenant Longdoz, in charge of the fort's anti-aircraft and machine gun posts, reported that the most of the men were at their posts, including the troops who normally manned the surface-mounted anti-aircraft guns. Twenty minutes later, Captain Hotermans, commander of the artillery battery, ordered Cupola Sud to begin firing their blanks. As they prepared to do so, gunfire was heard from the direction of nearby Maastricht and Major Jottrand realized that this was not just another drill. Standing orders demanded the immediate destruction of the barracks and administrative buildings just outside the fort's entrance in order to clear fields of fire and, short of manpower, gun crews were used to carry out the mission to clear the front entrance, leaving only skeleton crews in some positions and leaving others entirely unmanned. Then, at 0500hrs, reports came in from both the Canne Bridge and the fort's observation posts that aircraft were overhead but no engines could be heard and the aircraft appeared to stop in mid air. After hearing these reports, Major Jottrand ordered the Canne Bridge blown but his responsibility did not extend to either the Vroenhoven or Veldwezelt bridges which were under the command of Captain-Commandant Giedelo stationed at Lanaeken, too far away to be aware of the situation.

As dawn approached, the fort's anti-aircraft gunners reported 'airplanes with blocked engines' in sight but were told 'shoot only if you can identify them as enemy'. The unmarked gliders were within 200–300 m before the firing began. Almost immediately, one machine gun jammed and the three others were only able to fire their starter belts of 40–50 rounds before they, too, broke down. Fort Eben-Emael had seven authorized anti-aircraft guns, but only four were in position and brought into action too late. The first glider landed at 0525hrs. The Canne bridge crew reported that it had blown the bridge but was now under attack.

Soon after crossing the Rhine, Witzig's Ju52 towing aircraft went into a steep dive to avoid another plane, causing the glider's tow rope to break. Knowing that they could not make it to the objective, pilot Corporal Karl Pilz landed in a nearby grassy field as close to Cologne as possible. As his crew began clearing fences and hedges in hope of making a makeshift airstrip, Witzig commandeered a local civilian's bicycle and made his way to a nearby village. Luckily, the village garrisoned an army unit that gave him a car to drive back to the airfield some seventy kilometres away where he picked up a spare cable, a set of wheels for the glider (the DFS 230 jettisoned its wheels on takeoff) and arranged for a new Ju52 tug aircraft to be flown from the airfield at Goetersich. He then flew back with the tug to the rough landing strip prepared by his men and landed where his glider had been forced down. With the engines still running, the crews quickly fitted the cable, lifted the glider onto the new wheels and took off again for the fort. They finally arrived only two hours late. Glider 2 also encountered difficulties, the pilot, Fritz Bredenbeck, had been released too early by his towplane and had been forced to land near the town of Düren, still inside Germany. Commandeering a passing motorcycle, Feldwebel Maier found a nearby engineer unit and borrowed two staff cars. Arriving back at their landing site, the section piled their equipment into the cars and set off in a dash westward, determined not to miss the action.

At the fort, the remaining nine gliders had now all reached their targets and Witzig's men sprang into action. Gerhard Raschke, flying Glider 1, was forced to take evasive action as he came under heavy anti-aircraft fire. The resulting hard landing stunned Leutnant Delica, Feldwebel Niedermeier and the men of 1 Section but brought them directly alongside their target. Recovering quickly, the men followed the often rehearsed drill and placed a 50 kg hollow charge on Eben 3, the observation cupola on top of Maastricht 2, the south-west cupola with its three 75 mm guns. Theirs was the first explosion of the attack and the blast knocked Niedermeier and a comrade down and killed two of the Belgian defenders. Next, a 12.5 kg charge was placed on one of the guns where the blast hurled it against the back wall, killing more Belgians and creating a gap large enough for the Germans to enter. Niedermeier and two of his men threw grenades into the newly created entrance and entered firing their weapons before dropping 3 kg charges down the staircase. As artillery fire from Cupola Sud began to land near Maastricht 2 Niedermeier ordered his men inside the casement and sent a runner to find the platoon headquarters and inform Oberleutnant Witzig of their mission success. They would remain there throughout the day, holding back repeated counterattacks. Below them, Sergeant Poncelet, in charge of Maastricht 2, had already after lost three men dead and seventeen wounded when he ordered the building of emergency barricades to prevent the Germans from gaining

Rudolf Witzig

The commander of the assault pioneers who took Fort Eben-Emael went on to rise to the rank of colonel and commanded FJR 18 from late 1944 until its surrender in April 1945, adding the Oak Leaves cluster to the Knight's Cross he had won in 1940. In 1957 he rejoined the military in the fledgling Bundeswehr and again commanded airborne pioneers until his retirement in 1974. He died aged 85 on 3 October 2001 at his home in Oberschleissheim.

access to the fort's tunnel system, sealing the access door with sandbags and steel rods.

Alfred Supper circled the fort twice before he brought Glider 3 down just 60 feet from his objective, Maastricht 1, the westernmost cupola whose three 75 mm guns were being trained on the bridges. Feldwebel Peter Arent and his section immediately sprang into action but could not find a door or observation dome on which to affix a 50 kg charge. Instead, they tried to attach the charge to the muzzles of the guns but found them coated in preservation grease and the charges slid off. Eventually, Arent attached a charge to the ball joint at the base of gun number 3. It exploded and as black smoke poured out of a large hole, groans and cries could be heard from inside the cupola where the gun had been torn from its hinges and blown back into the casement wall. Arent dropped two hand grenades into the large opening and fired his machine pistol as he and two others entered the casement to find four heavily wounded Belgian defenders inside, all badly shocked. Soon artillery from Cupola Sud began falling outside Maastricht 1 and Arent took his squad under cover inside the casement. Noticing a staircase leading into the depths of the fort, he took two men and went down only to find two massive steel doors blocking the doors. Returning to the surface, the men found that the artillery fire from Cupola Sud had stopped and they immediately attacked and neutralized Block 2 with a hollow charge. The section then remained in the area between Maastricht 1 and Block 2 to harass incoming Belgian patrols with small arms fire and even managed to use one of the casement guns to fire onto those patrols.

The following morning, Arent again made the trip down the staircase. This time he took with him a hollow charge in an attempt to penetrate the fort's interior. Modifying the eight second ignition, Arent exploded it against the doors, killing six Belgian soldiers instantly as the door and steel beams were blasted across the passage. Shock waves blasted through the tunnels and convinced the defenders that the attackers had gained entrance to the underground chambers. By chance, the blast had also destroyed drums containing a chlorine-based disinfectant and the smell began to drift through the air vents, causing panic to spread among the defenders who feared a gas attack was under way. Although it also destroyed the staircase to the surface and prevented the Germans from taking advantage of the damage, it would be the turning point in the battle.

Casement Mi-Nord, the northernmost machine-gun bunker, was the responsibility of Oberfeldwebel Helmut Wenzel and Section 4. As their pilot, Otto Brautigam, brought their glider down, Sergeants Vossen and Bataille leapt out and immediately opened fire. Wenzel, who suffered a bloody nose during the landing, moved his men to the top of the casement and placed a 1 kg charge in the space which once housed a periscope. When this failed to silence the gun, Section 4 placed a 50 kg hollow charge on the steel cupola but this also failed to penetrate the armour plating. Although it was not enough to accomplish the Section 4 objective, it was enough to cause the Belgian crew to abandon the position. Not satisfied with partial victory, Section 4 exploded another large hollow charge. When the debris stopped falling and the dust settled, Oberfeldwebel Wenzel (forever after known as 'the cupola smasher') stepped through the newly created hole and heard a telephone ringing. Lifting the receiver, he couldn't resist answering the phone in English 'Hallo, here are the Germans!' A stunned silence at the other end was followed by a strangu-lated 'Mon Dieu!'[9] Within fifteen minutes, his section's mission accomplished, Wenzel ordered his men into defensive positions and waited for Oberleutnant Witzig to arrive at his position, which was designated as the platoon headquarters.

Section 5, led by Feldwebel Haugh, encountered a different set of difficulties as it made its final approach toward their objective. It was hit with machine-gun fire and glider pilot Karl-Heinz Lange recalled later that 'our first target was the antiaircraft guns, if we were on the short final [and] they shoot in my direction [then] it was easy for me to find my target because I could see the fire of the bullets if I looked over my shoulder, So I had to follow this direction.'[10] The pilot manoeuvred the glider towards the machine gun as they landed and, by sheer luck, the glider's wing caught the sandbag machine-gun emplacement, putting it temporarily out of action. The noise of the landing brought four Belgian defenders out of the nearby wooden barracks, only to find Lange standing next to his cockpit pointing his pistol at them.

Seeing the guns from Cupola Sud firing on top of the fort, Section 5 decided to attack, placing two 50 kg charges on its surface. The explosions shook the Belgian crew and dislodged the gun mounts but the gunners continued to fire, although their guns now required time-consuming adjustments after each salvo. The remainder of the Belgian defenders in the barracks fired a machine gun from the rear window towards Cupola Nord and at Section 8 as they landed.

Feldwebel Unger and Section 8's glider flew a wide circle, trying to avoid the fire and Hans Distelmeier flew in low and fast from the south, landing within 60 feet of Cupola Nord, the easternmost pair of 75 mm guns. It immediately came under heavy machine-gun fire from the north which killed Feldwebel Unger and one of his men. Taking charge, Oberfeldwebel Else placed a machine gun to provide covering fire for the assault. A 50 kg hollow charge was put on the top of Cupola Nord and a 12.5 kg charge against the steel entrance door but both exploded with no visible effects. A second attempt not only blew the door off its hinges, but also caused the surrounding concrete to collapse, sealing the entrance. Section 5 under Haugh then noticed that Unger's glider was in trouble, with a casualty lying on his glider's wing while heavy machine-gun fire pinned down the rest of his section. As Haugh moved to help Unger, his section also came under fire. The two sections united and destroyed the machine gun position, though the action cost the squads heavily with two killed, one seriously wounded and several injured. Artillery from the Cupola Sud, which Feldwebel Haugh thought he had destroyed, again began firing across the surface.

Inside Fort Eben-Emael, Major Jottrand ordered the 'general attack', a signal to shoot at any unidentified person and to be prepared to fire the artillery at a moment's notice. Sitting in his command post, he tried to figure out what was going on and to anticipate the Germans' next move. He could only wonder and wait for further information.

Elsewhere, inside Cupola Nord, Belgian defenders Sergeants Kip and Joris, the 75 mm gun crew, had been in position by 0430hrs and had reported seeing enemy activity before the attackers landed. Sergeant Joris, Cupola Nord commander, realizing what was going on top of the fort, was in the process of carrying anti-personnel ammunition up the staircase when the first hollow charge exploded. Luckily for the Belgians, no one was in the turret at the time. Oberfeldwebel Else, seeing no visible effect from the hollow charge directed another to be placed near the steel exit door. This second explosion damaged the electrical equipment and rendered the cupola inoperative. His mission complete, Else took charge of Section 8 and moved to the platoon headquarters near Mi-Nord. Twenty minutes after the first glider landed, Major Jottrand ordered the tunnel sealed and Cupola Nord abandoned.

Feldwebel Ewald Neuhaus and Section 9's glider had been shaken by Dutch anti-aircraft fire near Maastricht but pilot Gunther Schulz still managed to land within 150 feet of the objective, skidding to a halt entangled in the perimeter barbed wire. The wire was quickly breached and a 12.5 kg hollow charge was placed on the machine-gun embrasure of Mi-Sud, a bunker located in the north-west of the fort. Another 50 kg charge was then blown next to the neighbouring embrasure, creating a space large enough for Neuhaus to enter and find Mi-Sud had already been abandoned, its crew ordered away to assist in destroying the barracks and administrative buildings just outside the fort's entrance. His mission complete, he immediately organized his men for defence and sent a runner to find Oberleutnant Witzig to report his progress.

Feldwebel Willie Hübel and Section 10 were designated as the reserve. On landing without incident, a runner was sent to platoon headquarters to report their position. Oberfeldwebel Wenzel, now in charge since Witzig could not be found, ordered the attack on Vise 1, originally designated as the missing Section 2's objective. Within five minutes, the observation cupola was blown and the guns silenced. Feldwebel Fritz Heinemann with Section 7, and Feldwebel Siegfried Larlos, with Section 6, attacked what turned out to be false cupolas in the northernmost portion of the fort and set up defensive positions oriented towards the Geer River in the west. In the first thirty minutes of the attack, all anti-aircraft guns and surface-mounted machine guns had been destroyed. Mi-Nord, Mi-Sud, Vise 1 and Cupola Nord were neutralized. Cupola Sud was damaged and, though firing, was doing so at a reduced capacity. The German attackers had freedom of movement on top of the fort.

Wenzel now noticed the 120 mm guns at Cupola 120 in the centre of the fort, had not been attacked. Neutralizing Cupola 120 was another task assigned to Feldwebel Maier and Section 2. Inside it, Sergeant Cremers, casement commander, saw the gliders land and at 0530hrs ordered gunners to attack the Germans. When the Belgians tried to operate the gun's ammunition hoist and rammers they found that electric power was not available and frantically tried to fix the problem. Lange, the glider pilot from Section 5, was escorting prisoners to platoon headquarters as the 120 mm guns suddenly swung around toward him. Fire from Cupola Sud fell around him, wounding him in eight places, but Lange was more annoyed than hurt. Ordering the prisoners to lie down, he retrieved a hollow charge from his glider. Dragging it to the cupola, he lit the fuse and ran. The explosion caused no visible effect on the turret but attracted the attention of Ernst Grechza from Section 5, who came over to investigate. The night before, Grechza had filled his water bottle with rum and was now clearly drunk as he climbed on the huge guns and rode them as the Belgians swung them in a circle. Wenzel appeared and calmly dropped a 3 kg charge into each barrel. The explosion shattered the gunners inside and put the casement out of action. Two hours later, Sergeant Cremers returned and ordered the gun to resume firing. The first round split one barrel open and filled the casement with smoke. The casement was never fired from again.

Sturmgruppe Veldwezelt – Objective 'Steel'

The nine gliders carrying Oberleutnant Altmann and his men lifted off without problems but fog obscured the target and the gliders landed in a more dispersed pattern than planned. Glider 6 landed 1000 m from their target and the head-quarters group around 400 m away. As they approached the bridge at 0520hrs all encountered heavy anti-aircraft fire and the last glider, tasked with securing the southern edge of the bridge, took a direct hit, losing part of its left wing and splinters wounded the pilot in the head. It stalled and crashed from a height of around 10 m, disabling all but two of the section aboard.

Glider 2 spun around on landing, causing one man to break his arm in two places. All landing sites were wetter than expected and mud caused several stoppages so instead the Germans used captured Belgian weapons to lay down suppressive fire as a section under Ellersieck raced to capture the concrete bunker alongside the bridge by lobbing hand grenades and three 20 kg charges through the open door before taking out the pub and three houses next to it with two grenade boxes.

Engineer-Group A cleared the demolition charges from the bridge whilst more paratroopers took on and destroyed a machine-gun bunker west of the bridge held by fifteen Belgians. The engineers then cleared all obstacles on the bridge still under enemy fire. After all groups set up their defences they established contact with the Group HQ from a trench 150 m south-west of the bridge – all within the first ten minutes of the attack. Over the next thirty minutes a series of small, disorganized counterattacks were fought off but the planned support by artillery, Stukas and light bombers was slow to arrive.

At 0615hrs heavy machine gun teams were dropped by parachute to reinforce the bridgehead. One planeload jumped about 1000 m too far to the west with the planes under heavy ground fire. One soldier was killed, one lightly wounded and one parachute failed to open, but the newly arrived paras quickly cleared a trench in their landing zone as the second machine gun took up position and laid down flanking fire.

Fifteen minutes later, the enemy had begun to recover from the shock and began several small counterattacks which were fought off by small arms fire until, at around 0900hrs, the first strong, organized attack came from the town of Veldwezelt to the north-west of the bridgehead. Air attacks and fire from all weapons stopped it before it could build momentum but for nearly an hour, isolated firing from an area 500 m south-west of the bridge kept everyone alert as both sides gathered their breath.

At 1000hrs, Belgian artillery and mortar fire began to rain down but German air attacks suppressed them until contact was established with Flak-Abteilung Aldinger whose 88 mm guns were directed onto Belgian machinegun positions with great effect. Around noon the enemy artillery and mortar fire started again and again was stopped after air attack. Shortly before 1300hrs an artillery observer arrived at the bridge and guided artillery fire on Veldwezelt and the road to Vroenhoven. Ninety minutes later, the first infantry elements arrived and reinforced the bridgehead. A brief artillery attack at around 1900hrs was yet again ended by air support and, at 2100hrs, after fifteen hours on the ground, Sturmabteilung Koch was withdrawn and moved towards Maastricht. Altmann's men had achieved their mission at a cost of eight dead, fourteen severely wounded and another sixteen with lighter wounds. Belgian casualties included around eighty-five men killed and 200 captured.

Sturmgruppe Vroenhoven – Objective 'Concrete'

Leutnant Schacht's eleven gliders tasked to seize objective 'Concrete' took off from Cologne-Ostheim at 0430hrs but during the flight the glider carrying the pioneer troop under Oberjäger Kempa had to land at Hottdorf when the tow rope broke. The remaining gliders were released at 2,000–2,200 m between the German border and Maastricht – whose lights had acted as a navigational aid. At 1800 m the gliders began receiving heavy enemy anti-aircraft and machine-gun fire from the direction of Maastricht but the pilots managed to get through without casualties.

The bridge was clearly visible as they approached and, at around 100 m from the ground, a barrage of small arms fire from the trenches around the bridge began to hit home. The glider carrying OberGefreiter Stolzewski and Section 8 was hit, damaging the steering ropes and causing it to drop out of control from a height of around 12 m and seriously wounding three men. By around 0515hrs all the gliders were down near their targets, although that carrying the command group under Oberfeldwebel Hofmann – intended to land right beside the bunker guarding the bridge – came to a halt in a trench 150 m to the north-west. Three of the section were wounded and the machine gun, two rifles and one machine pistol put out of action. The crew quickly left the plane and cleared the trench back up to the bunker where Gefreiter Stenzel could see through the open door that the defenders were preparing to blow up the bridge. At the very last second, he managed to find and cut the detonator wire. The bridge was secure.

All the glider crews that landed near the bridge immediately put their carefully rehearsed assault into action. Two section commanders, Röhrich and Giese, led their teams against the flanking bunkers at the canal and put them out of action. Meanwhile, the engineer groups blew up houses next to the bridge to clear fields of fire. The command group under Schacht had been tasked to take buildings 1,200 m west of the bridge identified as barracks by Koch, but which actually turned out to be empty horse-stables. The group were now far from the supporting fire of the rest of the force and dangerously exposed. The second glider of the command section with the radio-group landed about 500 m west of the bridge and lost one man killed instantly by a headshot as the glider touched down. As a result, for the first hour the teams around the bridge operated solely under their NCO section commanders until Hofmann took command of the Sturmgruppe and OberGefreiter Orth brought the radios back to Hoffman's

Gerhard Schacht

'Owl' Schacht was commander of the team that seized Vroenhaven bridge on 10 May 1940. Wounded in the attack, Schacht recovered and served in Africa and the Mediterranean. In January 1944, a British commando raid in Italy led to a number of prisoners being taken. Hitler's infamous order to execute all captured special forces troops was in place but Schacht personally intervened to save Lieutenant Hughes as he faced a firing squad.

He later served on the Eastern Front and rose to the rank of colonel in command of FJR 25. It was men of this unit who reinforced the Breslau garrison in the closing stages of the war, making Schacht one of the first and last men to command combat glider assaults. He retired as commander when he was wounded on 16 May 1945.

In 1957, he joined the Bundeswehr and served as military attaché in Tehran before being given command of the 1st Air Landing Division with the rank of Generalmajor. He died after a short illness on 7 February 1972, aged 56.

position to establish contact with the other assault groups and 7th Airborne Division.

Combat patrols under OberGefreiter Borchardt cleared the area for around 600 m around the bridge whilst over to the east, machinegunners Haas and Schmidt held off an enemy counterattack. After a short but heavy firefight, the Dutch commander surrendered and ordered his troops to stop firing as they began to withdraw towards Maastricht. Half an hour after landing the bridge was secured.

It was not until around noon that it became possible to recover the survivors of Schacht's group. Three paras were dead, another six severely wounded. They regrouped around the bridge and the 300 or so prisoners they had taken were pressed into service clearing tank obstacles. Gahme's section dismantled the explosive charges and cables on the bridge and cleared a path through the minefields. As the work got under way, around 1250hrs the first regular infantry unit arrived.

At 1830hrs an unsuccessful barrage of heavy artillery attempted to destroy the bridge but it was too late. An infantry battalion arrived at 2140hrs and Sturmabteilung Vroenhoven began the move back to Maastricht, leaving behind them seven dead and twenty-four wounded. Around 120 defenders had been killed and 300 captured.

Sturmgruppe Canne – Objective 'Iron'

Leutnant Schächter's group left Cologne-Butzweilerhof in ten gliders. As they neared their objective, the glider carrying Section 1 was released too early at 2,000 m and couldn't make enough speed to carry it to the landing zone so the pilot landed on the heights south-west of the bridge. The rest of the force released too late and encountered heavy enemy anti-aircraft fire behind Aachen. The delay meant that Canne's defenders had been alerted and blew up the bridge around 0535hrs. At 0540hrs, the Sturmgruppe reported: 'Canne: reached objective, heavy resistance, bridge destroyed but passable with engineers help.'

Poor visibility had been a problem at all the bridges and again the gliders did not land as originally planned. Section 9's glider came down about 200 m south of the bridge at the village of Eben-Emael. The gliders of Sections 6 and 7 landed not on the northern heights commanding the bridge but on the middle heights below them. Section 3's aircraft was hit by a high explosive shell and caught fire as it crashed into its target area and burned out. In nearly every glider, casualties were taken as effective ground fire raked the aircraft before they hit the ground.

The Belgian trenches nearest the landing zone were quickly taken but machine-gun fire from the positions on the heights restricted movement until Section 8 silenced them using hand grenades. The valley and trench system on the northern hill were taken by Section 3, who also blew up three houses and the entrance to a bunker at the bridge and captured the crews of the two bunkers there.

Forty minutes after the landing, machine-gun teams parachuted in to reinforce the bridgeheads but the bad luck continued as Nollau's half-section dropped 500 m too far to the west and fourteen men were killed and eight wounded as they dropped onto Belgian positions. (One of the wounded found himself a prisoner of the Belgians, then the British, and was eventually found and released at Dunkirk.)

As elsewhere, counterattacks against the bridgehead were weak and dis-organized in the first hour after the landing, easily repulsed with air support, but this too was hampered by poor visibility and radio problems. Radio contact with 7th Airborne Division had been lost and, as a result, some of the air support failed to locate the friendly positions so that one strike by Hs-123 planes dropped bombs directly onto German positions.

Leutnant Schächter had been wounded in the head and arm while clearing the trenches at the landing area so Leutnant Meissner took command of the Sturmgruppe in his place, rallying the men so that a strong counterattack devel-oping around 1030hrs was broken up as it assembled by small arms fire and air support. More organized counterattacks from the west and south-west at 1500hrs and 1800hrs were held back by combined artillery fire and air support.

The paras remained in position as heavy artillery fire started at around 2000hrs and it would not be until 2330hrs that elements of the 51st Engineer battalion, part of the 151st Infantry Regiment Group, arrived at the bridgehead. The para-troopers had been trying all day to get in contact with these units in the village on the other side of the canal but the enemy fire was too strong. Under cover of darkness, soldiers of Section 8 swam through the canal and led the reinforce-ments forward.

The shelling continued, getting heavier throughout the night as another counterattacking force massed for an assault at 0030hrs on 11 May. This attack, too, was fought off by the combined infantry and paratrooper force but it was not until nearly twenty-four hours after they landed that elements of Sturmgruppe Canne got back to the eastern side of the canal. Twenty-two men were dead, twenty-six wounded and one missing. The defenders had lost about 150 dead, fifty wounded and around 190 prisoners.

By 0730hrs sixty-two Germans had been on top of Fort Eben-Emael for nearly two hours. Two soldiers were dead, eight severely wounded. Four more had slight wounds. Oberleutnant Witzig and Feldwebel Maier's Section 2 were still missing. Cupola Sud was still firing at a reduced capacity but the blockhouses around the fort's perimeter were inactive. Leutnant Delica had been directing Stuka dive bomber missions within forty-five minutes of landing and now guided in two aircraft for resupply of much needed ammunition and water. Oberfeldwebel Wenzel was in charge and talking to Hauptman Koch by radio to relay the status of ongoing operations. Koch knew that, although the Canne bridge was blown, the others had both been captured by 0530hrs and were being held.

Suddenly at 0830hrs, a lone glider appeared and landed near the platoon headquarters. Witzig and Feldwebel Schwarz's reserve Section 11 stepped out with just one more hour at the fort until the 4th Panzer Division was scheduled to arrive to relieve them. Thereafter, if the fort had not yet surrendered, the task would fall to them. The main task of the platoon now was to keep the Belgian defenders in the fort and to prevent them from recapturing the surface. After an initial update briefing by Wenzel, Witzig gave the order 'to blow in the fortified entrances and press the attack into the depths of the fortress, holding all captured positions until relief arrives'. Major Jottrand, still shaken by the explosions and casement damage, realized that only a few Germans were attacking the fort and ordered a counterattack to clear the top. A group of fourteen men under Lieutenant DeSloovere emerged from the woods in the north-west corner and immediately came under attack from Feldwebel Arndt. The Belgians quickly retreated. By 1030hrs a furious Major Jottrand launched two additional counterattacks in an attempt to dislodge the Germans from the top of the fort. Both met with failure, due largely to their lack of experience using infantry weapons and tactics as all the Belgians were trained solely as artillerymen. Jottrand now began to fear a German penetration into the fort and ordered all the tunnels blocked, calling for additional artillery fire from the neighbouring forts of Pontisse and Barchon to target the top of Eben-Emael and ordering in his reserve force from the nearby town of Wonck.

Meanwhile, driving through columns of advancing German vehicles, the missing Section 2 finally arrived at Canne only to discover the bridge had been blown. Feldwebel Maier was mortally wounded trying to cross the bridge but Meir, his second in command, made it over and stole a bicycle to ride towards the fort. Evading fire from both German and Belgian attackers, he made it to the gate but could not find a way in. Fearing no one would believe his story, he grabbed a copy of Fort Eben-Emael's daily orders and linked up with Feldwebel Haugh. Then he went back to Canne to meet his section and lead them forward. He never found his section, but ended up escorting 110 Belgian prisoners he captured in the vicinity of Canne to Bergen instead.

Early in the afternoon, Witzig saw lead elements of the German 151st Infantry Regiment trying to cross the Albert Canal in rubber boats near Blockhouse 17. This was built into the side of the cliff facing the Albert Canal and contained two 60 mm anti-tank guns, machine guns and searchlights. Feldwebel Harlos was charged with its destruction but had a challenge since it was built 120 feet below the top of the fort. Tying three 50 kg charges together, he lowered them by rope on top of the blockhouse and blew them with no visible effect. The gun crews in the blockhouse would continue to fire until the next morning when lead elements of the 51st Engineer Battalion destroyed it.

Lieutenant Levaque, in charge of the Belgian reserve force of 233 men, came under heavy fire from Ju87 Stukas as they assembled. The constant dive bombing disrupted the reserve force's movement by scattering them throughout the area – by 1600hrs, only fifteen men had reached the fort and it would be two more hours before roughly half of the original reserve was in position for the counterattack. As darkness fell, the Belgians found themselves under constant German machine-gun fire and only eight men carried through the assault, finally withdrawing back into the fort.

As darkness fell on Eben-Emael, the attackers lay exhausted in a defensive position near Witzig's glider. Incoming artillery fire and explosions kept the Belgian defenders in a state of fear. The interior of the fort was in shambles. The constant explosions cut off the power to the majority of the fort and the lack of ventilation and heat began to make work conditions unbearable. Smoke permeated every corner, reminding the defenders of their German adversaries above ground and threatening asphyxiation if the situation did not improve.

Throughout the night pioneers searched desperately for a way across to the paras in the fort. Using inflatable boats and rafts made from anything that might float, they forced their way across and at 0830hrs on 11 May Witzig was officially relieved by members of the 151st Infantry Regiment.

At 1000hrs that morning, Major Jottrand received a message from Liège that help would not come. General De Krahe, commander of the Belgian III Army Corps, signalled him that 'if the evacuation of the garrison is impossible, you are ordered to blow up the fort and all its men'. Jottrand summoned his officers and explained the situation as he knew it. Then he read Article 51 of the 'Instruction on the Defence of a Fort' which ordered that:

> The surrender of a fort is not justified unless it finds itself in one of the two following circumstances:
> When all defensive means of the fort and of its personnel are useless and non-reparable.
> When all means of subsistence of the garrison are exhausted.

In unison, the assembled council favoured surrender and agreed to the terms which they would present to the Germans. They would surrender on the conditions that the wounded would be evacuated and the garrison treated honourably as prisoners of war. At 1227hrs on 11 May, Fort Eben-Emael was officially surrendered to Colonel Melzer, commander of the 151st Infantry Regiment. Melzer told them 'I congratulate you on your courage. Someone must be defeated in war. I am sorry this must happen to you. But this is war. I must send you to Germany.' To keep the use of gliders and hollow charges secret, the Belgian prisoners of Fort Eben-Emael were kept in isolation until July 1944 at a prisoner of war camp in Fallingbostel, Germany.

For the loss of six dead and fifteen wounded, Witzig had achieved a stunning success. Several days after the platoon returned to its barracks in Hildesheim, it was ordered to report to a special ceremony where Adolf Hitler addressed the men and presented each officer with a Ritterkreuz (Knight's Cross), Nazi Germany's highest combat decoration, and each soldier with an Iron Cross. Everyone involved was promoted one grade, except Grechza, the drunken soldier who straddled the guns. Soon afterwards, the men received orders transferring them to other units and within a few months the platoon was deactivated. The platoon remained so until early in 1941, when Hitler ordered an attack on the Greek island of Crete and the men of Sturmabteilung Koch were in demand again.

Chapter Three

'Nothing is impossible':
The Glider Pilot Regiment

The British response was swift, if crude. Four days after Eben-Emael fell, the War Office announced the formation of a new force of Local Defence Volunteers to

> deal with the action of small enemy parties landed from the air . . . to help in the very earliest stage in preventing movement by enemy parties landed from the air by blocking roads . . . and by seeing that they were as completely as possible hemmed in from the moment they landed.[1]

By 7 June 1940, the weekly *War Illustrated* magazine was able to provide photographs and descriptions of German airborne forces and announce the likelihood of parachute and glider-borne attacks on Britain.

On 22 June, Prime Minister Winston Churchill sent a memo to the Chief of Staff:

> We ought to have a Corps of at least 5,000 parachute troops. I hear something is being done to form such a Corps but only on a small scale. Advantage must be taken of the summer to train these Forces who can none the less play their part meanwhile as shock troops in Home Defence. Pray let me have a Note from the War Office on the subject.[2]

Initially dismissed by many as simply another example of Churchillian folly – where, for example, were suitable aircraft to be found when the RAF was already stretched to its limit? – the idea was sound enough. Britain's army had lost heavily in terms of weapons and transport and its ability to respond to attack was limited. The use of airborne troops would allow for a rapid reaction force to support the spears and pitchforks of the Local Defence Volunteers in containing attacks before the enemy could establish an airhead.

Two days later, Major John F Rock of the Royal Engineers was summoned to the War Office and put in command of Britain's airborne forces. How, with what and where were not explained. 'It was impossible', he wrote in his diary, 'to get any information as to policy or task'.[3] Rock's previous experience of aircraft was limited to having travelled as a passenger and he knew nothing of parachutes or gliders beyond what had appeared in the *War Illustrated* and other newspapers. Nevertheless, he approached his task with enthusiasm and soon established himself at Ringway (now Manchester Airport) under its RAF Station Commander, Group Captain L G Harvey. Assisted by Squadron Leader Louis Strange and Wing Commander Sir Nigel Norman, Rock set up the RAF Central Landing School, starting at 'Rock bottom'. The school's existence and purpose caused confusion within the bureaucracy of the War Office and not least with the mail. In the early days, a letter arrived for recruit Private Crane, addressed to the Central Sunday School, and a name change to Central Landing Establishment (CLE) brought mail addressed to the Central Laundry Establishment.[4] Whether laundry staff were ever in receipt of instructions about taking part in dangerous combat missions is not recorded.

The CLE rapidly evolved and a Development School was quickly set up to explore methods of using parachutes and containers to drop men and supplies. A Parachute School under Group Captain Newnham began the first experiments using parachute troops on 13 July 1940. Alongside these, a Glider Training Squadron was formed on 19 September using donated Kirby Kite and other sailplanes, ageing Avro 504 and Tiger Moth biplanes and civilian instructors. On 26 October, a demonstration took place using two tug and sailplane combinations and almost immediately the Ministry of Aircraft Production issued specifications for an eight-seat assault and training glider. Within four months, General Aircraft Ltd (GAL) had successfully flown the GAL48 'Hotspur' Mk I and an order was placed for 400.

On 3 December, the first parachute exercise took place with 350 paratroopers dropping on a foggy morning from four converted Whitley bombers. Only one casualty was sustained in the drop and the men set off for their objective, commandeering the car of Norway's Crown Prince Olaf on the way. By 28 February 1941, under the headline 'Not All the Parachutists Are Nazis!', *War Illustrated* was able to report on a parachute raid against Southern Italy by a force of British paratroopers. The raid, on 10 February, consisted of seven officers and thirty-one men drawn from a long line of volunteers at the Central Landing Establishment against the Monte Vulture aqueduct and was intended to disrupt water supplies to Italian operations in Albania. It was not a great success and all the raiders were captured but it proved it could be done. Despite this, by April 1941, Churchill was becoming anxious about the airborne force and especially about the glider programme, asking 'is it being seriously taken up?' So far, his glider force consisted of a single Hotspur, delivered on 6 April and in use a few days later. A demonstration on 26 April consisting of a flypast of the Hotspur and five Kirby Kites in camouflage paint followed by a planned drop of forty paratroops (of whom six failed to jump) did little to inspire him – although the newly designed airborne dagger presented to him looked good.

Meanwhile, as glider development got under way, heated debates began about who should fly them. The RAF, firm in the belief that anything above head height is their realm, argued that gliders were aircraft and therefore must be RAF controlled. The army pointed out that glider pilots would crash-land a medium-sized aircraft into enemy positions and then have to fight alongside the ground troops until help arrived. This line of argument quickly helped broker a deal in which the pilots would be soldiers but would be trained by the RAF. The first recruits to the new glider pilot force were duly recruited from the Royal Army Service Corps. Lance-Corporals Morris, Baker and Harrison, along with Driver Cooper, would become the pioneers of what would become a truly unique unit: the Glider Pilot Regiment.[5] At first, there was a carefree atmosphere – early recruits joined without even a medical check – and it drew adventurous men with a love of flying in any form, such as the sergeant who became the first to solo in a glider who had earlier flown a Messerschmitt in the Spanish Civil War.

On 21 December 1940, John Rock – by now a lieutenant-colonel – became the Commanding Officer of 1st Battalion, The Glider Pilot Regiment (GPR). By now, the laid-back, academically minded Rock had been joined by the sharply contrasting character of Major George Chatterton, a former naval cadet at Pangbourne, RAF pilot with 1 Squadron until a crash in 1935 had ended his flying career, and most recently a veteran of France with the Queen's Royal Regiment. Recruited by General Frederick Browning to act as second in command of the GPR, Chatterton brought with him two Guards sergeant-majors and a belief in firm discipline, along with an intention, in his words, to be 'quite ruthless' in enforcing army standards. It was a source of friction between the two men that would last until Rock's death in a flying accident in October 1942 but which would, as Chatterton demanded, ensure that those who stayed the course were not simply men seeking to escape the boredom of garrison life by volunteering for anything but would be, as Jim Davies, an early volunteer, put it, 'men who would put up with anything for the sake of flying'.

Chatterton, described by one of his pilots as 'a super salesman who could sell you anything', persuaded Browning that the men of the GPR would be a force of 'total soldiers' – able to not only fly their gliders into action, but to operate any weapons they carried aboard and to lead airborne troops into combat with the motto that 'nothing is impossible'. One later volunteer, Alexander Morrison, recalled Chatterton's opening address to a new group of volunteers:

Please sit down. My name is George Chatterton and I am the Commanding Officer of the Glider Pilot Regiment. You are all volunteers and, at this moment in time, have no idea what you are letting yourselves in for! Well, the Glider Pilot Regiment is part of the Army Air Corps and will have the honour of delivering men, guns, vehicles and even tanks right into the heart of the forthcoming battle . . . This, then, will be your job and in it, you will be unique because you will not only have to be a top rate pilot, but also able to fight efficiently after landing. You will be taught to fly whilst, at the same time, master every type of weapon and vehicle. Associated with your training you must develop the highest form of personal discipline . . . you will find that the next few weeks will tax your strength and moral courage to the limit.[7]

Volunteers for the new force came forward in their thousands but were weeded out by an RAF selection board using the same standards as would be applied to RAF aircrews and by a rigorous training schedule that would eventually see just one in twenty-five volunteers achieve their 'wings'. Conditions at the GPR depot have been described by veterans as 'hostile' and some wondered whether they had mistakenly been sent to a penal unit. 'You had to be fanatical to stay there', recalled John Potts. 'One chap showed up on parade with a small cut on his face and was put on a charge for being "idle while shaving"!'[8] Legend has it that an entire parade jumped to attention when a dog barked, but it created a strong sense of confidence in the trainees and those who didn't like it were free to leave. Chatterton genuinely believed that such a regime was vital to developing the skills and discipline needed to carry out their tasks and, when the RAF appeared to be sneering at his trainees, he visited the station, flying in by Tiger Moth, to land 'in the most split arsed manner' and emerge in parade uniform, swagger stick under his arm and RAF wings prominently displayed on his tunic.

It had been decided that the large gliders planned for use would need two pilots – the first pilot, with the rank of at least staff sergeant, would be responsible for takeoff and landing, the second, a sergeant or above, whilst on tow or if the first were hit. After graduation from the Tilshead depot, first pilot trainees would spend eight weeks at an Elementary Flight Training School on Tiger Moth biplanes, followed by a further eight weeks at Glider Training School learning to fly Hotspurs. This would then be followed by a further four weeks conversion course to the new Horsa glider coming into service throughout 1941. Second pilots would undergo a shorter course of four weeks at Elementary Flight Training School and three to four at Glider Training School. Gradually, the discipline and high standards paid off and RAF disdain of the 'pongoes' in their midst and the equal Army distrust of the 'brylcream boys' began to fade. Glider pilots would be entirely dependent on their RAF tug pilots and close working relationships began to develop between the two services.

As the GPR grew, so too did its glider force. Plans had specified that they should be all wooden aircraft capable of being built by coach builders and furniture manufacturers to avoid putting strain on fighter production. Hotspurs and the new, larger, Horsa assault gliders were quick to build and by now even the huge tank-carrying Hamilcars were being delivered. Stockpiles grew to the point where production had to be stopped in 1942 by the Prime Minister who did not want 'a lot of these things standing around in the rain and spoiling'. It was time to find a use for them.

Operation Freshman – the attack on the Norsk Hydro-Electric Plant, Norway, 19 November 1942

In April 1940, the Germans had occupied Norway and seized the Norsk Hydro Electric Company's heavy water plant at Vermork in Southern Norway. Deuterium Oxide (D_2O or 'heavy water') was a vital component in the atomic research programme and, in 1942, it was decided that the plant must be destroyed. The plant itself was a fortress-like factory sited on a shelf of rock several hundred feet up the side of a cliff, surrounded by heavily forested mountains rising to over 6,000 feet. Bombers had failed to cause more than slight damage and so the plan for Operation Freshman called for a glider-borne force of men trained to identify and destroy the heavy water stock to land, meet up with the Norwegian resistance and attack the plant before escaping in civilian clothes to neutral Sweden, just over ninety miles away.

The Glider Pilot Regiment's first operation would test it to the limit. It required a 400 mile tow to the target, followed by a landing in mountainous terrain at night. On landing, each man would have to carry around 80 lb of equipment through three feet of snow to the objective. So great were the hazards that objections were raised to the plan by Special Operations, who described it as 'ill-conceived and susceptible to too many failures at too many stages'. Colonel John Wilson, head of the Norwegian Section of the Special Operations Executive, later wrote that

> of all countries, Norway is the least suitable for glider operations. Its landing grounds are too few, its mountains thickly clustered, precipitous and angry. The four hundred mile tow proposed was far longer than any ever attempted, even in daylight. The success of the operation demanded exceptionally favourable weather on the Hardanger Plateau, where in winter the weather was seldom favourable and hardly ever predictable.

Nevertheless, thirty volunteer sappers from the Royal Engineers under 20-year-old Lieutenant David Methven were gathered together and split into two teams of fifteen men each. Only one team would be needed to complete the task, but both would be sent to increase the chances of success. Two Horsas, one piloted by GPR pilots Staff Sergeant Malcolm Strathdee and Sergeant Peter Doig, the other by Pilot Officers Norman Davies and Herbert Fraser of the Royal Australian Air Force, would be towed by Halifax bombers to the Norwegian coast where they would be released at 10,000 feet and glide to a point alongside Mossvatn Lake, fifteen miles west of their target. They would be guided to the landing zone (LZ) by Norwegian resistance workers using the new 'Eureka' beacon, which would act as a homing device to guide them on to the 700 yard strip of flat ground selected for them.

After repeated delays due to bad weather and problems with their aircraft, the decision to go was made on 19 November, despite reports that poor weather was still affecting the LZ. At around 1745hrs, Halifax 'A-Able', towing Strathdee and Doig took off from Skitten, followed twenty minutes later by 'B-Baker' with the RAAF-crewed Horsa on the start of what was expected to be a five and a half hour journey. As they lifted off the ground, the glider landing gear was jettisoned to cut down on drag but still both bombers would need to fly at nearly full throttle to maintain height across the North Sea and fuel restrictions meant that the combinations would have to fly straight through any cloud or turbulence.

At 2341hrs, the Operations Room at Wick in Scotland picked up a signal from B-Baker asking for a course to return to base. The pilot, Canadian Arthur Parkinson, had been unable to locate the Hardanger Plateau and had begun to turn back with the glider still on tow (in fact, he had passed directly over the Norwegian group but the Eureka's battery had failed). Radio Direction Finding (RDF) plots gave his location as over the North Sea. Just before midnight, Squadron Leader Wilkinson, piloting A-Able, reported that his glider had been released in the sea but the RDF showed them to be over southern Norway, though off-course. At 0151hrs on 20 November, Halifax A-Able, flying now on its reserve tanks, reached base. Nothing more was heard from B-Baker.

At the end of the war, investigations into the fate of the Freshman teams found that A-Able's 'Rebecca' receiver, intended to pick up 'Eureka's' signals, had failed and the combination had flown on map reading alone. Heavy cloud cover had meant they were unable to identify the LZ and soon both Halifax and Horsa began to ice up, losing height and bringing increased risk that they would hit mountain peaks. The frozen tow rope snapped and Strathdee and Doig tried to bring the glider down near Fylgejedal but crashed, killing both men and six of their passengers. Four more were taken prisoner and either shot or poisoned by their captors on the night of 23/24 November, their bodies thrown into the sea and never recovered. The remaining five were shot without trial in January 1943 in accordance with Hitler's infamous *Kommandobefel* (Commando Order) of October 1942, which decreed that all Commando troops were to be executed immediately.

B-Baker, it was found, crashed into a mountain at Hestadfjell at around 2245hrs, killing all on board. Its glider crashed some distance away, killing three. The remainder were captured and executed within a few hours at the German barracks in Bekkebo, their bodies stripped and dumped in an unmarked grave, although they were later recovered and now lie in Egenes Cemetery, Stavanger, along with their comrades from the other aircraft and a memorial to the mission. At Nuremburg, two Germans were executed and a third, wanted for crimes on the Eastern Front, was handed over to the Russians for their part in the murders.

It was not a promising start for British glider operations, but as one report put it

> it must be realised that the glider pilots knowingly took on an adventure which meant great risk to their lives, and allowed only the smallest chance of escape. [The mission] would not have been undertaken at all but for the extreme importance of the objective, which justified the risk
> . . .

The Glider Pilot Regiment had adopted a motto that 'Nothing is Impossible' and set out to prove that with Operation Freshman – overambitious, perhaps undertaken more for political than military ends, it seemed the regiment had bitten off more than it could chew.[9] Yet worse was still to come.

Chapter Four

'The graveyard of the paratroopers': Mediterranean operations

With Operation Seelowe, the planned invasion of Britain postponed, Assault Group Koch, now expanded into 1st Battalion of the 1st Assault Regiment returned to its home station. The 7th (Airborne) and 22nd Luftlande (Airlanding) Divisions received orders to combine forces as the XI Flieger Corps with its own dedicated air transport groups and Student took over as Corps Commander. Recovering from a head wound sustained in fighting in Holland, Student had spent his days considering how his airborne forces could be employed and had concluded that a series of assaults across the islands of the central and eastern Mediterranean would allow the Germans to move ever closer to a final assault on Alexandria and the Suez Canal.

German ambitions in the Balkans at that time were limited to supporting the failing invasion of Greece by Italian troops and to securing their southern flanks and access to the Black Sea in preparation for the planned invasion of Russia, scheduled to begin on 15 May 1941. To achieve this, a plan was developed to seize control of Southern Thrace and the coast between Salonika and Alexandropolis using ground and airborne forces. In March 1941, as British imperial forces landed in Salonika to bolster the under-equipped Greeks, twenty-seven divisions of the German 12th Army under General List assembled in Romania, crossed the Danube into Bulgaria and prepared to attack the Metaxas defence line along Greece's northern border. Facing them were thirty-three Allied divisions, made up of three British, six Greek and twenty-four Yugoslavian formations, the whole supported by 200 aircraft against the Germans' 1,200. When, on 6 April, the Germans attacked, Allied forces in the north-east soon found themselves outflanked by the 12th Army's panzers and began to withdraw southwards. Like Leonidas before them, British troops fought a delaying action at the pass of Thermopylae but by 24 April they, too, were in retreat.

The capture of the Corinth Bridge, 26 April 1941

With Greece clearly about to fall, the Germans saw another Dunkirk in the making with an opportunity to trap a large number of British, Australian and

New Zealand forces by capturing the bridge spanning Corinth Canal – the main artery into the Peloponnese and the southern ports. If the Germans captured the ports north of the bridge before the evacuation was complete, the Allied forces would depend on the bridge for their very survival and its capture would effectively seal the escape route of thousands as well as enabling the tanks of the 12th Army to maintain their momentum and capture the whole of mainland Greece. A hasty plan was devised to take the Corinth Bridge using glider troops reinforced by paratroops on the same model as had proved successful the previous year in capturing the Albert Canal crossings. Three gliders, piloted by Leutnants Fulda, Brendenbeck and Mende would land on the north side of the bridge as three more flown by Leutnants Phenn, Lassen and Raschke approached from the south. On the morning of 26 April, a force of 270 Ju52 transports and six DFS 230 gliders began to take off at 0500hrs from the Greek airfield at Larissa for the two-hour flight to Corinth.

As a short but heavy bombing and strafing attack on the defenders softened up the positions around the bridge, the gliders carrying fifty-four *Fallschirmpioniere* (parachute engineers) under Leutnant Haffner were released twelve miles from their objective, swooping down to land on either side of the bridge at 0700hrs. Leutnant Phenn, aiming for a pinpoint landing, actually crashed into one of the pillars of the bridge, injuring one of his passengers, but the landing meant that, within seconds, the Germans were on the bridge.

The bridge's defenders, supported by three tanks, had prepared it for demolition but were taken by surprise by the speed of the German assault and eighty were taken prisoner as the northern group cleared through their positions. A brief firefight overwhelmed the British posts guarding the southern end and, even before they were taken, engineers had begun to search for the demolition charges. In a matter of minutes, eleven anti-aircraft positions had been taken and the bridge was in German hands. Leutenant Fulda ordered the wires and charges removed from the bridge but a lieutenant engineer refused to move them, stating that his orders were to only cut the wires to prevent their being detonated but to leave them in place in case of successful counterattack. The charges stayed put.

Recovering quickly, British and Greek troops began to counterattack and called in artillery and mortar fire on to the small force. It seemed as if the German gamble had paid off until the bridge suddenly exploded. The actual series of events remains the subject of controversy but some reports later claimed that a surviving Bofors gun crew, firing tracer rounds, had managed to close in on the charges. Leutnant Franz Phenn was among several Germans on the bridge when the Bofors hit its target. Simultaneous explosions at both ends dropped the bridge and it crashed to the canal floor far below. Although the bridge was destroyed, by 28 April a temporary structure had been put in place and German troops and vehicles poured south, taking the isthmus within just two days. The Allied forces were cut in two and the Germans were able to round up thousands of prisoners. For the loss of just eight men at the bridge and fifty-five in the parachute attack around it, the Peloponnese had been cut off. Thousands of British and Empire troops now faced a Dunkirk-style evacuation from Kalamata and other smaller ports to the, for now, relative safety of Crete.

Operation Merkur – the invasion of Crete, 20 May 1941

For Hitler, the campaign in Greece ended when the Allied armies had been pushed off the mainland. Europe was now secure and attention could be turned to the east. 'He wanted to break off the Balkan campaign after reaching the south of Greece', Student later recalled.

> When I heard this, I flew to see Goering, and proposed a plan of capturing Crete by airborne forces alone. Goering – who was always easy to enthuse – was quick to see the possibilities of the idea, and sent me on to Hitler. I saw him on April 21. When I first explained the project, Hitler said, 'it sounds all right, but I don't think it's practicable'. But I managed to convince him in the end.[1]

Many in the High Command felt that Crete was irrelevant and, if any attack was to be made in the Mediterranean, it should be against the British base at Malta. Goering, anxious to redeem himself after the Luftwaffe failures against Britain, now argued forcefully that Cretan airbases would put RAF bombers in reach of the much needed Romanian oilfields but could equally be used by German aircraft to dominate not only the eastern Mediterranean, but potentially provide a staging post for an attack on the Suez Canal. Hitler, still impressed by the performance of the airborne troops in the west, finally agreed to issue Directive No. 28, calling for 'Operation Merkur (Mercury)' to 'occupy the island of Crete, to be prepared with the object of using Crete as an air base against Britain in the Eastern Mediterranean'. The attack would take place before the end of May, led by the Luftwaffe and paratroops with a seaborne invasion by regular forces to support them.

The plan put forward by Student was simple and dictated largely by the rough terrain in Crete itself. Gliders would arrive first to seize Maleme airfield in the west of the island and secure it for the planned delivery of airlanding troops by Ju52. More gliders would attack nearby Canea and two waves of paratroop drops in four areas along the northern coastline would push outwards from each airhead until the forces spread 'like an oilspot', as Student put it at the briefing in the Hotel Grande Bretagne in Athens. The airborne force gathered was the greatest yet. The 7th Airborne Division would be supported by an air landing of the 5th Mountain Division (the 22nd Airlanding Division, so successful alongside the paras in Holland, had been sent to Romania in preparation for the Russian invasion) and was expected to arrive in eighty gliders and 493 Ju52s supported by fighters, bombers and Stukas – over 1,200 aircraft in all. By contrast, the seaborne invasion force was regarded as secondary and the motley collection of ferries, fishing boats, caiques and yachts made the invasion forces look, as one writer described it, 'like a reverse Dunkirk'. But that would not matter. Student was confident that by the time they arrived, Crete would have fallen. His confidence was boosted by reports that the defenders of Crete had been further weakened by sending troops to quell an insurrection that was under way in Iraq.

On Crete, General Wavell, Commander in Chief of Middle East forces, appointed Major-General 'Tiny' Freyburg, a six foot New Zealander commanding the 2nd New Zealand and the 6th Australian Divisions – both recently evacuated from Greece – to command the assortment of 28,500 British, Australian, New Zealand and Greek units on the island. Most heavy equipment had been left behind and morale was low but Wavell did what he could and sixteen light tanks of the 3rd Hussars and six infantry tanks of 2nd Royal Tank Regiment, together with forty-nine field guns and a battalion of the Leicestershire Regiment arrived on 16 May. Between the one obsolete squadron of Gladiator and Fulmar fighters and the Hurricanes of 33, 80 and 112 Squadrons, the RAF and Fleet Air Arm could produce between them just twelve serviceable aircraft with which to oppose the Luftwaffe. By 18 May, only four Hurricanes and three Gladiators remained operational and they were withdrawn to Egypt the following day. Top secret intercepts using the captured Enigma machines had alerted the British to German plans and Freyburg had now deployed his men along the coast, paying special attention to his airfields and possible landing zones.

Operation Merkur began at 0615hrs on 20 May with an hour-long attack by bombers and fighters. From Corinth, Dadion, Eleusis, Phaleron, Tangara and Topolis, Ju52s thundered into the air through clouds of choking dust that reduced visibility to a few yards and meant that each pilot needed to wait for the air to clear before starting his own takeoff run. Luftwaffe staff officers watched in frustration as their carefully planned timetable fell apart. From Tanagra, forty-eight DFS 230 gliders carrying 288 men of the 1st Assault Regiment began lifting off at 0503hrs for the two-hour flight. Twenty-six more lifted off from Megara and Eleusis and headed south. Even with the impressive air fleet available, two waves would be needed to transport the 750 glider, 5,000 airlanding and 10,000 parachute troops due to take part. Three groups would be landed during the day, Gruppe West would land and capture the airfield at Maleme and Gruppe Centre would take Canea and the Suda docks in the first wave that morning. Group East would land in the afternoon to take control of the airfield at Heraklion. Further drops to all three would extend their airheads throughout the afternoon and following day.

Gruppe West's three Glider Detachments were made up of men taken from the 1st Battalion of the Assault Regiment and scheduled to spearhead the attacks on Maleme. The dry bed of the Tavronitis was to act as an additional landing strip for the Ju52s following later and an anti-aircraft position at the mouth of the river was the target of 108 men in fourteen gliders commanded by Oberleutnant Wulf von Plessen. The second detachment was to be commanded by Eben-Emael veteran Major Walter Koch, with 120 men in fifteen gliders. Their objective was to land near the southern slopes of Hill 107 and capture the RAF camp there. Kampftrupp Braun, the third of Group West's glider detachments, under the command of Major Franz Braun would send ninety men in nine gliders to take and hold the bridge over the River Tavronitis to allow the paratroopers under General Meindl dropping to the west to link up with the airlanding troops.

Group Centre's headquarters staff under Generalmajor Wilhelm Süssmann would land by glider south-west of Galatas, whilst its two glider detachments attacked their targets. The first, under Leutnant Alfred Genz, with ninety men in nine gliders would attack and sieze British AA positions near Mournies, south-east of Chania and the second, 150 men in fifteen gliders led by Hauptmann Gustav Altmann, would neutralize positions on the Akrotiri Peninsula north-east of Chania, and make way for Oberst Heidrich's 3rd Parachute Regiment.

From the outset, the operation began to go wrong. The 7th Airborne's commander, Süssmann, died before even reaching the island when his glider crashed onto the Greek island of Aegina at 0600hrs after it caught in the slipstream of a Heinkel He-111 and the tow rope broke. Those who did make the journey soon found the island's defences were far stronger and more effective than anticipated, with Greek and Cretan troops and irregular forces swelling the ranks to around 43,000 and all fighting back determinedly – one story told of a German paratrooper beaten to death by an old man with a walking stick as he lay stunned from a heavy landing. German paratroopers still jumped with only a knife and a pistol with weapons delivered in a separate bundle and Hans Sack, who jumped near the airfield at Maleme, recalled that once he landed he took cover and soon heard the sound of a submachine gun close by. Thinking that his comrades were attacking British troops on Hill 107, he broke cover and was hit almost immediately, learning a few minutes later that a quick-thinking British soldier had found a weapons container, removed one of the automatic weapons and was now using it to good effect against the paratroops searching for their weapons bundles. Across Crete, paratroopers were being cut down before they could even find a way to fire back.

For the slow-moving gliders, this was no Eben-Emael. Only the first gliders reached Maleme without serious opposition. The defenders of Crete were both ready for action and experienced soldiers, and effective AA and small arms fire raked the craft as they came in to land, a reporter later describing the eerie experience of finding gliders crashed with everyone on board dead before they hit the ground. Some, though, obscured by dust and smoke, reached their targets.

The AA guns around the mouth of the Tavronitis were silenced at a cost of seventeen dead, among them von Plessen, and twenty-seven wounded. The iron bridge across the riverbed was taken, although Major Braun was among those killed doing so, and glider troops cut the main Maleme–Sphakia road but Hill 107 remained firmly in the hands of the New Zealand 22nd Battalion and continued to dominate the area. Major Koch's men had captured the RAF camp but failed to reach the summit of the hill. Koch was hit in the head within minutes of landing and handed command over to Oberleutnant Sarrazin, who was killed on the hill.

Further east, Group Centre ran into heavy and accurate fire as they approached their landing and drop zones. The transports broke formation to avoid the fire and their troops became widely scattered and easily pinned down by the defenders. The second glider group, tasked with taking control of the Akrotiri area, suffered 108 casualties out of the 150 men deployed, including Hauptmann Altmann and platoon commander Oberleutnant Ebner. Two more platoon commanders, Oberleutnant Möhr and Leutnant Rümmler, were captured and remained in captivity until the end of the war.

Back in Athens, though, initial reports suggested things were going well. Only seven Ju52s had been reported lost, although many showed some signs of damage by small arms fire, and word had not yet reached them that Süssmann and Meindl (commander of Group West) were dead. Delays at the takeoff fields meant that the second wave, due to drop around Canea immediately after a Stuka attack, in fact arrived an hour late. The bombing, far from keeping the defenders' heads down, merely gave them ample warning of the drop. (Captain Evelyn Waugh, the novelist, served on Crete and, finding himself under intense Stuka attack, observed 'like all things German it is very efficient, but it goes on much too long'.[2]) The loss of only seven aircraft was misleading. Seven had been shot down but many more had been hit or crashed when landing on Crete and Adolf Strauch, due to jump in the second wave, recorded in his diary for 20 May:

> Midday and it is boiling hot. Impenetrable clouds of dust lie above the airfield. The Ju52s have come back from the mission; but not all of them . . . Before we load the weapons containers we have to first remove the dead from the damaged machines. The aircrew do not say very much . . . the fighter planes which should be escorting us and which should beat down the enemy opposition when we drop pass us – flying back from Crete. Bad organization somewhere.[3]

At sea, the motley flotilla carrying two battalions of the Alpine troops along with elements of the 7th Airborne and their heavy weapons had been intercepted by the Royal Navy. The little boats were simply run down and the larger craft easy victims for the navy's guns, despite strenuous efforts by the Luftwaffe to provide air support. Only fifty-two men of the two Alpine battalions were to reach the fighting in Crete. In seven days of fighting, the 493 transport planes had been reduced to just 74 undamaged machines. Over half had been lost. More than half of Crete's 43,000 defenders escaped on naval ships, leaving behind a victorious but badly shaken enemy. Of the 22,000 German troops committed to Crete, an initial report claimed 1,915 officers and men killed, 1,632 wounded and a further 1,759 missing. Later estimates would claim up to 6,000 fatalities alone, nearly one-third of the attacking force. Crete, Churchill observed, had shattered 'the spearhead of the German lance'.

Crete, the island where Daedalus and Icarus had first taken to the skies, would clip the wings of the German airborne. Ironically, though, it would also spark enthusiasm among Allied advocates of airborne forces. Colonel Bonner Fellers, American Military Attache in Egypt, produced a 258-page report in which he could barely contain his excitement:

> The drama of Crete marks an epic in warfare. The concept of the operation was highly imaginative, daringly new. Combat elements drawn from Central Europe moved with precision into funnel shaped Greece. Here they reformed, took shape as a balanced force, were given wings. The operation had the movement, rhythm, harmony of a master's organ composition. On 20 May and succeeding days, this force soared through space; its elements broke over Crete in thundering crescendos – all stops out. For the first time in history, airborne troops, supplied and supported by air, landed in the face of an enemy, defeated him.[1]

But in assaulting Crete, as historian Milton Dank later put it, 'Hitler had skilfully opened a Pandora's box, and inside a genie was being born that would later grip him by the throat.'

Many still believe that Crete, the 'graveyard of the Fallschirmjager', so shocked Hitler that he refused to consider future airborne operations. Certainly, two months later, he rejected Student's plan to take Cyprus, telling him 'the day of the parachutist is over. The Parachute arm is a surprise weapon and without the element of surprise there can be no future for airborne forces' but in a postwar appraisal of German airborne operations for the American Office of the Chief of Military History, Generalfeldmarschall (Field Marshal) Albert Kesselring, commander of the German Second Air Force during the Netherlands campaign, commented that

> the airborne operation against Crete resulted in very serious losses which in percentage greatly exceeded those sustained by the Germans in previous World War II campaigns. The parachute troops were particularly affected. Since everything Germany possessed in the way

of parachute troops had been committed in the attack on Crete and had been reduced in that campaign to about one-third of their original strength, too few qualified troops remained to carry out large-scale airborne operations at the beginning of the Russian campaign. Air transportation was also insufficient for future operations. Furthermore, the German High Command had begun to doubt whether such operations would continue to pay – the Crete success had cost too much. The parachute troops themselves, however, recovered from the shock. Their rehabilitation was undertaken and lessons were drawn from the experience, so that a year later a similar undertaking against the island of Malta was energetically prepared.[5]

The invasion of Malta, 1942

By 21 April 1942, RAF aircraft of 69 Squadron had photographed glider strips in preparation at Gerbini in Sicily and Reinhard Hoffmann, serving in Russia with FJR-2 recalled that around this time his unit had been pulled out of the line. 'We all believed that we were being pulled out in order to be trained for new Para drops. According to rumour we would be attacking either Malta or Gibraltar . . .'[6] After moving from location to location, Hoffmann found himself still in Russia but the rumours of an operation against Malta were true. Colonel Freiherr von der Heydte, an outstanding field commander of German parachute troops, authored part of the same US appraisal and reported that

> in connection with the projected paratroop operation against Malta in 1942, six hours before the parachute jump, a battalion under my command was supposed to land by means of dive-gliders among the British antiaircraft positions on the south coast of the island and to eliminate the British ground defence. Over a period of months the Malta operation was prepared down to the smallest detail, and during that time the parachute troops practiced on mock-ups of these positions.[7]

Commenting on the problems of field communications, he noted that

> for the projected Malta operation of one parachute battalion, the engineering firm of Siemens-Halske supplied a portable radio set for maintaining contact with the base. It had a definite range of 180 miles, could be operated without interruption for six hours, and could easily be carried by one man.

The operation was never launched, not because of a lack of faith in airborne operations, but because men like Kesselring firmly believed airborne operations must always aim at surprise, which has become increasingly difficult but not impossible to achieve. Detection devices, for example radar equipment, can pick up air formations at a great distance and assure prompt countermeasures. Flights at very low altitude, such as were planned for the attack against Malta, are difficult to detect by means of such equipment . . . At this point, however, Hitler himself lost confidence in operations of this nature. He had come to the conclusion that only airborne operations which came as a complete surprise could lead to success. After the airborne operations against Holland and Crete, he believed surprise attacks to be impossible and maintained that the day of successful airborne operations were over. The fact that the Cretan operations came so close to defeat strengthened his opinion. Moreover, the Malta operation would have to be prepared in Italy and launched from there. Prior experience with the Italians had proved that the enemy would be apprised in advance regarding every single detail of the preparations, so that even a partial surprise was impossible. Since Hitler had no confidence at all in the combat value of the troops, which with the exception of the German parachute troops were to be of Italian origin exclusively, he did not believe the undertaking could be successful and abandoned its execution. The special circumstances prevailing at that time may have justified this particular decision, but the basic attitude in regard to airborne operations later turned out to be wrong . . .[8]

Nevertheless, the use of airborne troops for small-scale operations was still obvious and North Africa seemed the perfect place to use them.

Special operations in Tunisia, December 1942

Hauptman Fritz Von Koenen of the 13th Brandenburgers – the son of a farmer in South-West Africa, spoke fluent English and was already an experienced operative against the British in North Africa when, late in 1942, at Buerat, two hundred kilometres from Tripoli, he was briefed by Colonel Bayerlein on a special mission. Marked on a map were three blue crosses behind the enemy lines: three bridges over rivers and wadis at Tebessa, Gafsa and Tozeur on the railway line between Pray and Algiers. The railway was a vital link in the Allied supply lines and alongside it lay telephone and telegraph wires carrying all signals traffic between the front and the headquarters staff. If these could be cut, the Allies would be out of touch with their rear areas and their current offensive would stall.

Von Koenen's company were flown from Naples into the coastal town of Hammamet where they settled into a comfortable villa amongst the orange groves and lemon trees to plan the operation that would see them travel to their targets by glider and, after destroying them, make their way across the desert with the aid of Arab guides to the nearest friendly base. At midnight on 26 December, the mission got under way.

Three DFS 230s towed by Ju52s left Bizerta that night. Von Koenen sat directly behind his pilot, Unteroffizier Heinzel. Behind him was his trusted company sergeant-major, Hans Neumann, veteran of many missions with his captain. Next was interpreter Reginald Dade and behind him Sergeant Sloka and five more men. Between their feet lay their weapons and explosives. In the following gliders sat more of his men and their Arab guides. After flying a course over Cap Bon, the group crossed the bay south towards Sousse and Sfax and then over Gulf of Gabes to the west. During the flight, they met with a squadron of Ju88s and one Ju52 became disorientated and followed them by mistake, finally putting down to the north of Sfax when he realized his error and that it was too late to catch up.

The plan called for the gliders to release at around 2,500 m and use desert thermals to glide for the remaining seventy kilometres to the target. As they approached, at around 0200hrs, von Koenen could see the moonlight reflecting off the railway lines and the simple arc of the 300 m long bridge at Wadi el Kbir. At last the pilot put the glider down, its landing skids wrapped in barbed wire to shorten its landing run. The second glider landed alongside and it was only then that they realized the third had gone missing. Unloading the explosives, von Koenen and Neumann went forward to reconnoitre. Far behind the lines, the French garrison saw little reason to be on guard. Instead, they sat in the small station building of Sidi bou Baker.

Neumann then directed the demolition of the bridge. Two 3 kg charges of explosives to cut the railway lines, two more of 70 kg each in the widest part of the central pillar of the bridge. One man cut down the telegraph wires with an axe and narrowly avoided falling when the pole suddenly began to topple. Everything was going to plan until they realized that the fuses for the explosives were being carried on the missing glider. Neumann decided to improvise using cartridges but these gave, at best, just sixty seconds to get clear and each one had to be set off at the same time. At a signal to indicate the first was lit, Sloka set the fuse for the pillar charge and jumped from the bridge into the Wadi, a drop of around five metres, twisting his ankle in the fall. Neumann grabbed him and pulled him clear just as the bridge exploded.

As the dust began to settle, von Koenen ordered the team back to their rendezvous around the gliders. As they reached them, they found two men missing. Sloka went to look for them but whilst he was away, the group began to withdraw, heading off into the desert with their guides. Near dawn, the group lay up in a small wadi near Djebel bou Ramli and near noon, sentries saw Arabs approaching. The interpreter went to meet them and found instead one of the missing men. Brought up in Palestine, he had been able to make himself understood and anti–French Arabs had offered to find his comrades. That night, in a forced march of sixty-five kilometres, the men reached the city of Gafsa. Six days after the attack, Hannes Feldmann the other missing man arrived, well fed and riding an Arab donkey. The group eventually reached an Italian outpost and safety, their only casualty Sergeant Sloka, captured by a French patrol and shot.

A second mission, against a bridge near Kasserine, was less fortunate. One glider, flown by Unteroffizier Fissewert, was forced to make an emergency landing on the outbound leg and the crew were picked up and flown out the following day. Oberleutnant Hartig's glider crashlanded near the bridge, breaking both his ankles and seriously injuring two of his passengers. The attack went through but Hartig and the injured were left at the crash site and were taken prisoner. The fate of the third glider was never established.

The final bridge was destroyed by a mission by truck on 10 January. By now, the British had decided to put a stop to Brandenburger activity and launched an assault from a submarine against von Koenen's Hammamet base. It failed after a running battle over eight days. Von Koenen's men, with their Arab allies, fought on until the Germans withdrew from North Africa.

Operation 'Husky' – the invasion of Sicily, 1943

Whilst German commanders saw Crete as a disaster, the Allies saw the potential of large-scale airborne assault. Unfortunately, by the end of 1942, the Allied airborne divisions were still experiencing difficulties in recruiting, training and equipping their men. The official history of the 6th Airborne records that, by the beginning of 1943,

> 132 (jeeps) had not yet come to hand. They 'were reported to be standing on a quayside waiting to be delivered, but it could not be discovered on which side of the Atlantic this quayside was'. There were too few six-pounder anti-tank and 20mm Hispano guns, and there were no reserves for the Tetrach tank designed to be carried by the Hamilcar gliders . . . As with men and equipment, so too with aircraft. . . . Only half an Air Landing Brigade could be carried at one time, and no tugs capable of towing a fully loaded Horsa any length of distance had yet made their appearance.[9]

Nevertheless, Allied planners had by now decided that the first blow against occupied Europe should be led by an airborne assault.

Operation 'Husky', the invasion of Sicily, was scheduled for the summer of 1943. Montgomery had argued for a joint US/British force under his command to undertake the task but his arch rival, Patton, had decreed otherwise. Feeling he had not been supported strongly enough by Eisenhower, Patton later wrote that 'Ike is more British than the British and is putty in their hands . . . God damn all British and so-called Americans'. Montgomery was not surprised when, on 7

May, he was told at a briefing at the Hotel St Georges in Algiers that there would now be two invasions, one British, one American. Later, he cornered Eisenhower's Chief of Staff in the lavatory to argue that the two armies must land side by side to give cohesion to the assault. In view of what was to come, it was a highly appropriate venue. Browning had by now left his command of the British 1st Airborne to become Eisenhower's senior airborne adviser, his place taken by the energetic 'Hoppy' Hopkinson, a prewar amateur pilot and gliding enthusiast eager to prove his theories of gliderborne warfare. With Operation Husky under way, Hopkinson went to Montgomery to plead for a mass landing of his entire Air Landing Brigade to precede his divisional attack. Operation 'Ladbrooke', as this phase became known, would be led by Brigadier 'Pip' Hicks and would land outside Syracuse to capture and hold the important Ponte Grande bridge over the Anapo River until elements of the seaborne force reached them.

Montgomery agreed and Hopkinson returned to his headquarters a happy man – seemingly unconcerned that there was not one British glider available in the whole of North Africa to carry out the task. Both George Chatterton and his RAF colleague Nigel Norman had been summoned to a briefing on the upcoming operation but Norman had been killed when the engines of the Hudson he was travelling in failed soon after takeoff in the UK. Chatterton, without his friend's support, listened with dismay as the plan was put to him. Not least of the problems, he argued, was finding the aircraft in the first place. Hopkinson dismissed his concerns with the airy comment that 'the US air force are going to supply tugs and gliders'. For Chatterton, it was the final straw. A night landing in unknown terrain was bad enough, but doing it in a glider that the pilots had never even seen before was a recipe for disaster and he said so but Hopkinson was not one to accept criticism of his plan.

> Now look here, Colonel Chatterton, I'm going to leave you for half an hour and in that time you can study the photographs [of the LZs in Sicily]. If, at the end of that time, you still feel that this is too difficult for you, you can consider yourself relieved of your command.

Chatterton was aware that, technically, Hopkinson did not have the power to carry out his threat but that he could make life every difficult for him. Nothing he saw in the photographs encouraged him and his belief that the operation would be deadly for his crews grew but he knew that to refuse would simply mean that someone else would be placed in charge of the glider landings. There was no choice. When Hopkinson returned he said nothing but the general's mood changed dramatically. As Chatterton wrote later, 'he was like a little boy. He was *so* pleased.'[10]

With three months to prepare, Chatterton sent some of his men to collect the American Waco CG-4A gliders they would be flying into action. Arriving at the windswept airfield of Oran, the pilots found their aircraft – in crates. With only a manual and one American corporal to guide them, they began work building their planes. Chatterton, meanwhile, had been wrestling with the problems of the proposed landing zones. The Wacos were smaller than the Horsa, capable of carrying eighteen men to the Horsa's twenty-eight. Crucially, though, it could carry a jeep *or* an anti-tank gun – but not both. The assumption was that two gliders would land side by side and pair up their loads. In practice, it worked – but only in practice. In real operations, Chatterton decided, the risk of either being lost was too great. Horsas would be needed but immediately he hit the next problem. Space for the gliders could not be made on the supply convoys from the UK. The only option was to fly.

Operation Beggar/Turkey Buzzard – ferry operations to North Africa, June/July 1943

From RAF Portreath in Cornwall to the US base at Sale in North Africa – the shortest possible route – would mean a flight of 1,350 miles over open sea, then another 1,000 across the desert to Tunisia. It would mean flying for ten hours straight, at a height of around 500 feet across the Bay of Biscay and within a hundred miles of German fighter bases on the French coast. It was generally regarded as impossible until 'Freshman' survivor Squadron Leader Wilkinson carried out experiments around the UK, flying his aircraft and crew to the limits of their endurance to prove that a tow was possible over the distances required (later that summer, RAF Squadron Leaders R G Seys and F M Gobeil would complete Operation 'Voodoo' – a transatlantic tow of 3,500 miles – in a Waco glider during an epic twenty-eight-hour flight). Operation 'Beggar' (also referred to as 'Turkey Buzzard') could begin.

In April, 1943, the German Afrika Korps were being supplied in part by glider operations from their southern European bases. The problem of towing the huge Me321 had been resolved in part by simply adding engines to a number of them to create the Me323 cargo plane. The glider/tow combinations and the lumbering 'Gigants' formed a valuable, but vulnerable, link in the supply chain. On 22 April, Allied fighters had come across one such flight and destroyed sixteen planes in a single day. As they prepared for the long flight, the crews chosen to ferry the Horsas to North Africa heard the news and were now all too aware of the risks involved.

The first flights of Operation 'Beggar' began on 1 June but bad weather forced the combination back. Two days later, four more took off. Two reached Sale that afternoon, one returned because of weather and the last ditched in the sea when its tow rope broke. The crew, Major Alistair Cooper, Staff Sergeant Dennis Hall and Sergeant Anthony 'Harry' Antopoulos spent ten hours sitting miserably on top of the floating glider before being picked up by a Royal Navy frigate. Two weeks later, Hall and Antopoulos were again en route for North Africa, this time with Staff Sergeant Conway, when two Focke-Wulf Condors on patrol attacked their combination. Conway opened fire through a porthole with his rifle. 'We took evasive action', Antonoupolos later recalled,

> following the tug through some very steep turns. Finally, the towplane pilot spoke over the intercom and said, 'It's no good, Would you please pull off?' I pulled the rope release lever and the Halifax quickly climbed into the clouds and disappeared. One Focke-Wulf was just below me, and I dove at him. I don't know what was in my mind, but I thought 'I'll get this bastard'. It must have worried him because he stopped firing, and at the last second we both turned away. There was no problem landing – I was the greatest ditcher of all time and had written the definitive report on how to do it.[11]

It would be eleven days before the three men were picked up by a fishing boat off Spain and returned to England. Sympathetic colleagues encouraged Antonoupolos to 'keep trying, Harry, you'll make North Africa yet!'

By the end of June, twenty-five Horsas had been delivered to Sale and two more arrived on 7 July, just two days before the invasion was due to begin. A further 1,000 miles across the desert and mountains added to the losses but steady progress was being made on the 346 crated gliders delivered by the Americans to North Africa by ship. Enough would be ready to complete the mission.

At their desert base, Chatterton and his men had been joined by a few American glider pilots who had originally set out by ship for Australia and had been turned north only a day's sailing away from port, heading instead to India and eventually North Africa. Now on 'detached service' with the British, Flight Officer Bob Wilson was among those who found their names on the list of volunteers. Chatterton 'gathered us together and thanked us for volunteering for the invasion of Sicily. That's about as close to being scared to death as I have ever felt . . . we were issued red berets and Sten guns, which we had never fired before'. Chatterton made a point of introducing the men to the visiting Montgomery and 'the general fired a salute at us. That made me feel good.'[12]

Together, the pilots underwent flying training in conditions that were far from ideal. By the eve of the operation, Chatterton reckoned his men had an average of just two hours flying time in the Waco and no operational experience at all. The mood was not improved by their living conditions in a former POW camp or by the loads they saw being placed aboard their aircraft. Bob Wilson watched a trailer being loaded and looked under the cover. 'It really gave me a shock; it was material for marking graves – canvas bags, tags, and wooden crosses. Somebody already knew that we would not all be coming back.'[13] Worse still, Chatterton was shown tow ropes where black insulating tape had been wound around them. Peeling this off, he found that the intercom wires between the glider and its towplane had been cut – an Italian-American mechanic was later blamed.

Invasion of Sicily phase one: Operation Ladbrooke, 9/10 July 1943

The night of 9 July saw winds gusting up to forty-five miles per hour across the North African airfields where 136 Wacos and eight Horsas stood waiting to take off. Six Horsas were to land near the Ponte Grande bridge and two would carry General Hopkinson and his staff, along with seven jeeps and six six-pounder anti-tank guns. Twenty-eight Americans had volunteered to join the British effort, knowing that their allies had, at best, just five hours experience and only one at night. Wing Commander Peter May took time to seek out Colonel Chatterton just before takeoff. He had admired Chatterton's suede boots and wanted to make sure that they would go to 'a good owner' in the event of anything happening to him. 'Of course,' he was told, 'just ask my batman. They're yours.' At 1842hrs, the first combination took off, followed at one-minute intervals by the rest of the fleet, a steady stream of aircraft thundering into the sky until the last lifted off at 2020hrs. Like their German counterparts before them, the pilots soon ran into difficulties in the dusty conditions. 'Andy' Andrews wrote later that the 'first part of takeoff was in a sandstorm with zero visibility. We were dragged through this dirty yellow wall, mesmerised by the short length of towrope we could see.'[14]

At Malta, searchlights acted as a beacon to guide the flights to their rendezvous over the island. Flying low to avoid German radar, Chatterton remembered seeing the clifftops of Malta pass by at the same height as his aircraft. Breaking through a patch of cloud, he found himself flying alongside his tow, a potentially lethal position since the rope could easily snag either plane. Already some combinations had encountered similar problems and around 5 per cent of the attacking force failed to reach the Malta RV. Ahead, on Sicily, the garrison had spent the day on an anti-invasion exercise but had been stood down for the night. Weather conditions were not considered suitable for an airborne attack.

Approaching the island, the inexperience of both tug and glider pilots began to show. Gliders frequently found themselves in the same position as Chatterton – flying alongside their tugs and in great danger of collision. Aircraft jostled for position as the first flight neared the coast. Despite very specific instructions – the aircraft would not be expected to approach too close to anti-aircraft fire and so gliders were to be released 3,000 yards from the shore at a height of 5,000 feet for the Horsas and 1,900 for the Wacos intended for LZ 1 and 1,400 for those headed for LZ 2 – someone (it was never established who) in the US 51st Air Transport Wing made the decision to release them all at 1,800 feet. This would give the lowest gliders a theoretical extra two miles of range but also allowed the tugs to release even earlier.

The first seven gliders approached the coast but, as they crossed it, the Italian defenders opened up with every weapon to hand. The fire was wild and erratic but looked impressive. Later, Wing Commander May reported to the subsequent inquiry that not a single American tug plane sustained any significant damage and that there had been no AA fire at all within thousands of yards of the planned release point. Nevertheless, the unnerved pilots of the unarmoured, vulnerable tow aircraft were panicked by the sight of tracer rounds rushing into the sky. Some turned and fled, their gliders still on tow. Some dived to just 300 feet and released so that their gliders struggled to make landfall as others crashed down upon them. With communication with their tugs either lost or sabotaged, some glider pilots released without orders. The plan called for the gliders to release about two miles offshore but the frightened tug pilots cut them loose two or even three times that distance, with no hope of reaching the island. The gliders descended much more quickly than their pilots expected – the rates, and therefore the release point, had been based on their performance in training over the hot desert where thermals provided lift. Now, at night and over water, they were falling too fast.

Chatterton later wrote that 'the point of release, 3,000 yards from shore, transformed what, from a nearer point and in favourable weather would have been difficult enough, into flying on to a mantelpiece which one could not see'.[15] As his glider, carrying Brigadier Hicks and his staff, approached the shore Chatterton's co-pilot read out their height as they descended '300 . . . 200 . . . Hell! Look out sir, a cliff!' Chatterton pulled back on the joystick trying to bring the glider into a climbing turn to reach a small island nearby. As he did, machine-gun fire from positions on the cliff top blasted off part of his wing. The glider stalled and hit the sea. As the crew and passengers climbed on to the top of the slowly sinking aircraft, Brigadier Hicks turned to his brigade-major muttering 'all is not well, Bill'.[16]

As they lay on their glider, Chatterton and Hicks could see other gliders passing overhead and, with fire still being directed at them from the cliff tops, they decided to try to swim for shore. As they struggled through the sea, a voice was heard calling for Hicks to get down. 'I can't' came the exasperated reply, 'my ruddy Mae West's blown itself up too much. I can't get down!' Bobbing along 'proud and English like the bowsprit of Nelson's Victory, and in the half-light, just as grotesque', Hicks finally reached shore.[17] The humour of the situation evaporated as a Wellington bomber, ablaze from nose to tail, hit the sea behind them. Chatterton thought the fire reminded him of the brandy burning on a Christmas pudding. Laying up in the rocky shoreline, they soon met up with a boatload of Special Forces troops and joined them as infantry in an attack on the gun positions above them. Chatterton would later describe his contribution to the invasion of Sicily as 'wearing an Italian topee, armed with a Service rifle, I mounted guard over 200 or so Italian prisoners'.

Elsewhere, the glider carrying General Hopkinson had also ditched. A passing destroyer spotted him clinging to the wreckage and picked him up. The ship's captain, Lord Ashbourne, had been in the same boat crew as Hopkinson at Cambridge and welcomed him aboard. 'We wrung out his clothes, gave him a plate of eggs and bacon and then sent him off to catch up with the rest of his soldiers.' Dressed in the only clothes that could be found to fit – the second-best uniform of one of the ship's Maltese stewards – the general was not a happy man. Out at sea, other ditched glider pilots were also beginning the long swim to shore. Sergeant 'Andy' Andrews, though, had not ditched. He was about to but, warning his passenger, Colonel 'Honker' Henniker to make ready, he was told in no uncertain tone not to 'be a damn fool. We have to get on land. We can't get wet!'[18] Faced with such unarguable logic, Andrews turned towards a promontory where he could see a searchlight. He knew that, even if he reached it, they would land in the midst of enemy troops, but the alternative was to annoy the colonel even more. Andrews and Henniker would arrive at the bridge late the next day with a long line of prisoners and a donkey cart. Chatterton's deputy, Colonel O L 'Jonah' Jones, landed with part of the brigade headquarters on Sicily but also far from his intended landing area. Looking for something to do, he and his group of staff officers and signallers attacked a nearby coastal battery, quickly overrunning it and destroying five guns and an ammunition dump.

Such had been the chaos caused among tug pilots that gliders were landing far from their destinations. After making a smooth landing, the troops in one glider began to unload their cargo before the enemy opened fire only to be told firmly to vacate the runway by the irate RAF air traffic controllers of a Maltese airfield. Only twelve gliders towed by the RAF reached the island itself and of those, only one, a Horsa flown by Staff Sergeant D P 'Galp' Galpin, landed within sight of its objective at the Ponte Grande bridge. Galpin, carrying a platoon of the South Staffords under the command of Lieutenant Lawrence Withers, had been guided in by the light of a nearby searchlight. Nearby, another Horsa piloted by the popular Captain Denholm, crashed at high speed into the river bank killing all on board. Deciding not to wait, Withers ordered his men forward. As they dashed forward, another Horsa appeared. This one, carrying sappers and a cargo of Bangalore torpedoes to clear the wire, was riddled with machine-gun fire as it landed and disintegrated in an explosion that flung glider and body parts over hundreds of yards. Quickly briefing his little force, Withers took half his men across the river, swimming through the muddy waters to attack from the northern end, the other half assaulting from the south. They quickly formed up on the other side, still without the sentries being alerted and, as a signal flare arced into the sky, charged the bridge firing from the hip, shouting and screaming. The Italian defenders, convinced they were facing a much larger force, surrendered. Locking them up in a blockhouse, the men then severed the demolition charges. In a few minutes, twenty men had achieved the primary objective assigned to two thousand.

The following day, Chatterton's group came across Jones's and the two decided to attack a farmhouse they believed to be held by the enemy. Instead, as they approached, they found themselves invited to lunch by its owner, an American woman married to an Italian. She and her husband had been under the assumption that the noises were part of yet another exercise but were only too happy to treat their unexpected visitors to what Chatterton would remember as

> a wonderful lunch, while all around us were the sounds of the diminishing battle, the rattle of machine guns and explosives. I don't know how many bottles of Chianti we drank that afternoon or how much spaghetti we ate, but it was a very large and very, very good lunch.[100]

As the party made ready to leave, she directed them to a nearby barn. There they found a bright red 1900 vintage fire engine of the Syracuse fire department which, sporting a six-pounder gun attached to its rear, provided their transport to the Ponte Grande.

At the briefing in North Africa, Withers had been told that two companies of the South Staffs would hold the bridge until relieved at 0730hrs. By 0800hrs, his platoon, swelled by stragglers to a force of eight officers and sixty-five other ranks, remained alone on the bridge and could see the enemy massing for a counterattack. American volunteer Flight Officer Samuel Fine had already been hit in the shoulder as he landed but now found himself part of the defensive perimeter. With one 2inch and one 3inch mortar but only a few, mostly smoke, bombs, four Bren guns and a single Gammon bomb, the defenders held off massed attacks for the next seven hours until, with just fifteen men left unwounded and the ammunition gone, the force surrendered. Fine recalled:

> Just before we surrendered, I was wounded in the neck. As the enemy was marching us away along a dirt road through some woods, a British officer suddenly appeared from behind a tree right in front of us – he was at least 150 feet away – and took a shot with a pistol at the Fascist guard on point, smacking him right between the eyes. The other guards didn't know where the shot came from and while they were scurrying around among us, I grabbed two rifles from a couple of them. I tossed one to a trooper near me and the two of us shot every Fascist we could see. The rest of our captors were huddling in the woods behind trees and bushes and meekly surrendered.[20]

The seaborne force had arrived and the bridge was secure.

Standing beside the Ponte Grande bridge soon afterwards, Chatterton looked down at the remains of Denholm's glider and noted how 'the crew and passengers had been blown forward as if down a funnel but of the pilot there was no sign . . . I stood looking at this macabre and tragic pile of bodies.' Nearby the

H N 'Andy' Andrews

In 1942 22-year-old 'Andy' Andrews volunteered for the newly formed Glider Pilot Regiment to escape the boredom of waiting for the German invasion that never came. He had served with the Royal Engineers in France but, after evacuation from Dunkirk, he found service in England unexciting. He became one of the regiment's most experienced men, one of only six to have survived all four major operations (Sicily, Normandy, Arnhem and the Rhine crossing), during which his flying skills earned him the Distinguished Flying Medal and Bar

As the war in Europe ended, Andrews was assigned to fly gliders behind tow pilots under training for operations in the Far East and narrowly avoided a serious crash during one such flight. Afterwards, according to his *Times* obituary, he 'crisply' explained to the tug pilot that it would have been a shame had he been killed on a training mission after all he had survived on operations.

After demobilization in 1946, Harold Norman Andrews returned to his engineering studies and emigrated to Canada in 1953, where he was commissioned in the Royal Canadian Engineers and rose to the rank of major. He continued flying until 1965 when a helicopter crash left him stranded in a heavy snowstorm and he decided he had pushed his luck too far.

Working from a two-room trailer in a New Westminster car park, Andrews was instrumental in developing the town's Douglas College. After his death at the age of 80 in 2000, his wife Helen, whom he met while she was serving with the WAAF at Brize Norton in 1942, and their son and daughter were invited by the college to present the Andy Andrews Award to promising students in his memory.

burnt-out remains of the sapper Horsa lay in stark contrast to the relatively intact glider Galpin had landed. By now news was reaching Chatterton of the scale of the losses – at least sixty-nine of the 137 aircraft had gone down at sea. Just forty-nine Wacos and five Horsas had reached Sicily and several more were missing. As he surveyed the scene, General Hopkinson arrived by jeep. 'Andy' Andrews recalls that the general 'appeared small and tired. As he returned our salute, I could not help interpreting the look in his eyes with his own unspoken words, "Thank God, that's over. Not many left, are there?"'[21]

Back in North Africa, tempers were running high. General Sir John Hackett, then with the reserve brigade, wrote that

> glider pilots who were recovered from the sea came back looking for tug pilots' throats to cut. I saw no option but to confine them to camp until after the American parade for the award of decorations for gallantry, by

which time the admirable qualities always to be found in glider pilots had reasserted themselves and calm was restored.[22]

The award of medals to tug pilots who, they felt, had fled at the first shot was made all the more insulting for the glider pilots when Samuel Fine was refused any acknowledgement of his role in the defence of the Ponte Grande – despite the support of British witnesses – on the basis that glider pilots were not supposed to fight as infantry and so therefore could not qualify. He did, however, receive the promotion his British comrades recommended. Another American pilot has described how each unit was assigned a quota of awards given out on almost a lottery basis – he himself refused when asked to 'cut cards' to see who would be allowed to keep a Bronze Star award later in the war. Resentment would run deep for a long time to come.[23]

Invasion of Sicily phase two: Operation Fustian, 12/13 July 1943

Within forty-eight hours, the next stage of the invasion was under way with Operation 'Fustian'. Just as the taking of the Ponte Grande bridge 'saved the 8th Army seven days' in the capture of the port of Syracuse, taking the Primasole Bridge across the River Simeto and the Gornalunga Canal would allow tanks to head towards Catania and thus gain control of eastern Sicily. A *coup de main* attack would be made by paratroopers and airborne engineers in eight Wacos and eleven Horsas all towed by the RAF. Three days after the first wave, the next airborne element climbed into their aircraft and at 1935hrs on 12 July, C-47s of the US 51st Troop Carrier Wing began the lift followed at 2200hrs by the gliders towed by the RAF's 38 Wing. At first, all went well. The naval ships of the seaborne invasion fleet had been told of the 'Fustian' drop and of the routes and timings of the air fleet but somewhere off Cap Passero, some thirty aircraft strayed into the no-go zone established around the ships. Nervous gunners below opened up. Two aircraft were shot down immediately and another nine turned back because of damage and injuries. Six more turned back claiming they had been ordered to by their squadron commander. The firing had alerted the shore-based defenders and flak now added to the damage, another nine paratroop-carrying aircraft were shot down and three glider combinations went missing. Aboard one C47, Lieutenant-Colonel Pearson, commanding 1st Battalion of the Parachute Regiment, noticed the glow of Mount Etna below. Realizing they were off course, he jokingly asked one of his men, a former pilot, if he could fly the Dakota and was assured the man could. Moving forward, Pearson told the pilot that they had overshot the DZ.

His co-pilot was sitting with his hands over his face crying 'We can't, we can't' 'Can't do what' I said. 'We can't go in there'. I could see quite clearly blobs of fire. I knew what was going through his mind, it was going through mine as well, because on the ground were what I thought were burning Dakotas. I said to the pilot 'There's nothing for it old boy, we've got to do it. If your co-pilot's no good I've no hesitation in shooting him'. I pulled out my revolver. The pilot continued with his protests. So I said 'I could shoot you as well.' 'You can't do that, who'd fly the aeroplane?' I said, 'don't worry about that, I've got a bloke in the back who can fly this'. 'Yeah, but he won't know how to land it!' 'No-one has asked him to land the bloody thing – you don't think he's going to hang about to land it do you? He'll be stepping out very sharp!'[24]

Faced with the fact that none of their passengers expected to return with them to their base and that they were by now surplus to requirements, the pilots

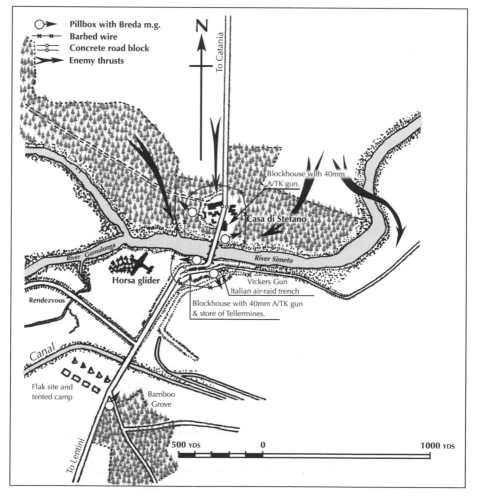

Sicily: map of the assault on the Prima Sole bridge.

reluctantly headed back towards the DZ but dropped the paras too low and at too high a speed, causing a number of casualties as they hit the ground hard.

Scattered over a wide area, the paras began to make their way to the objective. It would take General Lathbury nearly three hours to assemble a hundred men with which to attempt to take the bridge, only to find on arrival that Captain Rann had already taken it with fifty. By 0430hrs, it was in British hands but a battle for control was still in progress as gliders began to arrive. Major Cooper, survivor of the 'Buzzard' ditching, died when his towplane was shot down at only 500 feet, crashing into the dry riverbed but four glider loads arrived in time to contribute to the battle by carrying two jeeps and three six-pounders to the small force defending the bridge against a determined counterattack. By noon, the 250 men who had by now reached the perimeter around the bridge had been pushed back as their ammunition ran out and it would not be until dawn on the 16th that tanks and infantry would finally force their way back across it.

Sicily: the airborne counterattack

Even as the Allied airborne landed, German reinforcements began arriving by air from Italy in what would be the only time when both sides used airborne landings on the same target. In the confusion, on the drop zone near the bridge, a British soldier was approached by a shadowy figure asking 'haben sie meine Schmeisser gesehen?' (Have you seen my Schmeisser?) as he searched for the weapons bundle the Germans still dropped separately. Over the next few days, paratrooper would fight paratrooper in a fierce contest for the vital bridge.

On 11 July, three *Kette* ('flights') comprising eight Gotha Go242 gliders left their base in Italy at 0630hrs and flew without the promised fighter escort to Sicily, arriving over Messina at about 0930hrs and heading for Catania. Guided in by the smoke of an earlier bombardment, the first gliders touched down as planned. As the second and third groups arrived, firing started again and most were damaged by shell fragments. More followed on the 13th whilst larger landings began around Torre di Farro between 20 and 23 July. In Italy, glider units deployed from Pomigliano and Viterbo with more deploying to the Practica di Mare base near Rome in early August and raids on these bases over the coming months would damage or destroy around 250 glider combinations. Remaining accounts suggest that as many as eighteen Me 321 Gigants, 146 Go242 and nearly 300 DFS 230 gliders were available at Mediterranean bases to units involved in resupplying Sicily but little detailed information is actually known about the scale of glider landings against the Allies during the campaign.

The invasion of Sicily, the Allied Crete, could have spelt the end of glider operations. In many ways it failed just as the German invasion had two years before and for many of the same reasons, but it had achieved its goal. The larger capacity of Allied gliders meant that heavier weapons could be available from the outset and planners could see the potential even if they could not yet exploit it.

Back in North Africa, Lieutenant-Colonel Vladimir 'Popski' Peniakoff, the eccentric but effective founder of 'Popski's Private Army' had watched gliders in operation and had decided he could make use of them. Three weeks after the Sicily operations, he approached General Hopkinson with a plan to land six gliders on a deserted plain in Calabria to operate behind enemy lines to link up with the advancing Allies later. Twelve men would be detached from the Glider Pilot Regiment and Peniakoff would learn to fly a glider himself. Having gained his wings on a somewhat abbreviated course, he set about training his men for the problems ahead by deliberately having the heavily armed jeep teams landed anywhere in a thirty-mile radius of their target in daylight and at night in readiness for any eventuality. In September, though, the plan was shelved as Popski and his men were ordered into Italy along with the seaborne force.[25]

The problems in Sicily were summed up in Staff Sergeant Galpin's laconic analysis of the operation in a comment only he, as the only man to reach his objective, could have made: 'My observations at the time were that the following points were of interest in planning future night operations . . . Landing right on top of the objective is the best recipe for success.' With fifty-seven pilots dead and hundreds of their passengers lost at sea, the belief in a precision assault by glider had taken a sharp blow. The Glider Pilot Regiment had lost other friends, too. Freshman survivor Squadron Leader Wilkinson had disappeared flying in the second wave, as had Peter May, already wearing Chatterton's boots. In the aftermath of the disaster, Chatterton used his connections with the US military to secure an urgent flight back to the UK to examine the lessons and to rebuild confidence in his gliders as the invasion of Europe grew ever closer. The disaster had shown the chaos that could ensue if gliders were released en masse over an unmarked LZ and the need to mark sites correctly. One suggestion put forward was to use a clearly marked glider as a pathfinder, with the remainder of the serial using it as the aiming point to ensure that, even if they landed off target, they would still land together. At night, he had decided, paratroopers would need to land first to set up 'T's to indicate direction and zones for landing. Initial trials were undertaken but a mass exercise nearly went badly wrong when the 'T' was set up at an angle to the actual wind direction. Some pilots landed as instructed, others from the correct direction as dictated by the wind. Fortunately, there were no serious accidents. Chatterton also considered the use of decoys. Dummy paratroopers had already been used by both sides and Chatterton now suggested dummy gliders – four foot models to be released at night when height would be difficult to judge that would fool observers about the actual landing site. The plan was dropped before any trials could be carried out.

The Sicily operation had cast doubts on the effectiveness of glider operations but, just a few weeks later, the Germans would again carry out another operation, demonstrating with devastating effectiveness how they could be used.

Operation Eiche: the rescue of Mussolini, 12 September 1943

Allied advances in North Africa and Sicily had weakened Mussolini's control of Italy and he knew it. Meeting with Hitler at Feltre in the Veneto on 17 July 1943, he had intended to discuss withdrawing his support for the war but was overawed by Hitler's fervent belief in ultimate victory and so decided against it. Events were taken out of his hands on 24 July when the Italian Fascist Grand Council met and voted to grant military powers to the King of Italy. The following day, after an interview with the king, Mussolini was arrested and Marshal Pietro Badoglio was asked to form a government. Fearing that the new regime might surrender Italy to the Allies, thus opening up southern Europe to them, Hitler decreed that he would not let 'Italy's greatest son' down in his hour of need. His 'old ally and dear friend', he ordered, had to be rescued. With plans already in place for German forces to seize power in Italy if need be, Hitler chose to gamble that, if Mussolini were to be successfully rescued, then troops loyal to him might stay on the side of the Germans.

On 26 July, a young captain named Otto Skorzeny of the Friedenthal Special Formation of the Waffen SS, was called urgently to an airfield at the edge of a lake near Lotzen in East Prussia and from there taken to a room where five other officers, all strangers, were gathered. As they made their introductions, an aide appeared and ushered them into another room. 'You will now meet the Fuhrer, gentlemen', he told them, 'He will have some questions for you. Please follow me.' Hitler chatted briefly to the men before asking 'which of you knows Italy?' When the young captain answered that he had been there several times, the others were dismissed. Within minutes, Skorzeny was entrusted with a remarkable mission: to rescue Mussolini. Though Skorzeny was in the Waffen SS, for the purposes of the mission he was subordinated to the Luftwaffe. The mission was to be codenamed Operation Eiche (Oak) and it would be carried out with the assistance of General Student.[26]

Skorzeny had only recently returned from Iran, where he and his men had parachuted in to make contact with the dissident mountain tribes and lead insurgent forces in sabotaging US and British supplies of materiel bound for the Soviet Union. Within a few months of their arrival, interest had faded and Skorzeny, who remained behind to train more recruits, was forced to recognize it as a failure. Nevertheless, he remained the rising star of German special forces. He had entered the University of Vienna on his eighteenth birthday and graduated in 1931 with an engineering degree. Although his engineering background would prove useful later in planning sabotage attacks, it would be his time in the Schlagende Verbindungen (duelling society) that would be his most important college experience. Fighting his first duel during his freshman year at university, by 1928 he had earned the coveted *Schmisse* – the 'honour scars' that would later earn him the nickname of 'Scarface' among the Americans. Skorzeny would later recall how his time in the society shaped his attitude to combat:

My knowledge of pain, learned with the sabre, taught me not to be afraid. And, just as in duelling when you must concentrate on your enemy's cheek, so, too, in war. You cannot waste time on feinting and sidestepping. You must decide on your target and go in.[27]

When war broke out in September 1939, Skorzeny immediately volunteered for the Luftwaffe but at six foot four and 31 years old he was not accepted for flight training. Instead, he was assigned a job as a communications expert, which he hated. Five months later, he transferred to the Waffen SS, where he hoped to gain a commission. He was classified as an officer-cadet and would be commissioned if he proved himself. In operations in the Low Countries and Yugoslavia, he did so and was duly appointed as an officer. In late 1941, he was severely wounded in Russia and after recovering was summoned to Berlin in April 1943 to meet with Walter Schellenberg, head of the SD (the SS foreign intelligence service). Through his connections with senior Austrian Nazis, Skorzeny was offered the chance to take charge of the training of what would become known as Jagdverbande (Hunting Group) 502, whose members were drawn from the best men of the Reich's military units. Each man was to have basic skills in weapons from small arms to artillery, to be able to drive cars, motorcycles, boats and even trains. They had to be expert swimmers and be able to parachute from aircraft. Many were also trained in foreign languages, such as English, Italian, Russian, and Persian. The unit was based on the techniques found described in captured British commando documents, and from a few captured British commandos who were willing to switch sides. Skorzeny was the perfect man for the job.

Skorzeny flew to Rome under the cover of acting as an aide-de-camp in the German staff. As he did so, fifty of his men flew from Berlin to Rome via the South of France as replacements joining the 1st Parachute Division already en route to Italy. Skorzeny quickly prepared lists of equipment and weapons and hand-picked the officers who would go on the mission with him. The main problem, though, was finding where Mussolini was being held.

Rumours abounded that the Duce had been flown to Spain. Others claimed he had suffered a stroke and was under guard in a medical facility in the north. Intelligence sources in Berlin even tried consulting astrologers. In Rome agents of the Security Service were told to find him at all costs. After a month of searching, Skorzeny found his first lead. A reliable report suggested he was being held on the island of Ponza off the west coast of Italy but by the time investigations had been carried out he had been moved on, this time to the island of La Maddalena off the north-east coast of Sardinia. Plans for a rescue attempt were hastily put together but before they could be carried out Mussolini was once again spirited away to a new destination.

A Red Cross seaplane was seen landing on the Lago di Bracciano and a short time later, an intercepted coded message announced 'security measures around

Gran Sasso completed'. By 8 September, Skorzeny had tracked down his quarry to the Albero–Rifugio Hotel, part of a winter ski resort 6,000 feet up Gran Sasso d'Italia, the highest peak of the Apennines mountain range, some eighty miles north-east of Rome and only accessible via a cable car that ran up the side of the mountain from the valley below.

The high altitude location perched on the side of a mountain quickly ruled out a ground attack because of the number of troops that would be needed to secure the area. An attack via the cable car could not succeed and parachute assault was out of the question. The dangers involved in dropping through thin air at such high altitudes and in attempting to land on the tiny plateau around the hotel were too great. The only possible landing-site near the hotel seemed to be a small triangular field just behind it but senior staff officers soon declared that a landing on such a small and unprepared space would cause heavy losses among the troops and that the few who survived would probably not be enough to complete the operation. Luftwaffe experts declared that the plan was 'technically impossible'.[28] Skorzeny decided that assaulting the peak by glider was now his only option.

Four days later, on 12 September 1943, the nearest glider force, based at Grosseto, sent some of its aircraft to assemble on the Pratica di Mare airfield and only then were the pilots briefed for their mission. Joining them were SS troops supported by paratroopers of Major Mors's No. 1 Company. Student drew a sharp line between the military and political aims of the mission and had decided that his men would concentrate on the former, leaving Skorzeny to go in with the paras and act as bodyguard to Mussolini once he was rescued. Shortly before the 0900hrs briefing, Skorzeny and his men kidnapped the Italian general Ferdinando Soleti in Rome. Mussolini could be killed by his captors if the assault force were delayed by the Italian guards for too long and he hoped Soleti's presence would help ensure that the guards cooperated. Soleti, hearing what was proposed, became so upset he attempted suicide but finally agreed after reassurances that the operation was not intended to cause casualties among the guards. Student was confident that not a shot would be fired.

Twelve fully manned DFS 230 gliders, equipped with special rockets in the nose to act as brakes allowing them to land on extremely short LZs were prepared for the assault. They would be flying in men from Skorzeny's Friedenthal Battalion and men of the 1st Kompanie, 1st Battalion, 7th Regiment (the Fallschirm-Lehr Battalion), under the command of Oberleutnant Georg von Berlepsch. The remainder of the battalion under the command of Major Otto-Harald Mors were to travel by road and take the nearby airfield at Aquila and the cable car station in the valley below, whilst another group of Skorzeny's men was tasked with the job of freeing the Duce's family. To fly Mussolini out after the raid, Skorzeny secured the use of a new weapon in the German arsenal, the Focke-Angelis FA 225 'Stormbird' helicopter.

That afternoon, after narrowly avoiding an Allied air attack on the base, the gliders and their towing aircraft took off from the Practica de Mare airfield near Rome on their hour-long flight to the target. Gliders 11 and 12 never made it off the airfield – damaged during takeoff after hitting craters left by the Allied bombing raid just before H-hour.[29] Gliders 1 and 2 disappeared in dense cloud midway through the flight and separated from their tows, leaving Skorzeny in glider number 3 to take the lead. Eight gliders now remained to complete the mission. Visibility was bad as they approached the Gran Sasso and only the reconnaissance carried out by Skorzeny in the days before the attack allowed him to recognize any landmarks.

At around 1400hrs Skorzeny, looking through a hole he had cut in the skin of the lead glider, spotted the roof of the hotel. Both he and the pilot could see the triangular space planned as the LZ was not the flat ground it appeared to be from the reconnaissance photographs but a very steep hillside where a landing could be disastrous. The only other option was to crash-land on the rough but flatter ground in front of the hotel. Landing hard and taking casualties as a result, Skorzeny was one of the first out and running towards the hotel. The Italian carabinieri were everywhere, many dropping their rifles and already running away from their machine-gun posts as the Germans sprang from the gliders. As his men rushed into the hotel Skorzeny himself battered through the carabinieri with the butt of his machine gun and ran up the staircase to find Mussolini. Bursting through a door, he found him with another Italian officer.

By now the other gliders had crashed among the rocks and more SS men were streaming towards the hotel yet still not a shot had been fired. Skorzeny asked who was in command and an Italian colonel appeared, raised a glass of wine and said solemnly: 'To the victor'. Turning to Mussolini, Skorzeny introduced himself and told him 'Duce, the Fuhrer has sent me to set you free.' 'I knew my friend Adolf would not abandon me', replied Mussolini, hugging his liberator.[30] Still, not a shot. The hotel had been taken so quickly that by now gliders 6 and 7 were just coming in to land. Glider 8 made its approach shortly afterwards but crash-landed, badly injuring all those on board.

With Mussolini freed, the problem was how to get him away. The helicopter had broken down and was still at the airfield, leaving Skorzeny with three possible options for escape. The first, by road to Rome through the valley below (now in the hands of Major Mors and the Fallschirm-Lehr Battalion), was dangerous because of partisan activity in the area. The second was to transport the Duce to the nearby airfield at Aquila which was due to be captured by para-troops at any time. Skorzeny decided that this carried too much of a risk to his valuable prize and so chose the third option, using the Feisler Storch reconnais-sance aircraft piloted by Student's personal pilot Captain Gerlach to fly him directly off the Gran Sasso.

Captain Gerlach, flying overhead throughout the attack as observer, made an emergency landing on an improvised airstrip. Propaganda film shot by German war correspondents after the battle show the Italian soldiers who had acted as guards escorting him to the plane and helping to make the makeshift airstrip, along with the Duce being escorted to the Storch and secured in by Skorzeny himself. Whether this was staged later is uncertain but during the rescue itself Mussolini and Skorzeny climbed aboard the tiny, overloaded plane (the Duce insisted on taking his luggage) and took off barely making it off the plateau. Gerlach had to taxi off the edge of the steep drop and use the fall to accelerate enough to claw his way into the sky, flying straight back to the Practica de Mare airfield where they changed planes and carried on with the journey to Vienna, where Mussolini was reunited with his family. Whilst staying in Vienna Skorzeny was awarded the Knight's Cross for his part in the mission and later flew with Mussolini to meet the Fuhrer on 15 September at the Wolfs Lair in Eastern Prussia.

Although the Fallschirmtruppe played a major part in the planning and execution of the operation, it was Skorzeny who became the hero of the Gran Sasso raid. The next morning, he received a phone call from the Fuhrer to tell him 'you have performed a military feat which will become part of history. You have given me back my friend Mussolini.'[31] Practically overnight, Skorzeny's reputation reached near-legendary proportions. He became a national hero in Germany and earned the distinction of not only being regarded by the Allies as 'the most dangerous man in Europe', but also of having his operation discussed in the British Parliament where Winston Churchill himself spoke with admiration of the mission being 'one of great daring'. [32]

For Il Duce, one form of imprisonment was exchanged for another as he became a virtual puppet of the Germans. Briefly back in command in Italy, he had less than a year to live before partisans would hang his body from lampposts in the street in a defeated Italy.

On 5 October 1943, men of the Brandenburger 15 (Parachute) Company and elements of 22 Airlanding Division carried out Operation Polar Bear (Eisbär), a glider-borne assault aimed at neutralizing the British airbase on the Greek island of Kos, just off the Turkish coast. The aim was to deprive the Allies of a vital airbase in the Dodecanese but also to try to encourage Turkey to offer its support to Germany in response to the threat of Allied occupation. Polar Bear was a complete success, paving the way for Operation Leopard, a parachute attack on the island of Leros in November.

Operation Bunghole: liaison mission to Yugolsavia, 19 February 1944

The German invasion of Yugoslavia had met with strong resistance from guerrilla forces of the Jugoslav National Army of Liberation (JANL), an army strong enough to control whole regions of the country and a real threat to the German-occupied areas. Attempts to storm these strongholds with ground troops had met with little success since the tactics of the partisan forces were to avoid direct confrontation and to simply disperse into the mountains following any contact. As the JANL grew, though, it became increasingly difficult to disperse and regroup headquarters units at divisional and corps level and more difficult still when a National Headquarters was established under Tito. Throughout 1942 and 1943 German operations had forced repeated moves by JANL Headquarters and an offensive that opened in the autumn of 1943, codenamed Operation 'Fireball', had pushed them into the mountain stronghold of Drvar, where Tito's headquarters were now established in a 'cave' (actually a cleft in the rocks where a hut had been built to provide shelter). The cave was not only concealed from the air, making it an almost impossible target to detect and hit, it also had an exit through which the partisan leader could make good his escape if necessary.

In late January 1944, Captain Cornelius Turner of the newly formed 1st Independent Glider Squadron was dispatched with half a dozen pilots from their Italian base to an airstrip in Tunisia in search of three Horsa gliders left behind after the Sicily invasion of the previous summer. They found them, according to Turner, 'looking very lonesome and forlorn out there in the salt flats' and set about checking them out, although since no one was qualified to inspect them properly, 'checking them out' under the circumstances meant noting that 'nothing seemed to be hanging loose, so we plugged in the tow–ropes and took off on a wing and a prayer and flew them straight across the Med. to Sicily'.[33] After a 250 mile journey to Comiso in Sicily, the gliders were loaded with a jeep and anything else that would make up the 7,000 lb full payload and the loading was tested by simply hanging off the tail so that the front wheel lifted off the ground. Next, they lifted off and headed for Bari, in Italy, flying through high winds and driving snow, barely clearing the hilltops on the way, in a flight later described as 'an experience that was extremely unpleasant'.

Once at Bari, Turner was made aware of his mission. With Staff Sergeants McCulloch, Newman, Morrison, Hill and McMillan, Turner was ordered to prepare for a secret mission under the direction of a shadowy Cairo-based organization known as Force 133 to transport a Russian military mission of thirty-six senior officers to meet with Tito and his partisans at their mountain base at Drvar, a hundred miles inside Yugoslavia. Heavy snows meant that the landing strips were unusable by powered aircraft but gliders could make it. The plan called for three Horsas to land in the valley of Medenapolu two miles north-west of the town of Basan Petrovac, halfway between Zagreb and Sarajevo in the eastern Dinaric Alps, with a fighter escort of twenty-five Spitfires, another twenty-five P-51 Mustangs over the LZ and a diversionary raid by fifty B-17s on Zagreb providing cover.

After the difficulty of getting the Horsas to Bari, tug crews argued that it would be impossible to gain the height needed to clear the 8,000 foot peaks of the Dinaric Alps and so finally Wacos were substituted for the mission. At 1100hrs on 19 February the three combinations took off in clear weather.

Turner's tug pilot, Wendell C Little of Indianapolis wrote his name on the back fly-leaf of Turner's Bible and wished him luck, saying: 'You'll need it . . . it's all over town this secret of yours; I hope they don't jump us.'[34] Turner and his co-pilot 'Droop' Newman flew in silence apart from a few comments about course. Turner was uncomfortably aware of Marshal Korneyev sitting between them and the muzzle of a Russian machine pistol nestling six inches from the back of his neck.

Narrowly clearing the last peak and guided by straw fires below, the gliders put down within yards of each other. At 4,000 feet, the snow lay three feet thick, reducing the landing run of the Wacos to just twenty feet. Almost immediately, the pilots found themselves surrounded and 'forcibly embraced by almost un-believably dirty and bearded men'. Turner recalled partisans 'armed to the teeth, rifles, crossed bandoliers, knives and grenades, bearded and stinking they swarmed over us'.[35] The party set out in sleighs for the town of Petrovac where the Russians removed their greatcoats, revealing splendid dress uniforms that looked extremely impressive to the scruffy guerrillas. Later, Vladimir Dedijer in his biography of Tito wrote:

> what joy it gave the Yugoslavs to see the representatives of the Red Army! Headed by Generals Korneyev and Gorskov, the mission came by plane through Persia, Egypt and Italy. The journey was very slow, especially the last stage, because the winter in Yugoslavia had been severe; deep snow had fallen, and the planes were unable to land on the mountain airfield near Petrovac, not far from Drvar; so the military mission transferred to gliders which were cut free over Petrovac, where they slowly landed on a thick blanket of snow. That same night there was a formal public gathering in observance of the anniversary of the Red Army. The Soviet generals were the guests of Petrovac. The people carried them shoulder high and danced the Kozara kolo. [36]

The bemused British glider pilots looked on as the feast continued. One remembered:

> For three weary hours we ate course after course, drank tot after tot. It was a veritable banquet, disclosing General Korneyev's anxiety for his crates. When these were opened they were found to contain not valu-able weapons of war, but cases of vodka and caviar.[37]

For the next four weeks, though, life was very different. Food was in constant short supply and McCulloch, Newman, Morrison, Hill and McMillan, billeted together at the northern edge of the town, found their diet 'consisted exclusively of meat of every imaginable variety except beef, mutton or pork and of potatoes, unleavened rye and maize bread, and water'.[38] Turner found himself across the road with three other officers who were part of the resident Military Mission. They had a sergeant and half a dozen signallers not far away, and nearby was an American colonel with 'enough staff for two good poker schools'. These military missions were in place to collect baled-out aircrews and liaise with Cairo and Bari to arrange arms drops for the partisans. Night after night the pilots would join their comrades lying out on the hillsides, curled up in holes dug in the snow to get out of the bitter winds, waiting for the C-47s to make drops of arms, rations and agents.

During the first week of their stay, German Ju88 aircraft had carried out daily strafing attacks and Turner was aware that the Germans also had a force of gliders fifty miles away at Bihac. The three Wacos still lay where they had landed despite Turner's repeated requests for them to be moved out of sight. Now he decided to take drastic action. He and Claude Hill walked out to the LZ where they began tearing the canvas of one of the Wacos and set fire to the frayed ends. Within minutes, the fuselage was burning fiercely. The partisans were furious at the destruction of what they now considered their property and Turner found himself taken before Tito himself to explain himself. Having explained his reasons, Tito told him quietly that it 'was a pity, but you did well; give my thanks to your pilots'.

By March, the snows were beginning to thaw and arrangements were made to fly out the glider pilots. Landing in nine inches of snow, two C-47s, including one flown by Air Commodore Whitney Strought, a famous multi-millionaire and former Grand Prix racing driver, put down on the mountain airfield. At that height, in deep snow, every possible article had to be jettisoned if the planes were to be able to get off the ground and seats, doors, parachutes, weapons and kit were all abandoned but even so the Dakotas still skimmed the treetops as they lifted off at the very last second for the two-hour flight back to Bari.

Back at base, Turner found he had been posted missing after an administrative error had confused his aircraft with another shot down over Split on the day of the flight in, but fortunately enough doubt existed that his family had not been informed. Still in his now ragged uniform, he was debriefed by a man from Force 133 who, far from congratulating him, threatened with a court-martial for burning the glider. Turner explained the situation and pointed out that the partisans may have been annoyed that he had destroyed 'their' glider, but it was in fact American property and so, if anyone, it should be they who complained. Nevertheless, a commendation for him was torn up.

Soon afterwards, though, Turner's concerns about leaving the gliders in plain view of German reconnaissance planes would be fully justified.

Operation Rösselsprung: the attack on Tito's headquarters, 25 May 1944

In the spring of 1944, it was decided that the only effective way to deal with the partisan army was to decapitate its command structure. Ground offensives had proved too slow to trap them so an extremely risky plan was put forward for an SS unit of 600 men to launch an airborne attack into the heart of the partisan force, known to be at least 12,000 strong. Codenamed 'Rösselsprung' (Knight's Move), the operation would involve the dropping of 314 paratroops with the support of 340 glider-borne infantry directly onto the headquarters location, with the aim of killing or capturing as many senior commanders as possible. The date was set for 25 May 1944: Tito's birthday.

The unit chosen to undertake the mission has often been referred to as a 'penal' battalion but is more accurately described as a 'probationary' unit, made up of men convicted of military crimes but offered the chance to redeem their honour and clear their records by volunteering for service in the battalion and undertaking particularly dangerous missions. Officially formed on 6 September 1943, the 500th SS-Fallschirmjäger Battalion was composed of personnel of the SS-Bewährungs Abteilung (SS Punishment Battalion) officered by volunteers from various Waffen SS divisions, with half the men paroled prisoners from SS penal companies, the other half being genuine volunteers.[39] This newly formed unit was not held in high esteem, even within an organization as thuggish as the SS, because of its high rate of personnel with questionable records. Their main advantage was that they were expendable. In preparation for their new operation, all ranks of the battalion were trained or given refresher training at the Kralyevo Parachute School in Serbia and by May were ready for the mission. Under SS-Hauptsturmführer Rybka's leadership, the unit was to be landed by parachute and glider onto a hillside plateau near the target but a shortage of aircraft meant that two drops would have to be made. The first, at 0700hrs, would secure the area ready for the second at midday. These would secure the area whilst the glider-borne assault using all available DFS 230 aircraft would land and capture the headquarters.

Immediately following a short but intense dive-bombing attack on Drvar, Ju52s began dropping their paratroops and within minutes the deserted town had been captured. With the surrounding area secure, the forty gliders of the assault group began their descent. The glider force was divided into six groups, each assigned a special objective. The 'Citadel' (Tito's cave headquarters) was the target of the 110 men of Group 'Panther', along with Rybka and his detachment of paratroopers. Across the LZs, several gliders had crashed on landing, killing all their occupants, but the pilots of Group Panther's gliders had each landed safely within yards of the mouth of the cave and Rybka felt sure that a fast assault would succeed in capturing Tito himself.

Suddenly, the partisans reacted and poured heavy fire into the advancing Germans. As the last gliders made their approaches, they were riddled with gunfire as Rybka, firing a flare to bring reinforcements to him, continued to push forward but, faced with the heavy weapons and fortifications around the headquarters, the lightly armed airborne troops had no chance of reaching their target. As the battle raged, the second wave of paratroopers dropped only to find the DZ raked by machine guns and their losses were heavy. By late afternoon, Rybka reluctantly took the decision to withdraw from the cave area and his men began to regroup inside the walls of the town cemetery to await the promised relief force, although it was not until long after dark that the force was gathered together, by which time the SS paratroopers were exhausted.

The plan had called for the 1st Mountain Division and the 7th SS Freiwilligen-Gebirgs Division Prinz Eugen to link up with their airborne comrades within the first twenty-four hours, but they failed to reach them, finding themselves caught up instead in fierce fighting on the mountain roads. In Drvar, surrounded by a well-armed partisan army intent on annihilating them, the men of the SS battalion fought on. Throughout the night, successive attacks were fought off until, on the morning of 26 May, a battle group from the 13th Regiment of the 7th SS finally broke through. Only 200 men of the battalion answered roll call but it had achieved one goal – Himmler was so impressed by the fighting qualities the men had displayed that all ranks and insignia of the probationary men were restored and the unit redesignated as the 600th SS-Fallschirmjäger Battalion. Less than a year later, equipped with bicycles and panzerfausts, the unit would distinguish itself as a tank destroyer unit in the final throes of the war.[40]

By the time the paratroopers were relieved, Tito and his headquarters had already escaped and for the next ten days, German and Croatian forces slowly encircled him until on 3 June an RAF C-47 landed to evacuate key members of staff to Bari and then to a new base on the island of Vis. The offensive had cost both sides dearly, with over 3,000 partisans killed at a cost to the Germans of over 200 killed and nearly 900 wounded. Despite this, the nearest they came to their objective was the capture of Tito's dress uniform.

News of the operation reached the Allies via Force 133 and other intelligence sources and yet again seemed to prove the potential of glider attacks. Sicily had not gone as well as most hoped, but it had been successful. Now attention turned towards an attack on mainland Europe.

Operation Anvil/Dragoon – the invasion of Southern France, 15 August 1944

An operation against the coastline of southern France had first been put forward on 11 August 1942 at the Quebec conference where it was believed that a co-ordinated invasion of France on two fronts in May 1944 would trap German forces between the northern 'Hammer' and southern 'Anvil'. By late 1943, however, Churchill – who saw little need to open a second front in southern

France – was worried that it would take resources away from the proposed Normandy landings and was arguing that an attack against Trieste and from there into the Hungary would divert German forces away from the western front and so be of more value. His views were violently opposed by the American High Command who had already developed a plan in October 1943 to use three American divisions on Operation Anvil, assisted by seven French divisions. An agreement was secured at the Tehran conference that the major portion of the Free French forces would be given a chance in Italy to prove themselves ready. If so, they would be used in the invasion. The decision forced Churchill's hand as it met the demands of the Free French national liberation committee for a more visible part in the war. Responsibility for overall preparation and execution of the landing would therefore be the responsibility of the US 7th Army. Stories would circulate later that the code name for the operation was changed from 'Anvil' to 'Dragoon' to reflect Churchill's belief that he had been dragooned into complying.

The plan put forward called for the taking of Toulon and Marseille harbours as part of a bridgehead for the French arriving on D+3. The landing zone would be further along the coast to the east to avoid the Hyères Islands and the concentration of artillery covering the approaches to Toulon. This would also allow for the taking of the small ports of Saint-Tropez and Saint-Raphael, and control of the plain of Fréjus, ideal for the construction of airfields. The shortage of landing craft due to the demands of the Normandy operation provided an opportunity for the British to argue for the suspension of the southern landing and the final decision was put off until March 1944, with hopes high that the plan would be cancelled. Then General Alexander Patch, who had made his name on Guadalcanal, took command of the 7th Army and soon announced that Anvil would be the second highest priority of all US operations. In July, Field Marshal Sir Henry Wilson, the Supreme Commander of Allied Forces in the Mediterranean, received orders to go ahead with the invasion. Two events had finally swayed the argument. In early June, Rome fell to the Allies, freeing up large numbers of combatant troops, and in France Operation Cobra had succeeded in breaking out of Normandy. At short notice, Operation Dragoon's D-Day was set for 15 August 1944.

The 1st Airborne Task Force, a composite of around 10,000 British and American airborne troops, would lead the invasion, landing around Le Muy, a transportation hub about twelve miles from the coast. Once on the ground, the 1st Airborne Task Force would go after Le Muy itself and keep German reinforcements from reaching the beachheads by cutting roads and laying ambushes. Around 150,000 men of the 7th Army would then storm ashore in landing craft from a massive fleet of nearly 900 ships. Then, on the left, Attack Force Alpha, comprising the US 3rd Division, would land south-west of St Tropez, clear the small peninsula there, and move inland. In the centre, the 45th Division of Attack Force Delta would strike north of St Tropez, taking the coastal town of St

Maxime and linking up with the 3rd in a movement north-west. On the right flank, stretching to Antibes, Attack Force Camel's 36th Division would take St Raphael and Fréjus and secure the flank. With the beachheads established, De Lattre would lead his French troops through the VI Corps's secure left flank westward to capture Toulon and Marseille.

The first phase of the airborne assault, Operation Albatross, began at 0100hrs on 15 August when nine C-47s carrying three teams of British and American pathfinders took off from Italy intending to drop into the Argens river valley at around 0330hrs and prepare the drop zones around Le Muy, but heavy ground fog prevented the pilots from locating the drop zones and the aircraft were forced to circle the area time and again trying to find any landmarks. Eventually, the teams jumped with the last reaching the ground just fifteen minutes before the first wave of paratroopers arrived, but so far from their target that they were not able to link up to the main force until the following day. By 0530hrs, 5,600 paratroopers were on the ground but scattered over almost fifteen miles of coast.

The second phase, Operation Bluebird, was a glider landing at 0800hrs timed to coincide with the seaborne invasion. Thirty-five Horsas would land a Royal Artillery unit with the help of forty Wacos flown by Americans on double tow behind their tugs. Lifting off at 0400hrs, the gliders headed west but, as they reached Corsica, the Horsas were recalled because of the fog over their landing zones. A delayed release over the target could put undue strain on the tugs but for some reason the same did not seem to apply to the Wacos.

As the seaborne force charged across the beaches, thirty-three Wacos appeared overhead. Seven had either ditched when their tow ropes broke or had disintegrated in mid-air when their overloaded airframes collapsed. The survivors began to circle, looking for a place to release. The British paratroopers had cleared most of the LZs of anti-glider obstacles but there were still a number of accidents when gliders tangled in olive trees and vineyards in the poor visibility. An hour later, the fog lifted.

Phase three, Operation Dove, got under way that afternoon. The thirty-five Horsas recalled earlier were now in the air and all landed safely on their allotted objectives at 1645hrs, as another 800 US paratroopers dropped onto their drop zones. Richard Clarke, a Horsa pilot, recalled that

> we were proceeding to assemble in battle order when the American glider force appeared, all roughly at the same time. There were many collisions in the air and on the ground and jeeps and equipment rained down. It was all very hectic. [41]

'Hectic' was something of an understatement. As one American pilot later put it, the landing zone looked 'like Piccadilly Circus at high noon with the traffic being directed by an insane policeman'.[42] Seven serials of C-47s towing 332

Wacos carrying over 2,000 men, jeeps, guns and ammunition had assembled as planned over Elba at about 1630hrs and turned west. In one of the lead serials, a glider pilot had contacted his tug plane to report a violent tail vibration which would force him to abort. The tug pilot decided to try to release the glider over Corsica rather than ditch and executed a 180 degree turn without informing the rest of the serial of what he was about to do. The aircraft behind him followed suit. Realizing his mistake, the tow pilot released his glider and rejoined the skytrain, but now in the middle instead of the front. Aircraft following behind had to slow down to avoid running into the lost serial, others climbed to avoid collision. Other aircraft speeded up, pulling their gliders at over 150mph and causing them to begin falling apart. With four serials due to arrive over the LZ at ten-minute intervals, instead they arrived together, stacked anywhere between 1,000 and 3,000 feet. The lead serial had overshot and now turned back, headed directly into the following groups. At one point, 150 gliders were in free flight, all fighting for space on the crowded LZ – 'thick as flies around a dead road rabbit' as pilot Jack Merrick would later describe it.[43] Mid-air collisions were frequent, with one pilot reported being narrowly missed by a jeep, with its driver still aboard, falling from a shattered glider above.[44] By the end of D-Day, Operation Dragoon was declared a complete success.

Casualties were considered negligible for a large-scale invasion, but even so, landing in daylight without opposition, eleven glider pilots had been killed and thirty-two injured. With Le Muy captured for the loss of just one man and fifteen wounded, many asked whether such a massive airborne attack had been necessary in the first place and the US glider crews, angry at what they saw as the result of bad planning, sarcastically declared themselves the recipients of 'the Purple Shaft with Barbed Wire Cluster' for their efforts.

With the invasion of Southern France, the need for assault operations by airborne troops in the Mediterranean seemed to be fading. Towards the end of the year, though, they would again be stood by for an assault, not on the Germans, but on an ally.

Operation Manna – the capture of Athens, 13 October 1944

In October 1944, the partial withdrawal of the Germans from southern Greece left a power vacuum, with a variety of factions rushing to fill it. With civil war imminent, the British sought to stabilize the situation by installing the exiled Greek government back into power in Athens and launching an air and sea operation to take the city. Operation 'Manna' would involve a drop by 2nd Parachute Brigade on the Megara airfield twenty miles outside Athens. Ironically, it was from here that German gliders had left for Crete and now pilots of the Independent Squadron of the Glider Pilot Regiment would take a force of Wacos (Horsas were not available as they had all been used on Operation Dragoon) carrying guns and ammunition to the same airfield.

Cornelius Turner, the man who had flown into Tito's headquarters earlier in the year, looked nervously at his cargo. Carrying 4,000 lb of high explosives on Friday 13th did not seem like a particularly good omen. Nearing Corinth, a storm blew up, forcing the gliders back to Bari and the main parachute drop had to be delayed for twenty-four hours. Then, on 15 October, forty-four C-47s carrying supplies took off again from Bari, twenty of them towing gliders. Most carried jeeps and six-pounder guns but one brought in a small bulldozer for airfield repair work. The operation was a complete success apart from a few casualties among the paras dropped in high winds and, within days, the Greek government was in place. The gliders remained at Megara for a month until civil war broke out, when they were used to evacuate the pilots back to Tarquina. Other than resupply flights, the Mediterranean glider war was over.

Chapter Five

'Hitler's best friend in America': the US glider programme

In May 1943, *Time* magazine reported that

> during its harried 18-month career the Army Air Forces glider program
> has found the winds of public and official esteem as tricky as the thermal
> air currents over a mountain peak. Like many another new weapon, the
> glider was first overlooked, then over-dramatized, later over-disparaged.

By the end of the war, the US would field nearly 15,000 of its Waco CG 4 combat
gliders alone but before 1940, the US military had shown only a passing interest
in gliding for military training and none at all for its potential as a troop carrier.
Back in 1929, the War Department had considered using gliders as inexpensive
training aircraft but the instructors consulted could see no practical use for them,
reporting that 'military airplanes . . . are high powered and no beneficial result
would ensue from training our student pilots in gliding'. A few officers flew
gliders to keep their hand in but in 1931 the Air Corps demanded that any officer
flying them, even for sport, should obtain War Department approval first. By
1936, the sport had not achieved a measure of popularity even close to that in
Germany and there were only 413 gliders, mostly of foreign design, in America,
with 182 of them in just four states: Ohio, New York, California and Michigan.
There were fewer than 140 qualified glider pilots in the entire country.

Like their British allies, the Americans were shocked into action by the
German success at Eben-Emael but even so, it was not until February 1941 that
General Henry H 'Hap' Arnold was finally able to announce that 'in view of
certain information received from abroad, a study should be initiated on developing a glider that could be towed by an aircraft'.[1] As one staff officer put it, 'we've
got a lot of catching up to do'.[2] Arnold was firmly of the opinion that a civilian
expert was likely to know more about his subject than the military, so to advise
him on how to recruit and train glider pilots and on what sort of gliders to use
he recruited 35-year-old Lewin Barringer to coordinate the entire programme
and a number of other prewar sailplane enthusiasts to tackle other problems.
Champion glider pilot John Robinson quickly established the guidelines for a
detailed thirty-hour instructional course used to train the initial cadre at eigh-

teen civilian schools in eleven states, and which became the standard for all 6,000 recruits to follow.

The main problem, as in Britain, was the lack of aircraft to fly. Prior to the war gliders and sailplanes were not cost-effective to produce in large numbers and so there was no existing production capacity in place. Contracts were sent out for designs to meet two separate specifications. First, for an eight- or nine-seat transport with single prototypes of the Frankfort Model TCC-41 designated as the Experimental Cargo Glider (XCG)-1, the Waco NYQ-3 as XCG-3, the St Louis XCG-5 and the Bowlus XCG-7. Secondly, for a larger, fifteen-seat glider, the same four companies produced the Frankfort TCC-21 as XCG-2, the Waco XCG-4, St Louis XCG-6 and the Bowlus XCG-8. Of these, the Waco design was chosen and the CG-4 became the first and most widely used US troop glider of the Second World War. Just as in Britain, though, priority went to combat aircraft, so the Air Materiel Command (AMC) were forced to allow production contracts to virtually anyone who could promise rapid delivery, regardless of their lack of experience. Of the sixteen prime contractors involved in the glider programme,

Henry H 'Hap' Arnold

Major-General 'Hap' (a childhood nickname given him by an aunt and short for 'happy') Arnold suffered as a result of the enormous political pressures and physical burdens placed on him in creating the US Army Air Force, experiencing four heart attacks between 1943 and 1945. After the fourth attack, 'The Chief' as he was known to his staff, was allowed to remain in the service, but under conditions which amounted to light duty. With the war clearly in its final stages, Arnold reluctantly agreed. In December 1944 he was made a General of the Army, placing him fourth in the seniority of the US Army rank structure. In 1945, he founded Project RAND, a think-tank for military strategy which later developed into the RAND Corporation and, after further heart problems, retired in 1946. His successor, General Carl Spaatz, became first Chief of Staff of the United States Air Force when it became a separate service in September 1947.

Virtually penniless except for his pension, Arnold retired to a ranch near Sonoma, California, in the summer of 1946 and wrote his memoirs, published as *Global Mission*. In May 1949 Arnold was made the first (and to date, only) General of the Air Force and became the only American to serve in five-star rank in two of its military services.

Three of Arnold's sons were also graduates of West Point and served as colonels in the United States Air Force. He died on 15 January 1950 at his home and was given a state funeral in Washington, DC, at the Arlington cemetery where he was buried alongside his two youngest sons.

only two, the Ford Motor Company and the Cessna Aircraft Company, had any previous experience in the field. Even so, it took Ford six months to reconfigure their production line. Other contracts went to some unlikely candidates – to furniture and refrigerator manufacturers, to Steinway and Sons Pianos (for the wing and tail assemblies), H J Heinz Pickle Company (wings) and Anheuser-Busch (inboard wing panels). Quality control was an enormous problem and costly too. At a time when a combat-ready state-of-the-art P51 Mustang fighter cost the US government around $58,000, mismanagement and lack of direction meant that a Waco CG-4A glider could cost anywhere between $14, 891 (from Ford) to the single glider provided by the National Company at a staggering $1,741,809. With the exception of Cessna, which received sizeable government subsidies, none met the production deadlines.[3]

As the number of gliders available grew, Arnold had to tackle the problem of what to do with them. Because the gliders were a completely new weapon, any sort of doctrine for their use was virtually non-existent. General Arnold's 1941 memo had asked for a glider for 'transporting personnel and material and seizing objectives that can not normally be reached by conventional ground units' and went on to specify that the glider would deliver a self-contained combat team. In May 1942, the newly produced manual *Tactics and Technique of Airborne Troops* stated that

> an invasion force would require a large number of gliders. Initial estimates called for 1,000 gliders (thus 1,000 glider pilots) and 202 transports would be necessary to move a 14,000 man division. The gliders would carry three-fourths of the division while the other quarter would ride in the tugs. Half of the gliders would be eight-place versions and the other half would carry 15 troops each. 202 tugs for 1,000 gliders meant multiple tows would be the rule: 4 eight-place gliders or 3 15-place gliders for each tug.[4]

It emphasized the general concept that glider forces would only resupply parachute troops – completely ignoring General Arnold's original paper calling for them to act as a combat team. 'In training glider pilots, primary attention will be given to their training in the piloting role. The secondary function of these pilots . . . will consist of ground combat operations with the air-borne units which have been transported on their gliders.'[5] In other words, the doctrine evolving in the US was almost the exact opposite of British and German use of gliders as a combat weapon, with the newly formed I Troop Carrier Command (TCC) firmly of the opinion that glider pilots were 'aerial truck drivers' in 'air trailers'.

Finding the men to fly them was also becoming a problem. It was expected that glider pilots would be commissioned power pilots, immediately bringing the programme into conflict with the need for these men to fly combat fighters and bombers and few who had graduated in these roles wanted to now become 'aerial truck drivers'. At the time, the Army Air Corps required trainee pilots to be at least 21 years old with two years of college, the minimum thought necessary to allow them to be commissioned on graduation from the training programme. If the rapid expansion of the Air Corps, and especially the glider programme, were to meet the quotas set, entry requirements would have to be relaxed.

In December 1941, in the wake of the attack on Pearl Harbour, Arnold found his job becoming easier as war footing began to shake the rigid military bureaucracy. As a result, he was able to support a suggestion by Colonel Earl Naiden, commander of the Air Force Training Division, that enlisted volunteers should be sought, provided that they had not previously failed military flying training, held a Civil Aviation Administration qualification or at least thirty hours of civilian glider flight and could pass the medical and educational requirements of power pilot candidates. Even though the RAF was already successfully using sergeant pilots, many of Arnold's own staff had reservations. Some of Britain's enlisted pilots had found themselves commanding crews with commissioned officers acting as co-pilots and navigators and the American officers, products of a highly competitive and elitist prewar military, couldn't bring themselves to allow lower ranks to have that kind of responsibility.

The response, in May 1942, was to ask Congress to create a new grade above the enlisted ranks but below that of second lieutenant, then the lowest commissioned rank. On 8 July, Public Law 658 was signed by the President, creating the new grade of Flight Officer (F/O), equal in status to that of warrant officer junior grade.

> It is the desire of the Commanding General, AAF, that these new Flight Officers be accepted in the nature of 'Third Lieutenants' by all personnel and that they be required to comply with, and in turn to be treated in accordance with, all the customs and courtesies of the military service pertaining to commissioned officers.

This hybrid meant that the teenage graduates held neither warrant nor commission but Congressional appointments, referred to not by rank but as 'Mister', and not allowed to undertake the full responsibilities of commissioned officers. While second lieutenants and above were required to carry out additional duties such as Officer of the Day or Guard Commander when they were not flying, flight officers more usually had their time to themselves. They also enjoyed a 20 per cent increase in pay for overseas duty, as did enlisted men, instead of the 10 per cent paid to officers, meaning that their $150 per month basic pay was the same as that of junior grade warrant officers and second lieutenants, but when overseas, a second lieutenant collected $240 in combat, while a flight officer drew at least $255 and often more because of his added time in service. In the snobbish ranks of the Air Corps, socially they fell somewhere between the enlisted and commissioned ranks but in the wartime military, debate about social standing was the least of their problems.[6]

Despite these perks, the glider programme continued to have difficulty in finding recruits among those meeting the criteria for powered flight training and slowly began to reduce the entry requirements – accepting volunteers up to the age of 35, for example, instead of the 26 maximum for powered pilots, and quickly dropping the restriction on candidates who had previously failed military flight school. John Lowden, one such failed power pilot, was invited by the unit's Executive Officer to apply for glider training instead. When he turned down the offer, he found himself assigned to carrying out an inventory of thousands of blankets stacked in a warehouse where temperatures hit 90 degrees by mid-morning. After five days of this, Lowden finally reported back to the Exec.

'Sir, I have given careful consideration to your suggestion that I "enlist" in the glider corps and I have decided to do so'. He said 'I thought you'd see it my way' . . . When I went to check out with the sergeant who was caretaker of the warehouse, he shook my hand and said, 'Good luck. You held out longer than the others.'[7]

Successive reductions in entry requirements opened the trainee floodgates for men who were for various reasons unsuitable for air force training and, by the final revision published on 10 August 1942, a maximum pilot production rate of 12,000 a year was proposed. Shortly after that, it became apparent that pilot production was exceeding any existing or planned tactical need and glider pilot procurement ended on 16 November.

Independently of the efforts of the Army Air Corps, the US Navy had carried out experiments with gliders during the 1920s but by 1940 the programme had been dropped. As the army started its build up, the Marine Corps began to look at the possible use of parachute and glider-borne troops to support its seaborne role and at whether amphibious assault gliders could be developed for landings on enemy-held beaches. Like their army counterpart, marine and naval aviation training had not considered using sailplanes for the initial training of pilot candidates and so started their programmes from scratch, following the army's lead by buying thirteen Schweizer Model 2-8 two-seat, all-metal sailplanes in 1942. After tests with the Pratt-Read LNE-1 in 1942, it ordered a hundred although it appears probably only seventy-five were actually built, many of which were never delivered, and eventually most of the available planes were handed over to the army as the TG-32 trainer. The high-performance sailplanes were poor preparation for the heavy assault gliders the men were expected to fly.

Initially, the Marines glider programme was small, with just seventy-five gliders and 150 pilots, planned as enough to transport two battalions of infantry into action. Marine Glider Group Seventy One (MLG-71) had been organized at Marine Corps Air Station (MCAS) Parris Island, South Carolina, in April

1942 to oversee the growing glider programme and in May Marine Glider Squadron Seven Hundred Eleven (MLS-711) was organized under MLG-71 to put the programme into practice. With a training programme in place, the Navy and Marines now began to look for a suitable assault glider to meet their requirements. The Army's CG-4A was an obvious starting point and thirteen were acquired and redesignated as the LRW-1. Naval trials improved the towing bar for the glider, which was later incorporated into the Army's types. Further tests of the improved Waco CG-15 gliders (now designated the XLR2W) were also carried out, but with the beach assault role in mind the Navy issued its own requirements for twelve- and twenty-four-seat amphibious gliders. The results were technically successful, with Allied Aviation Corporation producing two XLRA-1s and Bristol Aeronautical Corporation four XLRQ-1s to fill the twelve-seat requirements and one hundred of each were ordered. The larger twenty-four-seat glider resulted in AGA Aviation's XLRG-1 and Snead & Company's XLRH-1 submitting plans for twin hulled amphibious gliders but neither was built.

By June, hopes for glider operations had expanded to a planned force capable of transporting 10,800 men in 1,371 gliders flown by a trained pool of 3,436 pilots. Among the hopeful candidates for glider training was film actor Tyrone Power, considered too old and poorly educated to be accepted by the Air Force, who instead enlisted in the Marines with the ambition of piloting a glider into combat. On 24 July 1942, construction began on 2,931 acres of former ranch land on the eastern shore of Eagle Mountain Lake in Texas to provide a base for Marine Corps glider operations and both units moved in the following November. At their peak, these units had between them just twenty-one gliders, thirty-six officers and 246 enlisted men to put together the planned airborne armada, until it became clear that Marine operations in the Pacific would involve assaulting small, widely scattered jungle-covered islands where the opportunities for glider landings would be limited. In May 1943 the programme was terminated, MLG-71 and MLS-711 disbanded and orders for gliders cancelled. Those already delivered were left at MCAS Eagle Mountain Lake for disposal.

By that time, the whole US glider programme was running out of steam. In June, many civilian and military officials had been dismayed to hear that Major-General William Lee, commander of the 101st Airborne and widely regarded as the father of the US Airborne, had been injured in a glider crash. In July, news of the heavy glider loss in Sicily reached them and, at the beginning of August, a public relations exercise had gone disastrously wrong when a CG-4A carrying local dignitaries had broken up in mid-air at a St Louis war bond rally, killing all on board. The cause of the crash was traced to a substandard wing strut fitting manufactured locally under subcontract, ironically enough to a company that had previously made coffins. Investigators found that a quarter of the fittings in the company's stockroom had also been poorly made. Jokers claimed that the man who had sold General Arnold the expensive and so far unproductive idea of using gliders must be 'Hitler's best friend in the USA'.[8] Just three days after the crash, General Arnold and the rest of the Air Corps staff arrived at the Lauringburg-Maxton Army Air Base in North Carolina for a demonstration of glider operations. Arnold was a worried man.

Arnold's guide for the visit was Major Michael Murphy, an experienced pilot but a recent convert who had graduated from the Twentynine Palms glider training centre in California the year before. Without wasting time, Murphy took his visitors out to the flight line for a demonstration of glider towing by a variety of aircraft ranging from C-47 transports to B-25 bombers and even the P-38 Lightning fighter followed by a glider pickup using the 'snatch' technique developed before the war for the US Postal Service, where a kind of rod and reel mechanism was used to collect sacks of mail attached to a towline suspended between two poles. A hook fitted to the aircraft would catch this towline and 'snatch' the sacks into the air and then a reel would pull them into the cargo doors. Between 12 May 1939 and April 1942, the US Postal Service had carried out 93,934 airmail pickups using this method without a single accident. Adapting the system for the much heavier gliders was a long process but by August experiments were well advanced and the generals were impressed. The visitors were then taken to a large pond at the edge of the base where a CG-4A fitted with flotation devices performed a landing on water. The VIPs then adjourned to the officer's club for dinner as the sun began to set.

As darkness fell, Murphy ushered them on to a waiting bus for a trip to a remote section of the base for a night landing demonstration – a touchy subject after Sicily. All the visitors expected was a lecture about flying distances and statistics but Murphy had something else in mind. The bus arrived at a row of benches near a thick stand of pine trees with nothing else visible for miles around. Murphy ordered all lights and cigarettes to be extinguished. In the darkness, unable to see Murphy or anything else, the visitors had to concentrate on the lecture he gave through a loudspeaker. Several miles away, ten CG-4As released from their tugs and headed towards a dim light concealed behind a barricade on the ground. The muffled thumps of the landings were hidden by Murphy's loudspeaker but, as he heard the last aircraft land behind him, Murphy finished his speech and called out 'Lights!' A hidden battery of searchlights flashed on to reveal to the visitors ten combat-ready gliders sat where less than half an hour before had been a wide and very empty field. As icing on the cake, a nine-piece marching band paraded out of one of the gliders playing the Air Corps marching song. Major Murphy's 'Pea Patch Show' (the field had previously been a pea farm) became legendary and Arnold returned to Washington more convinced than ever of the effectiveness of glider operations.[9] Now all he needed was an opportunity to prove that gliders could be used successfully in combat. That opportunity was not long in coming.

Chapter Six

'Any place, any time, anywhere': operations in the Far East

Although the US Marine Corps, tasked with island hopping across the Pacific, had already decided to cancel its glider programme as unsuitable for the type of operations it envisaged, the army still saw a role in its operations in the large mountainous islands of the western Pacific. General Douglas MacArthur had been appointed the youngest general officer in the US Army in 1918 for his distinguished command of the 42nd Infantry Division in France but now, at 62 years old, the distinguished commander faced defeat and humiliation when he was ordered to leave Corregidor and escape to Australia, leaving behind thousands of his men as the Japanese pushed the Americans out of the Philippines in March 1942. Arriving in Adelaide, he told waiting journalists that

> the President of the United States ordered me to break through the Japanese lines and proceed to Australia for the purpose, as I understand it, of organizing the American offensive against Japan, a primary objective of which is the relief of the Philippines. I came through and I shall return.[1]

Even as the American buildup began, the Japanese advance continued until, in July 1942, they reached New Guinea and within 300 air miles of the Australian coast. At the same time, forces on Guadalcanal began constructing airbases from which to strike at American supply convoys.

New Guinea, 4 September 1943

The Allied response was swift. Australian troops rushed to New Guinea as the US 1st Marine Division retook Guadalcanal against light opposition. The Japanese, finally halted, consolidated their forces around Lae and Salamaua where 10,000 troops were massed. MacArthur decided to feint against Salamaua to divert forces there and then to strike against his main objective, Lae, with a joint air and sea assault. The Australian 9th Infantry would land by sea twenty miles east of Lae and attack from there, and the following day a daylight jump by the US 503rd Parachute Infantry Regiment would seize an abandoned airfield twenty-two miles west near the town of Nadzab. The paratroopers would be followed by twenty-five CG-4As carrying their heavy equipment and link with Australian engineers to prepare the strip to take C-47s. The assault would mean that the Japanese commander, Lieutenant General Hatazao Adachi, would have to either fight against superior forces or withdraw to the north. D-Day was set for 4 September 1943.

The twenty-eight glider pilots selected for the mission had been in Australia since the previous January. Graduates of the first class of enlisted pilots at the Elmira base, they had been flown to Brisbane only to find no one was expecting them and no gliders in sight. Temporarily assigned to an aircrew replacement unit, a few days later they discovered their crated aircraft had surfaced at an air depot nearby. Flight Officer William Sampson found himself summoned before the commanding general of the Fifth Air Force who ordered a flying demonstration for the following Saturday, adding that he had 'plenty of Cubs to pull the gliders'.[2] Realizing that the general had no understanding of gliders and that he and his men had just a few days to learn how to put their aircraft together, Sampson spoke to an aide who arranged a C-47 tow. Working day and night, a glider was made ready and the demonstration went off according to plan. Two weeks before the Nadzab D-Day, twenty-five gliders were ferried 400 miles across the shark-infested Coral Sea to their final staging base. On 4 September, according to plan, the Australians landed and began their march westwards. The following day, the paratroopers landed to find the town deserted by the Japanese and the airfield in excellent condition. The glider mission was scrubbed – to the relief of pilots who had faced a 320-mile tow across mountainous jungle in over-loaded gliders. Lae fell to the Australians on 16 September and the gliders were put into storage at the staging field of Dobodura, their pilots reassigned to fly L5 observation planes for artillery units or as second pilots on C-47s. A year after arriving in Australia, the glider pilots went home. Even as the New Guinea operation wound down, another, far more successful glider force was about to grab headlines around the world – in the now almost forgotten invasion of Burma.

Operation Thursday – the invasion of Burma, 5 March 1944

At the start of the Second World War, Japan was determined to halt the expanding influence of the empires of the western nations in Southeast Asia and to forcibly create its own 'Greater East Asia Co-Prosperity Sphere'. British-held Burma was key to achieving this and its conquest would drive a wedge between the British in India and those in Malaya and Hong Kong, as well as isolating the French in Indochina. More importantly for the Japanese, Burma's deep mountains created a natural barrier to conclusively seal off China and starve her into submission after years of heavy fighting in resistance to Japanese expansionism. If the supply of arms and ammunition to Chiang Kai-Shek's army could be stopped, Japanese conquest of China would be certain. Burma could then become a springboard for further operations to grab the mineral rich states of Southeast Asia and westwards into the thriving industry of India, where independence movements against the British Raj were already active. It could also cover the flanks of the drive southwards through the Pacific rim. Ultimately, it was thought, the Japanese push west would link with German plans to expand into Persia.

In December 1941 the Japanese launched their attacks against the US Pacific fleet at Pearl Harbour and by February 1942 had gained control of Thailand, the Philippines, Guam, Wake and Hong Kong. British plans for the defence of their Burmese territory had relied heavily on the regional alliance structure of India, Thailand, Indochina and Singapore, assuming they would all be available to come to the aid of Burma if necessary, giving the British time they needed for the preparation of their defences. The existing forces already rapidly deployed there from India and Africa, along with two Chinese divisions under the command of American General Joseph 'Vinegar Joe' Stilwell, would benefit from the country's rugged geography and its climatic conditions – Burma's geographical features of high mountains and heavy jungle meant that the few roads and railways in the country, and even the navigable rivers, ran through natural chokepoints where an advance could be held up. Alongside this, the Burmese monsoon season seemed to offer a major natural defence. From mid-May to late October of each year, rainfalls varied from about 45 inches in the dry zone of north central Burma up to 200 inches in the area of Rangoon. During the monsoon season, it was reasoned, troops would find themselves mired in ankle-deep mud and movements would be brought almost to a standstill. In short, the British believed, military operations were limited to the dry season so, if they could hold up the Japanese advance with a relatively small defensive holding force, the monsoon season would finish the job and allow the Allies to strengthen their hold.

The British defence plan failed. Military planners had made some racist assumptions about their enemy that would prove disastrous. In the years before 1941, many in the West had ignored the rapid industrialization under way in Japan, regarding it almost as a backwater populated by characters from *The Mikado*. British defence plans for their Far Eastern empire assumed that any 'professional' army would behave as the British would, and any that didn't were likely to be little more than a native rabble. Instead, the Japanese, far from relying on the road and rail network, recognized the advantage of using the jungle as cover rather than seeing it as an obstacle – dividing their forces into small groups moving through the jungle to bypass British troop movements and getting behind British lines in much the same way as the German *blitzkreig* aimed to isolate units for later forces to clear up. The situation was made even worse because British Major-General William J Slim's command, preparing for war in the North Africa, had been trained for mechanized desert warfare rather than the jungle warfare it found itself caught up in.

As a result, Singapore fell because the British assumed that if *they* wouldn't attack the garrison overland, no one else could. Instead, a straightforward Japanese offensive plan, with the most basic equipment needed for transport, swiftly overcame barrier after barrier. Thailand fell after only eight hours of fighting. Singapore fell next on 15 February 1942 after seventy days and finally, by mid–May 1942, the Japanese had destroyed the weakest link in the defence plan, the regional alliance structure. They had established air superiority over Burma and raced against the oncoming monsoon season to remove the Allied forces permanently from the area. As the battered Allied army struggled into India, Lieutenant-General Joseph W Stilwell admitted: 'We got a hell of a beating. We got run out of Burma and it's humiliating as hell. I think we ought to find out what caused it and go back and retake it.'[3] It was easier said than done. If they were to stem the advance and take back Burma, the Allied forces would have to beat the Japanese at their own game.

Colonel Orde C. Wingate, a former artillery officer who had already led special units successfully in Palestine and Ethiopia, arrived in India as the retreat ended and immediately began studying everything he could about Burma and the Japanese. Geography, culture, tactics – anything, he felt, that could be useful. He quickly decided that the combination of Burmese topography and Japanese perimeter defence could not be assaulted head on but that the weak spot lay in the long and vulnerable Japanese logistics lines leading to the rear. Wingate argued that hit-and-run tactics by small highly mobile long-range-penetration (LRP) groups could seriously disrupt the Japanese and weaken their hold on Burma. Travelling with only what they could carry, these LRP units would be heavily reliant on continual aerial resupply and aerial firepower in lieu of artillery. Such operations would create widespread confusion behind the Japanese forward areas and, used ahead of the larger main Allied expedition, the chaos caused would gradually undermine the forward units and enable more conventional forces to attack head on.

Wingate's plan was accepted and work began developing a force to be known as 'Chindits' (named after fierce beasts of Burmese mythology) but a plan to coordinate with the Chinese fell through when Chiang Kai-Shek withdrew his pledge of forces for the main assault. Despite the setback, Wingate finally received permission to test his theory and Operation Longcloth (also sometimes referred to by some veterans as 'Loincloth', possibly a mishearing of the operational orders) was launched in February 1943. Wingate and his Chindit columns set out from Imphal with pack mules and bullock carts carrying their supplies in a trek that would continue until early June. In that time, Chindit raids successfully blew up over seventy-five sections of railway with very few casualties, frustrating Japanese attempts to find and engage them for nearly two months.

The operation was considered to be a great success, proving Wingate's theories and showing that small force could inflict damage on the enemy out of all proportion with its size, but it failed in many other key areas. First, the Chindits were intended to harass the Japanese in conjunction with a larger Allied attack. In this case, the Chindits were operating alone and thus the Japanese were able to concentrate all of their forces in operations against them. Secondly, the limits of the air support affected the effectiveness of the ground operation. With the Japanese having air superiority, supply drops were threatened and air strikes against identified enemy ground targets were difficult to arrange and direct. Finally, the lack of air support had another, potentially more serious effect on morale among the units, since there was no provision for casualty evacuation and all sick and wounded men had to be left behind, including some of Wingate's close friends.

Further afield, the Allied political leaders, and the US in particular, were desperate to keep China in the war. If it fell, the huge Japanese army currently tied up there would be freed for use elsewhere. An enormous, but very risky and expensive, supply mission was already under way to keep China supplied by flying in supplies from India over the Himalayan 'Hump' – by now the only supply route open. A safer and more efficient overland route would need to go through northern Burma and the US wanted to pressurize the British into greater efforts to retake the country. Prime Minister Winston Churchill, always a supporter of unconventional warfare, saw an opportunity and ordered Wingate to accompany him to the 'Quadrant' conference held in Quebec in August 1943.

A unified China–Burma–India (CBI) theatre command under the overall leadership of Lord Louis Mountbatten was established by the conference, which also laid out the principles of the Allied plan for the Far East which saw the retention of China as an ally as vital in an effort to ensure 'the destruction of Japanese sea and air forces, the blockade of Japan, and the large scale bombing of the Japanese homeland as a preliminary to the possible invasion of Japan'. US forces, it was decided, would advance towards Japan through the central, south-west, and possibly north-west Pacific approaches, whilst British forces would establish a Burma-to-China supply route and push north through the Straits of Malacca and South China Sea.

Churchill, ever the showman, introduced Wingate as a successor to 'Lawrence of Arabia' and, in a dramatic lecture, Wingate told the story of the first Chindit expedition and laid out his new plan for the formation of six LRP groups to disrupt Japanese communications and rear installations in Burma during the forthcoming 1943–4 dry season. Three of the groups would be held in reserve whilst the others would carry out twelve-week-long operations behind enemy lines. RAF air liaisons attached to these groups would be called upon to direct fighters and bombers to targets that would otherwise be undetectable by air. This time, he stressed, they would work in support of a much larger main offensive to successfully force the enemy out of Burma. Describing his ideas to the Chiefs of Staff Committee at the conference, Wingate claimed his aims were

> to disrupt the enemy's communications and rear installations. . . . [Furthermore], the consequence of their successful use [would be] widespread confusion and uncertainty behind the enemy's forward areas leading to progressive weakening and misdirection of his main forces.[4]

To do this effectively, he added, he needed US air support and asked for one bomber squadron per Chindit column, between twelve and twenty C-47s, and a sufficient number of light planes to perform a variety of tasks, including evacuation of the wounded. The British, he knew, could supply the bombers, but transport and light aircraft capable of using small jungle clearings were in short supply.

Having just recently denied 'Vinegar Joe' Stilwell (the senior US officer in the theatre) additional ground troops, Roosevelt sought a way of encouraging this renewed effort by providing material help. Moved by Wingate's descriptions of having to leave men behind, Roosevelt saw an ideal opportunity. Declaring that the Chindits would 'not have to walk out this time', he assigned General 'Hap' Arnold to confer with General Wingate to provide the necessary air support.

Arnold agreed on the need to revitalize the CBI theatre, believing that 'the previous campaigns had sapped the will of the British ground troops' and he immediately saw more than just a simple request for light aircraft. He decided that this was a chance to demonstrate the combat effectiveness of his air force and in so doing show the true capabilities of airpower if it could be coupled with a new way of thinking which cut across parochial lines and was solely dedicated to providing the necessary support for his operations. Wingate, it was agreed, would be provided with his own air force. Setting to work, Arnold identified a need for a leader of his new force who would be 'aggressive, imaginative, and endowed with organizational talent of a high order'. Whoever it was would need to share Arnold's vision of what properly used airpower could do. Two men came to mind.

Lieutenant-Colonel Philip G Cochran was an experienced fighter pilot who had fought in North Africa and who was the inspiration for the character of Colonel 'Flip' Corkin in the daily comic strip 'Terry and the Pirates'.[5] Summoned to Washington, Cochran, upset at the thought of missing the P-47 experience in Europe, set out to prove himself the wrong man for the job. Meeting the general, he decided to speak his mind, telling Arnold that he considered the task

> some doggone offshoot side-alley fight over in some jungle in Burma that doesn't mean a damn thing. The big show is in England and I've

got this job ready to go to over there and I think I can contribute a hell of a lot more with what I know and have been studying for seven years.[6]

Pushing his luck, he explained that he had run into his old friend from flying school, John Alison, the day before and found out that Alison was being considered for the same position. Cochran went on to tell Arnold that Alison was the man for the job because of his experience from his days in China. Arnold, by now tired of his attitude, dismissed him.

Cochran's friend, Lieutenant-Colonel John R Alison, had indeed served in China as part of Major-General Claire L Chennault's American Volunteer Group – the famous 'Flying Tigers'. When Alison arrived to meet General

---

Philip Cochran

Cartoonist Milton Caniff was old friend of Cochran's from their days at Ohio State University and was approached by Cochran to design an insignia for his squadron. Whilst awaiting approval for the design from Air Forces headquarters, Caniff was invited to watch the squadron perform a display. It was during this that Caniff struck upon the idea of a cartoon strip based around the adventures of a group of daring pilots led by Captain 'Flip' Corkin. The strip was an immediate success and when Cochran's citation for the Soldier's Medal was published and mentioned the connection, he began receiving fan mail addressed simply to Major Philip C Cochran, Army Air Forces, Washington, DC.

Following his death in 1979, his home town of Erie, Pennsylvania, campaigned for a special monument in his honour. Today, it stands on the west side of State Street, just south of the Glenwood Park Avenue turnoff, and next to the World War II Memorial:

COL. PHILIP COCHRAN
(1910–1979)
WWII hero. Cochran distinguished himself as a daring pilot commanding P-40 fighter planes in N. Africa and as the colorful leader of the 1st Air Commandos during the invasion of Burma. He became a colonel at the age of 33 and earned such honors as the Distinguished Service Medal and the British Distinguished Service Order. The Erie native inspired cartoon characters Flip Corkin in 'Terry & the Pirates' and Gen. Philerie in 'Steve Canyon.'

PENNSYLVANIA HISTORICAL AND MUSEUM
COMMISSION 2001

Arnold, he found Cochran waiting in the outer office. Arnold explained that a special air task force was to operate in support of the Chindits and that one of them was going to have to take the job of forming the group. This time, Alison objected, complaining that he had spent a lot of time training to be a fighter pilot and stating 'I don't think you need me and I don't want to go.' Both Cochran and Alison then each argued in favour of the other being sent until Arnold began to sell the idea in more detail. The project would have the highest available priority, he told them, and they would be given *carte blanche* authority for men and material to enable them to spearhead the entire air operation. As Arnold later put it

> I told both of them that they were going to Burma. Cochran immediately protested that he wanted to go 'where there was some fighting.' I informed him that he would get all the combat he wanted. I explained the unprecedented mission and ordered them to carry it out. 'To hell with the paperwork,' I added. 'Go out and fight.'[7]

Later, both men would recall interpreting what they had just heard differently – Cochran took it to mean 'go over and steal the show', whilst Alison understood it to mean 'transform the Wingate campaign into a new experiment in the use of air power'. Finally convinced, both men volunteered and, believing Alison was the senior, Arnold appointed him commander. When Alison corrected him about their respective seniority, he replied, 'Oh well, make it a co-command.'

They immediately set up an office in a nearby Washington DC hotel. To ensure they were working on the right lines, Cochran was sent to England to confer with General Wingate, who explained his requirements in detail. In return, Cochran promised Wingate any type of aircraft he wanted would be supplied by the new Air Commando organization. On his return to Washington, Cochran passed along concerns about the need to complete the operation before the onset of the next monsoon. If the original plans from the Quebec conference had called for number of light planes to aid General Wingate in support of his troops and the evacuation of his wounded for a period of about six months, the ambitious Cochran and Alison declared they would provide that and more. They wanted to US Air Commando to actually spearhead General Wingate's entire operation. Taking Arnold's vision and promise of unlimited resources to heart, the two men expanded the original plan for 100 light aircraft into a fully integrated and self-contained fighting unit, able to accomplish the entire mission, not just one part of it. Returning to Arnold with their proposal, they watched as he surveyed their work with his deputy, Colonel Vandenberg. Arnold read through it, then looked over to Vandenberg and asked, 'Van, does this thing make sense?' When Vandenberg agreed that it did, Arnold initialled it, slammed it on the table and said, 'All right, do it.'[8]

'Project Nine' became a source of resentment and dread across US air force bases as the best men and equipment were snatched away. Cochran and Alison toured bases asking for the best and brightest volunteers for a mysterious over-seas venture for a period of approximately six months which promised lots of excitement, hard work and combat. The response was overwhelming and, as men were selected, they in turn recommended other men whom they had served with and trusted.

Both Cochran and Allison independently thought of using gliders in the operation, Cochran seeing them as a means of flying in artillery for Wingate's forces into jungle firebases and Alison, with his past flying experience in the CBI theatre, saw the gliders as a means to transport Wingate's men into Burma and move them around in the jungle, using the transport planes for both aerial resupply and towing of the gliders. They turned to Major William H Taylor, who was conducting experimental jungle landings in Panama, to lead the glider force. Taylor travelled to Bowman Field, Kentucky, to the advanced glider school to interview over 200 applicants for the 100 places open to volun-teers who responded to the call for men who would return as 'dead glider pilots or live heroes'.[9] Among the successful applicants was Flight Officer John L 'Jackie' Coogan, the onetime child film star who had worked with Chaplin and was the former husband of Betty Grable.

In the space of less than three weeks, with the backing of the Chiefs of Staff, the new 5318th Provisional Air Unit, now comprising eighty-seven officers and 436 enlisted men, was formally approved on 13 September 1943. By that time, Cochran and Alison had secured the use of an impressive array of aircraft, including 150 CG-4A troop gliders, 100 L-1 and L-5 light planes, 30 P-51A fighters, 25 TG-5 training gliders, 13 C-47 transports, 12 UC-64 transports, 12 B-25H bombers and even 6 of the new, highly sought-after YR-4 helicopters. By then, the majority of the force had gathered together at Goldsboro, North Carolina, where they were issued with paratroop uniforms and jungle boots and began a six-week commando course. By late October, the orders arrived for the first men to go overseas.[10]

To facilitate the unit's movement, Cochran and an advance party left for India on 28 October, with the rest of the men and equipment due to follow by 1 December. Such was the priority that all members of the unit flew to India, with enlisted men of the Air Commando being given priority over full colonels of other units, and by mid-November 1943, 75 per cent of the unit had arrived. At a temporary base on Malir Airfield near Karachi, the men underwent acclimatization physical training before breakfast followed by lecture periods on a variety of subjects including jungle terrain, health care in tropical climates, communications procedures, weapons and pyrotechnics familiarization, and intelligence briefings from British Intelligence officers.

Equipment, supplies and aircraft began arriving by ship with all of the Project Nine aircraft going to Karachi except the gliders which were sent to an assembly area at Barrackpore Field, a British airbase near Calcutta. The crated aircraft needed to be assembled and, with only a hundred pilots and a similar number of ground crew available, everyone had to work. Arnold would later write an account of the operation for *National Geographic* magazine in August 1944 and described how

> visitors to our installations were confounded by the lack of 'rank.' Morale was high, and there was little paperwork. The men said, simply, 'If Phil or John says we do it, then by God, we do it!' Officers and men, hot, dusty, and bearded, lined up together at the chow lines, ate quickly, and went back to work. They sweated shoulder to shoulder unloading freight cars. For security reasons native help was kept to a minimum. At one base the headquarters was a bamboo hut, and the men slept at night on hard charpoys, or native cots.[11]

The British experience of Allied air support in Sicily meant that, before Wingate could fully trust the Americans, he had to know and understand their capabilities and the extent of their commitment to his forces. The 5318th set out to demonstrate new tactics they had developed for forces operating in the difficult Burmese terrain such as glider tow and pickup operations, aerial resupply and evacuation from difficult locations, and close air support and bombing by both P-51s and B-25s.

In the jungles, the Chindits used mules as transport. With their vocal chords surgically cut to ensure silence (and in some cases light-coloured animals being painted green as camouflage), mules were vital both for carrying heavy loads and, in emergency, as food. Wingate needed to know that the gliders could transport them. A CG-4A was rigged to carry three mules with a mechanic armed with a rifle standing by. Just before takeoff, the pilot reminded the mechanic 'if any one of those three critters starts raising hell up in the sky you shoot him right between the eyes before he kicks our glider apart'.[12] In the coming months, many mules would fly into combat but very few are recorded as having been shot – although toilet facilities proved another issue altogether.

Small-scale exercises were used to demonstrate glider capability, with a squad of troops being landed, setting up snatch poles and then being picked up again by their tow aircraft. Wingate watched the first demonstration before turning to Cochran saying 'I say, that was a jolly good show!' All that now remained was to convince Lord Mountbatten. Cochran set up another demonstration using twenty-four gliders, six mules and a battalion of the Black Watch. After a successful daytime landing, the exercise was repeated at night. Mountbatten, doubting that so many gliders could land with so little noise, was personally driven around each of the twenty-four aircraft, growing amazement evident on his face. The gliders had a new convert and full support.[13]

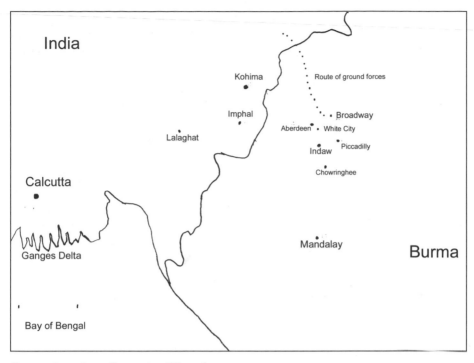

Burma invasion: Operation Thursday.

The plan called for the British 16th Brigade under Brigadier Bernard Fergussen, to make a gruelling 455 mile march from Ledow in India to 'Aberdeen' – a stronghold in the Burmese jungle twenty-seven miles from the village of Indaw, resupplied entirely by Cochran's men. Four weeks later, Brigadier Michael Calvert's 77th Brigade would make a night landing in gliders at two other strongholds named 'Piccadilly' and 'Broadway'. At the same time, Brigadier Walter Lentaigne and the 111th Brigade would make a night air landing into another stronghold thirty-five miles from Indaw, codenamed 'Chowringhee' after Calcutta's famous street. Each site was deep in the jungle and had large open spaces to facilitate a landing. Finally, 14th Brigade, led by Brigadier Thomas Brodie, together with the 3rd West African (Nigerian) Brigade under Brigadier Gilmore, would be flown four weeks later by C-47 to newly created landing strips around Indaw.

Operations moved to two British forward bases near Imphal in January 1944, with the fighters, bombers, light planes and the headquarters staff located at Hailakandi while the transports and gliders went to Lalaghat. Training was stepped up throughout January with all sections participating in demanding unit training exercises to smooth out all the rough edges and to develop relations with the Chindits. It was at Lalaghat that Jackie Coogan was to discover another hazard of glider operations in India. A flight of ten gliders had just landed after a training exercise and were waiting on the runway for the base's lone jeep to tow them to their dispersal points. The heat in the cockpits was unbearable so Coogan decided to pay one of the Indian labourers to use an elephant to tow his aircraft. The elephants were being used to move heavy logs on the airfield and the glider presented no great challenge to its strength. All went well until the elephant suddenly panicked – possibly seeing what seemed to be the shadow of a giant bird behind it – and began to run straight into a stand of trees, tearing off the glider's wings as the combination crashed into the dense forest.

Fergussen's 16th Brigade had been marching for two weeks when the Air Commando Group began practising landings for Broadway and Piccadilly with the men who would undertake the assault. Shortage of tow aircraft meant that the gliders were on double tow, two to each tug. During a night exercise, a glider broke free, killing four British soldiers, two pilots and a mechanic. Saddened by the loss of their friends, the glider pilots also worried about losing the confidence of the British. The next day, however, Major Taylor was relieved to find a note from the Chindits' commanding officer saying 'please be assured that we will go with your boys any place, any time, anywhere'. So proud were the commandos of this endorsement that it was adopted as their motto and remains the slogan of US Special Air Operations groups today.[14]

On 3 February 1944, air commando fighters and bombers began attacks on Japanese positions in Burma prior to the coming invasion that showed the versatility of the Air Commando. P-51s were fitted with rocket firing tubes and other fighters towed a dangling weight at the end of a cable to snag on telephone wires and tear them down. The light aircraft were used as spotter planes, finding likely targets and then leading attack planes to the location before dropping smoke to mark aiming points. These aircraft also carried adapted bomb racks to enable them to drop ammo, food, water and medical supplies to the Allied forces on the ground and were also called into action to evacuate sick and wounded men from the front lines, carrying more than 700 wounded men back from the battle area between 10 February and 6 March alone.

The success of the Air Commando meant that morale was high, perhaps too high. According to the unit history, the phrase ' "Blow it out – I'm from Project 9" was a sore spot at every [Air Training Command] base from Florida to Karachi.'[15] Although Cochran and Alison had gained the support of the highest levels, their success did little to impress the more traditionally minded air force commanders. In particular, Cochran and General William Old – commander of Troop Carrier Command (TCC) – had clashed. As the invasion got under way, Old complained about what he saw as lax standards among the men of the Air Commando. At Lalaghat on 5 March 1944, Old complained that Cochran's men showed no interest in dress and appearance. The men were not in uniforms, were growing beards, failed to salute and officers shared eating facilities and latrines with enlisted men. In response, Cochran issued an order to his men:

To: All Personnel and Attached Organizations.

Look, Sports, the beards and attempts at beards are not appreciated by visitors.

Since we can't explain to all strangers that the fuzz is a gag or 'something I always wanted to do' affair, we must avoid their reporting that we are unshaven (regulations say you must shave) by appearing like Saturday night in Jersey whenever possible. Work comes before shaving. You will never be criticized for being unkempt if you are so damn busy you can't take time to doll up. But be clean while you can.

Ain't it awful?

P.G. Cochran

Colonel, Air Corps,

Commanding.[16]

As the complaint came in, Cochran and his men had far more pressing concerns. The invasion of Burma was scheduled for early March, dependent on weather conditions. In February, the first glider mission of the war in Southeast Asia had inserted a sixteen-man patrol in a single aircraft on the east side of the Chindwin River and although four people were injured during the landing, the patrol successfully carried out its mission and the pilot walked back with them to the base fifteen days later. A second mission delivered nearly 8,000 lb of river crossing equipment, including folding boats, outboard motors and fuel, to a sand bar on the east side of the Chindwin near Singkaling Ekanti in support of a river crossing. The two gliders were collected the next day by snatch pickup. It was a good start.

Finally, on Sunday, 5 March 1944, after receiving favourable weather predictions, Air Vice Marshal Baldwin, the overall air commander, gave the order to go. The plan had originally intended for flights to start at 1740hrs with two pairs of gliders, both separated by a two-minute interval, departing the airfield – one pair heading for Piccadilly, the other Broadway. Twenty minutes later, more would begin lifting off with flights alternating between the two landing zones. Because there were only twenty-six tugs available, the rest of the glider force would wait until the transports returned from their first trips. As his men gathered for their mission briefing, Cochran gravely told them 'Nothing you've done, nothing you're ever going to do counts now – only the next few hours. Tonight you are going to find your souls.'[17]

Wingate wanted to achieve complete surprise and felt that any reconnaissance of the area might alert Japanese forces so ordered flights over the proposed landing sites should stop before D-Day itself. Captain Charles Russhon, the Air Commando's intelligence officer argued against it and eventually persuaded Cochran to allow one flight – without Wingate's knowledge. When the photographs came back, they showed that Broadway was clear but at Piccadilly (where the Chindits had operated before) the Japanese had dragged hundreds of logs across the open areas and laid a minefield in the middle of the area in case they returned. With forty minutes to go before takeoff, a hasty conference met to consider the options. Cochran, Alison and Wingate all agreed to send all the gliders into Broadway. As Cochran later put it; 'our decision was easy, really. . . . [If] those British soldiers had that kind of guts, and that kind of heart that they were going forward and going in there, it was up to us to take them in.' Calling his men together, Cochran cheerfully told them 'Boys! We've found a better place to go to!'[18]

Both Cochran and Alison had wanted to lead their men on this mission but eventually Alison had been able to convince Cochran that one of them had to stay behind with Wingate and that it should be the senior officer. Reluctantly, Cochran agreed and Alison, who had never flown a glider, spent the day before the invasion practising his landings. Now he would lead the initial glider assault into Broadway.

With all aircraft now tasked for Broadway, the first C-47 with two heavily laden gliders lifted off smoothly at 1812hrs. Almost immediately, though, problems began to surface. Broadway was over 200 miles behind enemy lines and the Chindits were taking no chances. Most carried more ammunition than the CG-4A's designers had expected and the overweight aircraft struggled to make height. When they did, turbulence around the mountains put additional strain on the tow ropes and several broke. Four gliders had crashed soon after takeoff because of broken towropes, three more broke loose on the east side of the Chindwin River and another two went down near the Irrawaddy River. Clearly, the double tow was not safe so Cochran ordered the use of use single tows for the rest of the operation, slowing down the insertion.

Almost as if planned, some of the lost gliders had landed inside the Japanese lines, creating an impression that an Allied attack was being made across several

John R Alison

Co-founder of the US Air Commando, Alison went on to set up two more similar formations and ended the war as operations officer for 5th Air Force, participating in the landings in the Philippines and in the air operations against Japan from Okinawa.

After the war his hometown of Gainesville, Florida, took over the military base there as a civilian airport, naming it after Alison. He served as an Assistant Secretary of Commerce, and as a major-general in the Air Force Reserve, retiring as vice president of the Northrop Corporation in 1984. In 1996 he was invited to give the keynote speech at the US Air Force's fiftieth anniversary convention as exemplifying the spirit of the service. He finally gave up working out in the gym three times per week at the age of 87.

areas. A later report claimed that 'the tactical advantage that must have resulted from the enemy being confused and bewildered at the idea of striking forces at ten different places in his rear was tremendous and gave impetus to the operation's success' but for the men aboard the gliders, the situation was desperate. Glider 19B, one of the early double tows, was piloted by Flight Officer Martin McTigue and carried men of the 1st King's (Liverpool) Regiment. At 7,500 feet, McTigue suddenly shouted that they had been cut loose and began circling to try to find an area to land. Finally, steering towards two high trees in the hope that they would act as a brake, he brought the glider down in thick jungle. Twenty-one-year-old Arthur House, one of the passengers, recalled what happened next:

> although we had been thrown about like rag dolls there was no panic at all. I kicked the glider door open and we stumbled out into the jungle. We were all badly shaken and nursing cuts and bruises . . . The pilot had no idea how far we might be from Broadway and as we had no maps (Sergeant) McGee decided our best chance of survival would be to head due west and try to march back towards the Chindwin River. This meant at least 150 miles through Japanese territory . . . [19]

In the co-pilot's seat had been the battalion's chaplain, Burmese-speaking former missionary Captain Patterson, but he had been killed in the crash. After burying him, the men set out on what would become a month-long escape through thick jungle, struggling through swamps and rivers and barely escaping their Japanese pursuers. After two weeks, the men ran into an ambush and, according to House, 'we were forced to scatter. I found myself on my own and could hear the Japs raking the undergrowth with their bayonets. How they missed me I'll never know.'[20] As the men regrouped, they found that McTigue and four others were missing. Later, the sole survivor was able to report that the pilot had been executed shortly after capture and Sergeant King, Privates Booth and Blundell all died in captivity. When the rest finally reached Imphal, they found it under attack by the Japanese and crouched in the jungle as the enemy fell back past them. House, the only member of the party fit enough to return to his regiment, would not rejoin them until July, four months after setting out for Broadway.

As their ordeal began, the first tow planes had arrived over Broadway. Shortly before midnight, the first pathfinder gliders, flown by Major Taylor and Colonel Alison, released and swooped down to land without incident to secure an area that had been identified as a likely ambush site. Soon, the rest began to arrive but it was only then that the dangers hidden in the tall grass made themselves apparent. Logs and deep log trenches littered the field, ripping off the glider undercarriages as they landed and creating a pile up as following gliders crashed onto those who had landed earlier. It was Alison's nightmare. Frantically, he and his crews ran across the landing zone reconfiguring the marker beacons in order to try to bring the gliders in to relatively safe areas. The brigadier was seen carrying smoke pots to where a corporal directed him in a race to minimize the chaos. With the Broadway landing zone quickly becoming blocked by wrecked gliders, Alison realized that the second wave would have no chance to land and so told his radio operator inform Cochran in India that they could not accept any more gliders until they could clear the field. In the confusion, the radio operator instead sent the prearranged 'Soya-Link' message indicating that the invasion force had met with disaster. The signal was received by an airborne C–47 and relayed back to Lalaghat, reaching Cochran and Wingate at 0227hrs. Believing that his men had met heavy resistance, Cochran's first reaction was to order in the rest of the force in an attempt to support the troops on the ground and win the battle but he was overruled by Wingate. Fearing heavy losses among his men, Cochran was devastated.

At dawn, Alison reviewed the situation. Of the fifty-four gliders not recalled during the night, thirty-seven had reached Broadway, carrying with them 539 men and 29,972 lb of equipment, including three bulldozers, airfield lighting apparatus and three pack mules. Eight aircraft had landed in friendly territory on the western side of the Chindwin River but of the nine that landed on the east side in enemy territory, two had been released just short of Broadway and had crashed in the jungle, killing all but two of their occupants. The fate of two gliders and their crews has never been discovered. In Arnold's August 1944 article for *National Geographic*, he wrote:

> Most of the crews landed in enemy territory escaped to safety. One medical officer, a glider pilot, and co–pilot, with 15 native troops, walked 85 miles to Broadway in ten days. Out of food at one point, they tossed a hand grenade into a pond and killed 60 fish. There was a soldier hero in one crew whose men were crossing a river in Jap-held territory. This man drowned rather than call for help and thus endanger the lives of his friends.[21]

So far, only thirty men were killed and thirty-three injured in the first night's operations. Looking around the landing zone strewn with wrecked gliders, Alison wondered whether their task of building an airstrip could really be achieved. Assured by the acting Airborne Engineer commander that it would be possible, he asked how long it might take. 'Well, if I have it done by this afternoon,' the engineer replied, 'will that be too late?'[22] True to his word, by 1620hrs that day Alison was able to send a message to base that 4,700 feet of runway would be ready that night for C–47 operations. An hour later, aircraft began to take off from Lalaghat and by 2111hrs, all of the Lalaghat aircraft had left and those from Hailakandi were on their way. Alison had organized the new airfield so well that on the first night sixty-two C–47s were able to land at Broadway.

Twenty-four hours after the first aircraft left, Wingate decided to move up the date for the second phase, believing that a counterattack against Broadway was likely. The second base, Chowringhee, was to be established fifty miles south of Broadway and, although it was recognized as being more vulnerable to enemy air and ground attack, with Piccadilly gone it was vital to open a second airfield.

That night, guided by a full moon, gliders landed at Chowringhee with only one serious incident. Unfortunately, the two fatalities of the insertion occurred when the special equipment glider carrying the heavy bulldozer for airfield construction and the radios for contacting the headquarters at Hailakandi crashed on landing. As Cochran arranged for another bulldozer to be flown in from Calcutta, Alison got the now redundant bulldozer from Broadway delivered. As before, the Airborne Engineers demonstrated a real dedication to the task ahead of them. The bulldozer flown in from Broadway was put straight to work until, as the official history reports; 'Fatty, the dozer driver, who had been operating his machine for 42 hours, finally collapsed while his machine continued to roll on and he was pulled off safely.'[23]

Back at Broadway, inbound flights were now increased to sixteen per hour, the maximum Alison thought could be handled safely. Ninety-two C-47s landed that night and the official report commented that

> nobody has seen a transport operation until he has stood at Broadway under the light of a Burma full moon and watched Dakotas coming in and taking off in the opposite direction on a single strip all night long at the rate of one landing and one takeoff every three minutes.[24]

Air strikes against Japanese airfields by the fighters and bombers of the Air Commando during 8 March were highly effective, dramatically reducing the threat to the inbound supply aircraft so that by the fourth night of the operation Broadway was able to accept eighty-five C-47s and Chowringhee another seventy-eight. The next night, Broadway managed ninety-five but Chowringhee reduced its number to the forty needed to complete the planned insertion of the equipment and personnel for that location. Its mission accomplished, Chowringhee was abandoned at 0800hrs on 10 March. That evening the empty site was attacked by the Japanese who, surrounded by the wreckage of the gliders, claimed a decisive victory. Having intercepted the message Air Commando fighters and bombers then pounced on the Japanese as they tried to work out what to do with their newly acquired position.

Operation Thursday was drawing to a close. Planners had decreed that another 129 C-47 missions would be needed to complete the insertion and every effort was made to finish the job. The last four flights arrived on the night of 11 March, by which time some 579 Dakota and seventy-four CG-4A Waco glider sorties had landed 9,052 men, 1,359 animals, 255 tons of supplies, a Bofors anti-aircraft battery and one 25-pound field gun battery, with the loss of a single C-47 which struck a water buffalo when taxi-ing. Of all the Air Commando crews, the glider pilots had suffered most. Fourteen had been killed and 90 per cent of their aircraft written off. After making certain that the Allied troops were in place and no longer under serious threat of counterattack, Cochran cabled Arnold that 'The aerial invasion of Burma was strictly an air show.'[25]

On 22 March, a Japanese offensive in the Assam area brought a call to reinforce Wingate's in-place forces by inserting the 14th and 3rd West African Brigades into the Aberdeen base in the Manhton area as well as White City at Mawlu. At Aberdeen (named after the hometown of Wingate's wife) ground forces had already built a glider landing strip so the plan was to develop this into an airfield for resupply transport flights. Gliders landed construction equipment and the strip was soon operational but two Transport Command aircraft overshot on landing and crashed, and one RAF aircraft was shot down. By now the Air Commando transport crews were feeling left out of the action and so began to carry three-inch mortar bombs, fragmentation clusters and incendiary bombs to throw out at any targets they might happen upon as they flew their assigned tasks. As one pilot put it 'we may not have done any damage but I'll bet we scared the hell out of them'.[26]

As the air operation began to wind down, Wingate signalled his men triumphantly to tell them 'our task is fulfilled. We have inflicted a complete surprise upon the enemy. All our columns are inside the enemy's guts . . . Let us thank God for our great success.' Not everyone, though, was under Wingate's spell. The War Diary of the 2nd Battalion of the Leicestershire Regiment notes simply 'long message from Force, impossible to decipher, but something about guts and God'.[27] Within weeks, Wingate was dead – killed when the B–25 he was travelling in crashed into a mountainside. His death meant that the driving force behind his vision was gone but he had proved his ideas could work.

Air Commando operations were expected to be over by May but the British asked for help in opening another airfield near Pinbaw and the exercise that had worked so well at Broadway and Chowringhee was repeated. By now, though, the Air Commandos were beginning to show the strain of the heavy workload and difficult living conditions. Malaria and exhaustion had reduced their effectiveness and, on 19 May, the last Air Commando flights in support of the Chindits took place. Cochran, Alison and their glider pilots had accomplished an enormous amount in a short space of time. The effect on the morale of the ground troops was a significant factor in the eventual success of the invasion of Burma and, as one observer later wrote; 'Col. Cochran and his men have fulfilled every requirement originally demanded of the air unit in the Wingate Plan and a great many more never believed possible.'[28]

Operation Thursday marked the peak of glider operations in the Far East. Other, smaller operations would be undertaken, such as the landing of heavy equipment to develop the runway at Luzon in the Philippines, but for the most part they were non-combat missions. One CG–13 glider was used to fly a general's staff car from base to base across thousands of miles and another

CG-4A to rescue the survivors of a plane crash in central New Guinea but, for the most part, the pilots were used for routine resupply. Then, in late 1944, rumours began to circulate about the biggest airborne operation yet – the invasion of Japan. Back in the United States, orders had been placed for 1,000 of the new CG-10 'Trojan Horse' gliders capable of carrying forty men or a jeep and howitzer, ready for the attack. The 11th Airborne Division was undergoing intensive training for the invasion in Manila when the atomic bombs devastated Hiroshima and Nagasaki. Two weeks later, the division and some of its attached glider pilots arrived peacefully in Japan as part of the occupation forces.

During the war, Japan, having briefly experimented with glider use in Manchuria in the late 1930s, developed its own airborne forces with German advisers and established a Glider Infantry Regiment, but although American forces at Luzon found cargo carrying Ku-8 'Gander' gliders on Nichols Field the *guridas* do not seem to have been used operationally other than for resupply.

As glider operations were beginning to prove their worth in Burma, the Commanding General of the Transport Carrier Command recommended developing protocols for their design and procurement, establishing a system for communication between the tug and glider, recovering landed gliders by aerial pickup and utilizing gliders as resupply vehicles. No one, though, gave much thought to their use in combat. Even as US glider pilots had prepared to go into action for the first time in support of their British colleagues in Sicily, their role after landing had not been completely thought through.

> The role of the glider pilot in combat will be primarily to land his glider safely, expedite the rapid debarkation of his passengers, secure his glider on the ground, assure that transport which may land after the glider-borne troops have secured the airdrome or locality to permit reinforcement by transport-borne troops. The glider pilot will participate in ground combat only in exceptional circumstances or after his glider has been wrecked in landing. [29]

The expectation appeared to be that he would return via army routes to his unit and training focused almost exclusively on the technical aspects of maintenance and 'the safe and proficient operation of the CG-4A glider'. In upcoming European operations in Holland and Germany, many American pilots, once they had landed their loads, simply left the battle area and went off exploring the delights of nearby towns and cities. If the glider-borne troop were to be used only as aerial truck drivers, this philosophy might have worked. However, as part of an assault airborne force, their fate was in their own, largely untrained, hands. In marked contrast to British and German pilots, it was not until 1945 that US glider training directives discussed combat missions and introduced weapons and combat team training as part of glider pilot syllabus. In 1943, five months after the invasion of Sicily, I TCC highlighted major problems with the training provided by Flying Training Command's glider programme, including even basic flight techniques and 'insufficient combat team training to function and NOT be a liability'. In Europe, the image of the glider pilot as truck driver would soon be dispelled.

Chapter Seven

Over the west wall: Europe 1944–1945

Operation Tonga: the British airborne assault on Normandy, 6 June 1944

The time was seven minutes past midnight. At 6,000 feet over the French coast, tug pilot Wing Commander Duder wished them luck and released the cable. In the cockpit of PF800, a Horsa glider with the chalk number 91 carrying men of the Oxford and Buckinghamshire Light Infantry, co-pilot John Ainsworth peered at his stopwatch, counting down the seconds; 'five . . . four . . . three . . . two . . . one . . . bingo, right turn to starboard onto course'. Pilot Jim Wallwork looked around and could see the moonlight glinting off the surface of the river and canal below him. He recalled:

> So then, to hell with the course. I knew my height; I knew how far away I was, so it was a case of by guess and by God from then on. I didn't complete the crosswind leg, so I bowled down and landed rather quickly. There was a feeling of the land rushing up and I landed probably at about ninety five instead of at eighty-five, and ten miles per hour in the dark looks like a lot.[1]

As the glider hit the ground, Wallwork shouted 'Stream' and Ainsworth released the arrester parachute which lifted the tail, forcing the nose into the ground. As they hit, the impact tore off the wheels and bounced the glider back into the air but the parachute did its job and they hit the ground again; this time on the skids. Wallwork shouted 'Jettison' and Ainsworth pressed the button to release the parachute. The glider had slowed but was careering along the ground at sixty miles per hour in a shower of sparks that made its passengers think they were already under fire. Eddie Edwards, one of those aboard, recalls:

> There was the usual slight bump, a small jerk and a much heavier thump, as the glider made contact with the ground, but only for a moment. It jerked again, shuddered, left the ground for a second or two, bumped over the rough surface and lurched forward like a bucking bronco. We sped forward, bouncing up and down on our hard wooden

seats as the vehicle lost contact with the ground, then came down again with another heavy thump, a tug and a jerk. For a few moments it appeared that we were in for a comparatively smooth landing, but just as that thought flashed through my mind the darkness filled with a stream of brilliant sparks as the glider lost its wheels and the skid hit some stony ground. There followed a sound like a giant canvas sheet being viciously ripped apart, then a mighty crash like a clap of thunder and my body seemed to be moving in several directions at once. Moments later the crippled glider skidded and bounced over the uneven ground to slide finally to a juddering halt, whereupon I found myself perched in a very strange position at an uneven angle. I peered into a misty blue and greyish haze. From somewhere out in endless space there zoomed towards me a long tracer-like stream of multicoloured lights, like a host of shooting stars that moved towards me at high speed. I realized after a moment that I was not being shot at. I was simply concussed and seeing stars! The noise from the landing had ceased very suddenly and was replaced by an ominous silence. No-one stirred, nothing moved. My immediate thought was 'God help me – we must all be dead' . . . The exit door had been right beside my seat. Now there was only a mass of twisted wood and fabric across the doorway and we had to use the butts of our rifles to smash our way out.[2]

The glider had come to rest within yards of its target, the impact so great that both pilots had been hurled through the windscreen. Jim Wallwork

went over headfirst and landed flat on my stomach. I was stunned, as was Ainsworth; I came around and he seemed to be in bad shape. I said, 'Can you crawl?' and he said, 'No,' and then I asked if I lifted, could he crawl out and he said, 'I'll try.' I lifted the thing and I felt that I lifted the whole bloody glider when probably all I lifted was a small spar, but I felt like 30 men when I picked this thing up and he did manage to crawl out.[3]

It was 0016hrs on 6 June 1944. D–Day had begun.

Hitler's Directive No. 40 of March 1942 ordered work to begin on what would become the 'Atlantic Wall' of 'Fortress Europe'. Under the direction of Fritz Todt, who had designed the Siegfried Line (*Westwall*) along the Franco-German border, thousands of forced labourers were put to work constructing huge concrete fortifications along the Dutch, Belgian and French coasts facing the English Channel with the aim of smashing any invasion attempt either on the beaches or immediately inland by a combination of strong defensive fortifications to delay an invasion and mobile forces inland, who would provide a massive armoured counterattack against the invaders once they had reached far enough

In the years immediately after the First World War, German gliding enthusiasts took to the air in very basic aircraft, often home-made. *(Author's collection.)*

As gliding developed as a sport, designers like Messerschmitt rapidly improved the performance of aircraft like this Condor II a glider seen during a flight over the Wasserkuppe. *(Author's collection.)*

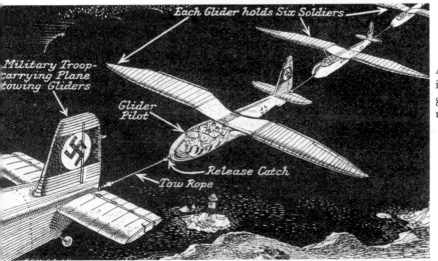

Each Glider holds Six Soldiers

Military Troop-carrying Plane towing Gliders

Glider Pilot

Release Catch

Tow Rope

An artist's impression of how gliders might be used against Britain.

The Nazis Show Us How They Took Eben-Eymael

German parachutists working under the protection of their own machine-guns paralysed the Belgian infantry defending the approaches to the fort. They also bored holes for mines in the massive concrete walls and eventually blew up the fort. Nazi soldiers are seen, left, by the partly destroyed fort.

On May 11 the German troops finally attacked the fort, after a terrific onslaught had been made by Nazi 'planes, which bombed and machine-gunned the garrison. The heroic struggle ended in a Nazi victory and the capitulation of the commander with 1,000 men. Some idea of the intensity of the attack can be gauged from the photograph below, which shows part of the damaged wall of the fort.

MOST powerful and modern of the forts of Liége, Eben-Eymael covered more than 200 acres and had an armament of two 12-centimetre guns (about 4·7-in.), over 30 of 6·5 and 7·5 cm., besides a large number of machine-guns, etc. Of its impregnability Belgium's military experts were convinced, and yet only a few hours sufficed for its capture by the Nazis. At first it was said that their parachutists descended on the cupola and threw hand grenades into the interior, but these photographs, reproduced from the German publication "Die Wehrmacht," prove rather that it was the severity of the aerial bombardment, combined with the mines laid by the parachutists, which broke the garrison's resistance, thus enabling picked storm troops to take the fort by assault. A Belgian soldier wounded in the defence of the fort confirmed the main outlines of the story.

The loop-holes in the thick concrete walls of Eben-Eymael were shattered as a result of mine explosions which went off with such force that the guns were broken out of their mountings. On the right, we see Hitler surrounded by some of the captors of the fort, who are proudly wearing the Iron Crosses awarded by the Fuehrer for their exploit.

How the British press reported the attack on Eben-Emael.

The victors of Eben Emael. (L-R) Lt Delica, Lt Witzig, Captain Koch, Lt Zierach, Hitler, Lt Ringler, Lt Meissner, Lt Kiess (glider pilot commander), Lt Altmann, Lt Jager.

German airborne machine gun team in action.

German infantry at Eben-Emael after the attack

A Kirby Kite prepares for takeoff. This type formed the nucleus of the British glider programme in 1940. (*Author's collection.*)

The King inspects the newly formed airborne force after a demonstration drop, 25 May 1941

A Hotspur training glider prepares for launch. Instructor Warrant Officer John Guest (wearing his best 'blues' in honour of the occasion) at Easter 1945. (*Eagle.*)

British troops in training with the Horsa glider

The Airspeed Horsa coming in to land. (Author's collection.)

Crete: a crashed DFS 230 and its crew.

General Kurt Student, founder of the German airborne forces.

After the invasion, aircraft and gliders litter Crete's Maleme airfield.

eneral Henry H 'Hap' Arnold (right) inspects the towrope of a CG-4A glider, August 1944. These ylon ropes were the main cause of the stocking shortage during the war – each 300ft rope contained nough nylon for over 1600 pairs.

Loading the Waco. Smaller than the British gliders, the Waco could carry a jeep or a gun. It was believed that the combination could be delivered by landing gliders side by side. Although it worked in theory, in combat it was a very different story. (*Author's collection.*)

glider 'snatch' pickup demonstration in the US. The technique had been used successfully by the US ostal service and was later adapted to pick up undamaged combat gliders such as the Waco and lorsa from their landing sites.

A wrecked German Go242 glider in the North African desert. Glider resupply to the Afrika Korps took a heavy toll on the vulnerable tow combinations.

An Me323, the powered variant of the Me321 Gigant glider, comes under attack as it crosses the Mediterranean. Fourteen were destroyed in a single ambush by Allied fighters and the news reached Britain just as British gliders were about to embark on the epic ferry operation to North Africa.

Skorzeny's men prepare for their mission.

Germany's 'most dangerous man', Otto Skorzeny (3rd from left in peaked cap) escorts Mussolini to safety following the daring glider-borne rescue mission ordered by Hitler. (*Signal* magazine, autumn 1943.)

Burma: a light aircraft recovers a soldier of the West African Brigade from a jungle airstrip. Casualty evacuation flights like this vastly improved morale among the Chindit forces.

Colonel Alison (left) with Wingate (in pith helmet) and staff on 'Broadway' during the invasion of Burma.

A bulldozer is loaded into a Waco glider in preparation for the invasion of Burma.

Russian paratroops prepare for operations.

Colonel Philip C Cochran, the inspirations for the cartoon character 'Flip' Corkin in the popular comic strip 'Terry and the Pirates' and commander of 1st Air Commando.

Europe: a pilot's eye view of 'Rommel's Asparagus' – the anti-glider obstacles put in place to prevent landings. Many poles were topped with explosive charges and linked by steel wire. *(Author's collection.)*

A high altitude shot of the British landing zones taken just after D-Day. The importance of Orne Canal bridge (bottom left) and river bridge (centre) in connecting the invasion beaches (out of shot to left) with Ranville LZs (right) is obvious in this picture. *(Author's collection.)*

British Hamilcar gliders prepare for Operation Mallard, the D-Day resupply mission. *(Eagle)*

A crashed Hamilcar in Normandy. *(Eagle.)*

WINGS ARE THE WHEELS OF TO-MORROW

THE **HAMILCAR GLIDER**

USED IN OPERATIONS ON D DAY, AT ARNHEM AND THE RHINE

A Product of

GENERAL AIRCRAFT LTD.

FELTHAM   MIDDLESEX

A contemporary advert for the Hamilcar glider. *(Author's collection.)*

A Hamilcar on 'high tow' behind a Halifax bomber. *(Author's collection.)*

ritish glider pilots after receiving awards at Buckingham Palace, December 1944. Left to right: Bruce obbs DFM, Stan Pearson DFM, W Herbert DFM, Jim Wallwork DFM and Tommy Moore MM. *(Eagle)*

Glider pilot and his tug captain. *(Eagle)*

This shot, showing a Normandy landing zone, demonstrates how difficult a safe landing could be. *(Larkin.)*

A Go242 prepares to cast off over Russia. The camouflage pattern is for the early winter period.

A DFS 230 and its passengers. In July 1944, a forc was landed by DFS and Go242 gliders to seize th rebel French stronghold of Vercors. (*Author's collection.*)

Allied glider fleet flying over the naval element of Operation Overlord.

A bust of Colonel Otway at the Merville Battery today. The gap in the hedgerow behind marks the landing site of the glider that overshot the battery as 9 Para attacked. (*Author's collection.*)

Pilot's eye view of a Horsa on tow. (*Author's collection.*)

A roadside marker overlooks the LZ north of Ranville where the 6th Airborne landed on D-Day. (*Author's collection.*)

A CG10 'Trojan Horse' on exercise in the US. A thousand of these aircraft were ordered and were expected to lead the invasion of Japan. *(Author's collection.)*

An artist's impression of the Hamilcar on tow behind a Stirling bomber.

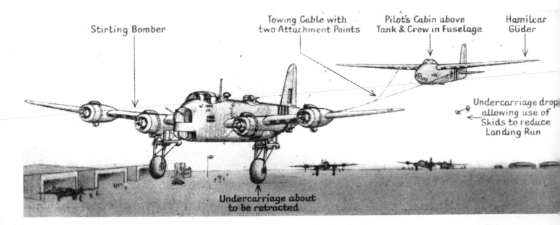

Jim Wallwork

Born in Manchester, as the son of an artilleryman veteran of the First World War, Jim volunteered for the British Army in March 1939. Against his father's advice, he joined the infantry but soon regretted it and, despite being promoted to sergeant, he tried to join the Royal Air Force. This was blocked by his commanding officer but in 1942 he was accepted for training in the newly formed Glider Pilot Regiment. By May 1942 he was at flight training school. Along with Andy Andrews, Wallwork was one of the few to take part in all four operations and his flight into the Orne bridges was described later as one of the greatest flying feats of the Second World War.

After the war he worked as a salesman and then in 1956 emigrated to British Columbia where, until retirement, he ran a small livestock farm near Vancouver. He remains active in the Glider Pilot Regimental Association and is a frequent speaker at conferences.

inland to be out of range of naval gunfire support. When, in 1944, Field Marshal Erwin Rommel was assigned command of the defences of the Wall, he considered them totally inadequate and immediately began intensive work to strengthen them. Soon, strings of reinforced concrete pillboxes were built along the beaches and slightly inland to house machine guns and anti-tank weapons. Almost six million mines were laid in northern France alone and every beach was studded with obstacles to destroy landing craft. Any areas that might be used for airborne landings soon sprouted *Rommelspargel* (Rommel's asparagus) – poles with mines or explosives attached to tear gliders apart. Low-lying areas were deliberately flooded.

Rommel firmly believed that any invasion would have to be destroyed on the beaches to prevent any build up of materiel able to overwhelm the defences. Even poor-quality troops could achieve this from strong fortifications with inter-locking fields of fire and nothing in the German experience to date had disproved this. In the *blitzkreig* operations in 1940, after all, the much vaunted Maginot Line had not been breached, it had been bypassed. Rommel wanted to force the Allies into attacking at a point which would stretch their resources, making them even more vulnerable and his planned counterattack more effective if they had to unload equipment under fire before it could be brought into action. Field Marshal Gerd von Runstedt, however, favoured allowing the Allies to move inland and then launching a rapid counterattack to cut off the supply routes. This, he argued, would remove the heavy gunfire support from the ships which would be brought to bear at the coast. Both men argued their cases to Hitler who decided to compromise. Rommel would be given three divisions of armour for immediate defence whilst another three would be held in reserve between Caen and the Pas de Calais, ready to be brought forward for Von Runstedt's inland attack should the beaches not be held. The significance of the Normandy area was recognized but the decision was taken that it was the Pas de Calais that should be the main focus for planning and construction of the Wall and Hitler insisted that he himself should remain in control of the panzers. By now a command structure had developed in which the large guns along the Atlantic Wall were under navy command until troops actually landed ashore, when they would be given over to the army, and the armoured forces could only move with direct orders from the Fuhrer. Rommel had no control over the Luftwaffe or its units of anti-aircraft artillery or paratroopers and command and control was fragmented at every level.

Realizing the potential threat posed to their eastern flank by the reserve forces stationed around Rouen, made up of over 1,000 enemy armoured vehicles, including the latest model of the fearsome Tiger tank, the British commanders decided that a force was needed to block the approaches to the planned invasion area. The nightmare scenario of a large, mobile force capable of outgunning most of the Allied armour running amok on the beaches had to be avoided at all costs. To reach the invasion beaches, the enemy would need to cross the Dives River at a number of points to the south of Cabourg before it could be brought into action and, if this approach could be denied them, would have to swing south around Caen itself. This would bring them head on to the invasion force rather than allowing them to attack the more exposed flank. A plan was developed to seize the ground between the Orne and Dives Rivers by an airborne assault.

Three key tasks were identified. The capture of the canal and river bridges at Benouville was vital to enable the airborne and seaborne troops to link up. Without these, the lightly armed airborne forces would be cut off. At the same time, bridges further east needed to be destroyed to prevent enemy armour from reaching the flank of the invasion force. The third task was to assault the battery of heavy artillery at Merville which dominated the landing beaches from across the mouth of the Orne. It was believed that the battery directly threatened the assault on Sword Beach at Ouistreham and had a wide field of fire across the sea offshore. So great was the threat that 10 per cent of all airborne troops to drop that day would be dedicated to the task which, even so, many considered impossible. In the spring of 1944, the airborne forces began to prepare.

That February, Squadron Commander Ian Toler of the Glider Pilot Regiment

> found a message from Wing Headquarters instructing me to provide three of my best crews for a very special operation. I was told they would have to release at 6000 feet and land by moonlight in a small field. As it had to be a surprise attack on an objective that had not yet been disclosed, no landing aids would be possible. I selected six staff sergeants whom I considered from their flying records to be the best pilots.[4]

In early March 1944 seven glider crews (six for the operation and one as backup) gathered at the Netheravon airfield and were met by their colonel, George Chatterton. Behind him were gathered a number of senior army and air force officers. Chatterton pointed out two small triangles marked with broad white tape on the airfield and gave them their briefing:

> You will be towed at one-minute intervals to 4,000ft, which will take about one hour. You will then release three miles away at a point decided by your tug, from where you will be able to see these triangles. Numbers 1, 2 and 3 will land in this one, making a right hand circuit, and 4, 5 and 6 on t'other from a left hand circuit. Now hop off for lunch. All gliders are ready and assembled on the towpath. Take off 1300hrs.[5]

To Chatterton's evident relief, all six landed exactly on target but some senior RAF officers were still doubtful so the exercise was repeated the following day. Again, the gliders landed exactly on target – surprising themselves as much as the RAF – and Operation 'Deadstick' was under way. The fourteen glider pilots were kept sequestered in one Nissen hut at Tarrant Rushton airfield with a lieutenant placed in charge. They had their own transport and their own independent operation directed by two RAF pilots, Flight Lieutenants Tom Grant and Keith Miller, both tug/glider specialists who provided the briefings, courses, winds and timings on every flight.

Jim Wallwork remembers that training for Operation Deadstick was

> all a bit half-arsed at first. A daylight tow was made at various times, apparently when Tarrant Rushton airfield was not too busy, which as two operational squadrons were based there, was not very often. Height was now set at 6,000ft, and two separate courses and times developed. Gliders 1–3 to fly a three sided path, and 4–6 a dog leg pattern. We were towed in line astern at one minute intervals. Broadly, 1–3 flew downwind leg of 180 degrees at 90mph for 3mins 40secs, then a 90 degree Rate One turn right on to second course for 2mins 5sec, and a last 90 degree turn right for the run-in, by which time the target should be directly ahead. Gliders 4–6 cast off at the same spot, operated half then full flap and in a dog-leg course flew in straight to the target.[6]

Soon, though, the crews were facing more of a challenge, working in heavily shaded goggles to simulate night flying into ever smaller landing zones. By June, they had flown forty-two practice missions and were confident they would pull it off. Whatever 'it' was.

Elsewhere, other glider exercises did not go so well. On 4 April, 'D' Squadron supplied thirty Horsas for Exercise 'Dreme', a mass landing on Salisbury Plain. The LZ was covered by low cloud and twenty-two gliders crashed and were written off during the landings. Worse, a Stirling tug and Horsa combination elected to fly below the cloud and slammed into a low hill at 140mph. The six-man crew of the tug, the glider pilots and their twenty-six passengers were all killed. Bill Musitano, another pilot on the exercise, wrote afterwards that 'it was said that the largest human remains were in their boots'.[7] It was a sobering omen for what was to come.

By now, men of 9 Battalion of the Parachute Regiment were preparing for their own mission – the assault on the guns at Merville. Lieutenant-Colonel Terence Otway, the battalion's commanding officer, gathered the men of 'A' Company in the mess hall and called for volunteers for a special task. Every man stepped forward. Gradually, the force was whittled down, selecting as many unmarried men as possible. Rumours of a 'suicide job' began to circulate. Fred Millward was relieved not to be selected.

> I didn't want to go in the gliders. I'd flown in one before. I had a trip in a Horsa and oh, the smell of the vomit! It was the actual movement of the thing, because not only did you go up and down, you also had the tugging. It wasn't a very nice feeling.[8]

The selected men, under Captain Gordon-Brown and known as G-B Force, would be required to land inside the perimeter of the Merville Battery in an echo of Eben-Emael attack and attack the bunkers using flamethrowers and small arms as the remainder of the battalion stormed the outer defences. Lieutenant Hugh Pond, one of those selected, was with the group when

> we were taken to a small aerodrome and made our first acquaintance with the glider and the glider pilots. We were horrified at the three-ply wooden structure and considered it more a joke, a toy, than a vehicle for going to war in . . . We climbed into the 'matchbox' and belted up. There were twenty-eight of us in all and we had a good laugh when we were introduced to the funnel which was the urinal. It doesn't take much to make a bunch of nervous parachutists laugh![9]

The flight went well and the men of G-B Force began to think their 'hazardous operation' might not be so bad after all.

For weeks, the pilots flew repeated practice landings into a circle painted on the airfield and joined the paras in street-fighting exercises in bomb-damaged areas of London. Pilot Bill Shannon was suffering a bout of flu at the time and passed out during one such exercise. He woke to find everyone had returned to barracks, leaving him to walk home. He remembered:

> It wasn't so much the walk, it was the fact that I was wearing German uniform and carrying a Schmeisser. Not one person challenged me, the whole way. In fact I lost count of the number of times I was saluted![10]

The exercises continued on a full-scale model of the battery built near Newbury but, as Hugh Pond recalls,

> when it came to live ammunition exercises we were told that we couldn't wreck a glider just for practice so we were marched into the centre of the mock-up battery and stood there, feeling rather silly, waiting for our comrades to arrive, and as one bright spark put it – waiting to be shot by our own people! [11]

To avoid that risk, passwords were hurriedly arranged. Captain Gordon-Brown, an architect in civilian life, came up with idea of painting a luminous skull and crossbones on the breast of their jump smocks. Improvising with toothbrushes and shaving brushes, G-B Force happily joined in the bravado – until someone pointed out what a great aiming point the bright insignia made.

The gliders would be guided in with the top-secret Eureka-Rebecca beacon, with the Rebecca set on the ground sending signals to the Eureka set aboard the glider. Things did not bode well, though, when the pilots joined the paras at their transit camp on RAF Broadwell in Oxfordshire a few days before the operation. On 1 June, pilot Joe Michie and the rest of the glider crews assembled at Netheravon for training on the system. They were told the course would take two weeks. After hasty phone calls, the course was speeded up but at the departure fields it was found that the gliders with arrester parachutes fitted didn't have Eureka and vice versa. Both were vital.

At 2249hrs on the night of 5 June, seven Horsas carrying the heavy equipment for 9 Para lifted off from Down Ampney heading for LZ 'V', followed at 2310hrs by four more from Harwell. At the same time, Dakotas of 512 Squadron took off with the paratroopers in thirty-two aircraft. The three Horsas of G-B Force lifted off at 0230hrs on 6 June, heavily overladen. The gliders provided were all meant to be new but what arrived were two new and one obviously well-used aircraft. All across the airborne force, men arrived carrying far more than the 'full equipment' schedule used by planners. Every man carried extra ammunition and haversacks – one pilot confiscated a bucket filled with grenades. Thirty minutes into the flight, the tow rope of the oldest of G-B Force's gliders fell victim to the weight and 'parted with a sigh more than anything'. Pilots Joe Michie and Arnold Baldwin put down at RAF Odiham at 0320hrs. Baldwin

> felt physically sick . . . I slumped in my seat feeling utterly dejected and said to Joe 'I don't give a f— what happens now'. When he responded, with a great deal of feeling 'Well I do and I expect those fellows in the back do as well!' I came out of my trance and began to think about what to do.[12]

Landing in the darkness, it fell to Baldwin to contact Chatterton by phone to report what had happened. They eventually reached France in a later lift that day.

As the remaining gliders continued, Chalk 28 began to experience its own problems. Gordon Newton, one of the passengers:

> We knew that something was not right. The glider was 'crabbing' from side to side. We didn't realize what the problem was but the light went on and the co-pilot came through, very calm and collected and said 'A knife please, any sort of knife, as long as it cuts'. I was sitting in the back seat. He said 'Just a minute mate', and pulled the back door open and cut the arrester gear off. We were about ten feet off the Channel.[13]

On the ground around Merville, the para drop had been widely scattered. Colonel Otway had not had the chance to jump but instead was blown from the Stirling Bomber that had carried his men from Berkshire by a flak burst. 'It didn't kill anyone, but it blew a great big hole in the fuselage of the plane and certainly encouraged my men to get out of the plane fairly quickly.' Off course and caught in the crosswinds, Otway found himself drifting

> straight into the side of a building at first floor level . . . As if that wasn't bad enough, the building turned out to be one of the company HQs of a German regiment and after I slid down the side of the wall and looked up from the ground, this fellow popped his head out of his bedroom window and stared at me. Fortunately, one of my corporals had landed right next to me and he had the presence of mind to pick something up, probably a stone, and chuck it at the chap, who popped his head back in. Then we vanished and never heard any more from them. [14]

Lance-Corporal Wilson, landing alongside Otway, had, in fact, landed on the roof of a glass hothouse in the garden of the farm, noisily crashing through it. The two men escaped and made their way to the RV, passing

> several men who had been caught in the floods, and were weighed down with their packs, just sinking. We tried to pull them out, but there was nothing we could do except watch them be sucked down by the mud. It was very unpleasant. [15]

Scores of men remain missing even today.

Reaching the RV safely, Otway waited for his men. By 0235hrs, only 110 of the expected 750 had made it and the gliders carrying the heavy equipment, including the engineers with their mine-clearing equipment, the mortars, machine guns, anti-tank guns and medical support were all missing. By 0250hrs, another forty men had found the RV. Otway surveyed his force – 150 men, one medium Vickers machine gun, a few Bren light machine guns and one container of Bangalore torpedoes. His men had only Sten guns, rifles, grenades and knives to take on an entrenched heavy artillery position whose defenders outnumbered the attackers. Weighing the damage the battery could cause against the men he had with him, Otway said later that 'it was a question of moving off, or give up. In the Parachute Regiment giving up is not an option.'[16] They set off on the ninety-minute march, Otway adapting his plan as he walked.

At Merville, pathfinder Major Smith was able to report that the battery was still active after bombing attacks by the RAF that left a pall of dust and smoke over the area but that the garrison did not appear to feel another attack was imminent. Smith was able to confirm the layout and strength of the battery and Otway used the information to modify his plan. The ground force would now have to destroy the battery with the limited explosives available to them. No mortar

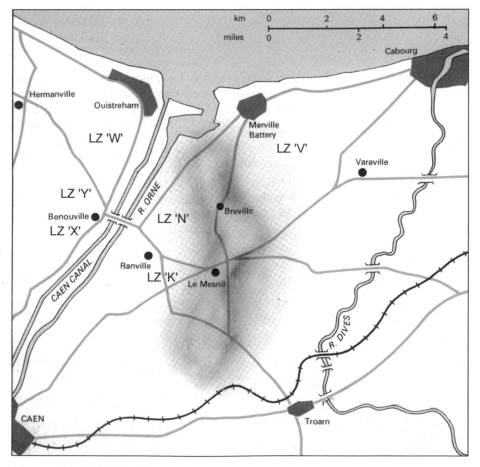

Normandy. British landing zones.

flares could be found and without these, the landing site for the gliders could not be illuminated and he could not rely on them being able to land on target.

As the paras moved into their assault positions, the gliders arrived overhead. Low cloud had forced them to fly at just 1,000 feet to the area where clouds of dust still hung obscured the LZ after the bombing raid earlier. Aboard the glider bringing in Captain Gordon–Brown, Gordon Newton, carrying a flamethrower, was becoming nervous as

> flak started coming up. It was coming through the floor and out the roof. Under the seats, which are along the full length of the glider, you had all the other equipment, and there were mortar bombs, high explosives, there were replacements for the flamethrowers . . . The whole thing was a tinderbox. [17]

Newton moved forward to sit with his fellow flamethrower just as flak ripped through the glider, straight through where he had been sat. The glider put down just 200 yards from the battery in a devastated landscape of bomb craters. When they found their bearings, the party set out for the target. Delayed by a firefight with a German patrol, they watched the success signal rise from the battery.

The final glider, flown by Staff Sergeant Dickie Kerr and co–pilot H Walker, circled the area searching for any indication of the LZ. At only 1,000 feet, there would be very little time to identify it and land. Under flak fire the whole time, tug pilot Flight Lieutenant Thompson circled the area six times, flashing his identification lights to try to establish contact with 9 Para. For the men in the back, glider flying could be a nauseating experience on even a smooth flight. Now, as the tug took evasive action, para snobbery about glider troops disappeared quickly but airsickness was the least of their worries. Sapper Alex Taylor, flying in the same glider as Hugh Pond, recalled being told that they were over the target and coming around for another run. 'We were in trouble! The flak was catching us again. Holes appeared in the thin plywood fuselage of the glider. Our tug was taking evasive action, causing terrific strain in the fabric of the glider.' The aircraft circled the site for fifteen minutes searching for a signal. Finally, a red triangle appeared and Kerr cast off, circling now to lose height: 'Three light flak batteries were now engaging us and the glider was hit frequently. We were hit about eight times in the fuselage with bursts of tracer and twice by cannon shells. The wings got a lot of tracer too. I could feel them quivering as the bullets hit them.' [18] Behind him, four men were wounded. Headed towards the casemates at 90 miles per hour, the men braced for impact when another flak shell hit the tail, forcing the aircraft to swerve. As it sped towards a nearby field, Kerr saw a skull and crossbones sign at the edge of a minefield and pulled back on the stick. Lifting again, they passed only feet above the men of the ground force before crashing into the orchard near the attack start line. Kerr was thrown twenty feet from the cockpit, landing in a bomb crater. A flak round had hit a box of smoke grenades and, as the stunned passengers clambered out, the glider burst into flames. Quickly gathering themselves together, the party set out for the battery but almost immediately encountered German reinforcements heading for the battle and another firefight began. Fortunately, they had landed in the ideal place to protect the ground force's flank.

Despite the setbacks, Merville Battery fell to the depleted paratroop force. A few miles away at the bridges, Major John Howard 'was a little worried about the position on the bridge over the river, till I got on my wireless the code signal for victory. "Ham and jam" said a voice, "ham and bloody jam". Then I blew the V-sign on my whistle.' The first objectives were secure, the battery under attack and already the next wave of gliders was about to land.

The gliders, including four of the massive new Hamilcars from 'C' Squadron, were on their way carrying heavy equipment for the paras tasked with sealing off the area by blowing the Dives River bridges. In a chaotic night, gliders sometimes landed far from their objectives – one as far afield as Le Havre. Before setting out, the men of 6th Airborne Division had been given the freedom to act on their own initiative by General 'Windy' Gale:

> You must remember that it is your plan, and that it is your duty to ensure that it is your plan which is being carried out. Your responsibility in this is not one that you can be permitted to shirk. Your natural tendency may be to fight shy of it. You cannot; for ultimately the edifice is yours, and its foundations and cornerstones must be laid by you. [19]

As 9 Para made their preparations, the pragmatic Brigadier Hill had told them 'gentlemen, in spite of your excellent orders and training, DO NOT BE DAUNTED IF CHAOS REIGNS. It undoubtedly will.'[20] Now scattered forces fought their own small wars to achieve their aims. At Truarn, Major Tim Roseveare and his team commandeered a jeep from a glider and used it to charge directly through the German garrison in order to blow the river bridge. At Varraville, the crew of Chalk 94 – originally intended for the Orne River bridge assault – had landed off course beside two bridges across the Dives. Arguing later that they had been sent to capture two bridges and had, nevertheless the party made their way slowly back to British lines, collecting stray groups as they did. One by one, all the targeted bridges were blown.

The US airborne assault, 6 June 1944

As the British consolidated their positions, at the other end of the invasion area their American colleagues had begun their mission to deliver support for the 82nd and 101st Airborne Divisions on the western flanks.

The American airborne assault had been controversial in the planning phase. Lieutenant-General Omar Bradley had been given command of the American

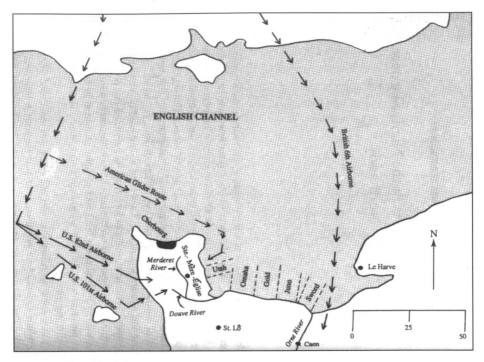

ENGLISH CHANNEL

British 6th Airborne

American Glider Route

U.S. 82nd Airborne

Cherbourg

U.S. 101st Airborne

Merderet
River →

Ste.-Mère-Église

Utah

Omaha

Gold

Juno

Sword

Le Harve

Douve River

St. Lô

Orne River

Caen

N

0   25   50

Normandy: US glider routes.

element of the ground assault and had decided that it was crucial to secure four causeways behind Utah Beach by the use of an airborne assault. Unlike the British landing zones, though, those around Utah would be in the Norman *bocage*. The countryside here was marked by small fields bordered by high hedgerows dating back hundreds of years and where the root systems had become so thick that German troops were able to cut holes and firing loops into them through which they were able to conduct strong defensive stands. Air Chief Marshal Leigh-Mallory, appointed by Eisenhower as overall air commander, felt that the area was unsuitable. A combination of terrain, flak concentrations and anti-invasion defences were expected to inflict casualties as high as 50 per cent among the paratroopers and 70 per cent among glider-borne troops. 'I cannot approve your plan. It is much too hazardous an undertaking. Your losses will be excessive – certainly far more than the gains are worth. I'm sorry, General Bradley, but I cannot go along with you.' Bradley, though, was insistent, telling Eisenhower that 'much as I favour the Cotentin assault . . . I would sooner see it go by the boards than risk a landing on Utah without airborne help.' Eisenhower, torn between commanders, eventually decided that the possible benefits outweighed the risks but even as late as 30 May, Leigh-Mallory went to Eisenhower's Portsmouth Headquarters for a final, last-ditch plea to prevent was he was convinced would be 'the futile slaughter of two fine divisions'.

Eisenhower, who had thought the matter resolved long before, deliberated into the night before deciding to side with Bradley.[21]

At 0119hrs on the morning of 6 June, fifty-one Waco gliders towed by Dakotas of 434th Troop Carrier Group took off from Aldermaston at the start of Operation Chicago. They would land ten miles inland of the coast at Hiesville in support of the 101st Airborne's mission to secure the causeways off Utah Beach. Among them, 'The Fighting Falcon' was carrying Brigadier-General Donald Pratt and flown by Lieutenant-Colonel Mike Murphy, architect of the 'pea patch' demonstration that had re-established confidence in the US glider programme the year before. Forty-nine arrived over the target area at 0354hrs, searching for the LZ markers. Landing on wet ground, Murphy was unable to control his glider's skid and it crashed headlong into a hedgerow. Murphy survived with broken legs but Pratt was among five men killed.

Operation Detroit, the 82nd Airborne's glider element, took to the air at 0159hrs with fifty-two Wacos from Ramsbury in Wiltshire. As they crossed the coast of France, seven were lost when their tow ropes broke or were shot through by flak. Seven more released early when their pilots mistook the flooded river areas for the sea on the far side of the peninsula, causing following tugs to release in the belief that the LZ had been reached. Now under small arms fire, the remaining gliders reached their target area and put down wherever they could find room. Flight Officer Francis Zinser was among them:

> I had a hell of a time finding my proper position behind the tow plane because of low cloud cover and turbulence. It wasn't long after we crossed the coast of France that we ran into a wild overcast so thick that it was like a dense cloud of black smoke. I couldn't see a thing, not even my own tow plane . . . I released the tow rope and turned toward my landing, but I evidently got a little too low in the darkness and I hit the top of the trees on the edge of the field. The trees tore off my left wing and we slewed around and hit the ground upside down. [22]

Twenty-two gliders were destroyed in the landing and another twelve damaged. One landed in the midst of a herd of cows with a bad outcome for all concerned but half the intended force was soon in action.

On the evening of D-Day itself, both the British and Americans launched massive resupply operations. The 6th Airborne, supported by Operation Mallard, were able to read about the invasion in the evening papers brought over by the glider crews. This third wave, arriving during the evening, were forced to land on the same LZ s used earlier, in fields littered with glider fuselages and where hundreds of vehicles were scurrying around. Accidents were common. Staff Sergeant G Heaton, flying a Hamilcar of 'C' Squadron, remembers there was a certain amount of small arms fire, including tracers, coming up at us, and the field in which we landed near Ranville had got telegraph poles erected in to hinder the landings. We came in rather fast with our wings hitting the odd telegraph pole, which proved to be no obstruction, but just as I thought we were going too fast and would end up in an orchard at the end of the field, a Tetrach [a light airborne tank] which had just driven out of the Hamilcar landing before we did, proceeded at right angles across our landing path. The tank commander, who was standing in his little turret, took one look, mouthed imprecations and leaped from the tank a second or two before we hit it at a speed of ninety to one hundred mph. My first pilot, Charles Channell, and I

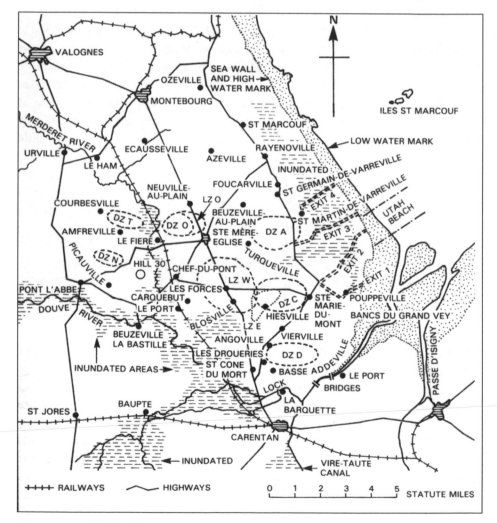

Normandy: US landing zones.

jumped from our cockpit, forgetting in the heat of the moment: (a) that my flying helmet with its intercom was still plugged into its socket, thus wrenching my neck; and (b) that the Hamilcar cockpit was situated on top of the glider, some fifteen to twenty feet above the ground.[23]

Fortunately, all survived and the driver was rescued. The light Tetrach tanks were advised to have the motor running during landing, ready to unload as soon as the aircraft came to a halt but this proved to be a dangerous decision. Glider pilot B Tomblin, of 'E' Squadron, had landed earlier in the day. Watching the arrival of the Hamilcars, he saw one come in 'very steeply, when a tank shot out of the nose of the glider followed by the glider helplessly out of control'.[24]

On the western edge of the invasion a second wave of US gliders, resupplying the 101st and 82nd in Operations Keokuk and Elmira respectively, brought in more heavy equipment using Wacos and British Horsa gliders flown by American pilots during the evening of D-Day. It had seemed like a fairly straightforward mission as Elmira's first echelon took to the skies above Ramsbury at 1920hrs. A total of fifty-four Horsas and twenty-two Wacos would deliver 428 troops, jeeps and anti-tank guns to LZ 'W' near Ste Mere Eglise, followed a few minutes later by the second echelon of eighty-six Horsas and fourteen Wacos. Unbeknown to the glider pilots, LZ 'W' was still being fought over even as they approached. General Ridgeway, whose radios were among the casualties of the previous night's drop, could hear the seaborne forces attempting to break through to him and the towplanes of the glider force approaching but could do little to warn them that the northern half of the LZ was in German hands and 88 mm guns on the nearby Hill 20 at Fauville were zeroed in. As the first echelon arrived, they were met with fairly light flak until they cut loose from their tows. By the time the second echelon crossed the coast, the flak batteries were ready and fire began to intensify three miles from the LZ and all the way in. The Horsas – known to the Americans as 'flying coffins'– lived up to their reputation. Only thirteen of the eighty-four Horsas that reached LZ 'W' were undamaged. Fifty-six were completely destroyed. But the glider pilots who had considered the Wacos' steel construction to be more of a guarantee of a safe landing were proved wrong – not a single Waco survived the landing intact. For days, many of the pilots found themselves pinned down among the paratroopers fighting for control of the area. Ten were dead, twenty-nine wounded, seven captured.

On D+1, Operation Galveston in support of the 82nd and Operation Hackensack for the 101st became the last glider operations of the invasion when thirty Horsas and twenty Wacos delivered supplies. By then, 1,030 US glider pilots had flown into France. Twenty-five were known to be dead and many more were fighting alongside the infantry in scattered pockets. Losses had indeed been heavy but thankfully not as bad as predicted. Both divisions had lost around 1,250 men each. Over 60 per cent of all supplies intended for the airborne assault had been lost. Like their British counterparts, the surviving pilots had been evacuated back to England to get ready for more flights as the Allies pushed inland. It was a strange experience for the survivors. British pilot Bob Cardy flew into Normandy with his co-pilot, 19-year-old Sergeant Sid Longworth. They had been instructed to return to the UK as quickly as possible to collect another aircraft and load. Along with a group of pilots, they made their way back to the beach. 'Young fellows were wading in as we were going home again. It hardly seemed reasonable; hardly possible that it had happened. Within hours we were in England, had showered and were boozing in a wayside pub.'[25]

The liberation of Europe had begun, to the joy of those held captive by the Nazis for four long years but the next glider operation in France would be a very different matter.

Assault on Vercors, 21 July 1944

On the other side of France, the combined resistance movements of the French Forces of the Interior (FFI) began receiving increased levels of supply drops in an effort to pin down German forces and prevent them reinforcing the Normandy beachheads and as preparation for a second invasion from the south. Back in 1943, the 'Plan Montagnards' (Plan for the Mountains) had already decided that the Vercors region near Grenoble would be strategically important for any Allied landings in Provence. At the beginning of the war, the Vercors had been located in the Vichy French free zone, and political and Jewish refugees had streamed into the area to escape purges in the north. When, in November 1942, the Vichy government handed power to the Germans, the isolated mountains of the Vercors welcomed an influx of volunteer Resistance workers who were later joined by draft evaders escaping forced labour under German conscription laws. In the deep forest of the plateau, the resistance camps were well protected from German attack and by May 1944, around 500 Maquis were operating in the region supported by regular supply drops and even landings by Allied aircraft flying from North Africa. With news of the Normandy invasion, the number rapidly swelled to over 4,000 during June.

On 21 June, members of a 'Jedburgh' special operations unit commanded by Major Desmond Longe parachuted into the Vercors region as part of an inter-allied mission codenamed 'Eucalyptus', intended to provide arms and training and to look for suitable landing and drop zones for airborne operations in the area. The British had been unable to drop mortars and other heavy equipment because of the risks involved in securing the bombs' sensitive fuses so instead, a landing strip was to be prepared on top of the plateau and supply flights would bring them in directly. As part of the preparatory operation, Second-Lieutenant Andrew E Pecquet (codenamed 'Paray') dropped as part of an American team and spent the night in a hotel in Vassieux. The next morning he woke to find the 450 inhabitants of the village were in the street. They had been making American flags during the night, so the Stars and Stripes floated in the breeze beside the French tricolour among the bouquets of flowers. In the Vercors they thought that these commandos in uniform – the OG [Operational Group –part of the Office of Strategic Services and forerunners of the CIA] – were the advance party of an army of paratroopers.[26]

Their arrival prompted a surge of nationalist pride among the inhabitants of the Vercors, an attitude fuelled at 0900hrs on Bastille Day, 14 July when seventy-two American planes dropped 860 containers of weapons and ammunition and even included a small tricolour parachute in the honour of the national festival. At the end of the drop, German planes attacked as the Resistance workers collected the containers but even this did not dampen enthusiasm. Vercors was declared by its population to be a free, independent republic.

Such behaviour could hardly be missed by the Germans. The Jedburghs had been warned at the start of the operation that Brandenburg troops had been seen in Pont St Esprit and now, slowly, the net around Vercors was being drawn in. In Grenoble, German General Karl Pflaum had carried out some small-scale operations in mid-June around St Nizier and Ecouges to test the size of the resistance force. Now he decided to strike a knockout blow. Between 18 and 20 July, two squadrons of I/LLG1 (1st Squadron, 1st Airlanding Group) arrived in Lyon equipped with twenty Do17/DFS 230 tow combinations and Go242s of I/LLG2. They were to transport paratroopers to the area around Vassieux, landing on the newly prepared airstrip and secure it so more troops could be air landed and then link up with ground units who had sealed off the area below. Rehearsals for the mission began at an airfield at Montelimar.

Fallschirm-Aufklärungs-Abteilung 12 under Major Hans Jungwirth (Kampfgruppe Jungwirth), a new formation of two companies, was created for the task in June 1944 and based in Lyon-Bron under the overall command of the Luftwaffe's special operations unit, II/KG200 based in Dedelstorf. It was made up of a company of paratroopers under Oberleutnant Friedrich Schäfer and another of the Brandenburgers of the 8th (Legionnaire) Company of the Brandenburg Division's 3rd Light Infantry Regiment. In this operation, they would be supported by the German Army's 157th Reserve Division currently based in towns in the region of the Vercors.

Further support would come from a third element made up of the German controlled SD (Sicherheitdienst) and SIPO (Sicherheitspolizei) police forces following in the wake of the combat troops. These elements included the combined Vichy French paramilitary police force known as the 'Milice Française' and an elite subsection of the Vichy 'Police Nationale' known as the 'Garde Mobile de Reserve' which had the specific task of actively combating known terrorist organizations; they were one of the most brutal enemies of the 'Maquisards' of the FFI, working enthusiastically alongside the SD and

Ordnungspolizei to infiltrate and mercilessly root out opposition to the Vichy regime.

Beginning on 18 July, the 157 Reserve (Gebirgs) Division, along with selected mobile units of the 9.Panzer-Division began encircling the plateau. Moving from Grenoble-St Nizier in the north and keeping pressure on three sides, they swept around to envelop and reduce the twenty by thirty kilometre FFI 'Republic' on the Vercors Massif. As they advanced, police troops moved in to mop up in their wake.

Three days later, just after 0930 hrs, the first wave of twenty DFS 230 gliders arrived over their target. Some were tasked to land on the plateau, others in Vassieux itself. Almost immediately, they came under heavy small arms fire and three were hit during the landing, causing several casualties among the paras aboard, which in turn hampered the street fighting that was now beginning. By evening, twenty-nine paras had been killed and another twenty badly wounded and they had been forced back into defensive positions. Bad weather the following day prevented reinforcements being flown in and it was not until 23 July that another flight of twenty DFS 230 and two Go242s could reach their beleaguered comrades.

On the 24th, a Go242 carrying a 2 cm flak gun arrived and within a few hours the weapon had turned the tide, destroying the resistance strongholds and forcing them to withdraw. The operation had been a success but had cost the lives of 101 paras, forty-six of whom died in the vicious fighting around Vassieux. Four glider pilots were killed in the operation, Eberhard Pyritz, Karl Rink, Unteroffiziers Metzen and Birzer. As the kampfgruppe left the plateau, the gliders were set on fire where they lay.

What happened next cast a shadow over the Luftwaffe's reputation as an honourable fighting force. In a brutal five-day campaign, Kampfgruppe Jungwirth burned houses and shot anyone suspected of being a maquisard or of aiding the resistance. Exact numbers of casualties have never been established but sources speak of 639 resistance fighters and 201 civilians killed as across the area, villages and farms were burned down, animals shot and farm machinery destroyed. On 27 July, a German plane spotted a Red Cross over the Luire cave and German troops arrived at around 1630hrs. Around fifty people were sheltering there, including one of the American Jedburgh troops and several German wounded. Despite pleas for mercy from the Germans, who had been well treated, twelve of the wounded were murdered and their bodies thrown into a nearby river. The nurses were later deported and two doctors and a priest executed in Grenoble.

Most accounts of the Vercors operation blame the SS but in fact, for once, they were not guilty. There were no SS troops in the area but the large numbers of civilians killed during the Vercors operation meant that it was one of four such attacks the French formally raised at Nuremburg. Because the other three massacres were definitely committed by the Waffen SS there has been assumption in most French writing that this atrocity was also their work. Within a few weeks, it all came to nothing when the Germans withdrew from the region.

Operation Dingson: French SAS insertion, 5 August 1944

Back in England, in the wake of D-Day, glider crews had stood ready to fly operation after operation, only to have them cancelled at the last minute as the objectives fell instead to ground troops. In August, however, a small operation in Brittany was under way that seemed as though it might set a new pattern for the men of the Glider Pilot Regiment. In late May 1944, eleven crews had been taken off D-Day training and reformed as 'X' Flight under the command of Captain 'Peggy' Clarke at Netheravon. Each was a veteran of Sicily – familiar with the Waco 'Hadrian' gliders they collected from an American base but knowing only that they would be taking part in a special operation. After intensive training, the crews moved to Tarrant Rushton on 7 June and continued training with Halifax tugs.

On 4 August, Colonel Chatterton arrived with Lieutenant Bodolec and thirty-five Frenchmen of 4th Battalion SAS in ten heavily armed jeeps to brief the men on their mission. The Frenchmen were part of a force who were to land nearly 200 miles behind German lines in the Vannes area of Britanny to link up with a force of around 3,000 French resistance fighters and harass the German supply lines. Other operational bases were already in existence and this one, Dingson, had already been the subject of many other air resupply flights. This would be Operation Dingson 35A.

At 2005hrs the following day, the force set off. At a small field about ten miles from Auray, resistance fighters organized by Special Operations Executive officer Richard 'Ruby' Rubenstein held off German patrols as the jeeps unloaded and sped off in the direction of Sainte-Helene to meet up with resistance HQ. One Waco carrying a team under Pierre Philippon, a former member of the Resistance Movement 'Réseau Bordeaux-Loupiac' was lost but the remainder arrived safely and were soon patrolling towards Auray, Quimper and Lorient, attacking convoys of retreating Germans and isolated pockets of resistance. Left to their own devices, the pilots – with a 20,000 franc bounty on their heads – spent the next week at the Maquis headquarters but they soon became bored.

The sometimes casual nature of the SAS (they frequently stopped at cafes and bars for a drink in full uniform) encouraged the pilots to take risks. Tired of being cooped up, Sergeants May and Beezum decided to take a chance to go into a village near Lorient only to narrowly escape a German patrol when a villager hid them, despite the fortune the bounty represented.

The SAS were soon involved in heavy fighting and John Batley found himself called upon to dig thirteen pieces of shrapnel from the shoulder of one man who then calmly picked up some bread and ammunition and went back out on patrol. Despite their undoubted courage, the pilots were less impressed with other aspects of their hosts, particularly after witnessing a brutal torture session of a young man suspected of collaborating. 'Feeling sick inside but too scared to say or do anything, we crept away to the barn and tried to sleep', Beezum later wrote.[27] They were more than a little relieved when, a few days later, they were told that an American armoured unit was nearby. Sitting on a wall, they watched as the tanks approached. A burly officer asked how long they had been there. 'Too long' was the heartfelt reply. Only later did they spot the officer's helmet with its stars – but Patton took them aboard cheerfully.

On 16 August, they returned home to Tarrant Rushton, just as another operation was about to set off from RAF Keevil where John Morrison had been given the task of transporting a British SAS squadron into the area around Falaise to harass the retreating German army. This time, however, it would need Horsas. Even with their armour stripped off, the armed jeeps weighed 4 tons – 50 per cent over the maximum load of the Horsa. To that was added the trailers filled with landmines and the men themselves. Practice runs showed that the tug combinations needed the longest runway available and that the gliders 'flew like a barge'. They dropped like a stone when released but it could be done. At 0800hrs on the 18th, Morrison briefed his flight. The Germans were effectively trapped in a pocket but for one escape route around Falaise. The SAS would land and attack any and all targets that presented themselves. The gliders would land wherever the opportunity arose and the jeeps would then make for a squadron RV. With no space on the jeeps for passengers, the glider crews would form their own fighting unit and link up with the advancing Canadians. At 1100hrs, the tugs began to roll but the gliders had barely cleared the runway when they were recalled. Morrison had mixed feelings as he returned to base, 'I always had the feeling that, as far as we were concerned, our Flight's plan for action once we had landed was a bit woolly!'[28]

For weeks, false starts and cancelled operations undermined morale. Operation Axehead, a plan to capture bridges on the River Seine, was followed by 'Linnet', a planned landing in Belgium. 'Linnet II' would encircle the enemy at Maastricht. 'Infatuate' would see troops landing at Walcheren. The list went on. For some pilots, fourteen, fifteen, sixteen, even seventeen operations had been made ready and scrubbed. Many wondered if they would see action again. Very shortly, they would.

Operation Market-Garden: the airborne carpet across Holland, 17–25 September 1944

The Fall of Paris on 25 August 1944 effectively ended the Normandy campaign and the closing of the Falaise gap had led to a massacre of the German 7th and 15th Armies in France. As the demoralized remnants fled, it seemed that the entire German effort in the west had collapsed and was in retreat but with the Allies still dependent almost entirely on the port of Cherbourg for supplies,

Eisenhower's 'broad front' strategy was running out of steam. Other harbours should have been available but Dunkirk would hold out until May 1945 and, although the massive port of Antwerp lay intact in British hands, it was unusable since the Scheldt estuary leading inland to it was still under German control. Eisenhower's problem was now to decide whether to pursue a broad logistical solution and clear the approaches to Antwerp or to concentrate on destroying German forces in a decisive tactical move. With the battered German armies seemingly on the run, most Allied commanders were in favour of a pursuit and the rapid destruction of their fighting ability. Both Patton and Montgomery now switched from the agreed 'broad front' advance strategy in place before the invasion, to each lobbying Eisenhower for priority on supplies in order to cross the Rhine River in a single decisive thrust by their own forces.

Montgomery argued for a thrust north through Holland and into Germany's industrial heartland that would also serve to eliminate the V-2 rocket sites currently bombarding London and Antwerp. Patton's 3rd Army were already into German territory and advancing on the German city of Aachen but had been stopped by the length of their supply lines (the 'Red Ball Express' convoys carrying everything needed to keep the army moving from depots at Cherbourg were by now making 1,700 mile round the clock trips to reach him). Loudly complaining that 'my men can eat their belts but my tanks need gas!', Patton claimed that, if he was given everything he needed, he could reach Berlin by pushing east from Metz and from there directly into the industrial Saarland, smashing through the Siegfried Line to the heavily defended Rhine. Allied air transport, it was argued, could be used to leapfrog any problems in the rear and quickly move supplies to the mobile front lines.

Both men made strong cases and Eisenhower was torn between the two plans. Ultimately, though, he was influenced by pressure from the US to use the airborne forces again as soon as possible. On average, the Allied airborne units had lost around 40 per cent of their men in Normandy before being withdrawn to England and were now in the process of reforming as the 1st Allied Airborne Army. Created on 16 August as the result of British demands for coordinated airborne headquarters, three US and two British divisions, along with a Polish Brigade, had been brought together under the command of Major-General Lewis H Brereton who, although he had no recent experience in airborne operations, had been involved in the planning of the proposed drop at Metz in 1918 and whose extensive command experience with the 9th Air Force gave him a working knowledge of the operations of IX Troop Carrier Command and an understanding of the needs of the airborne under his command. Under him, British General Frederick 'Boy' Browning and US General Matthew Ridgeway would act as corps commanders. Throughout that summer, the greatest airborne army the world would ever see, costly to train and equip, sat in England whilst plans were made and cancelled as ground forces overran their intended drop zones and the British 1st Airborne, who had rebelled when told they would not take part in the Normandy landings, were now becoming more and more frustrated at being kept in their barracks. Eventually, Eisenhower gave in to demands to use them and gave Montgomery authorization to try his narrow advance. Montgomery's plan was divided into two linked operations:

(1) MARKET: Three of the five divisions of General Brereton's 1st Allied Airborne Army would drop an 'airborne carpet' across Holland to seize bridges and other features under the tactical command of General Browning.

(2) GARDEN: XXX Corps under Lieutenant-General Brian Horrocks would spearhead a push by the British 2nd Army to move north and link with the airborne en route.

The operation would begin with the US 101st Airborne Division, under Major General Maxwell D. Taylor, dropping in two locations just north of the XXX Corps current position to take the bridges north-west of Eindhoven at Son and Veghel. Then, north-east of them at Grave and Nijmegen, Brigadier-General James M Gavin's 82nd Airborne Division would take two more bridges, allowing XXX Corps to push towards the British 1st Airborne Division, under Major-General Roy Urquhart and the Polish 1st Independent Parachute Brigade who would drop to take the road bridge at Arnhem and rail bridge at Oosterbeek. Then, the 52nd (Lowland) Division would be airlifted in to reinforce the position. With these bridges under Allied control over two million men of XXX Corps, 2nd Army and the US 9th Army would cross the Rhine and smash into the Ruhr – Germany's industrial heartland.

To achieve this, the British forces at the extreme northern end of the route would need to hold their positions long enough for XXX Corps to make the sixty-mile dash along the airborne carpet to link up with them. It was expected to take a matter of days. To take and hold the bridges, Operation Market would need to deliver over 34,600 men to the battlefield. The thirty-six battalions would need all fifteen aircraft groups of the US IX Troop Carrier Command and sixteen squadrons of the RAF's 38 Group – currently using converted bombers on special operations missions in support of resistance groups (it was they who had flown the tug planes for the Dingson mission) – and a transport formation, 46 Group. In all, 1,274 USAAF and 164 RAF C-47 Dakotas along with 321 converted RAF bombers would be used. With German forces in the area believed to be under strength and in disarray, confidence was high that this would be the winning blow that would carry the Allies to Berlin within months. D-Day was set for Sunday, 17 September.

In a final meeting between Montgomery and Browning on 10 September, Browning asked how long it would take for Horrock's armour to cover the sixty miles. Two days, he was told. Looking at the map, Browning considered that an advance of fifteen miles a day more likely. 'We can hold it for four' he told

Montgomery, 'but sir, I think we may be going a bridge too far.'[29] General Stanislaw Sosabowski, commander of the Polish Brigade, was even less optimistic and demanded his orders in writing so that he would be able to show that the disaster he foresaw was not of his making.

The following day, Brereton was advised that the glider losses of Normandy had been made good with 2,160 Wacos, 104 US and 812 British Horsas and sixty-four of the giant Hamilcars available to land over 20,000 glider troops, 1,736 vehicles, 263 artillery pieces and 3,342 tons of ammunition and other supplies. Pilots, however, were in shorter supply and this time no US glider would fly with two pilots. Worse, there would not be capacity in Troop Carrier Command for the full load to be carried in one lift. The drops and landings would have to be carried out piecemeal over three days.

To capture the Arnhem bridge, the British needed to be able to reach it quickly but heavy concentrations of flak around Arnhem had been reported and the only landing zones identified as suitable for use by the laden gliders lay six to eight miles from the bridge itself. Two days before D-Day, Major Brian Urquhart, the divisional intelligence officer, presented five photographs to Browning showing tanks in the Arnhem area but his concerns were dismissed. When he continued to express his belief that there were stronger forces in the area than previously reported, he was ordered to take sick leave for 'exhaustion'.

D-Day dawned bright and sunny in England. During the night, flak batteries along the air corridors had come under heavy air attack from RAF bombers. The attacks continued into the morning with 200 Lancasters and twenty-three Mosquitoes bombing more batteries along the Dutch coast. Immediately behind

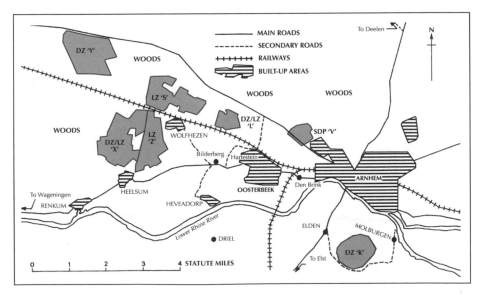

Arnhem landing zone.

them, 852 B–17s dropped 3,140 tons of bombs on 117 known flak positions. Barely had the dust settled when, at 1010hrs, pathfinders of the 21st Independent Parachute Company took off from RAF Fairford aboard Stirlings of 620 and 190 Squadrons. Arriving over Drop Zone 'X' and Landing Zone 'S' at 1240hrs, they dropped without difficulty and had set up the landing signals and Eureka beacons within fifteen minutes. As there had been no moon that night, the landings were planned to take place in daylight. The Luftwaffe threat was almost non-existent by this time and the lessons of Sicily and Normandy had shown that night drops carried a high risk of scattering forces away from their target areas. By shortening the time between successive waves and dropping in daylight, they would also be able to regroup far faster and more effectively to seize their objectives before the enemy could react.

Shortly after the arrival of the pathfinders, 143 troop planes carrying 1st Parachute Brigade and 331 Horsas, fourteen Hamilcars and nine Wacos bearing 1st Air Landing Brigade began to arrive in a formidable air armada. Thirty-nine gliders failed to reach the LZ but all those that made emergency landings were picked up safely by waiting air/sea rescue teams. Between 1300 and 1330hrs, gliders began to descend towards LZ 'S', north of the railway line through Wolfhezen and LZ 'Z' to the west amid small arms fire. The 7th Battalion King's Own Scottish Borderers landed safely, the only casualty on their LZ a pilot killed as he crashed into a tree. The cargoes were quickly unloaded and the men rallied to a piper playing 'Blue Bonnets over the Border' so that by 1500hrs, the battalion was fully formed and moving into a defensive perimeter around the LZ. By 1530hrs, 1st Airborne Division HQ was fully functioning.

Further south, Colonel Chatterton had been given permission to join the operation and was flying the glider carrying General Browning into Nijmegen, where he would assume control of Corps HQ. Browning made a somewhat incongruous figure:

> immaculately dressed in a Barathea battledress, complete with a highly polished Sam Browne belt, knife-edged creases to his trousers, leather revolver holster gleaming like fine glass, a kid glove on one hand with the other glove and a swagger cane in the other. He might have been on a visit to the Guards' Depot. [30]

Instead, he perched on an upturned Worthington's beer crate between the pilots' seats. Before leaving England, everyone had been given a tablet bearing the label 'Take it before you think you will be afraid'. Chatterton and his co-pilot, 'Andy' Andrews, had spent much of the previous evening trying to decide when this might be. They decided that halfway across the North Sea seemed a good time and downed their pills. The results were disappointing. Nothing happened.

Over Nijmegen, Chatterton released and came in for a bumpy but safe landing among cabbages in an allotment. Browning, his first glider flight over, got out quickly. Chatterton later described how

> I started to panic then. I couldn't get out of my seat. I couldn't find my Sten gun. In fact, I was the opposite of 'Boy' Browning. Suddenly, Andy shouted at me: 'You've still got your earphones attached'. I realised then why I couldn't leave my seat, and I've never snatched at anything quite so quickly. Then I dragged myself from the cockpit to the door and jumped down among the cabbages. [31]

Outside, there was no sign of Browning. In his younger days, Browning had been an Olympic class athlete. Now, with his glider down on the US LZ just yards from the Reichswald forest marking the German border, he used his speed for a very personal purpose. Returning a few minutes later, he explained himself: 'I wanted to be the first British officer to pee in Germany.' [32]

Firing continued from flak batteries deeper into the forest but, as the massed US tow groups appeared even they fell silent, awed by the sheer scale of the invasion. John Lowden, approaching the LZ with an infantry sergeant as co-pilot, was told quietly 'I wouldn't presume to fly for you, but I think you're about to land in a minefield'. [33] A very rapid pull on the controls lifted the glider into the next field and a gentle landing. The LZ at Nijmegen had been expected to be opposed by 4,000 SS cadets rumoured to be in the area but resistance was light. Instead of the fanatical cadets Lowden had feared, he saw a group of bewildered Dutch civilians in their Sunday best approaching with white, frightened faces. The welcome for others was rather warmer. US pilot Arthur Kaplan had landed in a field near Chatterton's under sporadic mortar fire. He helped unload his cargo and set off with his passengers towards their RV. Passing a barn, they heard suspicious noises from inside and burst in. 'There – in one of the stalls – a paratrooper was making love to a very willing Dutch girl. He was quite profane at being interrupted, so we apologized and left . . . The guy couldn't have been on the ground more than an hour.' [34]

Not everyone was so lucky. Donald Orcutt, flying a C-47 with eighteen men of the 82nd into a drop zone 500 yards from the edge of the forest, dropped to fifty feet for a fast turnaround and

> it was only then I spotted a German 88mm antiaircraft guncrew up ahead and only five hundred yards from the edge of the drop zone. The 88 was slightly off to my left and pointed directly at us. I distinctly remember the image of the gun crew. One man was naked from the waist up, the second guy had on only his long johns and boots, and the third guy, a sergeant who was completely dressed as though about to answer roll call, pulled the lanyard just a moment before we roared over. I didn't see the muzzle flash. The three Germans looked directly up at us as we

barrelled by. They must have taken a hell of a blast from our prop wash and wing down wash. The shot missed, obviously, or I wouldn't be here to talk about it. [35]

Elsewhere, a flak shell tore through the floor of a plane carrying paratroopers of the 101st. 'Now they give us a latrine!' one shouted to his fellow passengers. Private Robert Bryce, braced in the door of a low flying C-47, saw Dutch civilians 300 feet below making the 'V–Victory' sign. 'They're giving us two to one we don't make it!' he told the men behind him.

Across the airborne carpet, the landings were meeting varying levels of success. In marked contrast to the Normandy drop, the 82nd Airborne Division had 89 per cent of troops and 84 per cent of gliders landed on or within 1,000 yards of their correct landing zones. The 101st had had equal success in the drop, met only light resistance and captured four of the five bridges assigned to them. Then, after being held up by German anti-tank guns, they approached the bridge at Son. Suddenly, as they reached it, it exploded. Things had started to go wrong.

By nightfall, XXX Corps had covered only seven miles from their start point. They had been expected in Eindhoven by 1700hrs and already the advance was four hours behind schedule. Narrow roads choked with tanks caused considerable delay in bringing forward engineers and their equipment and it would be another twenty-four hours before they reached the Son bridge and could complete repairs. Five miles to their west, Colonel John Michaelis and the men of Company H of the 502nd Parachute Infantry Regiment had identified two more bridges and a fight for control was under way but for now they remained intact.

At Arnhem, as the paratroopers rushed towards the bridges across the Rhine against fierce opposition, the glider pilots, a battalion each of the KOSB and the Borders and half a battalion of the South Staffords formed a defensive perimeter around the LZs to secure them for the next lift. Whether their contribution to the battle in Arnhem itself could have influenced the final outcome is open to debate but certainly the additional punch they could have provided would have made the initial seizure of the bridge more likely. So, for the vital first twenty-four hours, they sat on their LZs and listened to sounds of fighting to the east.

On D+1, poor weather hampered the takeoff of the second lift in a delay that undoubtedly saved hundreds of lives. Copies of the operational plan had been found by a German patrol in a wrecked glider and were now in the hands of Generals Model at Arnhem and Student near Nijmegen. Both suspected the plans were fake because they were too detailed, too precise. The Luftwaffe, however, accepted them and, at 1000hrs, scrambled every available fighter to intercept the expected glider formations. A ground attack had also been launched from the Reichswald Forest that had temporarily captured the LZs around Nijmegen and might have created a killing field that made Normandy's LZ 'W' seem tame by comparison, had the weather delay not given the Americans time to counterattack. They were retaken shortly before the first aircraft arrived but the Germans could not be dislodged completely. A warning was sent to land on the western edge, away from the treeline, but it was too late. The second lift arrived under heavy fire. Tug pilots failed to spot hundreds of gliders littering the day before's LZs and General Gavin watched helplessly as twenty-five tow combinations flew overhead carrying badly needed guns deep into Germany itself. The 320th Field Artillery was forced to defend its landing position until nightfall and then try to make its way ten miles back to American lines, bringing with it 160 airborne troopers, twenty-two glider pilots, ten jeeps and two field guns.

Of 294 gliders setting out for the Arnhem LZs, 270 had landed by 1530hrs but this time, warned by Luftwaffe command, the flak was even heavier. Sergeant Tom Pearce landed after his glider was hit by a burst that punched a huge hole in his port wing and left 'a huge dent as if a giant had pushed with two fists' in his tail. From the ground, he watched as a Horsa cast off at 2,000 feet and was narrowly missed by flak:

> the glider almost immediately went into a vertical dive; I thought it was doing something like four hundred miles an hour. I thought it was going straight in, but suddenly at about five hundred feet it levelled off. The strain of the pullout was so great that it broke the back of the glider. It travelled along through the air in this V shape with the rear of the fuselage at a sharp angle to the rest of the glider. It went along for three or four hundred yards and then hit a ploughed field. The cockpit broke loose and barrelled along the ground like a huge top. The two pilots who had been strapped in got out without a scratch, but the four men in the back, the gun crew, were flung out of the sides of the Horsa. The only one who was hurt had a fractured ankle.[36]

At 0600hrs on D+2, the Guards Armoured Division began to cross the Son bridge. By noon they were within sight of Nijmegen. It seemed that the plan might work if the American troops could keep what some were already calling 'Hell's Highway' open. To do that, they needed resupply. Fog in England prevented takeoff and the lift was delayed in the hope that it would burn off by afternoon. It didn't. The weather got worse. With glider pilots unable to see their tugs and flying at just 200 feet across the Channel to try to get below the cloud cover, many gliders were lost or forced to put down at airfields in France. Flight Officer George Brennan recalls flying over the sea 'at an altitude of thirty feet, the tug prop blast kicking up a spray over our windshield'. Over Holland, flak hit the aircraft, wounding Brennan and puncturing petrol cans aboard his glider. A spark ignited the spilled fuel and caused flash burns to his face, eyes and hands. Beside him, an artillery sergeant was hit by a shell splinter which entered his scrotum. Despite the injuries, Brennan managed a good landing on the correct

LZ near Veghel. Scrambling out of the glider under fire, he began to crawl towards a nearby ditch. Turning to urge the sergeant to hurry, Brennan saw him calmly drop his trousers saying 'I want to see if all this hurrying is worthwhile'. It was and he was relieved to find a large wound in his thigh but nothing broken.[37]

As the weather worsened, so too did German resistance. Heavy artillery fire stalled the British tanks on the banks of the River Waal. Gavin proposed sending a battalion of men across in boats to attack the north end of the bridge as the British rushed the south. To do this, he needed to withdraw a battalion from the line. The only troops available to plug that gap were the glider pilots of the 50th Troop Carrier Wing under Major Hugh Nevins. The lightly armed pilots, bivouacked west of Groesbeek, were ill-equipped to do the job but at 2200hrs, Nevin spoke to them and explained the situation, asking for 295 volunteers. It was pitch dark. 'I don't know how many stepped forward, but with tears in my eyes, I selected the first two hundred ninety-five men in the line, touching and counting each man. I was very proud of them.' They held off an armoured attack by Tiger tanks until noon on 21 September.[38]

Over the following days, only a very few gliders were able to reach Holland. In England, tension rose among pilots waiting to go. At his Nottingham base, First Lieutenant Sam Davis Jr waited days but by the evening of 22 September had had enough. Slipping off base, he went to visit his girlfriend and stayed over at her parents' home. He woke the next day to the sound of aircraft engines and

---

George Chatterton DSO, OBE

After a twenty-one-year career spanning all three services, Brigadier Chatterton retired in 1946 and his Surrey home became an open house for former pilots. 'Himself', as he was affectionately known, later worked at the Mansion House under Sir Frederick Hoare, Bt. as Lord Mayor of London. In 1962, the mayor took as his theme 'Youth and Leadership' and as a result the Upward Bound Trust was born.

The trust was established to encourage young people aged 16–21 to experience flying at a glider school run by former Glider Pilot Regiment instructors recruited by Chatterton. Today it continues to provide gliding instruction for young people at around a tenth of the price charged by other organizations and is proud of its connections with the regiment.

As well as the Upward Bound Trust, he also became Chairman of the Lady Hoare Trust for Physically Disabled Children and was also a Trustee of the Army Air Corps Museum at Middle Wallop. His own account of the regiment, *The Wings of Pegasus: The Story of the Glider Pilot Regiment* remains widely available.

he raced into the street, frantically trying to flag down a passing car, imagining himself 'in Leavenworth or in front of a firing squad'.[39] Eventually, he managed to catch a bus, arriving just in time to grab a helmet and weapon and drag his replacement from his glider. Davis was probably the only man in Holland to fight in his full-dress Class A uniform.

By now, though, it was clear that the battle for Arnhem had been lost. Planners had counted on at least three consecutive days of good weather to achieve success. In England, General Brereton looked out of his office window and couldn't see a flagpole fifty feet away. In frustration, he hurled his hat at a map of Europe on his wall. In Holland the weather was clear as British tanks continued to push forward. Chatterton looked on as a Guards officer casually talked of rushing a bridge 'as though he were saying "Yes sir, I would like another glass of sherry"'.[40] Chatterton, forced into the position of spectator, could only stand idly by while 1,200 carefully selected and trained men of his regiment fought and died just a few miles away.

At Arnhem, the glider pilots had moved with their battalions into a defensive perimeter around the Hartenstein Hotel, the divisional headquarters in the suburb of Oosterbeek. A Glider Pilot Regiment unit had formed and had established positions on both the east and west flank but many other pilots had stayed with the men they had brought in, often taking command as casualties mounted. Sergeant-Major Tilley now commanded a battalion, Lieutenant-Colonel Murray an entire brigade. Major F A S 'Tony' Murray of the GPR led a defence against an armoured attack until he was wounded in the throat and taken to a dressing station where British and German orderlies were working side by side. His wound dressed, Murray calmly walked out of the dressing station (now behind German lines) and found his way back to his men. Everywhere, Chatterton's 'total soldiers' proved their worth, leading fighting patrols and steadying infantry under mortar barrages so heavy that at one point bombs landed at a rate of one every four seconds for hours at a time. Despite this, morale remained high. Louis Hagen, a German-born Jewish pilot whose identity discs claimed him to be 'Lewis Haig', was among those defending a row of houses near the Hartenstein. Published anonymously in 1945, his *Arnhem Lift* provides an excellent account of his experiences in which he describes the pilots he fought alongside, including

> our private miracle man. This glider pilot was the pride of our street, because by all the laws of nature he ought to have been dead, and instead he was doing the kitchen fatigues quite happily. A bullet had entered his right temple and exited through his left, leaving behind it a couple of neat little holes. He wasn't even knocked out of the fight by this, and had to be ordered sternly not to take part in combatant duties. Not only did he remain working in the kitchen all the time we were in our house, but he was able to retreat with us across the Rhine. The last we saw of him

was sitting perkily in the back of an ambulance in Belgium, making rude signs at us as he passed.[41]

Confusion reigned throughout the area. A German field cashier took a wrong turning and his motorcycle sidecar, crammed with Reichsmarks, was soon in the hands of the Independent Parachute Company. A German supply truck driver, wearing a Dutch farmer's smock, might have succeeded in sneaking past a British roadblock – if he had remembered to take his helmet off. Major Ian Toler, commander of 'B' Squadron, had been joined on Monday by the incongruous figure of an RAF Squadron Leader in his smart uniform. The officer had been in charge of a radar unit travelling by glider whose tug aircraft had been shot down south of the river. The aircrew and the glider party had then made their way to the battle by crossing on the still operating ferry – paying full fare for the privilege. A few days later, Toler, sheltering in a cellar of the Hartenstein Hotel's tennis pavilion, was to experience yet another unusual visitor. One of the Germans held as a prisoner was a woman auxiliary who had been on leave in Arnhem as the attack began. Unwilling to squat in front of the other prisoners, Major Toler was asked if he would mind leaving the cellar to allow her some privacy.

> Rather grudgingly I left the comparative safety of the cellar with my co-pilot S/Sgt Shackleton, for the lady's convenience. She was an unconsiously long time and must have been in extremis! When we returned to the cellar it appeared to be completely flooded with urine and uninhabitable![42]

The woman, he decided, 'must have had a very large bladder'.

Earlier in the week, pilot Maurice Willoughby had been startled to see a group of senior officers scrambling through a garden under fire. Major-General Robert Urquhart had been cut off from his men since the previous day when he had tried to get through to the 1st Parachute Brigade and instead became trapped in the attic of a Dutch family home as German troops swarmed into the area. Now, as Willoughby watched, the general made another attempt to climb the wall and rejoin his HQ. Suddenly, another pilot, Major John Hemmings, appeared, placed both hands on the general's backside and, with a mighty push, sent him flying over. With a grin, Hemmings proudly announced 'I'll dine out on this one for months!'

Despite the humour, things were becoming desperate, but even where the fighting was at its fiercest, humanity won out. The enemy were so close that at night the pilots could hear them talking. Sergeant 'Andy' Andrews recalls a night when one of them

> started whistling and the tune sounded vaguely familiar. After a few bars I realized that the last time I had heard it was when we were fighting

some German parachutists in a little town in southern Italy . . . I wondered if the whistler had been my enemy there too.[43]

The next day, Andrews found himself less than forty yards from a young German soldier looking through a hedge as though hunting for a bird's nest. Andrews lowered his weapon and let the man wander on, unaware of how close to death he had been.

The airborne troops had been asked to hold for two days. They had been prepared to stay for four. The divisional diary entry for 2144hrs on Thursday 21 September, the evening of the fifth day, recorded

> no knowledge of elements of Division in Arnhem for twenty-four hours. Balance of Division in very tight perimeter. Heavy mortaring and machine-gun fire . . . Our casualties are heavy. Rations stretched to utmost. Relief within twenty-four hours vital.[44]

They would hold for another four days. Rumours of a British breakthrough continued to give hope to the defenders but that night Staff Sergeant Leslie Gibbons wrote in his diary that 'we have already had too many false hopes'. Victory was a spent dream, what mattered now was survival. Urquhart sent two officers by boat across the Rhine to brief Browning on the situation.

With all hope gone, Montgomery ordered the withdrawal of the airborne from Arnhem on the morning of 25 September, four days after the final deadline for relief had come and gone. That evening, Captain Walchli gathered his pilots and told them 'keep your mouths shut, but we've had it; we're pulling out'.[45] He then explained what would happen. Glider pilots would act as guides, stationed at fifty yard intervals between the hotel and the river and would lead groups of men to waiting boats. The first groups would leave at 2200hrs. Their boots and equipment muffled by sheets and towels to prevent noise, slowly the airborne moved back in a shrinking perimeter. Discipline remained good and Les Gibbons, wounded in the hand, recalls a voice calling the wounded forward first. A paratrooper, spotting Gibbons's bandaged hand, pushed him forward. 'There was no panic, the others held back.'[46] When the boats were full, the stronger swimmers stripped and swam alongside but the strong current was too much for some. Lou Hagen remembers that 'the water was pleasantly warm, the air filling my battle smock kept me easily afloat' but the river was more dangerous than it seemed. Less than halfway across, Hagen found himself in difficulty. After a brief moment of panic,

> I turned over on my back to rest and pull myself together. I realised that I had to get rid of my Sten gun, but that it would be pretty difficult as it was strapped round my back. I had to let myself sink vertically, while I eased the gun up and over my head. A moment later

I heard it go bubbling to the bottom. Next I methodically rid myself of all the impedimenta that my battle smock contained, also my boots and steel helmet. There were Sten gun mags, hand grenades, writing materials, my fountain pen and every conceivable thing I had imagined to save.[47]

Considerably lighter, he made it. Setting out with Hagen, former long-distance-swimming champion Captain J G Ogilvie, similarly laden, with a wound to his shoulder and still proudly wearing the kilt he had worn throughout, did not. Hagen saw him drifting downstream. He was never seen again.

Ironically, the glider pilots had been ordered to leave at the first opportunity to return to their bases for further landings. Now, they were among the last out. Over half the 1,300 men tasked to land in Holland were killed, wounded or missing. Some would later find their way back after evading capture, often for weeks. 'Andy' Andrews was flown back to his British base.

We went to our Nissen huts where a fire was burning; blankets and sheets had been made up into comfortable looking beds. There were only two of us alone in a hut that held twenty-six beds. It was too much. Without a word, we dumped our kit and rifle on the bed and left.[48]

In the wake of Operation Market Garden, both sides evaluated the lessons. On 25 September, as British troops were beginning their withdrawal, General Gavin wrote to the commander of 9th Troop Carrier Command to complain about the behaviour of the US glider pilots.

In looking back . . . one thing in most urgent need of correction [is] the method of handling our glider pilots. Despite their individual willing-ness to help, I feel they were definitely a liability to me . . . They frequently became involved in small unit actions . . . or simply left to visit nearby towns. Glider pilots without unit assignment . . . .improp-erly trained, aimlessly wandering about cause confusion and generally get in the way. I believe now that they should be assigned to airborne units, take training with the units, and have a certain number of hours allocated periodically for flight training.[49]

John Lowden, who after landing a Waco near Groesbeek had refused to lead a combat patrol, hitched a lift with a British convoy into Brussels and stayed there until Military Police, specially flown in from England, were sent to round up the glider pilots.

. . . it was reliably 'rumoured' that a test case charging desertion in the face of the enemy had been brought against one of our own glider pilots who had visited Brussels. The case was dismissed on a technicality. The defence attorney proved that in the Market-Garden briefing, one of the glider pilots asked, 'After we hit the ground, what do we do then?' The briefing officer's response was, 'Don't worry about it, you'll find plenty to do!' This ambiguous statement was the key to the man's acquittal. It certainly saved a lot of us from going to trial.[50]

Many of the gliders had left Britain with slogans chalked on the sides – 'Up the Reds!', 'Up the fraulein's skirts!', 'We are the Al Capone gang' and more. A humourless German officer of the SS Panzer Grenadier Depot and 16th Reserve Battalion, evaluating the Allied airborne, was unsure whether this reflected 'the political convictions of the troops themselves, or whether it is due to Bolshevist opinions or American influence'. More usefully, the landings themselves had been accurately reported by ground troops and

> it may be learned from this that it is vitally important to attack the enemy immediately with any force available, not with any hope of destroying him, but to disturb his preparations for battle. It is not possible to destroy overwhelming forces with light forces, but one can pin him down to provide time to prepare counter-measures. The gliders are most vulnerable between casting off and landing.[51]

Expecting more mass attacks, the Germans began to prepare light mobile reserves to rush to the scene of any landings and hold them until heavier reinforcements arrived. Chatterton, though, had other ideas.

In the preparations for the Arnhem attack, Chatterton had proposed a *coup de main* landing alongside the bridge itself but his idea had quickly been dismissed.[52] Chatterton later recalled having been called a 'bloody murderer' by some fellow officers for even suggesting it. He remained convinced, though, that the strength of glider operations lay not in their being used as the airborne equivalent of landing craft – intended to deliver troops to the beach and nothing more – but that they worked best by allowing men to be delivered directly onto a given target. All the most successful operations to date proved it and the failure of Arnhem seemed to support his ideas. Fortunately, the RAF's 38 Group had now come under the command of Air Vice-Marshal Scarlett-Streatfield, a prewar acquaintance of Chatterton's and sympathetic to the needs of the Glider Pilot Regiment. Chatterton had, for some time, been working on a model he called 'tactical landings' which would involve gliders landing where company commanders wanted them rather than in massed LZs. They would land on top of the enemy according to the tactical requirements of the ground forces and with as little time between castoff and landing as possible. With the backing of Scarlett-Streatfield, the next operation would be a tactical landing.

Ironically, in the early days of the regiment, Air Vice-Marshal Arthur Harris,

Chief of the Air Staff, had claimed it would be disastrous to try to train army personnel to fly troop-carrying gliders, arguing that

> The idea that semi-skilled, unpicked personnel (infantry corporals have, I believe even been suggested) could, with a maximum of training, be entrusted with the piloting of these troop carriers is fantastic. Their operation is equivalent to forced landing the largest sized aircraft without engine aid – than which there is no higher test of piloting skill.[53]

Now, with glider pilot losses at Arnhem having devastated their ranks, Chatterton had no reserves. Training a 'total soldier' was a long process and time was a luxury he could not afford. With little choice if he were to bring the regiment back up to an effective force, he approached the RAF to request trained aircrews be transferred. Having first argued that gliders were too difficult for the army to fly, the RAF now claimed that, in the words of Sergeant-Pilot Lewis, gliders were 'an army job. To [the RAF] mind, gliders were boxes with wings on them'. It was only with the support of Air Chief Marshal Sir Peter Drummond, Director of RAF Training, that eventually 1,500 men were released for a rapid conversion course. Like their American counterparts, many glider pilots were now air force officers expected to become infantrymen for what promised to be the biggest operation yet.

As the new recruits began their training, a new threat emerged. In the winter of 1944, the Germans launched a counterattack in the Ardennes that threatened to stall the Allied advance. In 'the battle of the bulge', gliders would play an important role.

Operation Repulse – glider resupply of Bastogne, 26 December 1944

On the morning of 26 December 1944, pilots of the US 96th Squadron, 444th Troop Carrier Group were sleeping off their Christmas hangovers at their Orleans base when their glider officer came around requesting two volunteers for a combat mission. After many unsuccessful attempts to find anyone willing to fly, Second Lieutenant Charlton Corwin Jr and Flight Officer Benjamin Constantino asked him where to and were told that he didn't know. Nevertheless, they agreed to go. Within an hour they were airborne to Etain, where they picked up thirteen volunteer medics from the 12th Evacuation Hospital. When the request had been made there, it was assumed that the medical teams were to make a parachute drop. Untrained as paratroops, the doctors, medics and even several female nurses all volunteered anyway.

For the past week, men of the 82nd and 101st Airborne had been encircled in the town of Bastogne by a massive German counterattack through the Ardennes. Fighting had been heavy and by Christmas Day casualties were mounting to the point where existing medical resources were about to be overwhelmed. Brigadier-General Anthony McAuliffe had requested medical supplies be delivered by air and Corwin and Constantino now found that they were to be the first flight of Operation Repulse – the aerial resupply of 'the battered bastards of Bastogne'.

An hour later, the lone glider, escorted by four P-47 Thunderbolt fighters, arrived over the besieged town. Landing in a snow-covered field north-west of town without a shot being fired, the medics were quickly transported to the hospital and got to work.

At the 98th Squadron, First Lieutenant Wallace Hammargen was also having difficulty finding volunteers to fly with him that morning. Telling those who did come forward to 'get your combat gear together and draw your ammo and three days rations and report to the operations room in forty-five minutes', Hammargen joined them at 1315hrs for the briefing. Twenty pilots would be carrying petrol into the town that afternoon.

The Germans had chosen not to reveal their positions for a single glider earlier in the day but now heavy fire erupted towards the next flight to attempt to cross the lines. With a highly inflammable load, the pilots worried most about tracer. Sure enough, Hammargen recalls, 'we were picking up intense ground fire from our left and right – and there were a lot of tracers'. Landing safely just after 1700hrs, Hammargen reported to a nearby unit. 'The major in charge said, "What are you carrying?" I said, "Gasoline." He said, "Thank God! We're at the bottom of the barrel". Gasoline was so scarce that armour had to start off without warming the engines.'[54]

The next day, more gliders were sent, each with only one pilot (who had been given a parachute). Second Lieutenant Mack Striplin was tasked to fly artillery shells into the perimeter. Cutting loose from his tug, he hit the ground fast on a downward slope and slid along like a sled. Briefly becoming airborne again as his aircraft leapt over a fifteen foot drop, he skidded through a wire fence, coming to rest just ten yards from the artillery position he had been sent to resupply. When he landed, the gun had been down to its last twenty rounds. He was one of the lucky ones – the 440th Group took 42 per cent of its entire casualties of the war in that single afternoon. Of one serial of fifty tow combinations, fifteen gliders were shot down and seventeen tow planes failed to return to their bases but over 50 tons of supplies were delivered safely.

By that evening, tanks of Patton's 3rd Army had broken through the encirclement and further resupply flights were cancelled. Over a thousand tons of ammunition, fuel and medical supplies had been delivered, 94 per cent of it directly on to the designated LZ. On 28 December, acting as escorts for the 540 German POWs captured by the 101st, the glider pilots left Bastogne.

Operation Varsity – crossing the Rhine, 23 March 1945

The harsh lessons of Market Garden had been learned but, with the British 1st Airborne still out of action, the 6th fighting as infantry and the US 82nd and 101st regrouping after the German counterattack in the Ardennes, there seemed little scope for any more large-scale airborne operations until late February 1945. On 23 February Montgomery's 21st Army Group had started a successful push between the Meuse and the Rhine, clearing the western bank of the river in preparation for another thrust into Germany. Lieutenant-General Hodges's 1st Army had already seized the Ludendorff Bridge at Remagen (where glider snatches were being used to evacuate the wounded) and Patton's 3rd Army had established a bridgehead near Oppenheim. Montgomery's men would cross the Rhine in the north, trapping the Germans between his forces and those of Hodges and Patton driving in from the south. With the enemy caught in that vice, Eisenhower believed Eclipse, the planned airborne assault on Berlin, could probably end the war.

Montgomery offered Operation Plunder, an operation combining an airborne assault (codenamed Varsity) using the British 6th and the US 17th Airborne Divisions in support of a large-scale ground assault. He would control seventeen infantry, eight armoured and two airborne divisions, five armoured brigades, a Royal Marine brigade and another of Canadian infantry with support from over 35,000 vehicles. Thirty-six naval landing craft had been hauled forward on twenty-four-wheel low-loaders to ferry the force across the river from where it would strike east as an airborne armada brought in the paratroops to land on and around the Diersfordter Wald, an area of high, wooded ground overlooking the road and rail junctions at the town of Hamminkeln and the bridges over the River Issel. D-Day would be 23 March and the code to go would be a signal of 'two if by sea'.

The airborne mission looked quite simple. They were to seize the bridges over the Issel River (a task that once again fell to men of the Ox & Bucks Light Infantry) and rapidly clear the enemy from the Diersfordter Wald to prevent their reinforcements from reaching the beachhead. Once the crossing was secure, the ground elements would move forward and the airborne would join them, keeping the Germans on the run. The 17th Airborne was to land in the southern portion of the XVIII Airborne Corps zone, and the British 6th Airborne in the north. In all, the area measured just five miles deep and six wide, into which a total of nearly 22,000 airborne troops had to be inserted, making the airhead east of the Rhine the most congested airborne assault ever attempted. Unlike Arnhem's three days of lifts, the entire airborne drop, including resupply, would go down in just four hours.

During the night of 22 March, a giant smokescreen was laid down by artillery massed on the western bank as the land elements moved forward. For days, bombing attacks had sought to isolate the area but the sheer scale of the buildup was such that the Germans were aware of what was coming. Three divisions of

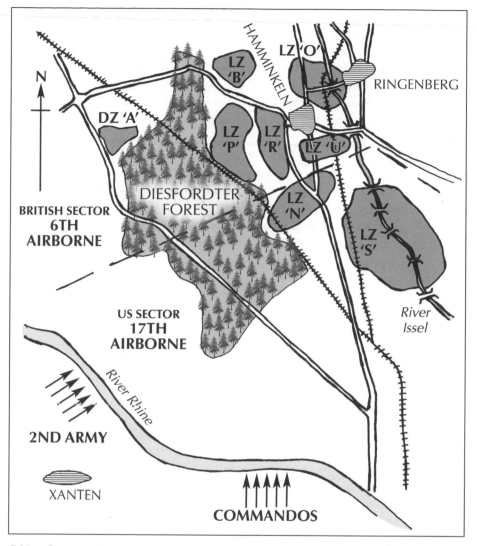

Rhine Crossing. Varsity landing zones.

the German 2nd Parachute Corps were in the area, supported by the 47th Panzer Division. It would be a tough fight.

At 0600hrs on 24 March, the first aircraft began to lift off carrying men of the 6th Airborne and formed an air fleet over Essex. The paras would jump at 1000hrs with gliders arriving between 1021 and 1100hrs. The first US gliders would land at 1036hrs and continue arriving until 1243hrs. At 0717hrs, the US 17th Airborne's aircraft began to lift off from their French bases to rendezvous with the British over the battlefield of Waterloo, by which time the British gliders alone formed a stream that took forty minutes to pass overhead. Together, they began the hundred-mile run to their targets, four to six miles east of the Rhine, the two streams forming an armada that would take two and a half hours to pass a given point. Chatterton had been asked to supply crews for 2,000 British gliders but had managed only 440 Horsas and forty-eight Hamilcars, the Americans using 906 Wacos. Even with only half the number requested, it was by far the largest air operation of the war. Lieutenant Sydney St John, at 32 the 'old man' of the GPR, remembers that 'visibility was perfect and everywhere you looked there were tugs and gliders. It was extraordinary.' Earlier, at one of the many briefings and pep-talks the men had endured, a brigadier had exclaimed excitedly 'won't those blighters be amazed when we cross the Rhine!' Looking around, St John couldn't help but feel that anyone would be amazed to find 1,300 gliders suddenly heading towards him.[55]

As the troop carriers approached the Rhine, the huge smokescreen stood out. Brigadier Bourne saw it ahead as his glider crossed the Meuse.

> From there, I could see the Rhine, a silver streak, and beyond it a thick, black haze, for all the world like Manchester or Birmingham as seen from the air. For the moment, I wondered whether the bombing of Wesel, which had preceded the attack upon that town by Commando troops, had been mistimed. If this was so, then the whole landing zone would be obscured by the clouds of dust which would be blowing from the rubble created by the attack.[56]

A reporter, flying aboard a Halifax bomber, described 'a gigantic curtain over the battlefield, hiding all that was going on underneath'. Vic Miller, flying a Horsa, 'hung on, hoping for a gap, a glimpse of something. It was a total blank.' Later, other pilots would talk of an anti-airborne ploy by the Germans but, whatever the source, hundreds of gliders would soon be trying to descend through the thick screen with no idea what lay beneath.

Reporter Howard Cowan was aboard a Horsa as it cast off. 'Now', his sergeant pilot told him, 'is when you pray.'[57] Searching for gaps, Vic Miller had given up hope of finding his designated LZ when the smoke parted and he caught a glimpse of a road he recognized from the briefing. Turning to his RAF co-pilot, he shouted, 'for God's sake, if you see a space with a glider on it, we'll have a go'. As they broke through the bottom of the cloud, Miller was shocked to find himself down in the very field he had been searching for. Arnhem veteran 'Andy' Andrews had a rough landing after flak wounded his co-pilot and badly damaged the controls of his Horsa. Landing in a crowded field, he clipped the wing of another glider and was sent cartwheeling across the LZ.

> I was thrown through the front, and finished by sliding along the left side of my face, slightly cutting the corner of my left eye, but was other-wise unhurt. I went round pulling out people from the wreckage, all of

whom were in a heap under the wings, on top of each other, with seating harness still strapped to their backs with part of the seat. I still cannot discover what happened to the three in the back. There were no bodies and they were not in their seats.[58]

The whole front of the Horsa was smashed, the wings had collapsed and the tail section had broken away and rolled into the middle of the field. Despite the smokescreen, 90 per cent of the British gliders landed as planned, but of the 416 that reached the LZs, only eighty-eight were undamaged by flak and small arms fire. Harry Antonopoulus, the ditching expert of Operation Buzzard, landed in one piece only to come under immediate machine-gun fire. 'That gun was so fast', he later claimed, 'that the bullets all came through one clean hole'. Scrabbling out, he found 'a nice, deep ditch with three or four American glider pilots in it' and decided to stay put.[59] By the evening, thirty-eight men of the GPR lay dead, seventy-seven more were wounded and 135 missing, a toll greater than either Normandy or Arnhem.

Before leaving, Major Ian Toler had visited his niece, Flying Officer Rosemary Britten, at the RAF base from which he would fly out the next day and asked her to come to watch his takeoff. Not content to watch the takeoff, Britten had managed to talk her way aboard *D-Dog* – a Halifax bomber that would act as a tug plane. Alongside her escape kit, she had packed powder and lipstick because, she recalled, 'I wanted to look like a German girl in case of baling out'. Over Holland, she saw the shattered towns and villages below and the vast smokescreen over the Rhine and wished their glider luck as it cast off towards the dust and smoke. Immediately, the Halifax pilot began evasive manoeuvres to dodge the flak now directed at them in ever increasing amounts. A shell hit the aircraft, almost severing the control column and peppering the fuselage but miraculously missed the fuel tanks and the crew. As *D-Dog* limped back across the Rhine it was clear they were out of immediate danger from the battle below but it seemed certain they would be forced to bale out soon.

> By that time, I knew I was going to be either killed or court-martialled, and was amazed to find I didn't really mind either. I remember thinking that now I wouldn't have to live to a dreary old age, which was a good thing. But I could do with a year or two, now it had come to the point . . . George went back to the turret to get his hat, so I got mine too, just in case we survived, in which event, one might as well put up as good a show as possible.[60]

Fortunately, the plane made a safe landing at an American base at Merville, near Lille and Britten was flown home later to find that four crews had reported *D-Dog* shot down. 'I felt rather bad about turning up after all, and decided to acquire an operational twitch at least!'

The operation would also be a landmark for the American pilots. At his briefing for Varsity, John Lowden recalls being ordered to

> take no prisoners for at least seventy-two hours' after landing. Asked what to do if Germans surrendered, they were told 'take them someplace out of the way, like a house or a barn, and get rid of them. Either knife them or strangle them. But for Christ's sake, don't shoot them. Some of their comrades might hear that and decide to fight it out, rather than surrender.[61]

It was a shocking statement for air force officers to hear but one that told them that, this time, glider pilots would be expected to be real soldiers.

Three weeks before, Major-General William Miley, commander of the 17th Airborne Division, had briefed the glider operations officers of the 53rd Troop Carrier Wing's five groups on the plans for Varsity. His 194th Glider Infantry Regiment would need an extra infantry company if it was to carry out its assigned objective. That company would be made up of glider pilots after landing, making it unique in military history – an infantry company made up entirely of officers. With so many chiefs, and not a single Indian, command would go to Captain Charles Gordon, glider operations officer of the 435th Troop Carrier Group. The pilots underwent two weeks of intensive training in weapons and tactics with the 194th GIR to prepare themselves. Organized into four platoons, one for each of the group's squadrons (75th, 76th, 77th and 78th), the men were to assist the 17th Airborne Division in securing a crossroads of the Helzweg and Hessenweg north-east of Wesel, establish roadblocks and make contact with British forces north-east of the town. They also knew that, this time, the LZs would not have been secured by paratroopers first.

The Group's 144 gliders came under ground fire as soon as they released from their tugs, causing heavy casualties among the infantry and glider crews. The survivors made their way to their objective – half a dozen brick houses in the middle of a wide, open area. The men dug in during the afternoon and evacuated the civilian inhabitants to the rear. All but one family had left and, in appreciation of their not being evicted, the remaining family, an elderly couple with their pregnant daughter, had prepared a meal of stew and potatoes for the Americans. Towards dusk, German patrols scouted up to their positions and were fought off with a murderous burst of fire from the pilots. Flight Officer William Horn remembers that, 'all of a sudden, the German infantry started hyping themselves up with a weird sort of yelling and cheering and came at us in a Japanese banzai charge and we really poured it into them'. One of the Germans, a teenager of around 17, began to plead in English that he was wounded and had an uncle in Milwaukee but, thinking it may be a trap, the pilots left him where he was. He died during the night.

Around 2355hrs, a Ju88 bomber crashed into a field next to the crossroads, coming to rest against the wreckage of a Waco. Flight Officer Oliver Faris was the first to reach the wreckage. Unable to see any markings in the darkness, he asked if the crew were British. 'No', answered one, 'we are Germans, but the war is over for us'. As the Americans rescued the trapped crewmen, a barrage of mortar fire fell around the site, heralding the start of an attack.

A few minutes later a German tank, supported by a large number of infantry, hit the crossroad defended by the 75th Platoon. A tank round hit a .50 calibre gun emplacement and another set fire to a crashed glider. By the light of the flames, Flight Officer Joseph Menard watched in horror as the barrel swung slowly towards him and began to fire his rifle at it, hoping against hope that a round might enter the muzzle and explode the shell before it could be fired. Then suddenly, an explosion rocked the tank and its gun fired early, hitting the ground and ricocheting over Menard's foxhole, missing him but leaving him with a slight wound and temporarily deafened. Flight Officer Elbert Jella's bazooka round had been enough to make the tank fall back, running over the 20 mm gun it was towing and, seeing what had happened, a second tank behind also withdrew.

At daybreak, Horn saw 'a lone German medic was out in front of us desperately trying to minister to a number of his wounded comrades but it was a losing battle'. Thirteen enemy dead lay around the crossroads and a sweep later recovered forty-five wounded. British forces reached the glider pilots and the 'Battle of Burp Gun Corner', as the forces newspaper *Stars and Stripes* called it, was over.[62] Although it received coverage in the 1 April edition of the paper, the fight soon faded into obscurity. It would not be until fifty years later, at the 435th Troop Carrier Reunion in October 1995, that Flight Officers Jella, Deshurley, Campbell and Hurley each were awarded the Silver Star for their defence against the tanks at a range of only fifteen yards. All the others who fought in the battle were awarded the Bronze Star, but many of the more than 280 men had died before their heroism was finally recognized.

In the British sector, Ian Toler found himself surrounded on his LZ by misplaced American troops but without hearing a shot for the first few minutes. He had landed short of an area raked by 88 mm fire but soon small arms rounds began to hit the glider. With a Bren gunner covering them from behind the wheels, Toler and his co-pilot, RAF Flying Officer George Telman, struggled to unload their Horsa, sawing through the joints to get it open. Once clear, he made his way to a nearby farmhouse where the German farmer's wife began to scream at him in German. Angrily, Toler shouted back 'Das is deine Kreig – this is your bloody war. You started it. If we want to use your house we jolly well will.' Realizing that there were pigeons in the loft that might be used for messages, he ordered them killed but relented when he found they were the pets of the farmer's young son, his anger suddenly gone as he saw the tears in the child's eyes and realized that these people were not his enemy.

For Toler, Varsity did not involve any fighting. Within a short time we heard the unmistakeable noise of tanks. Surely we weren't going to be attacked by Panzers? Then they appeared. The Sherman tanks of the Guards Armoured Division. What a wonderful sight. It brought a lump to my throat to see them as they roared past and to realise that they were now advancing into Germany.[63]

It was then that he was informed of the death of one of his fellow officers. Toler was now the only officer in the squadron to have survived Arnhem. Gathering together as many pilots as he could find, he led them back towards the Rhine, passing a large group of prisoners being herded along by an American trooper stripped to the waist and riding bareback on a horse. Amphibious trucks took them back to the western bank where a camp had been set up offering hot food and showers at the 'Rhine Hotel – Glider Pilots a Speciality'. Arriving back at their Down Ampney base, the pilots found a customs official demanding to know if they had anything to declare. He quickly got the message. American pilots of the 440th Group, meanwhile, established themselves in a Parisian brothel and cut cards to determine who would get the unit's allocation of medals for the operation.

Back in Britain, Chatterton immediately began planning the next operation. Even larger than Varsity, Operation Arena would land troops near Kassel to seize the airfields there and use them to fly in infantry deep inside Germany. The Allied advance soon made the plan redundant. Next would be Operation Eclipse, the attack on Berlin itself. It had barely reached the end of the planning stage when the Russian steamroller reached the city. The Allied glider war was over.

Chapter Eight

War behind the lines:
Russian glider operations 1941–1945

In 1923, Soviet authorities sponsored the first all-Soviet Union gliding contest at the Moscow Gliding Club as a way of encouraging sport gliding. Within ten years, they could claim 57,000 trained glider pilots at ten gliding schools and 230 gliding stations and a glider factory capable of producing 900 primary trainers and 300 training gliders per year under the management of leading designer Oleg Antonov. In January 1931, the Ninth Party Congress announced a massive expansion in its glider programme with the aims of building a pool of pilots, developing new designs and techniques and establishing as many world records as possible. Almost immediately, eighty leading pilots and designers gathered at Koktabel airfield and began a rigorous thirty-six days of flight testing of over twenty types of glider, setting six new Russian records in the process. Throughout that year, Russian pilots continued to push the boundaries of glider flight – V A Stepanchenok looped his glider 115 times and flew upside down for over a minute and B Borodin flew two passengers for four hours in a single flight as, behind the scenes, the military took a great interest in their progress. Following a series of exercises conducted in 1929 and 1930, M. N. Tukhachevsky, then commander of the Leningrad Military District, prepared a study on the 'Action of Airborne Units in Offensive Operations' and presented it to the Revoensovet (Revolutionary Military Soviet), along with a plan for an airborne motorized division for use as an operational landing force. Alongside Tukhachevsky's work, an article by the Chief of Staff of the Voenno-Vozdushnvi sil (Red Army Air Force), A N Lapchinsky and N P Ivanov investigated the more detailed aspects of airborne operations and, in a country as vast as the Soviet Union, the concept of airborne warfare was very attractive. In 1931, just one year after a trial jump had been demonstrated, a fifteen-man team dropped by parachute in a raid on a bandit stronghold at Basmach in Central Asia. The raid was such a success that in February 1932 a Red Army order 'Temporary Regulation on the Organization of Deep Battle' discussed the use of airborne forces, describing them as 'army operational-tactical units that coordinated closely with ground forces'. In the event of war, it was suggested, the airborne forces would undertake sabotage missions and raids on enemy lines of communication, depots and headquarters, as well as blocking enemy reinforcement or withdrawal.

Having set out their ideas of airborne operations, the Red Army command set about tackling the problems of how they could be put into practice. The Training Directorate issued a series of directives that outlined four operational categories of training needs: parachute, glider, airlanding and combined operations. In April 1932, the 'Regulations Concerning the Special Design Bureau (OKB) of the VVS, RKKA' (Raboche-Krest'yanskaya Krasnaya Armiya, Workers and Peasants Red Army) handed responsibility for developing air assault equipment to the OKB, with a particular emphasis on the production of gliders and modifying the TB-1 bomber to transport airborne troops. By the end of the year, an 18-year-old designer, Boris Dimitiyevitch Urlapov, working as part of a team at the Institute of Narkomtyazhproma had developed an idea from the head of the OKB, Pavel Ingatievitch Grokhovski and produced the G-63 glider. With a 28 m wingspan, the glider could be towed by reconnaissance aircraft and carry between sixteen and eighteen troops lying prone in spaces in the wings, ready to drop by parachute over the target. The aircraft was named the 'Jakov Alknisa' after the Commanding General of the Red Army Air Force and took part in the autumn manoeuvres of the Red Army in 1933. Despite these initial advances, Tukhachesky, the founding father of the Soviet airborne, and Alknisa both fell victim to Stalin's purge of the military in 1937–8 that robbed the Red Army of some of its best thinkers. The result was that the development of glider and airborne operations stalled – but not before Soviet displays had inspired men like German observers Student and Udet.

In 1939, small groups of Russians made combat jumps into action near Summa and Petsano in Finland and by 1941 five corps of airborne troops had been created with a Military Glider Training School at Saratov and nearly 50,000 parachute-trained men available but it was not until after the German invasion began in June 1941 that the Russian High Command abruptly ordered the development of transport gliders to be stepped up. A project competition had been set up in January 1940 and work was already under way, so within two months, designers Vladimir Gribowski and Oleg Antonov had produced troop-carrying gliders capable of transporting men and equipment inside the fuselage. The G-11 (Gribowski, eleven man – also known as the G29) was first flown on 1 September 1941, and over 300 would eventually be produced in two factories at Shumerlya (factory no. 471) and Kozlovka village (factory no. 494) between late 1941 and mid-1942 when production was switched because the demand for combat aircraft overtook the need for transport. Production started again in 1944 in Riazan and by October of that year a dual control training variant, the G-11U glider, appeared and remained in production until 1948.

Designated the A-7 (Antonov, seven passenger – also known as the RF-8, Rot Front-8), Antonov's glider was based on a 1939 design and was similar in appearance to the German DFS 230. The A-7 was an enlarged variant of a prewar sports glider, the RF-7, and experiments showed it capable of carrying seven men or around 900 kg of equipment. In all about 400 were built, including an experimental tanker variant carrying 1,000 litres of fuel but this did not go into production. Production began in the Lithuanian city of Kaunas but had to be hastily evacuated as the country was overrun.

During experiments over the previous decade, the Soviets had been among several countries attempting various means of delivering heavy equipment and armour by air. The American engineer Walter Christie had experimented with a design for a flying tank and the Royal Air Force had tested a one-third-scale prototype known as the 'Baynes Bat', a flying wing intended to carry a light tank. It flew well, but no suitable tank was available for the project to be taken further. Small 'tankettes' such as the T-27 could simply be strapped into the bomb bay of heavy bombers like the TB-3 and dropped with or without parachutes from low-level (some reports suggest that during the 1940 occupation of Bessarabia, light tanks may have been dropped from a few metres by TB-3 bombers, to roll to a stop with the clutch in neutral). The problem was that the crews dropped separately and could be unable to reach their vehicles to bring them into action. Gliders, on the other hand, would allow crews to arrive at the drop zone along with their vehicles and minimize exposure of the valuable towing aircraft to fire. The Soviet Air Force ordered Oleg Antonov to design a glider for landing tanks.

Instead of designing a glider to carry a tank, Antonov came up with an ambitious design to turn a tank into a glider, the result was the Antonov A-40 Krylya Tanka (winged tank). A T-60 light tank was given a detachable cradle bearing large wood and fabric biplane wings and twin tail with the idea that the tank could glide into the battlefield, drop its wings and be ready to fight within minutes. A stripped-down prototype flew on 2 September 1942 piloted by the 'Honourable Master of Gliding', Sergey Nikolayevich Anokhin. The design flew well but the weight – even with weapons, ammunition and all non-essential parts removed – proved too much for the tug aircraft to maintain the glide speed of 160km/h needed to keep it flying and the project was abandoned.

The rapid advance of the Germans forced the Russians to evacuate their production lines further east and, with priority given to combat aircraft, glider production fell and very few air operations were carried out. Those that were proved disastrous. On 27 January 1942, as the Soviet counteroffensive got under way, the 4th Airborne Corps began a series of night drops of paratroopers in the German rear in the area south-west of Vyazma using forty civilian and twenty-two military aircraft with a small fighter escort. From the outset, the operation went badly and after six nights, only 2,100 men from the 10,000-man airborne corps had been dropped. A combination of bad weather and the pilots' inexperience with night navigation meant that, of those, most landed twenty kilometres south of the intended drop zone. The intended five or six sorties each night had not taken into account the weather conditions, aircraft failures or combat losses, all compounded by the failure to conceal the buildup of troops at the airfields, which led to an attack by German bombers that closed one and damaged others, reducing their capacity so only two to three sorties per night were actually possible. The paratroops who landed, however, did succeed in interdicting lines of communication in the German rear area for almost three weeks, in part because of their linkup with the 1st Guards Cavalry Corps on 6 February.

A second series of night landings near Yukhnov between 17 and 23 February also saw paratroops spread out over a large area because of inaccurate drops and the loss of most of their supplies. Some eventually joined partisan groups in the area whilst the main body, lacking artillery and air support, found itself restricted to night operations. The planned two- to three-day operation stretched to almost five months until, with the help of a battalion of reinforcements dropped into the area on 15–16 April, the battered remnants of the 4th Airborne Corps managed to break through two encirclements and reach the Russian lines in late May. Although it had created considerable havoc in the German rear, the corps had been decimated.

Despite the problems at Vyazma, the Soviets attempted a second night drop using an entire airborne corps on 24–25 September 1943 to seize a bridgehead at the Bukrin Bend on the Dnieper. The mission of the airborne corps, as established by General Vatutin, was to secure a bridgehead on the right bank of the Dnieper River near Velikyi Bukrin and specifically to prevent German counterattacks from penetrating the west bank of the Dnieper in the sector from Kanev to Traktomirov. A defensive perimeter thirty kilometres deep and fifteen to twenty kilometres wide would be set up with Colonel Krasovsky's 1st Guards Airborne Brigade landing near Lazurtsy, Beresnyagi and Grishentsy to prevent enemy counterattacks towards Kurifovka and Bobritsa and Colonel Goncharov's 3rd Guards Airborne Brigade preventing a German advance to Chernyshi and Buchak by securing a line from Lipovyi Rog to Makedony. The 3rd Brigade would then hold the line until units of the 40th Army arrived from Traktomirov and Zarubentsy. Meanwhile Lieutenant-Colonel Sidorchuk's 5th Guards Airborne Brigade would secure a defensive line from Gorkavshchina through Stepantsy to Kostyanets and to prevent an enemy advance to the Dnieper from the south and south-west. The landing would take place over two nights and would require fifty PS-84 aircraft, 150 IL-4/B-25 aircraft and around forty-five A-7 and G-11 gliders carrying heavy weapons. The aircraft would lift the force from Smorodino and Bogodukhov airfields near Lebedin, a distance of 175–200 kilometres from the drop zones and would be expected to make two or three sorties each night. The 1st and 5th Guards Airborne brigades would land on the first night, 3rd Guards Airborne Brigade the next. The gliders carrying artillery would land during the intervals between the drops of the parachute echelons. Although the concept was excellent, the planning, timing and execution of the operation produced results similar to those in 1942.

On 19 September, General G K Zhukov approved the plan, stressing that the operations had to be coordinated with those of the Voronezh Front and ordering Vatutin to update brigade missions accordingly. As the plans were being drawn up, the Soviet advance had seen lead elements cross the Dnieper River on 21/22 September. A series of unforeseen events then followed which threw the carefully laid plans into chaos. First, there were not enough rail transport cars to move the corps and its supplies to the airfields in time. Bad weather then prevented the transports from assembling the necessary aircraft at the correct airfields and only eight planes arrived at the right place at the right time. Plans were hastily changed and new orders issued by General Vatutin from 40th Army Headquarters on the morning of 23 September. Consequently, instead of three brigades dropping over two nights, only the two brigades that could complete their movement to the departure airfields in time were to be used. The drop itself was delayed by twenty-four hours to take place the next night and the delays and the last-minute changes in plans caused near chaos in command channels. The corps commander and his staff needed time to adapt missions and make decisions in response to the changes, which meant that orders to subordinate units could not be issued until the 24th. At brigade level, commanders needed to study the changes and issued new orders just one and a half hours before the troops loaded onto the aircraft. As a result, company commanders had only fifteen minutes before takeoff to brief their platoon officers and they, in turn, passed the information to their men during the flight to the drop zone itself.

Throughout the day, men, supplies and support aircraft were being assembled at the departure airfields but by the time the 5th Guards Airborne Brigade had assembled, bad weather had prevented many aircraft getting through and only forty eight of the required sixty-five LL-2 transports had arrived. Aircraft commanders, for safety reasons, insisted on cutting back on their loads, allowing only fifteen to eighteen units of men or cargo instead of the planned twenty on each aircraft. As these changes disrupted planning calculations, commanders were forced to reallocate loads just before takeoff, resulting in piles of supplies being left sitting on the runway.

At 1830hrs, 4,575 men of the 3rd Guards Airborne Brigade finally took off, with the lead elements of 5th Brigade starting out two hours later. As the lift got under way, it became apparent that the capacity of the fuel trucks at the airfields was less than expected, reducing the number of refuelled aircraft available so that the first wave, due to takeoff ten minutes before the second, could not complete its launch on time. As soon as an aircraft had been fuelled, it took off and soon both waves became intermingled. As they returned for the next sortie, the refuelling problems meant that paratroopers shifted from one plane to another in search of an earlier departing flight. Only 298 of the planned 500 sorties took off that night, leaving around 30 per cent of the two brigades behind.

Of those who did take off, the inadequately trained pilots – despite exercises held late that summer along the Moskva River on terrain similar to the Dnieper – were ill prepared for the heavy flak they encountered. One aircraft dropped its men into the Dnieper River, another into Russian positions on the eastern bank. Two more dropped their men in what turned out to be a relatively safe area far behind the German lines. A total of thirteen aircraft simply returned to their base without dropping their men, further complicating the already confused flight schedule. Among those who reached the drop zones, the pilots' sometimes violent evasive action did not improve the accuracy of the drop, with the paratroopers jumping from aircraft flying at 200km/h at altitudes anywhere between 600 and 2,000 m. Instead of landing in the planned, lightly defended and relatively compact, ten by fourteen kilometre area, they found themselves scattered over an area nearer to thirty by ninety kilometres infested with German defensive positions and right on top of three German divisions. The storm that had prevented reconnaissance flights noticing the buildup of German troops also prevented the use of pathfinder teams and the lead elements of the Russian paratroop force jumped into the Dubari-Grushevo area just as the first troops of the main body of the 19th Panzer Division reached it. Colonel E Binder of the 19th Division later recalled:

> [Our] Reconnaissance Battalion was fighting west of Zarubentsy. The armoured personnel carrier battalion of the 73rd Panzer Grenadier Regiment, with elements of the division staff of the 19th Panzer Division, was advancing by way of Pii-Potaptsy-Dudari [Dubari]-Kolesishche; it was followed by the main body of the 73rd Panzer Grenadier Regiment, and the 74th Panzer Grenadier Regiment. Behind these forces came the rest of the division, including the 19th Panzer Regiment. After the Germans had reached Dudari [Dubari], the first Russian parachutists jumped from a transport plane flying at an altitude of 600 to 700 metres directly above the little village. While these parachutists were still in the air they were taken under fire by machine guns and a 20mm four-barrelled flak gun. A half minute or a minute later, the second plane came over and thereafter at like intervals other planes followed, flying in single file; only seldom did two crafts fly side by side.
>
> The parachutists were fired on while they were still in the air with all available weapons, including rifles and the flak guns which had in the meantime been set up. As a result the fourteenth or fifteenth plane turned off in a northerly direction and dropped its parachutists in the area of Romashki. These parachutists were immediately taken under fire by men of the supply trains, repair teams, and maintenance sections of the 19th Panzer Reconnaissance Battalion. The jumps, which continued for one to one and a half hours, steadily became more irregular, one of the reasons being the swift German counteraction and another the signal lights going aloft on all sides. The parachutists were dropped without any plan. Wherever they landed they were immediately attacked. Those who could took cover in the numerous clefts in the ground. With the parachutists split up in small groups, the fate of the undertaking was

sealed. During the night great numbers of prisoners were brought in. The rest of the parachutists were destroyed the next day.[1]

In all, 120 gliders and their B-25, Il-4 and LI-2 tugs had been assembled on airfields around Kharkov ready to follow up on the jumps but the strong winds dispersed them. Some did manage to link up with the ground forces but by then the operation was already a failure. Between Dubari and Rossava, the Germans reported finding 1,500 parachutes in the first twenty-four hours, as well as 692 Soviet dead and 209 prisoners, whilst near Grushevo, the 3rd Company, 73rd Panzer Grenadier Regiment suffered heavy losses to eliminate an estimated 150 Soviet paratroopers. Once on the ground, the paratroops and whatever equipment they had managed to find were too scattered for any hope of a cohesive action and their lack of radios meant they were unable to establish contact with each other or with 40th Army HQ so instead they began fighting a guerrilla war from the deep forests, operating in approximately thirty-five small groups and gradually regrouping into a corps unit. Around 1,000 paratroopers finally linked up with the advancing forces of the Second Ukrainian Front in mid-November. The attack had been a fiasco and a furious Stalin banned any further attempts at large-scale drops.

Gliders had not played a major role in the Dnieper assault and they do not appear to have been used in other offensive operations. Instead, like their German counterparts, Russian glider pilots found themselves involved in high-risk resupply operations, such as Operation Antifris in November 1942 when a fleet of A-7 and G-11 gliders under the command of Dmitri Koshits were towed from the Medveshii Osero airfield outside Moscow to Saratov and from there to Stalingrad. The delivery of much needed antifreeze for the Soviet tanks enabled the stalled counterattack to continue. More dangerous still, gliders provided the vital link between the Soviet High Command and partisan groups operating deep in enemy territory. The German advances of 1941 had rapidly overrun huge areas of the country, trapping thousands of Russians behind German lines. The remnants of Red Army units, Communist and Komsomol officials and Soviet activists formed the core of what would become a massive partisan movement and, as early as August 1941, Soviet estimates claimed some 231 detachments were already operating. By the end of 1941, 437 'seed' detachments had been formed with over 7,000 guerrillas in Belarus alone.

The difficulties facing the partisans grew as the frontline moved further away, leaving them with virtually no logistical support from the Soviet lines. Without any means of making contact with other groups and short of ammunition, medicine or food, the partisans fought brave but isolated and uncoordinated actions from the forests. Resupply flights by powered aircraft began but, as winter drew in, deep snow meant that they could no longer land. Parachute drops of supplies continued but there was still a need to land some items. Gliders offered a means of doing just that.

A headquarters was set up at Staraja Toropa, north-west of Moscow, commanded by Brigadier-General A Scherbakov and under the operational control of Colonel P Tsybin of the 3rd Air Force to organize resupply flights deep into enemy territory. One flight landed members of the Lithuanian Supreme Soviet over 600 miles behind German lines and between 6 and 20 March 1943, the Kalinin Front was supplied with 50 tonnes of ammunition, 150 demolition specialists, 106 key personnel, five printing presses and sixteen radio stations for the production of propaganda in ninety-six combat missions with transport aircraft towing thirty-five A-7s and thirty G-11s. The pilots were later recovered by light aircraft and returned to Staraja Toropa. The following month, a request from partisans in the Polotsk-Lepel area led to a glider force being assembled at the base and nearby airfields of Lushi and Andreapol but bad weather prevented the operation taking place until the night of 2 May. Six gliders, guided by just four signal fires, landed at Begoml that night and were immediately attacked by waiting German fighters, although their cargoes were unloaded safely later. The next day, a fierce German attack closed the landing site. Another 600 by 200 m area was found and over the next three weeks a train of gliders brought in supplies. When a German anti-partisan operation reached the area around the village of Beresyouka later in the year, it found the remains of 100 burnt-out Russian gliders. It was during this operation that test pilot Sergey Anokhin completed the only known Russian glider extraction when he evacuated two wounded partisan commanders by being towed behind an SB bomber piloted by Yuriy Zhelutov on a 10 m rope and using a frozen lake as a runway.

The Dnieper operation and a second series of partisan resupply missions lasting until April 1944 were the last uses of gliders by the Russians. The pilots were awarded the title of 'Guards Regiment' and reassigned to fighter units until the end of the war but Russia would then maintain a glider force for another twenty years – the first and last country in the world to use them.

Chapter Nine

Into the cauldron:
German operations on the Eastern Front

On 20 March 1941, Sumner Welles, the American Undersecretary of State, informed the Soviet ambassador in Washington of an impending attack on Russia by Germany based on information supplied by the American commercial attaché in Berlin. A month later, Winston Churchill, alerted by intercepts of German messages, sent a personal note to Stalin that reached him on 19 April. US legations in Bucharest and Stockholm reported during the first week of June that an invasion of Russia was coming within a fortnight, information that American Ambassador Laurence Steinhardt passed on to the Soviet foreign minister, Molotov. On 16 June, the German embassy evacuated all non-essential personnel as the Luftwaffe continued to make over 300 reconnaissance flights over Russian territory. Despite this, Stalin's government chose to ignore the warnings and continued to supply its former ally with raw materials right up until 0315hrs on 22 June 1941, when German artillery and air strikes began to hit Russian airfields at the start of Operation Barbarossa. From the outset, it seemed, Moscow failed completely to grasp the dimensions of the catastrophe that was unfolding.

After the initial shock of invasion, the Russians regrouped and began a counteroffensive that would drag on for years. Over the coming months, like all German forces, glider groups frequently fragmented and reformed, making a continuous narrative of German glider operations in Russia difficult to achieve and what follows is merely an overview of the work of dozens of such units in often *ad hoc* formations created for short operations and then reabsorbed into larger squadrons and groups.

Throughout June, three German armies rapidly pushed eastward into Russia. Army Group North punched through the gap between two Soviet armies with the 600 tanks of 4th Panzer Army sweeping towards the Rivers Neman and Dvina – the two largest obstacles en route to Leningrad. By the end of the first day, German tanks crossed the River Neman and had penetrated another fifty miles. A counterattack by 300 Soviet tanks near Rasienai held them up for four days but by the end of the month the Germans had reached the Dvina and were poised to take Leningrad.

Meanwhile, Army Group Centre was headed towards Smolensk and Moscow and, by the end of June, the 2nd and 3rd Panzer Armies had met up after advancing 200 miles into Soviet territory and were now about one-third of the way to Moscow. A vast pincer movement had encircled thirty-two infantry and eight tank divisions in a pocket between Minsk and the Polish border. It was a costly clearing up operation for the Germans but by the end 290,000 Soviet prisoners had been taken with 1,500 guns and 2,500 tanks destroyed, but around another 250,000 Soviet troops managed to escape.

Army Group South, pushing towards Kiev, found their task more difficult. Soviet commanders had quickly reacted to the German attack and mounted a determined resistance by three Soviet armies. On 26 June, as 1st Panzer Army attempted to capture Brody, a massive counterattack by five Soviet mechanized corps with over 1,000 tanks pounced. The four-day-long battle was among the fiercest of the invasion with heavy losses on both sides, but the Germans eventually succeeded in pushing the Russians back, costing the latter their last tank reserves in the south. By the end of the first week, all three German army groups had won major battles and were well on the way to success.

Army Group North, moving into position around Leningrad, now turned its attention towards consolidating the ground it had taken and mopping up resistance. High on its list of priorities was a group of islands in the Gulf of Finland where Russian guns threatened the German supply lines.

The capture of Ösel Island: 24 September 1941

During the advance, the Russian garrisons of the Baltic islands of Vormsi, Muhu, Saaremaa (known to the Germans as Ösel) and Hiiu had been by-passed and left alone. The islands had long been a strategic position, fought over in 1790 during the Russo-Finnish war and again in October 1917 when the Imperial German Army launched Operation Albion – an amphibious assault by the Nordkorps on the seaward side which ultimately ended up capturing 20,000 Russian POWs and established a base for the capture of Tallinn. In 1941, the islands were estimated by German intelligence to be garrisoned by approximately 15,000 Russians and held ten coastal and sixteen mobile batteries of artillery under the overall command of Major-General A B Elisseyev. The batteries threatened the air and sea approaches to the ports of Riga and Pernau but also provided an airfield from which several bomber raids on Berlin had been launched between 7 August and 4 September. Saaremaa is approximately 1000 square miles of flat, sandy and sparsely populated terrain connected to the smaller island of Muhu by a two and a half mile causeway. It held coastal batteries and the 3rd Independent Rifle Brigade commanded by Berzarin, with support from the 79th Rifle Regiment on Muhu. Elsewhere, the second largest island at around half the size of Saaremaa, Hiiumaa was held by two Rifle Battalions and another two companies on Vormsi to the north-east. In all, the Russians could muster some 24,000 defenders.

Operation Beowulf, the German assault on the islands, was essentially a reverse of the 1917 attack, with 18th Army capturing Tallinn first and then using the Estonian mainland to mount their attack against Saaremaa. The operation was held up by heavy fighting in the 18th Army area and the Kriegsmarine's difficulty in assembling amphibious craft but by September, with the islands by and large cut off from the mainland for ten weeks, an attack force was ready.

On 10 September, Vormsi Island, closest to the mainland, fell quickly to an attack by elements of the 217th Infantry Division. In an attempt to make Elisseyev think the Germans were simply repeating the plan for the 1917 seaborne attack, Operation Sudwind was launched on the 13th when the Cruisers *Leipzig*, *Koln* and *Emden*, together with a force of minesweepers and torpedo boats, feinted to the south and west of Saaremaa. At the same time, their Finnish allies undertook Operation Nordwind off the north shore of Hiiumaa island with two Monitors, two armed Icebreakers and a variety of smaller vessels. During this phase of the operation, the Finnish flagship, the ten inch gun monitor *Ilmarinen* struck two mines and sank in minutes with a loss of 271 crewmen but the plan had worked and had diverted attention away to the coasts when the real attack came early next morning.

On 5 July, ten DFS 230 gliders of 6./LLG 1 (6 Squadron, Air Landing Group 1) had left their base at Halberstadt and made their way to a variety of airfields before arriving at Pernau as 'Sudwind' began. Here the glider commander, Leutnant Flucke, met with Hauptman Benesch of the 16th Brandenburger Regiment to discuss an operation against the coastal guns of Fort Kübassaare on Saaremaa. Five gliders carrying pioneers would land near the coast and eliminate the guns there whilst another eighty pioneers with heavy weapons would land from a force of eighteen fishing boats and attack the coastal batteries. Other positions identified from aerial photos would be attacked by Me110 'Destroyers' from II/ZG26. As the Brandenburgers attacked, the 61st Infantry Division under Haenicke and comprising the 151st, 162nd and 176th Infantry Regiments and Auflarungs Abteilung 161 were to launch an amphibious assault on Muhu island at 0400hrs on 24 July and would link up with the airborne later in the day.

The five gliders, under the command of Unteroffizier Haag, with pilots Thielmann, Rösler, Kommander and Hertwig, lifted off on schedule from Pernau for a forty-five-minute flight through low cloud and poor visibility. Over the target, the gliders released at 400 m, each following their leader to a smooth landing without any resistance from the Russians but coming to rest around 800 m from where they expected to be. Rösler asked Haag why and was told that Benesch had told him to land there but Haag didn't know why. On the way in, no one had seen the boats bringing the rest of the Brandenburgers and now they were further from their objective than expected. Rösler realized things were not going to plan. In fact, heavy seas were hampering efforts on all the islands. The 151st Infantry Regiment took 180 boats and AA 161 another 90 to cross the six-mile sound but as the 151st IR landed at Kuivastu the first wave in four six-man boats missed their intended beach by a mile as a result of strong winds and currents and the second wave got so disorientated that they circled back to the Estonian mainland. The pioneers headed for Saaremaa had been forced back by rough seas and strong currents.

After the initial surprise, the Russians reacted. As the group set out for its objective it came under heavy fire and was soon under fire from three sides as trucks brought Russian reinforcements to the bunkers around the battery. The Germans began to withdraw towards the coast, the only route left to them, and within minutes the thirty men still capable of fighting had formed a 'hedgehog' defence as the Russians pushed to within 400 m of the landing site. For the rest of the day the force remained pinned down among reeds along the coast. At around 1600hrs, a message reached them from a circling Me110 to 'hang on, the boats will attempt a landing'. The glider pilots had rescued the life rafts from their aircraft and now got ready to use them to reach the expected boats but none appeared. Air support by Ju88s and naval gunfire support held off Russian attacks until, at around 1800hrs, three Ju52s appeared and dropped nine rubber dinghies, each designed to carry four men. Four of these, together with all the

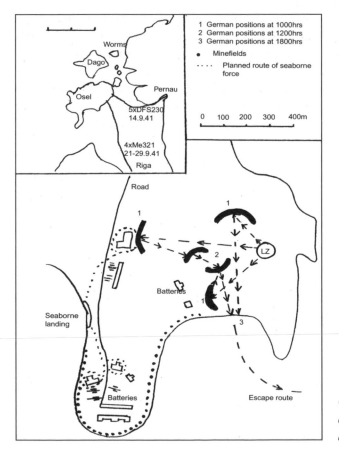

Osel Island: sketch map of the glider force assault and movements.

paddles, dropped into Russian hands but five were recovered and the men were told to use the dinghies and head for Muhu where, at around 2300hrs, they would be picked up by three fishing boats.

At 1900hrs, with darkness falling, the last Me110 left. Hauptman Benesch and some of his pioneers scouted the beach to find an area where they would be able to put to sea. Using the inflated dinghies as stretchers for the wounded, the survivors dragged themselves 300 m to the beach under sporadic rifle and cannon fire as they moved. All the boats were damaged and overloaded and the unwounded men in each boat were forced to take turns to swim alongside in the freezing water as others baled. Lacking paddles, the men had to use their hands to row and a spade as a rudder. The strong currents that had hampered the sea landing now pushed the boats back towards shore and it was only with great effort that the group reached open sea after jettisoning everything possible. At around 0700hrs, a ship was spotted and a white flare fired. Within an hour, three cutters arrived to pick the men of four boats up but the fifth had drifted back to shore and the nine men in it were captured. They were dragged in front of the Soviet Commissar who ordered them to be shot. Two, though, were not hit, managed to escape and were picked up later by seaplane. During the battle, Haag was shot through the neck and eleven of the pioneers were killed, with another nine wounded. Muhu fell the following day and the 151st IR attacked across the causeway to Saaremaa against a now disorganised resistance. A beachhead was finally secured on the island by 1100 on the 16th but it was not until the 21st that the town of Kuresaare fell, by which time Me321 Gigant gliders of GS1 (Special Squadron 1) under the command of Oberleutnant Melzer had undertaken their first combat mission, flying in 20,000 litres of fuel and four tonnes of ammunition to support the ongoing battle. More followed the next day and four of the giant gliders would take part in the operation over the next week.

The following day the Soviets retreated into the Sorve Peninsula, a one and a quarter mile wide isthmus to the south and began a last ditch defence with around 15,000 men. The assault on the isthmus started on the 23rd and fighting continued for four days. On the 27th, two Me110 tugs of GS1 were hit by Russian flak whilst towing the lumbering Gigant but that evening the 151st IR, with heavy Luftwaffe close air support from I/KG77 and II/ZG26 and naval gunfire from Cruisers in Operation West Storm, began a final push. The Sorve peninsula finally fell on 5 October with the capture of 5,000 POWs although another 1,500 Russians managed to escape by sea to the island of Hiiumaa. A week later, after another naval feint (Operation East Prussia) the 176th IR, supported by fire from the cruiser *Koln*, landed on the east side of Hiiumaa island at 0500hrs at the start of Operation Siegfried. That afternoon, AA161 and the 151st IR landed on the southern side of the island and Hiiumaa fell after another nine days. Only 570 of the original 24,000 Russian defenders of the Baltic Islands remained. By the end, the operations against the Baltic islands had captured around 15,000 POWs and 200 guns at a cost to the Germans of 2,850 casualties.

At the end of June there were very few Soviet soldiers between the Germans and Moscow and the entire Soviet army in European Russia was down to 800,000 men and 770 tanks. By the autumn, though, the situation had changed radically. On 5 October, Stalin received a radio message from his spy Richard Sorge in Tokyo that the Japanese would go to war with the United States in the next few months. Realizing that the huge army currently based in eastern Siberia and Outer Mongolia to deter Japan was no longer needed, Stalin ordered twelve divisions with around 250,000 men, 1,700 tanks and 1,500 aircraft to come to the defence of Moscow. Two days later, the first snows began to fall. It melted quickly, but was followed by heavy rains. 'The roads rapidly became nothing but canals of bottomless mud,' Guderian later wrote, 'along which our vehicles could only advance at a snail's pace and with great wear to the engines.'

Then, on 2 November, the weather began to improve. A light frost permitted the troops to become mobile again as artillery pieces were dragged out of the mud and trucks could roll once more. So confident of quick victory was Hitler that he had not prepared for even the possibility of winter warfare in the Soviet Union. The entire German plan assumed that within five weeks the German troops would have full control of the country once the Red Army collapsed. Logistical support would then only be needed to meet the fuel requirements of the few mobile units required to occupy the defeated state. Despite this confidence, the German army suffered more than 734,000 casualties (about 23 per cent of its average strength of 3,200,000 troops) during the first five months of the invasion, and on 27 November 1941, General Eduard Wagner, the Quartermaster General of the German Army, reported that 'We are at the end of our resources in both personnel and material. We are about to be confronted with the dangers of deep winter.' German commanders called for a final great exertion to reach Moscow in an offensive that would go down in the annals of the German army as the 'die Flucht nach vorn' (the flight to the front) – a desperate attempt to get the troops into the shelter of Moscow before the onset of winter.

The three German armies had entered Russia with over 3,500 tanks but only around one-fifth of the force was motorized. The 600,000 large western European horses the Germans relied on for supply and artillery movement did not cope well with the freezing weather, unlike the small ponies used by the Red Army which were much better adapted to the climate and could even scrape the icy ground with their hooves to dig up the weeds beneath. German troops had the equipment for winter conditions, but the severely overstrained transport network failed to reach the men who needed it most. Precious fuel that was difficult to resupply went to keeping fires burning as soldiers had to pack newspapers into their jackets to stay warm in temperatures falling to record levels of around -30°C (-22°F). Then the Russians attacked.

The newly arrived troops from Siberia, supported by wide-tracked T-34 tanks, had no difficulty in coping with the mud and snow and their attacks began to penetrate deep into German lines. The counterattack hit the worn-out

German divisions at their moment of greatest weakest and everywhere the Germans began to fall back. Writing of the disaster of Napoleon's 1812 retreat from Moscow, Swiss military analyst Antoine-Henri Jomini commented that: 'Russia is a country which is easy to get into, but very difficult to get out of.' Mindful of the fate of Napoleon's troops, Hitler issued what became known as the 'stand or die' order, demanding that German forces fight 'breakwater' actions to stem the tide of Soviet counterattacks. It prevented a rout, but resulted in heavy casualties from battle and cold and, as winter set in, the already over-stretched supply network virtually collapsed. Vehicles and horses struggled to make progress in deep mud and the Luftwaffe assumed more and more of the burden. The Me321 Gigant gliders, originally designed to support the invasion of Britain, were now redeployed to the Russian front with each army group being allocated a squadron of six of the massive aircraft; Sonderstaffel GS1 under Oberleutnant Melzer had been sent with its Me110 towplanes to Riga to support Army Group North with a replacement unit (Sonderstaffel GS2) under Oberleutnant Baumann moving to join GS1 at Merseburg in January 1942. Army Group Centre was supported by Oberleutnant Pohl's Sonderstaffel GS4 operating out of Winniza and Army Group South by Sonderstaffel GS22 at Orscha-Sud under the command of Oberleutnant Schäfer. Along with the Gigants, the Gotha Go242 glider had entered service in 1941. The GO, as it was known, could carry twenty-three equipped soldiers and its size allowed it to be converted into a mobile workshop to maintain aircraft at rudimentary airstrips or into a field medical unit. DFS 230 gliders were also used to transport ground crews and every Stuka squadron was allocated a glider (which could be towed by the Ju87). Flying supplies in and wounded out, gliders became a routine part of the aerial resupply operation but as the Russians attacked in a series of en-circlement movements, they found a more demanding role. The glider war in Russia would become a series of heroic but desperate flights by glider pilots into siege after siege, each more dangerous than the last and all based on the early success achieved by the Luftwaffe at the small town of Suchinitschi.

The Suchinitschi resupply flights:
December 1941–January 1942

On 29 December 1941, part of Army Group Centre's 216th Infantry Division found themselves outflanked and withdrew into a defensive perimeter around the village of Suchinitschi, about 230 kilometres south-east of Smolensk where five thousand soldiers with another thousand wounded were dug in but trapped in an area seven kilometres long by three wide. VIII Fliegerkorps command ordered a resupply of desperately needed ammunition and so on 16 January Oberfeldwebel Held set out in a Go242 but was forced back when bad weather prevented the tow finding the landing zone. A second, more successful attempt was made by Unteroffizier Ulmer carrying 120 rounds of 10.5 cm heavy artillery shells, small arms and ammunition and a powerful radioset. Green flares fired by the infantry guided him safely onto the landing zone and, half an hour later, another GO arrived. Two days later, two more GOs were attacked by Russian fighters as they approached but were saved by their Me109 escorts. Over the next few days, five gliders would land in the encirclement whilst a sixth landed in Russian lines when its cable broke (although the crew managed to evade capture and reach safety). Panzer forces broke through the siege on 24 January and the glider crews returned to their Smolensk base, warmly congratulated by the officers of the division, as were the crew of the sole Ju52 that had managed to land inside the perimeter to evacuate the wounded. The operation had been a complete success but, even as Suchinitschi was being relieved, the Russian 3rd Shock and 11th Armies had forced a breach of German lines on the Waldai plateau and reached the Lovat River via Ostachkov. The Russian counteroffensive was well under way and the resupply work was not over. More encirclements were to come.

The Demjansk 'Kessel' (Cauldron) resupply, 18 February–19 May 1942

The Germans had not expected the Red Army to be capable of launching a wide offensive and the sudden attack through a previously quiet sector took them by surprise. General Kurochkin, commanding the Soviet North-Western Front,

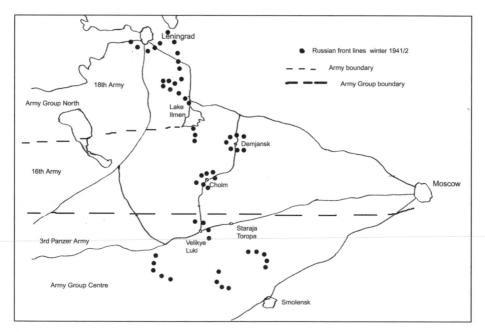

Eastern Front 1941/2: main areas of glider operations.

had been tasked with breaking out of his position south of Lake Ilmen and advancing directly west through Staraya Russa to split the German 18th and 16th Armies in support of the Volkhov and Leningrad Fronts in order to break the siege of Leningrad. This was to be followed by a thrust by the 33rd, 3rd and 4th Shock Armies in a south-westerly direction towards Vitebsk with the aim of encircling the German Army Group Centre. As they pushed south, the Russians exploited every opportunity, overrunning the forward two regiments of the German 123rd Infantry Division, which was covering a line of thirty kilometres and capturing the vital supply depot at Toropets. Every available German reserve was rushed to the area by train and aircraft to create strongpoints in an attempt to break up the Soviet attack. The 81st Infantry Division, a reserve formation, was brought forward by rail at the end of December and disembarked at Toropets and Andreapol. The 189th Infantry Regiment under Colonel Hohmeyer, along with the 2nd Battalion of Artillery Regiment 181 and the 3rd Company of the Engineer Battalion 181 then moved up to Okhvat where, on 14 January, it was encircled and completely destroyed so quickly that their presence was not even added to German situation maps. Over a thousand bodies were later found in the forest around Okhvat and just forty survivors from the artillery battalion made it back to the German lines.

On 8 February the Soviet operation encircled the Germans at Demjansk, trapping around 100,000 men of the 2nd and 10th Army Corps. The garrison, under General der Infanterie Walter Graf von Brockdorff-Ahlefeldt, commander of the 2nd Army Corps, prepared defences and requested urgent resupply to enable them to hold off the repeated Russian attacks. Assured by the Luftwaffe that the pocket could indeed be supplied with its daily requirement of 270 tons by air, Hitler ordered that the surrounded divisions hold their positions until relieved and the task was assigned to the First Air Force with three groups of Junkers Ju52 transport planes and their DFS 230 and Go242 cargo gliders. The chief supply officer of the air force formed a special air transport staff under Colonel Fritz Morzik which, in liaison with the army, carried out the supply operations in accordance with requests received from the encircled units.[1]

The Demjansk *Kessel* (literally meaning 'cauldron') was a pocket containing two landing fields capable of handling Ju52 flights and a number of drops were made by parachute and supported by special bomber squadrons dropping additional supply canisters. The weather remained clear and the resupply operations were generally very successful but used up most of the available Luftwaffe transport and much of their bomber capability. On their return flights, the carrying capacity of the aircraft was taxed to the limit with heavy loads of sick and wounded, official and soldiers' mail, and sometimes even with equipment in need of repair. Few planes were lost to enemy action but the rate of attrition from wear and tear was very high, requiring constant replacement of the transport planes and the increased demands by other sectors of the front along with the low rate of production meant that it was even necessary at times to use training aircraft to fill the gaps that developed. Between 18 February and 19 May, when the siege was finally lifted, the Germans transported an average of 302 tons of supplies per day, flew some 30,500 men into the pocket and 35,400 wounded men out in over 32,427 missions at a cost of 265 aircraft and 385 Luftwaffe crewmen, including two group commanders. It was a stunning achievement but, as Morzik later commented, it effectively set the Luftwaffe up to fail by raising expectations about the feasibility of aerial resupply in every situation. Round-the-clock flights by bombers dropping their containers at the lowest possible altitudes were costly in aircraft losses and put the personnel to a severe test, but worse, during February alone, I Air Corps had flown 1,725 bomber sorties in direct support of ground operations and 800 supply missions for the Army. By March, the supply missions had taken up 1,104 bomber flights, diverting them from their primary offensive tasks to join the improvised supply operation. After the Demyansk pocket was relieved, top-level army experts concluded that the air supply operations had been of decisive importance in enabling the encircled forces to hold out. Now, in the coming months, they would be expected to repeat their success on ever greater scales in very different circumstances.

The Cholm Kessel, 21 January–5 May 1942

As the Russians encircled Demjansk, other units pushed another hundred kilometres to the south where the German 39th Corps was being forced back to the south-west of Cholm (or Kholm), a small town in a swampy area to the south of Lake Ilmen. Built where the Rivers Lovat and Kunya met and a crossroads for the major north–south and east–west roads, Cholm was a major transport hub at the boundary between Army Groups North and Centre and provided a jumping off point for the attacks on both Moscow and Leningrad. It was also a key point in the land bridge between Demjansk and the small city of Velikye Luki, located further down the Lovat River. Velikye Luki had a prewar population of around 30,000 and was one of the most westernized of Russian cities – the point where the wide West European railway gauge was changed to that of the narrower East European network. Control of Velikye Luki meant control of the supply routes east and west.

Russian ski units cut the road linking Cholm with Velikye Luki on 21 January, forcing units of 39th Corps to the west back into the town where, with elements of the 123rd and 218th infantry Divisions, Reconnaissance Battalion 218, a Luftwaffe field regiment and the 65th Reserve Police Battalion, around 5,500 men reformed as 'Kampfgruppe Scherer' under the command of Generalmajor Theodor Scherer and prepared to hold out against a massing Russian assault.

The first serious Russian attacks against Scherer's men began two days later when, from all four sides of the perimeter, infantry supported by tanks probed for a weak point to exploit. Fortunately for the Germans, the ground conditions prevented the Russians using heavy armour and although the attacks managed to gain some ground in the north-western part of the town, they were held every-where else. During the day, 200 mountain troops from the 10th Machine Gun Battalion joined the Kampfgruppe after fighting through the Russian lines, providing men for a counterattack that managed to recapture most of the lost ground.

Heavy Russian artillery bombardments quickly reduced most of the buildings within Cholm to rubble and there was little shelter for the defenders against temperatures that dropped to almost -40°C at times. Trenches had to be blown out of the ground using explosives and most movement could only be made using Russian Panje horses and sleds. Frostbite became commonplace and, more seri-ously, diseases such as typhus and dysentery began to appear in the unsanitary conditions. The small field hospital was forced to move into bunkers after its first base burnt down during an artillery strike.

Outside support came from the artillery of 'Gruppe Uckermann', sited around eight kilometres west of the town around the villages of Tarakonovo and Dubrowo and directed by a radio link to artillery observers in the city church who were able to call down 1,000 rounds per day in support of the forces inside the pocket. Air support was also available using a kilometre-wide meadow to the west of Cholm as a landing strip which enabled Ju52s to evacuate some 700 wounded men in the early stages of the encirclement. Soon, however, pressure on the Germans forced them back and the landing strip became part of no man's land. Even then, Ju52s risked landing during quiet periods, drawing the inevitable artillery, mortar and small arms fire but managing to deliver vital supplies. In the middle of February, one attempted landing alone cost the loss of five aircraft and, on 13 February, Luftflotte 1 signalled the General Staff that 'artillery and mortar fire on the landing strip resulting in heavy losses in trans-port aircraft was a compelling block to transport landings in Cholm. We ask [Luftwaffe Staff Headquarters] to cause LS [lastensegler = glider] use to be stepped up.'[2] Immediately, the commander of Luftwaffe Transport Command in the area, Colonel Morzik, ordered gliders to be moved to Pleskau under the command of GO-Kommando/Luftflotte 1 (GO Unit, 1st Air Fleet). The first Go242 glider, flown by pilots Seidel and Jauch, had landed in Cholm on 16 February and was followed by more at a rate of two or three gliders a day flying in weapons, ammunition, medical equipment and other supplies.

On 23 February, the Russians launched their heaviest attack of the siege with an entire infantry division supported by tanks committed to the assault. With just a few 37 mm Pak and one 50 mm Pak anti-tank gun, the Germans struggled to fight off the armour, firing at almost point-blank range into the well-armoured Russian tanks in order to have any effect. As the first attack broke down, the Russians regrouped and pressed home a second until eventually they fought their way into the eastern outskirts of the town itself. Over the next two days eighteen more attempts to break the perimeter were held back with the support of Luftwaffe ground attack aircraft and General Uckermann's artillery.

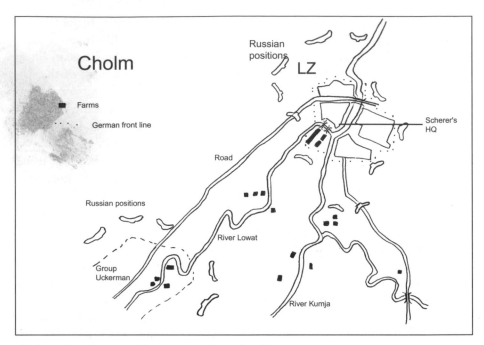

Cholm: sketch map of the area and Landing Zones.

The next day, Luftwaffe Ju52s again landed to bring in reinforcements and evacuate the wounded but Russian pressure on the landing strip was now so intense that aircraft losses reached 30 per cent of those committed. Further flights were suspended by the Luftwaffe General Staff. The small size of the pocket meant that parachute drops risked losing supplies to the Russians so supply canisters were being dropped by special bomber groups equipped with He111s and even, where the lines were particularly close, by Ju87 Stukas. For heavy supplies, though, the only option was by glider. The suspension of flights by Ju52 meant that, from then on, glider flights into Cholm would be a one-way trip for their crews.

Between 9 and 12 March, a complete infantry company was flown into the pocket and one of the passengers later recalled his journey. Early on the morning of 21 April 1942, twenty men were taken to a glider on the airfield where a Luftwaffe officer assured them that they could expect a nice quiet trip and that everything was under control. They sat facing each other on benches along the sides of the aircraft with ammunition piled between them and nervous banter gave way to silence as they prepared for their first flight. A jolt was felt through the glider and slowly it began to move. The engine noise of the JU tug rose and through the windows they could see the earth scurrying past. The stern of the glider lifted and then, with a jump, it began rising rapidly. Another jerk as the wheels were jettisoned and it climbed to around 500 m. As the tension eased, there was laughter but the passengers knew they were in business. The glider

> hung quietly behind the tugplane and I could make out a second glider and there was a fighter I was told was an Me109 but I couldn't see it, only the light blue of the sky. The pilot shouted something unintelligible and pointed with his thumb below us. We dropped quickly, like an elevator in a store as the Russians opened up with machine gun and rifle fire. I could feel the excitement rising but there was nothing to be seen out of the window and there was much to do . . . Through the cockpit we could see the JU banking away to the left, then the pilot called 'We're landing!'. We hit the ground and were jolted around as we landed with a crash and the aircraft splintered. I was sitting tight and when we stopped jumped out and lay stunned in a small bunker. It was a comparatively good arrival, no-one was killed.[3]

On 16 March, GO pilot Werner Sinhart flew from Riga to Pleskau where his glider was loaded with 1,000 kg of Teller mines, five mortars, two hundred-weight of chocolate and some woolsacks – 'and then eighteen men climbed in'. All flights into Cholm were now taking place in the early morning or at dusk to reduce the risks of effective anti-aircraft fire and Sinhart left at 1645hrs. After flying for eighty minutes, the glider skimmed over the outlying German positions at a height of just 20 m. The glider quickly put down and Sinhart watched the tug disappear. In the half-darkness, he saw a horse sleigh coming towards him. Anxiously he wondered whether they were Russians and was enormously relieved to find them to be Germans – his precious cargo was safe. At that point, he had no idea that he would be stuck there for the next 'fifty-one often troubled and sorrowful days' until the encirclement was broken. Two weeks later, 29 March was a bad day for Sinhart. His friend Gunther Langmann was landing close by when he hit a telegraph pole at about two metres off the ground. The glider rolled left and broke its back, killing six pioneers but Langmann survived and was rescued, seriously injured, from the wreckage.

On 1 May, another large Russian attack was launched against the pocket, which by now had shrunk to less than 1,000 square metres and the defenders were almost overrun as Russian forces came within a hundred metres of the eastern bank of the Lovat River. For Sinhart and his fellow glider pilots, now sheltering as best they could and fighting alongside the infantry, it was a desperate time. Uninterrupted fire from artillery and Stalin Organs (multi-barrelled rocket launchers) kept them pinned down between 1 and 3 May. Glider pilot Unteroffizier Langguth was working in front of his bunker when he was hit in the abdomen and knee. He died very quickly. Max Pfeiffer was next door and was hit by an incendiary shell, and a house facing Sinhart where forty-five wounded men were sheltering was hit and burned down, killing everyone inside.

The outlook for the wounded was bleak. By the end of April, there were around 1,500 injured men but no means of evacuating them and it was only reinforcement by a team of volunteer medics that prevented a total collapse of the medical system.

Then, on the morning of 5 May, lead elements Grenadier Regiment 411, commanded by Oberstleutnant Tromm and supported by Sturmgeschutze assault guns and Luftwaffe ground attack aircraft, broke the encirclement. Rapidly reinforced, the garrison was replaced and taken out of the line after a 105-day siege but it would be another month before the front was stabilized in that area. Only 1,200 were left of the original 5,500 men trapped in Cholm back in January. In recognition of his command of the defence of Cholm, General Scherer was awarded the Knight's Cross. On 1 July 1942, Hitler ordered the award of a special decoration consisting of a shield emblazoned with a eagle with outstretched wings holding in its talons an Iron Cross with a swastika and the words 'CHOLM' and '1942' below it to 'all who were involved in the defence of the city of Cholm'. Sinhart and the surviving glider crews were among the proud recipients.

Across the Eastern Front, the power of the Russian winter offensive had caused panic among the German army and, as a result, a number of senior German commanders were dismissed. Field Marshal von Brauchitsch, Commander in Chief of the Army, was formally removed by Hitler on 19 December 1941, who then assumed the position himself and ruthlessly enforced his order to stand and fight. Slowly, as the German army recovered during the spring of 1942, the front stabilized and it could be argued that Hitler had saved the army from total collapse during those crucial months. Unfortunately for the Germans, the success of his inflexible approach and of the air resupply of the trapped 'cauldrons' clouded his judgement – setting the precedent for all future crises.

Among the commands replaced by Hitler was that of the 6th Army, part of Army Group South. General Paulus, a staff officer at German Army High Command was recommended for the post by Field Marshal von Reichenau, the former commander of 6th Army and newly appointed commander of Army Group South and duly given the command on 6 January 1942. Paulus had no experience at this level, had never even commanded a division or corps and even Hitler expressed reservations about the appointment, but Paulus had a reputation as an exceptional operations officer and had been responsible for evaluating the options for Operation Barbarossa. Whatever his paper ability, as a commanding officer he lacked initiative and could be indecisive – character traits that would bring serious repercussions on his army as they became embroiled in the war's bloodiest battles.

The Stalingrad airlift

By late spring, 1942, the Germans were once again ready to begin their offensive but by now, plans to attack Moscow directly had been shelved. Army Group Centre had suffered too many losses to be able to take on the task just yet. German military doctrine insisted on attacking where least expected so that rapid gains could be made and an attack on Moscow was seen as too predictable by many, including Hitler. Aware that the United States had entered the war, Hitler wanted to end the fighting on the Eastern Front or at least minimize it before America became involved in the war in Europe. So, acting against the advice of his generals, Hitler suddenly shifted the main German effort south. Army Group South's 6th and 17th Armies and the 1st and 4th Panzer Armies were ordered to sprint forward through the southern Russian steppes into the Caucasus and capture the vital Soviet oilfields in a summer offensive codenamed *Fall Blau* (Case Blue). In 1941, Army Group South had conquered the Ukraine and was well positioned for the offensive. Hitler now intervened, ordering Army Group South to be split into two separate forces. Army Group South (A), under the command of Paul Ludwig Ewald von Kleist, was to continue advancing south towards the Caucasus as originally planned, with the 17th Army and 1st Panzer Army. Meanwhile, Army Group South (B), under General Maximilian von Weichs would use Friedrich Paulus's 6th Army and Hermann Hoth's 4th Panzer Army to move east towards the Volga and the city of Stalingrad.

After delays to allow units required for the offensive to disengage from besieging Sebastopol in the Crimea, the attack finally got under way on 28 June. It started well, with Soviet forces offering little resistance and the vast empty steppes proving ideal tank country. Soon, disordered Russian troops were streaming eastward as attempts to form defensive lines were quickly outflanked and destroyed in two major pockets, the first north-east of Kharkov on 2 July and a second around Millerovo and Rostov Oblast a week later. Three days later, the city of Voronezh fell to the Hungarian 2nd Army and the German 4th Panzer Division.

This initial advance by 6th Army was so successful that Hitler again intervened, ordering the 4th Panzer Division south to join Army Group South (A). In an area of few roads, thousands of vehicles of both the 4th and 6th Army ground to a halt in a massive traffic jam that would take up to a week to clear. With the advance now slowed, Hitler again changed his mind and reassigned the 4th Panzer Army back to the attack on Stalingrad. By late July the Germans had pushed the Soviets across the Don River and, together with their Italian, Hungarian and Romanian allies, had established a line only a few dozen kilometres from the city. Originally, Stalingrad did not feature significantly in the German operational plans. The intention had been simply to reduce it by artillery and air bombardment to destroy its armaments production and the harbour on the Volga. The capture of the city would now serve a useful military purpose in securing the left flank of the German armies as they advanced into the Caucasus but the fact that the city bore Joseph Stalin's name would also make its fall a potentially fatal propaganda coup against the Russians. When reports indicated that the attacks had progressed better than expected, the plans were yet again changed and the city became a focal point for the German effort.

Stalin obviously also had his own interest in defending the city that bore his name, having himself played a prominent role in the Soviet defence of Tsaritsyn (as Stalingrad was then known) during the Russian Civil War. The fact was that, with panzers sweeping across huge tracts of Russia, Stalin was fast running out of time and resources and he knew that luring the Germans into a drawn-out battle in a large urban area dominated by short-range small arms fire and artillery would disadvantage German forces geared up to highly mobile operations. By the end, though, over and above the actual strategic significance of the battle, for both Hitler and Stalin, Stalingrad would come to be about prestige. The Soviet command transferred aircraft from the entire country to the Stalingrad region and moved their strategic reserves from the Moscow area to the lower Volga. On 27 July, Stalin's Order No. 227 decreed that anyone who retreated or otherwise left their positions without orders could be summarily shot. Every able Soviet citizen in the city was told to pick up a rifle and defend Stalingrad or die, with the slogan 'not one step back!' 'Workers militias' made up of those not directly involved in war production became frontline troops, with tanks produced in local factories driven directly from the factory floor to the frontline, often without paint or even gunsights, by volunteer crews of factory workers.

For the next few months, German and Russian troops fought a bitter hand-to-hand battle for control of the ruins of the city. By the end of August, as Army Group South (B) finally reached the Volga north of Stalingrad, the life expectancy of newly arrived Russian reinforcements to the city had dropped to less than twenty-four hours. The strain on both military commanders was immense and Paulus developed an uncontrollable tic in his eye whilst Chuikov experienced an outbreak of eczema so severe that his hands were bandaged completely. Neither side appeared to be making any significant gains until, in the autumn, Soviet generals Aleksandr Vasilyevskiy and Georgy Zhukov concentrated massive Soviet forces in the steppes to the north and south of the city. The German northern flank, defended by Italian, Hungarian and Romanian units that suffered from inferior equipment and low morale, was particularly vulnerable and the plan was to keep the Germans pinned down then strike the overstretched and weakly defended German flanks, thus surrounding the Germans inside Stalingrad. Operation 'Uranus' would be launched in conjunction with Operation Mars, against Army Group Centre and was similar to that used by Zhukov three years earlier at Khalkin Gol when a double envelopment manoeuvre had destroyed the Japanese 23rd Division. The offensive began on 19 November.

Three complete Soviet Armies, the 1st Guards, 5th Tank and the 21st Army, with a total of eighteen infantry divisions, eight tank brigades, two motorized brigades, six cavalry divisions and one anti-tank brigade crashed into the northern flank of German 6th Army where the thinly spread, outnumbered and poorly equipped Romanian 3rd Army mounted a spectacular but ultimately futile day-long defence. The following day, to the south of Stalingrad, the infantry of the Romanian IV Corps collapsed almost immediately as a second Soviet offensive using two armies hit them. Both Soviet forces raced west in a pincer movement that met two days later near the town of Kalach and closed the ring around Stalingrad, trapping about 250,000 German, Romanian, Croatian and other foreign volunteers inside the pocket along with around 10,000 surviving Soviet civilians and several thousand Soviet POWs captured earlier by the Germans. Nearly 50,000 German soldiers from 6th Army were pushed aside outside the pocket and the Soviet units formed two defensive fronts, facing 'inward', to defend against breakout attempts and another facing 'outward' to defend against any German relief attempt.

In September, Hitler had declared that the German army would never leave Stalingrad. At a hastily gathered meeting on 20 November at his Berchtesgaden retreat in Bavaria, he met with Colonel-General Hans Jeschonnek, Chief of Staff of the Luftwaffe, and asked if an operation like that at Demjansk could be mounted. Jeschonnek replied, without much thought, that the Luftwaffe could supply the 6th Army with an 'air bridge' provided that suitable airfields could be found and every available transport was drafted into service, allowing the Germans in the city to fight on while a relief force was assembled. Two days later, Goering announced, 'Mein Fuehrer, the air bridge to 6th Army in Stalingrad is personally guaranteed by me. You can rely on the Luftwaffe.' Later, Goering would claim that, if he had not agreed, the Luftwaffe, and especially Goering himself, would have been blamed for the fall of Stalingrad.[4]

The situation at Stalingrad was very different to that at Demjansk. That operation had supplied a corps-sized unit in good weather and in an area without any significant Russian fighter cover. General Oberst Wolfram von Richthofen, head of the 4th Air Fleet (Luftflotte 4), tried in vain to overturn the decision to attempt to resupply the city by air, arguing that the resources to do so were simply not available. Even if every Ju52 aircraft from all fronts were assembled for the operation, including the ones from Europe and North Africa where they could not be spared, only 750 aircraft would have been made available and success would still not have been guaranteed. General Paulus had already reported that, in order to defend Stalingrad, his army would require 650–1,000 tons of supplies per day depending on the scale of activities expected of them and whether the 50,000 horses within the pocket could be used as meat or if fodder also had to be flown in for them. In fact, a supply of between 300 and 350 tons per day may have been enough, but even these levels could not be achieved. The 6th Army, deep in Russian territory, was by now closer to the borders of India than to their own homeland and supply lines were stretched to breaking point.

The air supply mission failed almost immediately as many German transport aircraft fell to heavy Soviet anti-aircraft fire and fighter attacks. The winter weather was atrocious and flying only possible for a few hours or a few days in succession, restricting not only the transport aircraft but also the fighters protecting them and the Stukas and bombers attempting to destroy enemy tanks and gun emplacements on the supply routes into the city. Even if the weather at the airfields outside the city was clear or passable, the airfields within might be fog-bound or covered with deep overnight snow and then the aircraft had to turn back. If the airfields in Stalingrad were open, fog and storms forced aircraft to remain on the ground at the jump-off points and then bitter complaints from the defenders came thick and fast. The aircrews flew whenever possible, always dicing with death, especially at landing strips which were often blocked by crashed aircraft, shell craters and snow drifts, and losses were high.

As long as there were airfields available as jump-off points outside the city and landing sites inside it there was still hope, but it did not last long. One by one the Russians wrested the airfields from the Germans until, by January 1943, the Luftwaffe was forced to rely on air drops of supplies, which did not always reach their targets. The Russians constructed decoy drop areas complete with correct flare patterns that lured German aircraft to drop supplies outside German-controlled areas. Often, the bomb canisters converted to carry rations dropped by He111 or Stukas disappeared into snow drifts or the soldiers were simply too weak to carry them back to their trenches.

Despite the best efforts of the aircrews, only around 10 per cent of the required amount of supplies could actually be delivered. Mistakes were common (one aircraft arrived carrying 20 tonnes of vodka and a consignment of summer uniforms) and pilots were shocked when they managed to land to find starving soldiers too exhausted to unload the food. By November 1942, the German soldiers in the Stalingrad pocket were rationed to 200g (about 7oz) bread, 200g horsemeat (including bones), 30g cheese, 30g fat and 3 cigarettes. By mid-January 1943, this already insufficient diet for fighting under extreme winter conditions had to be cut drastically by to just 75g bread, 200g horsemeat, 24g vegetables, 12g fat, 11g sugar and 1 cigarette.[5] In a gesture of solidarity, back in Berlin General Zeitzler limited himself to their level of rations but after a few weeks had become so emaciated that Hitler personally ordered him to start eating regular meals again.

As all available Ju52s headed east in November 1942, glider squadrons received their orders to join the airlift. Leutnant Raschke, an officer of 1st Airlanding Wing based in Saporoschje, later noted that in December 1942 orders reached Hauptman Kiess from General Student to send a liaison officer to the area of operations north of the Sea of Azov (the sea area between the Crimea and the Volga River) and that the glider groups were to take up position at jumping-off points around Stalino, Taganrog, Rostow and Nowotscherkask to speed up the Stalingrad airlift. Fighting positions were planned at Makejewka, then Stalino and later Saporoschje. In early January 1943, at different times and by different routes, the DFS 230 gliders flew in to Russia, with reserve aircraft being transported by rail. In all, 170 towplanes and around 350 gliders, including Me321 Gigants, gradually assembled at the designated airfields around Stalingrad after flights of up to 5,000 kilometres from their home bases. Leutnant Dittebrandt flew an He111Z, the specially created 'Siamese twin' Heinkel bomber designed to act as tug for the Me321 of GS2. The two He111s, joined at the wingtips, were the only aircraft capable of towing the huge gliders and flying via Reichshof, Schitomir, Poltawa and Stalino to Makejewka. Dittebrandt knew that every mile east increased the risk to his slow, ungainly towplane from the Russian fighters now crowding the skies around Stalingrad. 'Besides those worries, we kept receiving nonsensical orders to hurry up!'[6]

As the gliders gathered, arguments raged about whether they should be used at all. Bad weather and heavy anti-aircraft fire around the city meant that the risks to the gliders were even higher than those to the powered aircraft. By now, the desperate Luftwaffe had transferred any aircraft it could find to the Russian Front, including He177s, totally unsuitable for the intended use as transports and even FW200 Condor aircraft from French coastal bases. Field Marshal Milch arrived from Berlin and told the glider crews 'I remain of the belief that my plan for a relief operation by glider should go ahead with strengthened support from fighters and [Me110] Destroyers in the city.' Officers of the Airlanding Wing pointed out that their gliders 'would be obstructed by other aircraft. No-one seems concerned about gliders lying about (on the landing zones).' Milch refused to accept the logic, demanding that new landing zones be established in the Stalingrad suburbs and that an officer of the group be sent to find them. The fact that no strengthened fighter escort was available made little difference.[7]

On 23 January, three He111 tugs stood by at Makejewka, each acting as tug for fully laden Go242s of 4 Supply Squadron carrying around 5 tonnes of medical and food supplies. The previous day, Gumrak, the last German held airfield, had fallen to a Russian attack and with it went the last air route in or out of the city, so this mission would be the last effort to reach the trapped men. In the poor weather and darkness, Leutnant Raschke had improvised a system to guide the gliders using torches in the back of the Heinkels. A green signal showed they were dropping low, red meant too high and white that they were in the right position. The weather was bad and deteriorating so much that every hour from 1630hrs throughout the night, the He111 engines had to be started to prevent them freezing. Midnight came and went. Around 0300hrs, VIII Fliegerkorps finally cancelled the mission. The three Heinkels would go ahead and drop supply canisters, but the gliders would stay behind.

Four days later, another Russian attack split what was left of the 6th Army in two. German doctors were ordered to stop feeding the estimated 25,000 wounded men. Finally, on 30 January, Paulus surrendered. Some sources claim that over 11,000 German and Axis soldiers refused to accept the surrender and continued to resist, fighting on from cellars and the city sewers until March 1943, believing that fighting to the death was better than the prospect of a slow end in a Soviet POW camp. Soviet documents later claimed that another 2,418 Germans were killed in the fighting to clear these isolated pockets of resistance and over 8,500 finally taken prisoner. It would not be until 1955 that the last of these men was repatriated and, by that time, of the 91,000 men taken prisoner at Stalingrad, only 6,000 had survived captivity.

The loss of the 6th Army at Stalingrad was a bitter blow to the Germans but it did not put an end to fighting in the region. German Army Group (A) was now off-balance and in danger of becoming trapped in the Caucasus by the rapid advance of Russian reinforcements. Alexander Werth observed Red soldiers on the move through the dark and frost, the path lit by a string of bonfires along the road:

> Such was the endless procession coming out of Stalingrad; lorries, and horse sleighs and guns, and covered wagons, and even camels pulling sleighs – several of them stepping sedately through the deep snow as if it were sand. Every conceivable means of transport was being used. Thousands of soldiers were marching, or rather walking in large irregular crowds, to the west through this cold deadly night. But they were cheerful and strangely happy, and they kept shouting about Stalingrad and the job they had done.[8]

Further north, another Russian offensive was again threatening the Leningrad front. As the 6th Army lay trapped in Stalingrad, the desperate airlift had taken up most of the Luftwaffe's resources and throughout that winter, other German units found themselves equally hard pushed but now without the air support they might have expected. The situation came to a head along the supply lines of Army Group North, this time at the town of Velikye Luki.

The Velikye Luki Kessel, 24 November 1942–16 January 1943

In early November 1942, the German 11th Army had arrived to reinforce the badly mauled units around Cholm, Demjansk and Velikye Luki after the heavy fighting of the previous winter. It was a massive boost to morale to be joined by the victors of Sebastapol under von Manstein, widely regarded as one of the most able German field commanders and taken as a sign of an impending offensive to remove the Soviet threat to the line. Almost immediately, though, the 11th were redirected south to support forces around Stalingrad, leaving a gap in the line from Cholm in the north to Velizh in the south. The only forces left in the area were the 83rd Infantry Division around Velikye Luki in the centre and the 3rd Gebirgsjäger (Mountain) Division slightly to the south. The LIX Corps, renamed Group von der Chevallerie, was given the added responsibility for defence of the entire area the 11th Army had evacuated without any additional troops. With the 11th Army gone, LIX Corps was left to its fate.

Both the 83rd Infantry, commanded by Major General Scherer, now wearing his Knight's Cross for his defence of Cholm, and the 3rd Gebirgsjäger were experienced divisions. Under strength after the fighting of the previous summer, the 83rd in particular was dangerously overstretched, with companies each defending up to three kilometres of the front directly west of Velikye Luki. The 3rd Gebirgsjäger, tasked to defend an area so bleak that there were not even farmhouses to provide some shelter from the winter snows, was also split between commitments in Norway and Russia and had left one of its infantry regiments and an artillery battalion behind after being badly hit during the drive on Murmansk.

The Soviet attack would be led by the 9th, 19th, 21st and 46th Guards Divisions, with several ski-equipped battalions, tank brigades and nine rifle divisions in reserve, all relatively new troops. The Soviet policy of allowing units to burn out, then withdrawing them to be rebuilt, meant that most of these divisions had been destroyed and reconstituted at least once and in the battle for Cholm, for example, the 249th Estonian Rifle Division had started the battle with 8,000 men but by the end of the month had been reduced to just 1,400 – a casualty rate of over 82 per cent. With that loss rate, unit cohesion was a major problem.

Despite the strength of the Russian force, Velikye Luki was ready for a siege. Since its capture by 11th Panzer Division in August 1941, the Germans had constructed concrete bunkers and tank traps, stockpiling supplies of food and ammunition for use only if the city was encircled. Key locations such as the West Railway Station (actually located in the eastern part of the city and which doubled as a bunker and supply depot) and the medieval fortress known as the Citadel, located in the western quarter, were fortified. The Citadel, guarded on three sides by the River Lovat and whose thick earth-and-mortar walls made it a strong defence against artillery fire, had a commanding view of the bridges over the Lovat and could control access to the city itself. The plan of defence was terrifyingly simple: force the Soviets into a bloody battle of attrition by a fight to the death for each strongpoint, then fall back to the next prepared position.

In early November the Soviets began attacking the German supply lines with artillery and air strikes. At this stage of the war, though, the Soviet Air Force restricted itself to operations less than twenty miles behind the front on such missions and this meant that the rail network itself was largely undamaged, although the Germans had difficulty in actually getting supplies to their most forward units. Then, on 24 November, strong Soviet forces began moving on Velikye Luki from north and south, skirting the screen of fortified positions east of the city and meeting only scattered resistance, so that, by nightfall, the Soviets had Velikye Luki nearly surrounded. German units dug in along the Kuban stream were quickly overrun and the Soviets were able to launch their attack into the city the following day. The attack was held off and the Soviets suffered heavy losses but more assaults came on 26 November and, on the 27th, the Soviet 357th Rifle Division completed the encirclement of the city. The last telephone call into garrison headquarters came that day but after that all communication with the outside world was by radio only. Almost daily for the following seven weeks, the Soviets pressed home attacks, each one beaten back with steadily mounting losses.

Far to the south, Stalingrad was eating up German resources so that there were only a few Luftwaffe units still flying on the Velikye Luki front. These performed a superb job of resupplying the city as best they could with the basics. A composite *Gefechtsverband* (battle group) was formed under the command of Colonel Wilke with aircraft drawn from bomber and Stuka groups to drop supply canisters of food and ammunition, since this time there were no airfields within the perimeter. Bad weather hampered these flights and increasingly desperate calls for ammunition were being received: '6.12.1942 – Ammunitions to last for another eight days, when gliders? 9.12.1942 – Ammunition urgently! 12.12.1942 – Supply canisters not reaching us! Absolutely necessary glider operation takes place!'[9] The supplies that LIX Corps needed were being dropped to the 6th Army and all that was available to Leutnant-Colonel Freiherr von Sass of the 277th Infantry Regiment, commander of the garrison, were encouraging words. On 16 December, Sass received a radio message from the Fuhrer to tell him: 'I commend you and your soldiers for holding so bravely. I am convinced that you will hold like iron, just as General Scherer did in Cholm, until you are relieved.' Sass had little choice but to assure Hitler that 'Velikye Luki will be held until the last man' but went on to beg for supply drops to be made by the Luftwaffe.[10] By 18 December, the ferocity of the fighting meant that the Soviet 20th Motorized Division and 291st Infantry Division had a combined strength of only 6,200 men, the 21st and 46th Guards divisions were destroyed, the 9th and 19th Guards divisions were at breaking point and the 249th Estonian Rifle Division had suffered some 1,100 desertions going over to fight under the Wehrmacht against their Russian masters. The already weakened German forces had also suffered terribly – one Gebirgsjäger regiment had lost all but two of its officers and sixty of its 786 other ranks.

Eventually, Go242 gliders of 1.(GO)/VK (S) V were brought from the south to join the resupply missions, landing around the goods yard of the railway station where Unteroffizier Lorenz had gone in ahead to prepare landing lights to guide them in. The ring of anti-aircraft guns around the city had already taken a heavy toll and the glider pilots had adopted a new tactic that seemed to offer some chance of reaching the LZ by 'dive gliding' – releasing high and diving rapidly into the target area – a technique resurrected by US pilots attempting to reach the besieged Marine base of Khe Sanh in Vietnam twenty-five years later. Oberfeldwebel Rademacher, who flew into Velikye Luki with his co-pilot Obergefreiter Weyermanns on the day Hitler's message was received, piloted a glider carrying a load of 3 tonnes of medicine and post. It was a dark night and after about two hours in the air they were over Velikye Luki at a height of about 2,000 m. The tow pilot circled to make sure they were over the LZ and then released them. Below, the green and red lamps marking the LZ could be seen and they began to fly towards them.

> Then the first illumination round was fired. I made a fast turn as green flares were fired from the Russian positions. At about 1000m the machineguns opened up but fortunately they didn't reach us. I was terrified as I pushed the GO down and our speed reached 370 km/h. I pulled into a high bank to the left and applied full flaps and airbrakes as I reached the edge of the LZ.[11]

The biggest danger at this point was overshooting the LZ and crashing outside the German perimeter. As he steered towards a small hut at the edge of the LZ, Rademacher hit a stone column and his glider swerved across the ground, breaking up as it did so. As the glider slid to a halt,

> Pioneers got us out and sent us to the medics as they quickly unloaded the glider. From there we went to the command post and stayed there three hours until an air strike began. It was an eerie bombardment and it was there in the command post, with dead and wounded lying all around, with the noise and the stench, that I learned the terror of war. We glider pilots ended up fighting as a group on the ground.[12]

More GO crews brought in light anti-tank guns, artillery, *Nebelwerfer* ammunition and even squads of specialists into the city. Unteroffizier Mayer had landed near the station and watched as two more aircraft came in, taking heavy flak as they landed. The engineer of the first was reported killed on the approach and the aircraft skidded right up to the windows of the railway station before settling. The second (flown by Unteroffizier Hirschmann) was carrying artillery rounds and Russian tracer rounds sparked off a fire in his fuselage as he came in to land. Hirschmann later reported that his engineer had watched as the slipstream had blown the fire out. Minor miracles like this kept the flow of supplies to the city coming but in the end it was not enough. Luftwaffe losses were very high. More than 80 aircraft, including a number of priceless He111 bombers and Ju52 transports, were lost during efforts to free the city.

A second army corps, commanded by the chief of staff of Army Group Centre, Leutenant-General Otto Wohler, was pushing from the south-west toward Velikye Luki, suffering 9,940 casualties by mid-December, its only replacements coming from those wounded who could be quickly returned to action but, despite their heavy losses, Wohler's men were determined to rescue their surrounded comrades. By January, Sass was still sending out long, detailed situation reports describing how, although the hundreds of wounded soldiers were being protected as much as possible from the weather and the enemy, there was little more that could be done for them. The medical staff had been so badly hit that captured Estonians had been pressed into service to tend the injured but there was almost no medicine left. Food rations were minimal, and what little horse meat remained was rotten. Disease was rife. Ammunition was in short supply and the Russians maintained a constant barrage of artillery and mortar shells and air attacks in any type of weather.

On 15 January, the last radio messages came from the eastern sector. At 0440hrs Sass radioed that, 'a breakout appears out of the question; because almost 2,000 wounded would fall into Russian hands . . . help must immediately come from the outside. Urgently request reply.' A few hours later, he again asked for help: 'We cannot break out. You must immediately break through to us.' At 0840hrs, a last, despairing message from the beleaguered garrison: 'Urgently request artillery fire.' That was the last heard from the force. Velikye Luki was officially declared lost the next day.[13]

By now, STAVKA, the Red Army high command, had recognized that one of the key factors in successfully fighting the Germans would be neutralizing the Luftwaffe's air superiority. To do this would require an almost total restructuring of the Voyenno Vozdushnye Sily (VVS, or Soviet Air Force), both in its organizational framework and its tactical and strategic doctrines and General A A Novikov was appointed in the summer of 1942 to do the job, in recognition of his effective and innovative use of airpower on the Leningrad front. By the end of the year, the Red Air Force had become a much more effective force but had yet to face a major test. That test would not be long coming. Early in 1943, Novikov found the perfect testing ground for his theories: the Kuban.

The Kuban bridgehead: February–October 1943

On 4 February 1943, a Soviet assault group established a beachhead just southwest of the Black Sea port of Novorissisk, catching the Germans offguard and putting them in danger of being encircled. Since the port anchored the southern flank of their bridgehead over the Kuban River, Kleist, commander of Army Group A, was all too aware that the Red Army was now ten times closer to Rostov, his only escape route from the region, than he was and he knew he had to withdraw immediately. Hitler, convinced his earlier intransigence still held good, demanded instead that he stand and fight. Kleist knew it was a death sentence and fortunately Hitler quickly came to realize that any action other than withdrawal would be futile now that the strong Russian thrust south to capture Rostov had driven a wedge between the Donets Basin and the Kuban region of the Caucasus. The Germans launched immediate local counterattacks, but the Soviet beachhead held, aided by the region's foothills and rugged terrain, and soon reinforcements in increasing numbers from both sides began to arrive at the sector, threatening to create a full-scale campaign. The opportunity Novikov needed for his air force to make the transition from a defensive to an offensive force had arrived.

The German-held Kuban bridgehead, situated along the Taman peninsula, was an area of extreme importance to both sides. The Germans saw it as essential to protecting the eastern approaches to the Crimea, the Soviets as a launch-point for another possible German offensive into the northern Caucasus, but the campaign on the Kuban was an inconclusive round of limited ground offensives that today is almost unknown in the West. The air battles fought there, though, would be a turning point for the growth of the Soviet Air Force. So much so that some Soviet sources claim the battle – so intense that General K V Vershinin, the main Soviet air commander of the sector, claimed on some days he could see an aircraft fall every ten minutes in up to 100 air battles a day – to be as important to their war effort as the battle of Midway was to the Americans.

The German Fourth Luftflotte, which included glider groups equipped with DFS 230 and Go242s, was responsible for this area but this time warned army commanders from the outset that a full airlift was impossible. Gliders of 1st, 2nd and 3rd Groups of 1st Airlanding Wing had already begun limited operations in late January from the Bagrevo and Kerch IV airfields in the Crimea and now stepped up their efforts, flying in food for the troops and fodder for the horse transport of the Mountain Division. Flying a shuttle service into the Kuban, glider pilots flew two or three missions per day, always, in accordance with standing orders, returning to their home bases at the end of the day.

Again, all available aircraft were pressed into service and flights by FW200 Condor aircraft began on 4 February, supported by their newly arrived ground crews. Originally intended to help with the Stalingrad lift, their journey from France had lasted several weeks and saw them make the last part by car from Poland, where their train had been halted. With the Kuban rapidly turning into a battle for air superiority, gliders provided a vital link in maintaining German fighter power. The Go242 was capable of carrying an Me109 fuselage and could be used to transport damaged fighters back for base repair at specialist depots around Bagrevo as well as maintenance crews out to unprepared, isolated and remote airstrips. They became a vital factor in maintaining Luftwaffe capability.

On 26 May a huge Soviet ground offensive got under way with a powerful armoured infantry thrust. Within hours, the Germans had launched a determined counterattack that soon stalled the Soviet drive with the loss of more than a hundred Soviet tanks on the first day alone. In the air, both sides launched an all-out effort to break the other. A Soviet raid by 338 aircraft was met by up to 1,500 German sorties on the same day. German sources claimed the Russians lost 350 combat aircraft that day, but Luftwaffe losses were so high that by 7 June they had to withdraw their own aircraft. A new German offensive was launched in July but failed to achieve its objectives and Hitler called it off after just twelve days. Sensing victory, the Russians pressed home a new counteroffensive.

Fighting on the ground continued until October, with gliders still running the gauntlet of enemy fighters, when German forces evacuated the Kuban.

The tide was turning. German forces were being pushed back as they attempted to disengage from the determined Russian onslaught. Time after time, Russian forces encircled the Germans and glider flights were sent in to deliver supplies. In most cases, they were supplying strategic points in towns and cities but, as the withdrawal continued, found themselves being asked to supply a moving target.

In March 1944, Russian advances had effectively cut off the 300,000 men of the 1st Panzer Army from their rear areas and the formation began an epic fighting retreat. DFS 230 gliders of Towgroup 2 helped resupply the force with fuel and ammunition, flying out wounded on the return trip, always under threat from Russian fighters. Feldwebel Sandvoss of 1.(DFS)/Schleppgruppe 2 recalled flying at low level, day after day, sometimes with loads hanging out of the doors of his overladen aircraft. As well as the 1st Army, gliders based in Romania were also attempting to support the encircled Tarnapol garrison and flying daily missions there. As the long retreat from Russia began, the list of names of towns and cities the glider crews supplied – Tiraspol, Nikolajew, Rostov, Kerstch, Sebastopol – grew ever longer.

Back in Germany, gliders were also being considered for use for more than just supply runs. Kampfgruppe 200, a Luftwaffe special operations unit, was giving serious consideration to a proposal by Oberleutnant Karl-Heinz Lange, a former glider pilot who had been wounded in Sicily, to create a suicide unit to fly glider bombs into hydro–electric plants deep in Russia as part of Operation Joseph. In April 1944 Gothaer-Waggon-Fabrik, builders of the Go242, had put forward plans for a guided 3,000 kg bomb with a cockpit, wings and controls and designated Type P55. The weapon was never put into production but at least 120 volunteers had already stepped forward and were undergoing glider training at Hildesheim under the code names of 'Totaleinsatz' (Operation Total), 'Selbstopfer-Staffel' (Self-sacrifice squadron), 'Staffel Leonidas', 'Kommando Lange' and 'So-Staffel'. How much this was a true suicide unit in the same sense as the Japanese Kamikazes is open to question but men of the unit eventually flew FW190 fighters into action against US B-17s in late April of 1945 with devastating results.[14] By now, though, the risks being run by glider crews were tantamount to suicide in any case. By the winter of 1944, German forces had been pushed further back and were now facing yet another encirclement. This time, it would be among the bloodiest of the war so far.

The siege of Budapest, 7 November 1944–13 February 1945

Despite the loss of 120,000 Hungarians alongside them at Stalingrad, Germany still regarded Hungary as an 'unwilling satellite', and on 16 October 1944, Hungarian Regent Miklós Horthy was forced to resign. Germany installed

Ferenc Szálasi, leader of Hungary's fascist Arrow Cross (Nyilaskereszt) party as Prime Minister and any hopes Hungarians may have had of escaping the war were gone. Two weeks later, more than a million Russian soldiers were pushing forward in a pincer movement around the capital, Budapest.

On 7 November, they began to move into Budapest's eastern suburbs, advanced through the town of Pest, twenty kilometres from the city's old town and halted. Once again, Hitler demanded that Budapest be held and declared it a Fortress City. When the offensive got under way again at Christmas and the road linking Budapest to Vienna, its last link with the outside world, was cut, there were nearly 80,000 German and Hungarian soldiers as well as over 800,000 civilians trapped in the city. The Russians sent two men to discuss surrender but they were never seen again. Both sides blamed the other for their loss but the consequence was a more determined Russian effort to take the city. Progress was slow but steady – so slow, in fact, that István Deák, then a child in the city, later recalled that

> generally life in Pest returned to something like normal at an astonishing speed: peasants began to bring in food, expecting to be paid in gold or family possessions, and while the fighting was still continuing in Buda a movie house opened in central Pest. It showed the Soviet film *The Battle of Orel*, in which the audience was treated to the double thrill of being able to watch Soviet airplanes machine-gun and bomb the enemy first on the screen and then outside the theatre.[15]

Attempts to break through to the garrison failed and by January 1945, intense fighting was taking place. Ferihegy airport had been taken by the Russians just before the start of the siege and resupply was fast becoming a problem. At first, some supplies were brought up the Danube by barge under cover of darkness, but when the river froze the Luftwaffe was called upon once again to provide an airlift. Using some of the main avenues and the park next to Buda Castle as landing zones for planes and gliders, a link was maintained until early January when heavy losses meant powered flights into the city were stopped.

Gliders continued to make hazardous trips into the Blutweise Park landing strip near the castle throughout January. On the night of 20/21 January, towplane pilot Hauptman Reich made four sorties by Stuka over the burning city to deliver DFS 230 gliders, twenty of whom set out that night. Three were shot down over Russian lines. Heavy fog prevented flying the following night. During 22/23 January, another eleven set out but this time only four reached German lines. The next night, nine left and six made landings in the Blutweise Park. The LZ was small and often covered in smoke or fog and many pilots failed to reach it. Feldwebel Filius crashed into the roof of a house in the city centre. Obergefreiter Schiermeier made an emergency landing on the Russian side after his tailplane was damaged by a breaking tow rope. Albert Schlupmann circled the city looking for the landing lights and eventually landed near a Soviet anti-aircraft battery. He almost managed, after several adventures, to reach German lines but ended up in captivity anyway. Those who made it into the LZ were directed to Luftwaffe command posts in the cellars of the Belle Vue Hotel for reassignment as infantrymen. Unteroffizier Jäger flew into Budapest on the night of 23/24 January. After reporting to the command post, he was sent to join other pilots manning a machine-gun post in the cellars of the ministry building on the banks of the Danube. Making his way there through a maze of ruins, cellars and sewers, Jäger found people who had been living underground for a month.

> From the sick bays came the wails of the wounded. The air was unbearable. Then there were the cries of the little children. Here and there, people had managed to find snow and were melting it to at least make a kind of thin soup and smoke from woodfires filled your eyes. I was happy to finally reach the ministry and meet up again with my comrades from the squadron.[16]

Thirty-five glider pilots eventually reached the cellar and held that position for the next three weeks as the battle of Buda raged.

By the beginning of February, it was clear that, for pilots flying into the city, there was no way out. Still, they flew in. Five left on the night of 4/5 February but only two made it into the LZ. Two more left on the night of the 7th. By now, Russian troops were pouring accurate fire onto the LZ and landing more gliders would be futile. On 11 February, Gellért Hill finally fell after six weeks of fighting to a vicious simultaneous Soviet attack from three sides. Soviet artillery now dominated the entire city and shelled the remaining defenders, concentrated into an area less than two square kilometres, mercilessly. On 10 February, after capturing the southern railway station, Soviet marines established a bridgehead on the castle hill, cutting the remaining German forces in two. Facing a hopeless situation, the German commander, General Karl Pfeffer-Wildenbruch, decided to go against Hitler's orders and attempt to break out of the city. Jäger and his fellow pilots fought until the night of 11/12 February and then tried to join the breakout, following a half-kilometre-long canal but found a blockhouse there and no way out.

Using a heavy fog as cover, German and Hungarian troops and those civilians able to make the journey attempted to escape in three waves. The first wave was successful and a great many escaped but the Soviets were alerted and bracketed the following groups with shellfire. Only around 1,000 men managed to survive to reach the wooded hills north-west of Budapest and escape towards Vienna. Finally, on 13 February, the remaining garrison was forced to surrender. For the Germans, the siege of Budapest marked their last major operation on the southern front and for the Russians a dress rehearsal for the attacks on Vienna and, eventually, Berlin. In all, seventy-three DFS 230 gliders had flown to Budapest, forty-one actually making it into the city. Eleven were known to have been shot down by flak and others lost to weather, mechanical failure or emergency landings. At the beginning of March, forty-nine pilots were formally listed as missing.

The siege of Festung Breslau, 8 February–5 May 1945

Just as the battle for Budapest was reaching its climax, far to the north Soviet forces were nearing the city of Breslau (now Wroclow in Poland). The city was the capital of Silesia and an important industrial and communications centre housing a number of important industrial plants manned by prisoners from nearby forced labour camps such as Brugweide and the Gross-Rosen concentration camp. The city was outside the range of Allied bombing and had gained a reputation as the 'air shelter of the Reich' to where many government and civil offices had been relocated from bombed western and northern German cities. It was not until autumn 1944 that the first Soviet bombers appeared.

In July 1944, Hitler had issued secret instructions that Breslau must be turned into a *festung* (fortress), to be defended at all costs as part of his 'Eastern Wall' on the River Oder, still thought to be an insurmountable barrier to Soviet invasion. The Gauleiter of Silesia, Karl Hanke, was appointed by Hitler as the city's *Kampfkommandant* (battle commander) with authority even over the military commanders of the garrison. Work on the defences of the city had begun in June but it was not until the formal announcement of 'Festung Breslau' in September that work really got under way. At first, the people of the city were not aware of their new status but Stefan Kuczynski, a Polish doctor who had lived in Breslau since the First World War, recalled

> in our streets, into our domestic life, something strange began to creep in. We saw cattle herds, which were driven to the slaughterhouse. One saw truck columns, which transported mysterious cargoes covered with tarpaulins. Other lorries carried crates and bags with food, which was accommodated in cellars.[17]

In December, the military commander of Breslau, General Krause, suggested evacuating the civilian population but was overruled by the city's political master, Hanke, who then replaced Krause with General Niehoff. Instead, the civilian population – men women and children –were put to work building two defensive rings twenty kilometres from the centre of the city and helping to stockpile supplies for long-term siege.

On 12 January 1945, Soviet forces crossed the borders of eastern Prussia and began to advance into Silesia itself. Suddenly, on 20 January, with refugees from the east crowding into the city, Hanke changed his mind about fighting in a city crammed with civilians and announced 'Men of Breslau! Our state capital has been declared a fortress. The evacuation of the city of women and children has started and must be completed quickly.' All that day and the next, loud-speakers declared 'Attention! Attention! Women with children march by foot on the road from Opperau toward Kanth! You should gather in the south suburb.' Around 630,000 were expected to pack and leave with virtually no warning and no transport to help them. In January temperatures falling to -20°, old people, the sick, women and children began to cross the Oder bridges. German propaganda about Russian atrocities fuelled the fear and soon the evacuation became a panic. Hans Joachim Terp, a civilian in Breslau at the time, later described how people had crammed into the Freiburger station, whose tracks led west:

> You couldn't get onto the platform, because the crowd was all moving one way. Children were rolled over and crushed. A railwayman told me 'yesterday they took away twenty four children here, dead children', they had been just trampled on the stairs. It was cruel.

On 22 January, voluntary worker Vera Eckle was ordered to take part in a supply trip to the refugees.

> A snowstorm raved, the snow lay a metre high, and it was ice cold. The children had put on several dresses one above the other and stood help-lessly beside their mothers. Here an old woman, who could hardly breathe, there an old man on crutches, who slipped continuously, because it was so icy. It was a dreadful sight. Then the Volksturm man cried, 'Hurry girls, carry the bedcovers forward and gather up the dolls!' 'Which dolls does he mean', I asked myself. And at that moment I tripped over a bundle before me. I picked it up to throw to one side – 'God's sake, those are children, child corpses!', I cried. It was the greatest misery which I had seen ever in my life.

Unofficial estimates suggest the 'Breslau Death March', as it came to be known, cost up to 90,000 lives as many of those who survived the cold later disappeared into the inferno of Dresden on 14 February when Allied bombers pounded the city to destruction.

As the Soviets closed in, Breslau's defences were manned by a 45,000-strong garrison under the overall command of Field Marshal Schoerner of Army Group Centre but consisted of a ragged mixture of troops, including the newly formed 609th Infantry Division, elements of 269th Infantry Division, school and reserve units, an improvised SS regiment (SS Festung Abseiling 'Besselein'), thirty-eight battalions (each 400-strong) of Volkssturm volunteers, boys of the

Hitlerjugend, Police, Luftwaffe ground units and the remnants of several destroyed combat formations. Troops on leave or in transit were hurriedly reassigned to defence units. Its heavy weapons were thirty-two artillery batteries using obsolete German guns and a mixture of captured Soviet, Polish, Yugoslav and Italian artillery pieces and a total of fifteen assault guns and two Tiger tanks currently at a repair workshop in the city.

The Russian attack began on 8 February against heavy resistance from LVII Panzer Corps and counterattacks from 19th Panzer Division from the direction of Raciborz (Ratibor) and 20th Panzer Division from Jawor (Jauer) and Strzegom (Striegau). Although they slowed the advance, the panzers could not hold back the Russian tide and on 13 February, the Soviet 6th Army defeated the 19th Panzer Division's desperate defence of the autobahn in the area of Kostomloty – the only remaining link between encircled city and the remainder of the German forces – and completed the encirclement of Breslau. Two days later, the Luftwaffe began yet another airlift of supplies into an encirclement. This one would last another seventy-six days.

The following day the Soviets launched an attack on the city from the south and then from the west, which soon turned into bloody and savage fight for each house and street with the heaviest fighting in the area of the city's airbase and industrial district. The Soviets were reported to have lost seventy-six tanks in the first three days and at least another hundred the following fortnight when they tried to use tanks in the street fighting. Soon their tactics changed to using artillery to destroy enemy positions and engineers along with Marines to clear enemy strongpoints. By late March, the fate of city was sealed as the last strong German formations south-east of Opeln (Opole) were destroyed. Fighting continued as Soviets pushed German defenders deeper into the city and they, in turn, destroyed every house and city block behind them to slow the Soviet advance.

Jürgen Hempel, a 12-year-old Hitler Youth, had remained in the city with his mother. His father was serving in Russia and his older brother had fought at Monte Cassino and, as he put it later, 'I was as a twelve-year-old boy serving among soldiers and found it all a completely wonderful adventure.' From his home on Schweidnitzer Strasse, he was assigned to work with an infantry unit to provide food, run messages and other errands whilst his mother acted as medic. 'There was always something exploding somewhere', he recalled, and he and other Hitler Youth continuously ran the gauntlet of shell, sniper and air attack to find water from the broken pipes, waiting in the entrance of the stock exchange until the air was clear, then running with buckets to the well – and back. Air raids had burst pipes in the houses and he and his comrades were tasked with acting as a kind of fire brigade. Soon, the adventure wore off. Four hundred Hitler Youth, many of them his friends, died within weeks. His priorities changed and now the German people 'did not want to win the war, we wanted to only survive'.[18]

Another boy, identified only as Werner, later described life in the city for civilians:

> My mother, my six year old sister and I lived in the cellar and my father
> a baker released a few weeks before by the army – was soon conscripted
> into the Volksturm. They had just one rifle for seven men. The supply of
> food was sufficient both for the soldiers and for the civilian population,
> because the stores had been supplied with enough for up to two years
> storage and at first there was still electric current in the cellars, which were
> connected [by] holes through the wall to those of the rest of the block.
> Later the current failed because of the ever increasing bomb and shell
> impacts. We made do – and very well – with carbide lamps, petroleum
> and candle light but our constant companion in the cellar was fear.
>   The Russians worked by the clock: From midnight to the early
> morning it was mostly relatively calm. Then from six to ten am it was
> mostly artillery bombardment into the city centre, with continuing dull,
> rolling explosions, sometimes further away, sometimes more near. From
> ten to one pm came the airplanes, fighters first, then bombers. The cellar
> walls and the soil trembled again and again and we were all scared that
> the basement ceiling came could collapse and kill us all. The Soviet
> airplanes did not have far to travel because they were based just outside
> the city's defence ring and could land and refuel quickly. Around two
> pm, the bomb attacks would break off until around six. About ten pm,
> German airplanes, mostly Ju52s, came and brought medicines and
> ammunition, and perhaps also post.[19]

Breslau's airfield, at Gandau, was in the frontline. Fritz Morzik reported that

> any aircraft, regardless of the direction from which it approached the
> field and regardless of whether it cut its motors at high altitude and
> glided in for a landing or tried to come in at hedge hopping altitude, was
> soon caught in the cross beams of some thirty searchlights and subjected
> to concentrated fire. On the ground there were additional obstacles to be
> overcome. The landing strip itself was under constant artillery fire,
> since the Russian main front lay only half a mile from the edge of the
> field. The unloading of supplies, and the loading of wounded personnel
> for the trips back, had to be carried out under constant enemy fire and
> with the help of improvised lighting arrangements.[20]

The only alternative airstrip, a landing field on the Friesenweise and the Kaiserstrasse, two broad streets in the city, could be used in an emergency by skilled pilots but was of no real use most of the time, although light 'Storch' aircraft were able to use it to recover the wounded. The response, on 7 March, was to order the construction of a new airstrip using the Kaiserstrasse in the city centre. Houses in the area were blown up and boys aged 10 and over, girls from the age of 12 and all available adults were put to work. Rations were only provided for those who had cards marked to prove they had been working. Under repeated air attack and artillery bombardment, an airstrip was slowly carved out of the rubble. Even before it was complete, gliders began using the new strip.

Gliders had been arriving in Breslau from the start and had flown in two battalions of 9. Fallschirmjaegerdivision in mid-February. By that time, the Luftwaffe had sixty-six towplanes, 204 Go242 and 233 DFS 230 gliders left, with 233 crews to fly them. After the loss of the Gandau airbase on 1 April, gliders became the sole means of getting supplies into the city but at a high price. On the night of 7/8 April, twenty-nine gliders set out for the city but only ten reached it. Russian searchlights and anti-aircraft guns were proving to be deadly effective. Where possible, Storch reconnaissance planes were sent to bring back the pilots and unconfirmed reports even suggest that FA 223 helicopters may have made attempts to recover downed airmen.

On 23 April, Unteroffizier Stephan volunteered for a flight into his home-town, reporting to Hauptman Reich at the Alt Lonnewitz airfield where he was shown aerial photos of the LZ taken by day and night. The night pictures were taken on a clear night like the expected weather for his flight. Standing out were the fires and the bend in the river that would be a useful marker for the flight. Beacons on the landing strip would only be visible at fairly low altitude (1,000–1,500 m) and he was warned that the Russians had built decoy strips that had claimed several earlier crews. The tow planes would be Do17 and He111s and, like many glider pilots, Stephan had little experience of working with these aircraft. Flying at low altitude behind a He111 in the early hours of the morning to avoid hostile fighters he remembered being captivated by the sight of the burning city whose flames reflected off the clouds. Suddenly, searchlights caught him and lit the cockpit brightly as, instinctively, he banked quickly and lost himself in the darkness. Turning east, he had enough height to allow slight detour and followed the river from the south-east towards the fires burning in the north-west. The LZ was a section of tidal channel in the city's river.

Reaching the city at a height of about 1000 m, Stephan could soon make out the landing lights on the LZ and the unmistakable flashes of artillery strikes on the Friesenweise and the Kaiserstrasse. To the north, a clear landing area was being lit by the Russians as a decoy, but too far away from the channel to entice him to land there. The problem was that the channel was lined with trees and presented a difficult place to put down. 'I circled to lose height and, on my last turn, clipped a house with my wing and needed to constantly correct myself as I came in fast. The trees along the channel slipped past me and the red lamp marking the end of the LZ was coming up very fast.'[21] Up ahead, he could see a bridge and, as a Breslauer, knew it stood on thick stone pillars. He quickly put down and, after a landing of just a few metres, the glider stopped near the bridge and at the water's edge. A truck pulled up and men with axes and other tools approached, clapped him on the back and set about unloading the cargo. Stephan was directed to an artillery command post and given a very welcome shot of schnapps as he watched his glider being cut up and pushed into the river to clear the LZ so that the Russians would not be alerted to it. A second glider then tried a landing but missed the channel and came down hard, its wing broken and cockpit shattered. The heavily injured pilot was rescued and taken to the medics. Another glider that had started out with him never made it to the city. At the end of April, Stephan managed to find a place aboard a Storch flying wounded from the Friesenweise.

As the siege of Breslau dragged on, attempts to maintain morale included the issue of a chocolate ration to celebrate Hitler's birthday on 20 April but by now most knew that time was running out. On 4 May, when the city's senior clergy – Pastor Hornig, Dr Konrad, Bishop Ferche and Canon Kramer – pleaded with the garrison commander, Niehoff, to surrender the town, most military commanders agreed, but Hanke ordered Niehoff not to have any further dealings with them. The next day, Hanke fled the city in a Storch, using the runway he had forced the citizens to build. By then, over two-thirds of Breslau lay in ruins.

The fall of Berlin, May 1945

Meanwhile, Russian forces had continued their advance and by now were fighting in Berlin itself. By 25 April, Germany's glider forces were down to just thirteen DFS 230s and six Go242s yet still from the bunkers in Berlin came ridiculous demands for air supplies to be flown in. On 17 March for example, General Reinhard demanded a delivery of 500 tons of supplies a day to be sent to the Berlin garrison. To do this would have required 250 Ju52 flights each day at a time when the Luftwaffe could only muster 250 aircraft in total. It would require 1,000 tons of fuel for the aircraft when the Luftwaffe was rationed to only 800. A single attempt to carry out a large-scale resupply on 16 April was a disaster and, after that, only isolated attempts could be made. At night, gliders were still arriving in the capital whenever possible but heavy fire often prevented landing. On the night of 28/29 April, five DFS set out from their base at Rurik, each pilot carrying a letter from Luftwaffe High Command giving him priority on any flights leaving the city so that he could return to his unit for further attempts. Unteroffizier Kugler, navigating by the light of the fires raging all around, managed to find a landing place in the Tegel District, his load of ammunition quickly collected by the crew of a nearby flak tower. Unteroffizier Heim was forced down in the Mecklenburg District when his towplane crashed. The fate of the others is unknown. Kugler was on one of the last flights out of the city before it fell.

The next night, two DFS left Rurik in another attempt. Wilhelm Schneider was badly hit on landing and dragged from his crashed glider by the Russians. The other pilot, Unteroffizier Göbel, was killed as he brought his aircraft in to land.

Then, at 0200hrs on 1 May, a single DFS 230 started out from Hohenmauth airfield and flew via Koniggratz towards Breslau carrying a load of Panzerfaust anti-tank weapons and ammunition. At the controls was Unteroffizier Thies; flying the He111 tug was the squadron commander of Tow Group 1, Oberleutnant Hönig. Flying towards the city, Theis saw flames reaching high into the sky miles before they reached the defence rings around it. He released over the city and began to circle to lose height when suddenly, at a height of around 700 m, searchlights found him and a flak round hit the cockpit wounding him in the head. Dazed, he managed to keep control of his glider and began to look for somewhere to land. It seemed everywhere below him was ablaze but finally he found a clear area and began to land. As he approached, he realized he was about to land in a cemetery and braced himself. Crashing into tombs and vaults, his glider came to rest with its tail jammed between two large gravestones. Everything was quiet. Theis clambered out of the wreckage and looked around him. The clock read 0305hrs.

Back at Rurik, the crews of the glider group knew the end had come. On 1 May they boarded a He111 and flew west to Eggebck in the Schleswig region where they surrendered to British forces. The glider war was over.

Epilogue

Even as Operation Varsity marked the high water mark of the 'bamboo bomber', its days were numbered. In March 1945, the Airborne Forces Experimental Establishment began testing the new Sikorsky R4 'Hoverfly' helicopter. Later, six army captains from 'C' Flight, 657 Air Observation Squadron, traded in their Auster aircraft and began a conversion course to the R6 helicopters that had performed so well in Burma. Army aviation had taken a new turn.

In the years after 1945, other countries experimented with glider use – Argentina, Australia, Canada, China, Czechoslovakia, France, India and even Turkey maintained glider forces or produced aircraft but never again would they fly on operations. Gradually, the Glider Pilot Regiment wound down until by 1950 it existed only as a headquarters and a small training section. It was disbanded to re-emerge in 1957 as the Army Air Corps, the badge unchanged from that of the original corps of 1942 but gone was the maroon beret of the airborne and in its place a sky blue beret of its own – chosen, it is said because it was felt that brawls against soldiers of other units who dared mock it would be good for esprit de corps. In April 1949, Operation Tarheel, a month-long series of exercises around Fort Bragg saw the last American use of gliders. They were formally deleted from the US armoury on 1 January 1953. In October 1949, the experimental sixty-seat XCG20 glider was equipped with engines and became the C-123 Provider that saw service throughout the Vietnam war and is still in operation today. The Russians maintained a glider force of three glider infantry regiments and Yak-14 gliders for twenty years after the end of the Second World War, finally disbanding them in 1965. In recent years, military theorists have been considering the use of gliders for 'Operations Other Than War' (such as disaster relief) and have concluded that they may be a more cost-effective means of delivering supplies than the helicopters and aircraft currently used.

The combat use of gliders is also not entirely a thing of the past. On 25 November 1987, two motorized hang gliders crossed the Lebanese border carrying guerrillas in an attack on the Israeli military base. Six Israeli soldiers were killed in the attack and the guerrillas were able to fly out of the compound and evaded search helicopters for hours before being killed. Israeli intelligence believed up to 200 fighters had been trained to fly. Gliders are back on the agenda. One, in particular, leads the way. The US Space Shuttle crews were recently awarded honorary membership of the American WWII Glider Pilots Association. The shuttle does not land under power. After re-entry it glides to earth – the ultimate glider.

Of the thousands of gliders produced, only a tiny handful remain in museums around the world. Few books on the aircraft of the Second World War even think to include them. In 1962, replica Horsas built for the film *The Longest Day* were refused permission to fly across the Channel. The Air Ministry considered the design 'inherently dangerous'. What, then, of the men that flew them?

On 29 July 1945, the sleepy Sussex village of Stedham, near Midhurst, was the venue for a memorial service for the men of the Glider Pilot Regiment. Four hundred pilots, all that remained of the 1,200 recruited just a few years earlier, had been based near the home of George Chatterton. Now a brigadier, he had taken the opportunity to open his home to them all and to arrange a private service for the regiment to remember their fallen. He told them: 'In this regiment we aim at the discipline of the Guards, the toughness of the Commandos, individual intelligence and initiative of the Intelligence Corps' and spoke movingly of

> the things I have watched as the Commander of this regiment – the wonderful qualities of patience, discipline, and fortitude of all concerned. I have always wanted you to have the better qualities which are given to men. By that I mean simplicity, faith, and that good courage on which you would have to fall back when the real trial came – and you had them.[1]

Reporter Edward Denny of the *Evening News* watched as the men lay up their regimental flag in the small church and filed out. One man in twelve had made it through selection and of those select few, just one in three remained. As they marched into history, Denny believed that 'it gave one a nagging sense of dissatisfaction not to have been privileged to be of that goodly company – and a quiet pride in a country which can still produce such men'.[2]

Notes

Introduction

1   Benjamin Franklin quoted in B Gregory and J Batchelor, *Airborne Warfare 1918–1945* (London: Phoebus Publishing 1979), p. 8.

2   See Barbara Cartland, 'The First Towed Transport Glider', in the Glider Pilot Regimental Association journal *The Eagle*, 6/5 (April 1990).

Chapter 1

1   For a discussion of early airborne operations see Gregory and Batchelor, *Airborne Warfare*.

2   For an account of German airborne development, see R Edwards, *German Airborne Troops* (London: Macdonald & Jane's, 1974). Also W. Gericke, *Soldaten Fallen vom Himmel* (Berlin: Schützen-Verlag, 1940).

3   A Wood, *History of the World's Glider Forces* (Wellingborough: Patrick Stephens, 1990).

Chapter 2

1   J E Mrazek, *The Fall of Eben Emael* (Novato, CA: Presidio Press, 1999), pp. 35–6.

2   Ibid., p. 29.

3   Ibid., p. 36.

4   See Major-General W Wider 'Auftragstaktik & Innere Führung', *Military* Review (Sept.–Oct. 2002), 3–9.

5   C Ailsby, *Hitler's Sky Warriors German Paratroopers in Action, 1939–1945* (Dulles, VA: Brassey's, Inc., 2000), p. 37.

6   W H McRaven, *Spec Ops Case Studies in Special Operations Warfare: Theory and Practice* (Novato, CA: Presido Press, 1995), p. 37.

7   See T B Gukeisen, 'The Fall of Fort Eben Emael: The Effects of Emerging Technologies on the Successful Completion of Military Objectives', Master's Thesis presented to the Faculty of the US Army Command and General Staff College, University of South Dakota, Vermillion, SD, 1993.

8   The following account of the seizure of Eben-Emael and the canal bridges is drawn from Gukeisen, 'Fall', Mrazek, *Fall*, and G Schlaug,

Die deutschen Lastensegler-verbände 1937–1945 (Stuttgart: Motorbuch Verlag, 1985).
9   Gukeisen, 'Fall', p. 44.
10   Ibid., p. 42.

Chapter 3

1   For more details of the formation of the Local Defence Volunteers see D Carroll, *Dad's Army: The Home Guard 1940–1944* (Stroud: Sutton Publishing, 2002).
2   HMSO, *By Air to Battle: The Official Account of the British Airborne Divisions* (London: HMSO, 1945), p. 7.
3   Ibid., p. 7.
4   Ibid., p. 8.
5   R Seth, *Lion with Blue Wings* (London: Panther Books, 1959), p. 39.
6   A Morrison, *Silent Invader* (Shrewsbury: Airlife Publishing, 1999), p. 15.
7   M Dank, *The Glider Gang* (London: Cassell, 1977), p. 44.
8   'Operation Freshman', *The Eagle*, 6/4 (Dec. 1989), 5–6.
9   *The Eagle*, 6/5 (April 1990), 19–20.

Chapter 4

1   Dank, *Glider Gang*, p.32.
2   R Edwards, *German Airborne Troops*, p. 95.
3   J Lucas, *Storming Eagles: German Airborne Forces in World War Two* (London: Guild Publishing, 1988), p. 54.
4   Dank, *Glider Gang*, p. 38.
5   'Airborne Operations: A German Appraisal', CMH Pub 104-13 Historical Division, EUCOM, Washington, DC, p. 22.
6   Lucas, *Storming Eagles*, p69
7   'Airborne Operations', pp. 54–5.
8   Ibid., p. 5.
9   HMSO, *By Air to Battle*, p. 50.
10   Dank, *Glider Gang*, pp. 63–4.
11   Ibid., p. 65.
12   Ibid., p. 68.
13   Ibid., p. 73.
14   Ibid.
15   Seth, *Lion with Blue Wings*, p. 22.
16   HMSO, *By Air to Battle*, p. 57.
17   Seth, *Lion with Blue Wings*, p. 24.
18   Dank, *Glider Gang*, p. 77.

19   J L Lowden, *Silent Wings at War: Combat Gliders in World War II* (Washington, DC: Smithsonian, 1992), p. 50.

20   Chatterton's account of the assault appears in G Chatterton, *The Wings of Pegasus* (London: Macdonald, 1962).

21   Dank, *Glider Gang*, p. 82.

22   General Sir John Hackett in the Foreword to K Shannon and S Wright, *One Night in June* (Airlife Publishing, 1994), p. 7.

23   Lowden, *Silent Wings at War*, p. 157.

24   M. Arthur, *Forgotten Voices of the Second World War* (London: Ebury Press, 2004), p. 231.

25   V. Peniakoff, *Popski's Private Army* (London: Reprint Society, 1953), p. 285.

26   For Skorzeny's own account of the mission, see O Skorzeny, *Skorzeny's Secret Missions* (New York: E P Dutton & Co., Inc, 1950).

27   C Whiting, *Skorzeny* (New York: Ballantine Books, 1972), p. 17.

28   Skorzeny, *Skorzeny's Secret Missions, p. 85.*

29   The German propaganda magazine *Signal* (2 Nov. 1943), pp. 9–10, featured a photo essay about the rescue showing German troops sheltering from the raid just prior to takeoff.

30   G B Infield, *Skorzeny: Hitler's Commando* (New York: St Martin's Press, 1981), p. 43.

31   J Toland, *Adolf Hitler* (New York: Ballatine Books, 1976), p. 1033.

32   Whiting, *Skorzeny*, p. 64.

33   A personal account of Captain Turner's experiences is available on the BBC 'People's War' website at: http://www.bbc.co.uk/ww2peopleswar/stories/93/a4374993.shtml

34   Ibid

35   Seth, *Lion with Blue Wings*, p. 109.

36   V Dedijer, *Tito Speaks* (London: Weidenfield & Nicholson, 1953), p. 211.

37   Seth, *Lion with Blue Wings*, p. 111.

38   Ibid.

39   For details of the battalion, see A J Munoz, *Forgotten Legions: Obscure Combat Formations of the Waffen-SS* (Boulder, CO: Paladin Press, 1991) or R Michaelis, *Das SS-Fallschirmjäger-Bataillon 500/600* (Berlin: Michaelis-Verlag, 2004).

40   A photographic record of the assault is included in A Kunzmann and S Milius, *Fallschirmjäger der Waffen-SS im Bild* (Osnabrück: Munin-Verlag, 1986).

41   Lowden, *Silent Wings at War*, p. 89.

42   Dank, *Glider Gang*, p. 156.

43   Lowden, *Silent Wings at War*, p. 91.

44   Ibid., p. 90. A similar incident, possibly the same one, was reported by

Flight Officer Leon Luczak as he prepared to land on LZ 'O'. See G Devlin, *Silent Wings* (New York: St Martin's Press, 1985), p. 225.

Chapter 5

1   Army Air Forces Historical Study No. 47, *Development and Procurement of Gliders in the Army Air Forces 1941–1944* (Washington, DC: AAF Historical Office, 1946), p. 5.
2   Devlin, *Silent Wings*, p. 38.
3   For details of production costs of the CG-4A, see J E Mrazek, *Fighting Gliders of World War II* (New York: St Martin's Press, 1977), appendix III.
4   FM 30-31, *Tactics and Technique of Airborne Troops* (Washington, DC: War Department, 1942).
5   See Army Air Forces Historical Study No. 47, *The Glider Pilot Training Program 1941–1943* (Washington, DC: Assistant Chief or Air Staff, Intelligence Historical Division, 1943).
6   J H MacWilliam and B D Callander, 'The Third Lieutenants', *Air Force Magazine*, 73/3 (March 1990).
7   Lowden, *Silent Wings at War*, pp. 7–8.
8   The remark is attributed to the head of glider procurement by Dank, *Glider Gang*, p. 51.
9   Devlin, *Silent Wings*, pp. 135–6.

Chapter 6

1   Speech to journalists on arrival in Australia, 17 March 1942. See G Perrett, *Old Soldiers Never Die: The Life of Douglas MacArthur* (London: Andre Deutsch, 1996), p. 282.
2   Devlin, *Silent Wings*, p. 340.
3   W Yust, *Ten Eventful Years* (Chicago: Encyclopedia Britannica, 1947), vol. 4, p. 164.
4   Brigadier-General Orde C Wingate, memorandum, to Chiefs of Staff Committee, War Cabinet, 'Forces of Long-Range Penetration: Future Development and Employment in Burma, 10 August 1943' (Maxwell AFB, AL: AFHRA file 145.81-170, 1).
5   In R W Boltz, 'Phil Cochran and John Alison: Images of Apollo's Warriors', thesis presented to the School of Advanced Airpower Studies, Air University, Maxwell Air Force Base Alabama, June 2001, p. 38.
6   Ibid., p. 74.
7   General H H Arnold, 'The Aerial Invasion of Burma', *National Geographic Magazine (Aug. 1944)*.

8   Boltz, 'Cochran and Alison', pp. 75–6.
9   Devlin, *Silent Wings*, p. 138.
10   Ibid
11   Arnold, 'Aerial Invasion'.
12   Devlin, *Silent Wings*, p. 140.
13   Ibid., pp. 141–2.
14   The phrase was adopted by the 5318th Provisional Unit (Air) and has become the motto of the USAF's Special Operations groups. See P D Chinnery, *Any Time, Any Place: Fifty Years of the USAF Air Commando and Special Operations Forces, 1944–1994* (Annapolis: Naval Institute Press, 1994).
15   'Unit History of the First Air Commando Force' (Maxwell AFB, AL: AFHRA file GP-A-CMDO-1-HI).
16   Boltz, 'Cochran and Alison', p. 87.
17   Ibid., p. 71.
18   Ibid., pp. 88–9.
19   P D Chinnery, *March or Die: The Story of Wingate's Chindits* (Shrewsbury: Airlife Classic, 2001), p. 113.
20   Ibid., p. 114.
21   Arnold, 'Aerial Invasion'.
22   Boltz, 'Cochran and Alison', p. 92.
23   Unit History.
24   L S Dure, Jr., 'Air Conquest of Burma', Unit History, Eastern Air Command (Maxwell AFB, AL: AFHRA file 820.04C).
25   Boltz, 'Cochran and Alison', p. 95.
26   Unit History, p. 12.
27   J Thompson, *The Imperial War Museum Book of the War in Burma 1942–1945* (London: Pan Grand Strategy Series, 2002), p. 229.
28   Letter from Major-General George E Stratemeyer, in New Delhi, India, to General Arnold, Washington, DC, dated 31 March 1944 (Maxwell AFB, AL: AFHRA file 815.452).
29   AAF, *Development and Procurement*, p. 20.

Chapter 7

1   Jim Wallwork, personal account at: www.britisharmedforces.org/ns/ns/nat_jim_wallwork.htm
2   D Edwards, *The Devil's Own Luck* (Barnsley: Pen & Sword, 2002), p. 41.
3   Wallwork (see n. 1).
4   I Toler, *Gliding into War* (Warrington: Horseshoe Publications, 1998), p. 193.
5   Wallwork (see n. 1).

6   Ibid.
7   Shannon and Wright, *One Night in June*, p. 25.
8   N. Barber, *The Day the Devils Dropped in: The 9th Parachute Battalion in Normandy D-Day to D+6: Merville Battery to the Chateau St Come* (Barnsley: Leo Cooper, 2004), p. 27.
9   Shannon and Wright, *One Night in June*, p. 29.
10   Ibid., p. 31.
11   Ibid., p. 30.
12   Barber, *Devils Dropped in*, p. 73
13   Ibid.
14   Interview with Colonel Otway, *Daily Telegraph* (6 June 1994). See also Arthur, *Forgotten Voices*, p. 302.
15   Ibid.
16   See www.pegasusarchive.org/normandy/terence_otway.htm
17   Barber, *Devils Dropped in*, p. 79.
18   Ibid., p. 80.
19   HMSO, *By Air to Battle*, p. 72.
20   Barber, *Devils Dropped in*, p. 40. See also Brigadier Hill's account at www.bbc.co.uk/ww2peopleswar/stories/16/a2523016.shtml
21   For discussion of the debate, see C J Masters, *Glidermen of Neptune: The American D-Day Glider Attack* (Carbondale, IL: Southern Illinois University Press, 1995).
22   Lowden, *Silent Wings at War*, p. 71.
23   P. Warner, *The D-Day Landings* (Barnsley: Pen & Sword, 2004), p. 51.
24   Ibid.
25   A Lloyd, *The Gliders* (London: Corgi Books, 1984), p. 98.
26   P Gaujac, *Special Forces in the Invasion of France* (Paris: Histoire & Collections, 1999), p. 292.
27   Lloyd, *The Gliders*, p. 170. See also *The Eagle* (Dec. 1989), p. 7 and (Aug. 1990), p. 19.
28   Morrison, *Silent Invader*, p. 47
29   C Ryan, *A Bridge Too Far* (London: Book Club Associates, 1975), p. 79.
30   Seth, *Lion with Blue Wings*, p. 124.
31   Ibid., pp. 125–6.
32   Ryan, *A Bridge Too Far*, p. 189.
33   Dank, *Glider Gang*, p. 175.
34   Ibid., p. 176.
35   Lowden, *Silent Wings at War*, p. 98.
36   Dank, *Glider Gang*, p. 181.
37   Ibid., p. 189.
38   Ibid., pp. 191–3.
39   Lowden, *Silent Wings at War*, p. 106.
40   Seth, *Lion with Blue Wings*, p. 173.

41   *Arnhem Lift*, published anonymously in 1945 but later identified as the work of Louis Hagen (London: Pilot Press, 1945), p. 74.

42   Toler, *Gliding into War*, p. 224.

43   Dank, *Glider Gang*, p. 195.

44   HMSO, *By Air to Battle*, p. 128.

45   Lloyd, *The Gliders*, p. 158

46   Ibid., p. 159.

47   Hagen, *Arnhem Lift*, pp. 86–7.

48   Dank, *Glider Gang*, p. 204.

49   Devlin, *Silent Wings*, p. 279.

50   Lowden, *Silent Wings at War*, p. 112.

51   Seth, *Lion with Blue Wings*, p. 144.

52   See Dank, *Glider Gang*, p. 206. Chatterton had proposed flying fifty gliders in a *coup de main* attack, expecting that at least half (carrying 750 men) would survive.

53   Quoted in Wallwork (n. 1). See also the history of the GPR at: www.89fss.com/affiliated/gpr.htm

54   Lowden, *Silent Wings at War*, p. 127.

55   Lloyd, *The Gliders*, p. 183.

56   Ibid., p. 188.

57   Ibid., p. 190.

58   Seth, *Lion with Blue Wings*, p. 154.

59   Dank, *Glider Gang*, p. 245.

60   *War Diary 1939–1945* (London: Marshall Cavendish, 1995), pp. 232–3.

61   Lowden, *Silent Wings at War*, p. 140.

62   For details see J L Frisbee, 'Operation Varsity', *Air Force Association Magazine*, 79/3 (March 1996).

63   Toler, *Gliding into War*, pp. 242–3.

Chapter 8

1   This account is taken from 'All the World's Combat Airborne Operations' available at: www.geocities.com/Pentagon/7963/para-trooper.htm See also O von Knobelsdorff, *Geschichte der niedersächsischen 19. Panzer-Division 1939–1945* (Bad Nauheim: Podzun, 1958) and R Hinze, *Die 19. Panzer-Division 1939–1945* (Bildband) (Eggolsheim: Nebel Verlag, 2003).

Chapter 9

1   For details of the air supply operations, see Generalmajor D F Morzik, *German Air Force Airlift Operations* (Hawaii: University Press of the Pacific, 1961).

2 Schlaug, *Die deutshen Lastensegler*, p. 70.
3 Ibid., p. 71.
4 Ibid., p. 81.
5 B. Barry, 'Stopped Cold at Stalingrad', *World War II* (Jan.–Feb. 2007), 32–41.
6 For details see J S A Hayward, *Stopped at Stalingrad: The Luftwaffe and Hitler's Defeat in the East 1942–1943* (Lawrence, KS: University Press of Kansas, 1998). Also available via http://www.joelhayward.org
7 Schlaug, *Die deutshen Lastensegler*, p. 129.
8 Ibid., p. 130.
9 Correspondent Alexander Werth's account of his experiences at Stalingrad have been republished as *The Year of Stalingrad* (London: Simon Publications, 2001).
10 Schlaug, *Die deutshen Lastensegler*, p. 91.
11 W A Webb, 'Battle of Velikye Luki: Surrounded in the Snow', *World War II*. Available at www.military.com/Content/MoreContent?file= PRsovietf
12 Schlaug, *Die deutshen Lastensegler*, p. 92.
13 Ibid.
14 Webb, 'Battle of Velikyc Luki'.
15 See R O'Neill, *Suicide Squads* (Guilford, CT: Lyons Press, 1999).
16 I Deak, *The Siege of Budapest: One Hundred Days in World War II* (New Haven, CT: Yale University Press, 2005). See also his homepage at www.columbia.edu/~id1/
17 Schlaug, *Die deutshen Lastensegler*, p. 220.
18 The civilian accounts that follow were discovered in an article published on 2 Dec. 2001 at the online newspaper www.welt.de/print-wams/article617628/Eine_schlesische_Tragoedie.html
19 Article in *Weisbadner Kurier* (12 Feb. 2005): www.wiesbadener-kurier.de/region/serie/kriegsende/objekt.php3?artikel_id=1786681
20 Werner's account was accessed via www.zobten.de/index.htm and can be found at www.zeitzeugenforum.de/Krieg%20%20 Nachkriegszeit,BI/sitewerner
21 Morzik, *German Air Force Airlift Operations*, p. 274.
22 Schlaug, *Die deutshen Lastensegler*, p. 229.

Epilogue

1 In *The War Illustrated* magazine, 9/214 (31 Aug. 1945).
2 Ibid.

Appendix A:

Flying the Horsa

A pack of gliders sat tightly packed together on the runway, tow ropes already connecting them to their tug aircraft parked in a herringbone pattern along either side so that, as the formation took off, the whole would unravel like knitting. Bombers like the Lancaster, Wellington, Stirling, Whitley and Albemarle were all used as tugs during the war, along with the C-47 Dakota transports, but the closest working relationship had grown up between the men of the Glider Pilot Regiment and the Halifax aircrews of the RAF's 38 Group. On some operations, the Halifaxes would carry a small bomb load so that they would appear to be just another bomber formation and divert attention away from the gliders, but for this training mission they would fly empty.

To its crews, the cockpit of the Horsa felt 'like a greenhouse'. Its huge wind-screen gave a 180 degree view from side to side and 90 degrees ahead and above – essential if the crew were to maintain visual contact with their tug aircraft and find their way onto a crowded LZ, but offering no protection at all for the pilots if they hit any of the dozens of obstacles that might be waiting for them. Behind the cockpit, a long, slim tube-like fuselage, 'for all the world like a London tube train', could accommodate twenty-eight fully equipped infantrymen on remov-able bench seats along either side or 7500 lb of equipment – enough to carry a jeep or small gun. It was an aircraft built to be expendable and had earned itself the nickname 'the flying matchbox' because of its flimsy plywood construction. In 1962, during the filming of the Pegasus Bridge assault for *The Longest Day*, replica Horsas were built but refused permission to fly across the Channel by the Air Ministry because, they said, the design was 'inherently dangerous'. More bluntly, the Americans, who flew a number of Horsas, were more used to the steel frames of their Wacos and soon re-christened it 'the flying morgue'. Dangerous or not, it would carry thousands of troops safely into battle.

Loading the Horsa Mk I was a tricky business. Manhandling vehicles and equipment into the narrow fuselage could be time-consuming and difficult. This became easier with the Mk II's hinged nose section which simply swung the cockpit to one side for access. Loads had to be secured and balanced correctly and the consequences of them moving in flight could be disastrous. Even more difficult, in some ways, were the problems of dealing with passengers. Weight loads were crucial to both glider and tugs and worked out on the basis that an infantryman in full battle order should weigh 210 lb, a sapper around 250 lb.

Unfortunately, this did not take into account human nature and pilots found men carrying all kinds of extra weapons, ammunition or equipment and even stow-aways managed to find a way on board on some missions. Checking and reporting the load to the tug pilot was the final preparation before takeoff.

Clambering aboard through a door in the port side and stowing the ladder in the cabin, the first pilot – a staff sergeant or above who had completed the full training programme and wore the lion with blue wings badge of a qualified pilot – took his place in the port side seat. He would be responsible for the takeoff and landing of the aircraft. Beside him, the second pilot – a sergeant who had completed an abbreviated training course – wore the winged 'G' of a qualified glider pilot and would fly during the tow and assist the first pilot as required. The first pilot could, when needed, fly the aircraft solo, the second seat filled with ballast. In front of each seat was a steering column and rudder bar and between them a simple instrument panel consisting of an air speed indicator, compass, air pressure gauge, altimeter, artificial horizon, rate of climb/descent indicator and finally the tow cable angle indicator – usually known as the 'angle of dangle'. Attached to this were the tow release, flap and elevator control levers. A quick check of the locking levers holding the cockpit in place and of the controls and the aircraft was ready to go.

Communication between the tug and glider was by means of an intercom cable woven into the hemp tow rope and a TR9 radio in the Horsa cockpit. As the Halifax roared into life (engines were not run prior to takeoff to avoid the risk of overheating during the strain of getting both aircraft off the ground), the first pilot gave the signal 'take up the slack'. Keeping the wheel brakes on as the tug slowly pulled forward, the pilot waited until the rope went taut before signalling 'takeoff' and releasing the brakes. Immediately, the tug pilot opened up to full power to ensure the rope did not become slack or the glider accelerate into the rear of the tug.

At around 70mph, the glider would reach takeoff speed and begin to rise, climbing quickly to the 'high tow' position above the tug. This eased the drag on the heavier bomber and allowed it, too, to lift off. Together, the two aircraft would climb steadily to their assigned altitude. By the time they began to roll, the glider pilots had attended three separate briefings on the mission given by the army, the RAF and by the glider unit commander, so they were clear about their routes, timings and landmarks but command of the combination went to the tug pilot and it was his navigator who would determine the release point. Once at the cruising altitude, the glider would descend into 'low tow', passing through the bomber slipstream to fly 'directly behind the tug and one half the wing span of the tug below it'. This was the preferred method, the Horsa seeming to settle naturally into position and allowing visual contact to be maintained with the tug. Above 200 feet, if necessary, the undercarriage could be jettisoned to reduce drag and the glider would land on skids instead. Below this height and they risked the wheels bouncing back and hitting the rear of the aircraft.

In poor conditions, the 'angle of dangle' became vital, indicating when the glider was in danger of overtaking its tug and allowing the pilots to maintain the correct position. Overtaking the tug could wrap the tow cable around its wings or engines and could even pull the two aircraft together in mid-air, as happened to some during the Sicily invasion. Generally, though, the Horsa 'behaved' in level flight but it was never intended to be comfortable. A 'sanitary bottle' was clipped to the bulkhead behind the first pilot and a 'sanitary tube' was available for passengers in the main cabin. Crews quickly learned to provide a bucket for the inevitable airsickness that followed the buffeting of crossing the slipstream. Travel sickness tablets were provided before takeoff but a combination of the motion and natural nervousness were often too much. In-flight catering included a thermos flask for the pilots and flasks and ration packs stowed under the passenger seats (in Normandy, one unfortunate passenger had to endure comments about his courage when a flak splinter pierced a flask nearby, spilling hot tea into his lap and soaking his trousers).

As the combination approached their target, the tug flew on the required course that the glider should follow and passed the course to the glider crew. Three points, 'A', 'B' and 'C', each about five miles apart, were marked on the navigator's map and the glider would be released only at point 'C', worked out to ensure that the glider would reach within 1,000 yards of the target at a height of between 1,200 and 1,500 feet. This gave the pilot a left-hand turn through 90 or 180 degrees onto the LZ. The glider's own compass could be severely affected by the loads it carried, especially radios or other electrical equipment and this was an opportunity to note any deviation. The glider moved into 'high tow' and waited for the order from the tug pilot. On release, the tug continued in level flight and jettisoned the rope at a designated point.

The Horsa had a 'glide ratio' of 1:7.2, which broadly meant that it would travel 2,500 yards along the ground for every 1,000 feet of altitude it lost. In Normandy, two groups of gliders destined for the Orne bridges cast off together at 7,000 feet, giving them around twelve miles of flight. Those aiming for Pegasus Bridge flew inland, turned and came back towards the coast, landing exactly on target. Those aiming for the river ('Horsa Bridge') had only five miles in which to lose the same amount of height. By applying full flaps, a pilot could use the Horsa's maximum 1:1.5 glide ratio to put his aircraft into a 45 degree dive to lose height, pulling out at the last moment to touch down on target – a process one pilot described as 'dropping like a streamlined brick' – highly effective but nerve-wracking for the passengers and certainly adding to the pools of vomit that washed throughout the cabin on most flights.

Night flying was an important element of glider operations and pilots trained frequently with special RAF goggles heavily shaded to recreate darkness – although tales of pilots being ordered to wear them even when playing football were exaggerated. As far as possible, gliders only operated when there was at least some moonlight over the LZ and at night pilots used 'The Funnel', an imaginary area 500–1,000 yards from the entrance to the LZ and worked out by calculating the height and glide ratio and confirmed by landmarks identified on air reconnaissance and maps. If the glider reached the Funnel at the right height, he would reach the LZ. In addition to this system, gliders would normally expect to be guided in by pathfinder paratroopers setting up the Rebecca/Eureka homing system and a flarepath of eight electric lamps in the shape of a 'T'. Three lamps set seventy-five yards apart formed the crossbar, five more fifty yards apart made up the stem. Three hundred yards from the stem of the 'T' a flashing light indicated the Funnel. All the lamps were designed to direct their beams straight up and would remain invisible on the ground.

The lessons of Crete were hard-won but later captured German assessments showed that they were very much aware that in free flight the glider was highly vulnerable. Their gliders were armed with machine guns (the Gigant routinely carried four air gunners and both the DFS 230 and Go242 could have machine guns mounted on top of the cabin). The Horsa had two hatches, one on the roof and another through the floor at the rear, where guns could be positioned, but they were rarely if ever used. Anecdotal evidence suggests that some soldiers may have simply fired through the sides and at least one Waco is reported to have landed with everyone aboard firing blindly through holes torn in the fuselage, but more often they relied on speed and surprise to get down before the enemy could react.

The ideal LZ was on arable land 2,000 by 1,000 yards square giving space for 300 gliders to land. Each LZ was subdivided into four squares, allowing commanders to direct their loads into specific spots. Landing in smaller LZs was possible and various methods were used to shorten the landing run. The Germans wrapped barbed wire around the skids to act as anchors and later fitted retro rockets as emergency brakes. The Allies developed arrester parachutes to deploy on landing and force the nose of the glider down, bringing it to a halt in a very short distance.

On landing, the first task was to unload. In theory, this was achieved by swinging open hinged sections of the nose or tail but in practice a rough landing could wreck the aircraft or jam the hinges so that the vehicles inside could not be extracted. Modifications to the Mk I included a bolted-on tail section that could be cut away if the nose section were damaged and this was backed up with a ring of cordex explosive known as a 'surcingle' to blow off the tail in an emergency. Powerful wirecutters were stowed aboard and one of the crew or passengers assigned the task of cutting away the glider's control wires on landing. Although generally successful, unloading could still be a frustrating experience and one crew, aided by some of their passengers, spent nearly an hour trying to open the rear of their Horsa, attacking it with axes, saws, boots and even standing on it and jumping to no avail. Later, a passing paratroop officer stopped to see if he could be of any help. When he gave the tail an experimental push with one hand, the whole section swung gently aside.

After unloading, glider pilots reverted to their secondary role as infantrymen and had to be competent in using whatever weapons they were carrying, from grenades to anti-tank guns. They would rendezvous with the glider commander and act as an individual unit (although many found it more practical to remain with the unit they had carried). Where possible, they were to be evacuated as soon as practical so that they could return to fly in reinforcements. Some, though, were needed to remain available for the recovery of aircraft by 'snatch' tow, a technique developed from the US Postal Service.

Any glider not damaged on landing could be recovered by using a specially adapted Dakota fitted with a winch and a cable ending in a large hook attached to the port side of the aircraft. On the ground, two light poles, painted yellow, were set up with yellow strips 9 feet by 3 feet laid on the ground to make them visible to the tow aircraft. A nylon rope was attached to these poles and laid out so that the glider was 300 feet behind and slightly to one side of the poles. The tow plane then flew low over the poles, snagged the rope with the hook and 'snatched' the glider off the ground. The nylon rope stretched enough to absorb the initial shock and a braking system on the winch ensured that the slack was taken up gradually and the glider pulled into the air in the 'low tow' position. The cable paid out through the floor of the Dakota instead of, as with other tows, the tail and so, although casting off was from the 'high tow' position, extra care was needed to avoid snagging the tailplane of the Dakota.

Unlike their RAF counterparts, glider pilots measured their experience not in flying hours but in 'lifts' – the number of successful takeoffs and landings made. Just six British pilots are known to have survived the four major operational 'lifts' of Sicily, Normandy, Arnhem and the Rhine Crossing.

Appendix B:

Towing techniques

The standard combination throughout the war for all nations was a powerful tug aircraft (usually a transport or bomber) towing a glider on a cable approximately 130–60 feet long. However, where circumstances demanded it, variations on the theme developed. The German DFS 230, for example, was usually towed by the Ju52 transport but could be used in combination with the He126 reconnaissance aircraft, the Ju87 Stuka, the He111 bomber or even the Me109 fighter.

Known to the Germans as the 'Seilschlepp', this was the standard tow configuration for all forces. In this case the common combination of Ju52 transport and DFS230 glider using a 131 feet cable.

Lighter gliders, such as the Waco CG-4, could be flown in 'double-tow' formation. Towed behind a C-47 Dakota, glider 1 flew on a 350 feet tow rope and glider 2 on a 425 feet rope, both aircraft staying 75 feet apart. It was a dangerous technique and not widely used on operations.

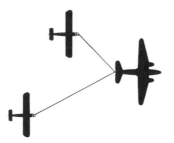

In poor weather or at night, the Germans used the 'Starrschlepp' – a rigid bar connecting the two aircraft via an articulated joint at the rear of the tug. Some flights were carried out by US aircraft using the same technique but it was not used operationally by the Allies.

To raise the enormous Me321 Gigant off the ground, the terrifying 'troika' tow required very skilful pilots as three Me110s had to take off in formation along a 4,000 feet runway. The lead aircraft towed a 328 feet cable, the others 262 feet cables. Hydrogen–peroxide rockets attached to the glider gave extra thrust.

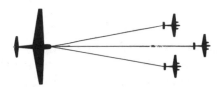

The 'Mistletoe' or the Parasite tow proved effective but was never used operationally.

In 1947, tests were carried out in the United States using the P-38 Lightning fighter and the British Hamilcar glider. Later still, the Space Shuttle, the ultimate military glider, was transported in a similar fashion atop a Boeing 747 Jumbo Jet.

Appendix C:

Technical details

Airspeed AS51 Horsa Mk I and Mk II

Wingspan	88 feet
Length	68 feet
Height	20.3 feet
Crew	pilot, co-pilot
Weight (lb)	total 15,750, cargo 7,380
Loadings	28 troops, two jeeps or one jeep and one 6pdr gun (or equivalent)
Tow speed	160mph
Glide ratio	7.2
Towplanes	Albemarle, Wellington, Dakota, Lancaster, Stirling, Halifax

The Horsa glider first flew on 12 September 1941, just ten months after the start of the design process. Originally designed as a paratroop aircraft from which the men would jump and the glider return to base, experiments were also conducted into using it as a bomber with a single 12,000 lb armour-piercing bomb. In all, 3,655 Horsas were produced, 2,960 by furniture factories. It remained in service after the war, operating in support of British forces in Palestine.

General Aircraft Limited (GAL49) Hamilcar

Wingspan	110 feet
Length	68.5 feet
Weight (lb)	total 36,000, cargo 17,500
Height	20.3 feet
Crew	pilot, co-pilot

Loadings	40 troops or one Tetrach Mk IV (or M22 Locust) tank or two scout cars (or equivalent)
Tow speed	150mph
Glide ratio	11.5
Towplanes:	Halifax, Lancaster, Stirling

First flown on 27 March 1942, the Hamilcar was the largest wooden aircraft built during the war, prompting the US Army's glider procurement officer to call it 'the biggest hunk of airplane I have ever seen put together'. It featured a nose-opening door that opened automatically. Tanks carried aboard started their engines during the approach and could be in action in just fifteen seconds after landing. In 1949, experiments were conducted in the US using a P-38 fighter mounted on top of the fuselage to act as a tow, as had been done with the German DFS 230 and a Me109 fighter. A total of 412 aircraft were produced.

Deutsche Forschungsanstalt für Segelflug (DFS) 230

Wingspan	72 feet
Length	37.5 feet
Weight (lb)	total 4,600, cargo 2,800
Height	9 feet 4 inches
Crew	pilot
Loadings	9 troops or equivalent
Tow speed	120mph
Glide ratio	18
Armament	One passenger-operated machine gun
Towplanes	Ju52, Ju87, He111, He126, Bf110

First flown in 1937, the DFS 230 was a development of the German Institute for Glider Research's earlier 'flying observatory'. It saw widespread service in all theatres and was light enough to be towed by a range of improvised tow aircraft. Some experiments were carried out using Me109 fighters to launch them by carrying them as underslung loads but this was never used operationally. The fuselage was also the basis for the Focke-Achgelis Fa225 Tow-Copter – a rotary wing version of the glider using the blades of the Fa223 helicopter. Although one stood by for the rescue of Mussolini, there were few advantages to the design and it was never put into production. In all, 2,230 DFS 230 models and variants were produced.

Gothaer Waggonfabric, AG (Gotha) Go242

Wingspan	79 feet
Length	52.5 feet
Weight (lb)	total 15,000, cargo 8000
Height	14 feet 5 inches
Crew	pilot, co-pilot
Loadings	23 troops or one Kubelwagen vehicle or equivalent
Tow speed	150mph (186mph max in dive)
Glide ratio	16
Armament	up to 8 MG15 machine guns could be mounted, but no more than 4 were used at any one time – one roof-mounted, one each side of the fuselage and another firing through the rear loading door.
Towplanes	Ju52, He111

To meet the demand for a larger capacity than the DFS 230, the Go242 was designed as an assault and transport aircraft and first flew for the Luftwaffe in mid-1941. Nine variants of the basic design were produced, mainly featuring changes to the landing gear, and some 1,530 were produced. Around 133 gliders were fitted with two radial engines and another 43 specially built and these flew as the Go244 transport aircraft.

Messerschmitt Me321 Gigant

Wingspan	181 feet
Length	93 feet
Weight (lb)	total 70,000, cargo 44,000
Height	33 feet 4 inches
Crew	pilot, co-pilot, radio operator, loadmaster, two airgunners
Loadings	200 troops or a tank or an 88 mm gun and tractor
Tow speed	110mph
Towplanes	Ju90, He111z or three Bf110s

Until the arrival of the Boeing 747 Jumbo Jet, the Gigant was the largest aircraft ever flown. Designed for the invasion of Britain, the Me321 was one of two designs in preparation, the other being the Ju322 Mammut (Mammoth) with an even bigger wingspan of 203 feet. Trials of the Mammut were abandoned and the Gigant adopted after it first flew on 25 February 1941. It was used widely in

Russia later that year but production stopped in 1941 after 200 had been delivered. Problems in finding a powerful enough tow led to the development of the He111z 'Twin' – two He111 bombers joined at the wingtip to produce a five-engined aircraft. At times even this needed help from rocket packs attached to the glider to get it airborne. Later, a four-engined variant of the Me323 was produced and 198 went into service.

Kryliatyi Tank (KT) Antonov A-40

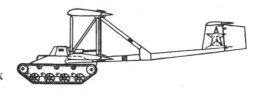

Wingspan	49.2 feet
Length	37.7 feet
Weight (lb)	total 18,000, cargo 13,200
Loadings	one T-60 tank
Tow speed	100mph
Towplanes	TB-3 Bomber

The 'winged tank' concept originated in 1939 and was based on the idea that a tank could be delivered to the battlefield by attaching biplane wings to it. Trials were successful but the 6 ton payload was too much for the towplanes and the project was abandoned. Similar British projects were attempted but these did not get beyond the production of a 1/3 scale model.

ANTONOV A-7 (also known as the Rot Front RF8)

Wingspan	62.2 feet
Length	37.7 feet
Weight (lb)	total 3,782, cargo 1,980
Crew	pilot
Loadings	8 troops
Glide ratio	18 (some sources suggest as high as 22.5)
Speed	186mph
Towplanes	Li-2, SB-3

Designed in 1938, the A-7 was Russia's most widely used glider, with over 400 being built, mostly in 1942 for operations behind German lines.

Waco Cargo Glider 4 (CG-4 or 'Hadrian')

Wingspan	83.6 feet
Length	48 feet
Weight (lb)	total 7,500, cargo 4,060
Height	7.3 feet
Crew	pilot, co-pilot
Loadings	13 troops or one jeep with three troops or one 75 mm howitzer with a crew of three. Alternatively, six stretchers could be carried.
Tow speed	120mph
Glide ratio	8.2
Towplanes	C-47, C-46, C-54, A-25, B-25, P-38

The Waco glider was the most widely used aircraft in the Second World War, with nearly 14,000 being delivered by 1945.

Laister Kauffman Aircraft Corporation Cargo Glider 10 (CG-10 'Trojan Horse')

Wingspan	105 feet
Length	67 feet
Weight (lb)	total 23,000, cargo 10,850
Height	26.3 feet
Crew	pilot, co-pilot
Loadings	40 troops or one 2.5 ton truck or one M1 155 mm howitzer or one jeep and 75mm howitzer.
Tow speed	180mph
Glide ratio	8.1
Towplanes	C-47, C-46, C-54

Larger than the B-17 Flying Fortress, the CG-10 was intended for use in the invasion of Japan and an order was placed in 1942 for 1,000 aircraft. It grew out of a challenge by Colonel Fred Dent when he asked Jack Laister to produce copies of the Horsa under licence. Laister said he could do better and the result was the CG-10, first flown in early 1942. Its rear-loading ramp and low floor – just two feet off the ground – meant it could be loaded and unloaded very easily. Only ten were completed and ninety more were in production by the time Japan surrendered but these saw postwar service as medical facilities and airborne workshops. Every rear-loading military aircraft since has used the CG-10's design features.

Index

A-40 'Winged Tank *See* gliders
'Aberdeen' 91
Ainsworth, Sgt John 101–5
Air Commando (5138th Provisional
     Air Unit) 89–100
Alison, Col. John R 87–100
Andrews, H N 'Andy' 55, 130–1, 132
Antonopoulos, Sgt 'Harry' 49–50,
     139
Antonov, Oleg 144–5
Arnhem *See* Operation Market-
     Garden
Arnold, Gen. Henry H 'Hap' 74–80

Bastogne *See* Operation Repulse
'Baynes Bat' 145
Berlin 184–5
Binder, Col. E 148–9
Brandenbergers 45–7, 153
Brereton, Gen. Lewis H 3, 4, 121, 123
Breslau 179–184
Brittany *See* Operation Dingson
Britten, Flying Officer Rosemary 139
'Broadway' 91–100
Browning, Maj.-Gen. Frederick
     'Boy' 121–34
Budapest 176–9
Burma 82–100
'Burp Gun Corner' 140–1

Canne 14, 25–6
Cartland, Barbara 2
Central Landing Establishment 31
Chatterton, Brig. George 32, 48–56,
     105, 119, 124–5, 128, 133, 142,
     187
Chindits 85–100

Cholm 160–4
Cochran, Col. Philip C 86–100
Corinth Bridge 37–9
Crete *See* Operation Merkur

Demjansk 158–60
Deutsche Forschungsanhalt Für
     Segelflug (DFS) 7
Dneiper 146–9

Eben-Emael 8–29
Edwards, 'Eddie' (Ox & Bucks Light
     Infantry) 101

Flight Officer 77
Force 133 65–7
Franklin, Benjamin 1

Goering, Herman 5, 167
Gale, Gen. Richard 'Windy' 111
Galpin, Sgt 'Galp' 53–5
'Glide ratio' 198
Glider Pilot Regiment: Disbandment
     187; Formation 32; Training 33
Gliders: Airspeed 51 Horsa 33–6,
     101–42, 196–200, 203; Antonov
     A-7 (RF 8 'Red Front') 144–5,
     149, 206; Antonov A-40
     (Winged Tank) 145, 206; CG-
     4A (Waco) 51, 55, 65–7, 71–2,
     207; CG 10 (Laister Kaufman
     'Trojan Horse') 99, 207; CG 13
     98; DFS 230 2, 7, 15–28, 38, 40,
     46, 58, 62, 68, 153–85, 201, 202,
     204; GAL 48; Hotspur 31;
     GAL49 Hamilcar 113–15, 138,
     203–4; Go 242 (Gothaer

Waggonfabrik) 58, 157–84, 204; Me321 (Gigant) and Me323 49, 58, 155–7, 169, 205; XCG 1 75; XCG 3 75; XCG 5 75; XCG 6 75; XCG 7 75; XCG 8 75

Gordon-Brown, Capt. (9Para) 106–11

Gran Sasso 62–4

Gribowski, Vladimir 144

Gurida 100

Hadrian (Waco CG 4A) *See* Gliders

Hagen, Louis (Lewis Haig) 129, 131–32

Hamilcar (General Aircraft Limited 49) *See* Gliders

Heinz Pickle Company 76

Helicopters: Focke-Wulf FA 223 183; FA 225 'Stormbird' 62–3; Sikorsky YR 4 89; Sikorsky YR 6 186

Hempel, Jurgen 181

Hopkinson, Gen. 'Hoppy' 48, 52–6

Horsa (Airspeed 51) *See* Gliders

Hotspur (GAL 48) *See* Gliders

House, Pte Arthur (Liverpool Regt) 95

Howard, Maj. John 111

Iraq, airborne operations in 3–4

Italy, development of airborne force 4

Jager, Unteroffizier 178

Japan 100

Jedburgh Special Operations Team 116

Koch, Hauptman Walter 13–29

Kuban 174–6

Lange, Karl-Heinz 20, 22

Leigh-Mallory, Air Chief Marshal 112

Lowden, Flight Officer John 78, 125, 132, 140

Luzon 98–9

Maleme 39

Malta 44–5

Marine Glider Group 78

Marine Glider Squadron 79

Merville Battery 106–11

Miller, Sgt Vic 138–9

Morzik, Col. Fritz 159, 161

Mountbatten, Lord Louis 85, 90

Murphy, Maj. Michael 80, 113

Mussolini, Benito 60–4

New Guinea 81

Newton, Pte Gordon (9Para) 108–11

Norway *See* Operation Freshman

Operations: Albatross 71; Antifris 149; Anvil/Dragoon 69–72; Barbarossa 151–7; Bluebird 71; Bunghole 64–7; Detroit 113; Dingson 119 20; Dove 71; Eiche 60–4; Elmira 115; Freshman 34–6; Fustian 56–8; Galveston 115; Granit 13; Husky 47–58; Keokuk 115; Ladbrooke 51–6; Mallard 113; Manna 72–3; Market-Garden 120–34; Merkur 39–44; Repulse 134–5; Rösselsprung 68–9; Thursday 85–100; Tonga 101–11; Turkey Buzzard/Beggar 49–51; Varsity 136–42; Voodoo 49

Orcutt, Donald 125–6

Ösel Island 152–7

Otway, Lt-Col. Terence (9Para) 106–11

Partisans 149–50

'Pea Patch Show' 80

Pearson, Lt-Col. 56–7
Pegasus Bridge 101
Peniakoff, Vladimir ('Popski') 59
Philippines 98–9
Pond, Lt Hugh (9Para) 106–7
Project Nine *See* Air Commando

Rademacher, Oberfeldwebel 172–3
Red Army airborne operations 4,
    145–50

Saarema *See* Ösel Island
Schacht, Gerhard 'Owl' 24
Scherbakov, Brig.-Gen. A 150
Shannon, Sgt Bill 106
Skorzeny, Otto 60–4
Special Air Service 119–20
SS Fallschirmjager Battalion 500
    68–9
Stalingrad 165–70
Staraja Toropa 150
Stephan, Unteroffizier 183–4
Student, Gen. Kurt 6, 12–13
Suchinitschi 157–8

'Third Lieutenants' *See* Flight
    Officers
Tito 65–9
Toler, Maj. Ian 104, 130, 139, 141,
    142
Tunisia 45–7
Turner, Capt Cornelius 65–7, 73

Veldwezelt 14, 22–3
Velikye Luki 170–4
Vercors 116–19
Vroenhoven 14, 23–5

Wallwork, Sgt Jim 101–5
Wenzel, Sgt Helmut 14–29
Wilson, FO Bob 50
Wingate, Gen. Orde 84–99
Witzig, Hauptman Rudolf 13–29

'X' Flight Glider Pilot Regiment 119

Yugoslavia *See* Operation Bunghole

Zinser, FO Francis 113

THE
NIGHTWALKER

SEBASTIAN FITZEK

Translated by Jamie Lee Searle

sphere

SPHERE

First published in the English language in
Great Britain in 2016 by Sphere
Originally published in German as *Der Nachtwandler*
in 2013 by Droemer Knaur
This paperback edition published in 2016 by Sphere

1 3 5 7 9 10 8 6 4 2

This book is published by agreement with AVA International GmbH, Germany
(www.ava-international.de)

The moral right of the author has been asserted.

A CIP catalogue record for this book
is available from the British Library.

ISBN 978-0-7515-5682-7

Typeset by Palimpsest Book Production Ltd, Falkirk, Stirlingshire
Printed and bound in Great Britain by Clays Ltd, St Ives plc

Papers used by Sphere are from well-managed forests
and other responsible sources.

MIX
Paper from
responsible sources
FSC
www.fsc.org   FSC® C104740

Sphere
An imprint of
Little, Brown Book Group
Carmelite House
50 Victoria Embankment
London EC4Y 0DZ

An Hachette UK Company
www.hachette.co.uk

www.littlebrown.co.uk

For Manuela

By a route obscure and lonely,
Haunted by ill angels only,
Where an Eidolon, named NIGHT,
On a black throne reigns upright,
I have wandered home but newly
From this ultimate dim Thule.

'Dream-Land', Edgar Allan Poe

Prologue

The patient hadn't even been on the ward for half an hour, and already he was causing trouble. Sister Susan had *tasted* it, almost as soon as the ambulance opened its doors and the stretcher was pushed out.

She could always taste it when problems rolled into the psychiatric department. She would get this strange sensation in her mouth, as though she was chewing on aluminium foil. It could even be unleashed by patients who at first glance seemed more like victims and not aggressive in the slightest; much like the man who had just activated the alarm in Room 1310.

And at five to eight, of all times.

If he could just have waited another five minutes, Susan would have been on her break. Instead, she had to rush along the corridor on an empty stomach.

Not that she had much of an appetite in the evenings anyway. She took great care not to gain weight, even though she wasn't much bigger than some of the anorexia patients being treated on the ward. The tiny salad and half an egg were part of her evening routine – as was, admittedly, a paranoid schizophrenic with hallucinations, but she would have gladly relinquished the latter.

The patient had been found lying naked in the snow outside a supermarket, covered in blood and with lacerations on his feet. He had appeared bedraggled, disorientated and dehydrated, but his gaze was alert and steady, his voice clear, and his teeth (teeth, as far as Susan was concerned, were always a sure indication of the state of the soul) showed no signs of alcohol, nicotine or substance abuse.

And yet I could still taste it, she thought, with one hand on her bleeper and the other on her bunch of keys.

Susan unlocked the door and entered the room.

The scene before her was so bizarre that she stood in shock for a moment before pressing the bleeper to call the security team, who were trained especially for situations such as these.

'I can prove it,' screamed the naked man in front of the window. He was standing in a pool of vomit.

'Of course you can,' answered the sister, taking care to keep her distance.

Her words sounded rehearsed rather than genuine, because Susan had indeed rehearsed them and didn't intend them to be genuine, but in the past she had often been able to win time with empty platitudes.

Not this time, though.

Later, in its final report, the inquiry panel would establish that the cleaning woman had been listening to music on an MP3 player, something strictly forbidden during working hours. When her supervisor came by unexpectedly to do a hygiene check, she had hidden the device in the water meter cupboard next to the shower.

But in the moment of crisis it was a mystery to Sister Susan how the patient had come into possession of the electronic device. He had ripped open its battery compartment and was holding a bent alkaline battery, which he must have chewed open with his teeth. Although Susan couldn't actually see it, she pictured the viscous battery acid flowing over the edges like marmalade.

'Everything's going to be OK,' she said, trying to placate him.

'No, nothing's going to be OK,' the man protested. 'Listen to me. I'm not crazy. I tried to throw up to get it out of my stomach, but maybe I've already digested it. Please. You have to take an X-ray. You have to X-ray my body. The proof is inside me!'

He screamed and screamed until, eventually, the security team came in and restrained him.

But they were too late. By the time the doctors rushed into the room, the patient had long since swallowed the battery.

A few days before

Somewhere in the world.
In a town you know.
Maybe even in your neighbourhood . . .

1

The cockroach was creeping towards Leon's mouth.

Just another few centimetres and its long feelers would touch his open lips. It had already reached the fleck of drool he had left on the bed sheet in his sleep.

Leon tried to close his mouth, but his muscles were paralysed.

It's happening again.

He couldn't get up, raise his hand or even blink. He had no choice but to stare at the cockroach, which was lifting up its wings as if extending some friendly greeting:

Hello, Leon, I'm back. Don't you recognise me?

Yes, of course I do. I know exactly who you are.

They had christened it Morphet, the gigantic cockroach from Réunion. He hadn't realised that these repulsive things could actually fly. When they looked on the internet afterwards they found all these crazy discussion threads on the topic, and from that day on they were able to add their own unequivocal contribution: cockroaches from Réunion were certainly able to, and it must have been one of these flight-enabled specimens that Natalie had brought back from holiday nine months ago. The monstrosity must have crawled into her suitcase while she was packing, and when she opened the case back at home, Morphet had been sat there on her dirty washing, cleaning his feelers. Natalie hadn't even had time to draw breath to scream before the cockroach flew off, hiding itself in some unreachable corner of the old building.

They had searched everywhere. Every nook and cranny, of which there were many in the high-ceilinged rooms of their three-bedroom apartment: under the skirting boards, behind the washer-dryer in the bathroom, among Leon's architectural models in his study – they even turned the dark room upside down, despite the fact that Natalie had sealed the door to her photography lab with light-excluding material and always kept it locked. But it was all in vain. The gigantic insect with its spider-like legs and bluebottle-coloured shell could not be found.

On that first night Natalie seriously contemplated leaving the apartment they had moved into only a few months before.

The apartment where we wanted to make a fresh start.

Later, after having sex, they had laughingly reassured one another that Morphet was sure to have flown out of the window to the park, to discover that those of his kind in this town were a little smaller and less hairy than he was.

But now he's back.

Morphet was so close now that Leon could *smell* him. Nonsense, of course, but his disgust at the cockroach was so great that Leon's senses were playing tricks on him. He was even convinced he could make out on its hairy legs the faecal remains of the countless dust mites it had hoarded beneath the bed under the cloak of darkness. Its feelers still hadn't made contact with Leon's dry, open lips, but he already thought he could feel the tickling sensation. And he had a premonition of how it would feel when the cockroach crept into his mouth. It would be salty and scratchy, like popcorn when it clings to your palate.

Then Morphet would slowly but surely force himself into Leon's throat, bashing his wings against his teeth along the way.

And I can't even bite.

Leon groaned, trying with all his might to scream. Sometimes it helped, but it usually took more than that to free himself from the sleep paralysis.

He knew, of course, that the cockroach wasn't real. It was early in the morning, a few days before New

9

Year, and pitch black in the bedroom. It was physically impossible to see even his hand right in front of his face, but none of these certainties made the horror any more bearable. Because disgust, even at its most intense, is never material, but instead a psychological reaction to some external influence. Whether this influence is imagined or really exists makes no difference at all to how it feels.

Natalie!

Leon tried to scream his wife's name, but failed miserably. Just as so many times before, he was imprisoned in a waking nightmare from which he couldn't escape without help.

People with ego weakness are particularly prone to sleep paralysis, Leon had once read in a popular psychology magazine, partly recognising himself in the article. Although he didn't have an inferiority complex as such, he secretly saw himself as a 'Yes, but' person: yes, his dark hair was full and thick, but its numerous kinks ensured that he tended to look as though he had just fallen out of bed. Yes, his chin and its gently sloping V-shape might give his face an attractively masculine appearance, but his beard resembled that of a teenager. Yes, he had white teeth, but when he laughed too hard you could see that his fillings had paid for his dentist's SUV. And yes, he was six feet tall, but seemed shorter on account of the fact that he never stood up straight. In brief:

he wasn't bad looking. But women who were looking for a good time, even though they may have given him a smile, never gave him their telephone numbers. They gave them to his best friend Sven instead, who had been blessed with a royal flush in the game of genetic poker: great hair, teeth, lips, a strong build . . . everything like Leon, except without the 'but'.

Natalie? Grunting, Leon tried to fight his way out of the paralysis. *Please help me. Morphet is about to crawl across my tongue.*

He was taken aback by the unexpected sound coming from his mouth. Even when dreaming, he only ever spoke, grunted or cried out in his own, familiar voice. But the whimper he was hearing now sounded softer, higher. More like the voice of a woman.

'Natalie?'

All at once it became light in the room.

Thank God.

This time he had managed to free himself from the clutches of his nightmare without kicking and screaming. He knew that at some point in their life most people would suffer from the same thing, imprisoned in the shadowy world between sleeping and waking. A world you could only escape with the greatest strength of will. Or through some paradoxical disturbance from the outside. If someone turned on a bright light in the middle of the night, for example, or if loud music was playing, or if an alarm started or . . . *if someone was crying?*

Leon pulled himself upright and blinked.

'Natalie?'

His wife was kneeling in front of the wardrobe opposite the bed with her back to him. She seemed to be looking for something among her shoes.

'Sorry, sweetheart, did I wake you?'

No response, just a long drawn-out sob. Natalie sighed, then the whimper quietened down.

'Are you OK?'

She silently pulled a pair of ankle boots from the cupboard and threw them into . . .

. . . *her suitcase?*

Leon flung back the blanket and got out of bed.

'What's wrong?' He looked at the clock on his nightstand. It was only a quarter to seven. So early that not even the light in Natalie's aquarium had come on.

'Are you still angry?'

They had argued repeatedly throughout the whole of the previous week, and two days ago things had escalated. Both of them were so busy at work that they could barely see straight. She had her first big photography exhibition looming, and he was preparing for the architecture pitch. Each had accused the other of neglect, and each thought their own commitments the most important.

On Christmas Eve the word 'divorce' had been uttered for the first time, and even though neither of them meant it seriously, it was an alarming sign of how raw their nerves were. Yesterday Leon wanted to extend an olive branch by taking Natalie out for a reconciliation dinner, but she'd come home late from the gallery yet again.

'Listen, I know we have our problems at the moment, but—'

She spun round to face him and the sight of her hit him like a blow to the gut.

'Natalie, what—' He blinked, wondering if he could still be dreaming. 'What the hell happened to your face?'

The skin around her right eye was deep violet and her eyelids were swollen shut. She was dressed, but it looked like she had thrown everything on in a rush. The flower-patterned blouse with the ruffled sleeves was buttoned up unevenly, her trousers were missing the belt, and the laces of her high-heeled suede boots were flapping around loose.

She turned away from him again. Moving awkwardly, she tried to close the suitcase, but it was too small for all the things she'd tried to cram into it. A red silk slip, a scarf and her favourite white skirt bulged out of the sides.

Leon moved closer and went to pull her into his arms in a reassuring embrace, but Natalie flinched away in fear.

'What's wrong with you?' he asked in confusion as she hastily reached for her suitcase. Four of her fingernails were painted a mud-like colour. The thumbnail was missing.

'Jesus Christ, your thumb!' cried Leon, trying to grab her injured hand. Then the sleeve of Natalie's blouse slid upwards and he saw the cuts.

From a razor blade?

'For the love of God, Natalie. Have you started with that again?'

'Me?'

It was the first question he had asked that actually prompted an answer.

In her gaze was a mix of bewilderment, fear and – the most confusing thing to Leon right now – pity. She had opened her lips by only a narrow slit, but it was enough to see that a large part of one of her front teeth was missing.

'*Me?*'

He froze in shock, and Natalie pulled herself free from his touch. She grabbed her mobile from the bed. Her good-luck charm swung from the smartphone, a pink artificial-pearl chain on which each bead was decorated with a letter from her name – Natalie's name band, which had been fastened on to her wrist in the hospital the day she was born twenty-seven years ago. With her suitcase in the other hand, she rushed across the room.

'Where are you going?' he cried, but she was already half out the door. He tried to run into the hallway after her, but stumbled over a crate of building plans that he had been going to take into the office.

'Natalie, please just explain to me . . .'

She ran down the steps, not turning around to him even once.

Later, in the days of horror that followed, Leon was no longer sure if it was his imagination or if his wife really had been dragging her right leg as she hurried to the door. Although it could equally have been because of the suitcase, or the fact that her shoes weren't properly fastened.

Once Leon had picked himself up again, she had disappeared into the ancient lift and had pulled the manual door across in front of her like a protective shield. The last thing he saw of his wife, the woman he had shared the last three years of his life with, was that horrified, fearful (and pitiful?) gaze: '*Me?*'

The lift began to move. After standing there for an instant, frozen in shock, Leon ran to the stairs.

The wide wooden steps, coiling their way downwards around the lift shaft like a snake, were covered with sisal carpet, the coarse fibres of which pricked the soles of his feet. Leon was wearing nothing but a loose pair of boxer shorts, which were threatening to slip down over his slim hips with every step he took.

Taking several steps at a time, he reckoned he could reach the ground floor in time. Then old Ivana Helsing on the second floor opened her apartment door, admittedly only by a crack and without taking off the safety chain from the inside, but it was still enough to break Leon's rhythm.

'Alba, come back,' he heard his neighbour calling out, but it was too late. The black cat had slipped out of the apartment into the stairway, running between his legs. So as not to fall flat on his face, he had to grab on to the handrail with both hands and bring himself to a halt.

'Good God, Leon! What's wrong?'

He ignored the concerned voice of the elderly woman, who had now opened her door completely and stepped out. He pushed his way past.

There was still time. He could hear the creaking of the lift's wooden cabin and the crackling of the steel cable from which it was hanging.

Arriving on the ground floor, he veered around the corner, slid across the smooth marble and ended up huddled on all fours, wheezing and panting, in front of the lift door. The cabin slowly sunk down to rest in its standby position.

And then . . . nothing.

No rattling or clattering, no sound at all to indicate someone was about to get out.

'Natalie?'

Leon took a deep breath, pulled himself to his feet and tried to peer through the colourful art nouveau stained-glass panes set into the door, but all he could see were shadows.

So he opened the door from the outside. Only to find himself staring at his own reflection.

The mirrored cabin was empty; Natalie had gone. Vanished.

How was that possible?

Leon looked around in search of help, and at that moment Dr Michael Tareski came into the empty hallway. The chemist – who lived above Leon on the fourth floor, never greeted him and always looked listless – was wearing a tracksuit and trainers instead of his usual blazer and white linen trousers. A glistening brow and dark flecks around the armpits of his sweatshirt betrayed the fact that he had just been for an early-morning run.

'Have you seen Natalie?' asked Leon.

'Who?'

Tareski's wary gaze wandered from Leon's naked torso down to his boxer shorts. Presumably the chemist was running through a mental list of the medication that could be responsible for his neighbour's confused state. Either that, or the ones that could put him right again.

'Oh, you mean your wife?' Tareski turned away and went over to the mailboxes on the wall, which meant that Leon could no longer see his face as he replied: 'She just left in a taxi.'

Feeling dazed, Leon scrunched up his eyes as if blinded by the beam of a torch, then went past Tareski to the main door.

'You'll catch your death out there,' the chemist warned him, and as Leon opened the door and stepped out on to the stone steps leading down to the pavement every muscle in his body cramped up in agreement. The building was in a reduced traffic zone in the old town, with lots of boutiques, restaurants, cafés, theatres and art-house cinemas like the Celeste, the malfunctioning neon sign of which was flickering on to the neighbouring house above Leon's head in the early-dawn light.

The antique-looking street lights, modelled on gas lanterns, were still burning. At this hour on a weekend very few people were around. In the distance a man was walking his dog, and opposite a man was just pulling up the shutters of his newspaper kiosk. But most people weren't even awake yet, let alone out and about. This year the Christmas holidays had fallen so that just a few days of holiday had been enough to bridge the time until the New Year's celebrations. The streets looked abandoned, whichever direction Leon looked. No cars, no taxis, no Natalie.

His teeth began to chatter, and he wrapped his arms around his upper body. By the time he stepped back into the shelter of the lobby, Tareski had disappeared into the lift.

Shivering with cold, confused, and unwilling to wait, Leon took the stairs instead.

This time no cat ran across his path. Ivana Helsing's door was closed, even though Leon felt sure the old woman was watching him through the peephole. Just like the Falconis on the first floor, the childless, melancholic couple who he was sure to have woken with his stumbling and clamouring.

It was very likely they would make another complaint about him to the building management, just like they had when he celebrated his twenty-eighth birthday rather too loudly back in the spring.

Confused, exhausted and trembling all over, Leon reached the third floor, thankful the door was still ajar and he hadn't locked himself out. Natalie's perfume, a subtle summery scent, still hung in the air. For a moment he lost himself in the hope that he had just dreamed it all, that the woman he wanted to spend the rest of his life with would still be sleeping peacefully, wrapped up in the thick quilt. But then he saw Natalie's untouched side of the bed, and knew his wish would not be granted.

He stared at the ransacked wardrobe, the lower drawer of which was still open. It was empty, as was the small bureau next to the window which, until yesterday, housed her make-up brushes. Now it held only the laptop they watched DVDs on now and again. A compromise, because Natalie hadn't wanted a TV in the bedroom.

The clock on Leon's nightstand jumped to 7 a.m., and the fluorescent lamps above the tall aquarium flickered on. Leon saw his reflection in the shimmering, green-tinged glass of the tank. There was no longer even a single fish swimming in the four hundred litres of fresh water.

Three weeks before, all the angel fish had perished due to a persistent fungus, even though Natalie had tended to her precious possessions meticulously, checking the water quality on a daily basis. She was so despondent afterwards that Leon had doubted she would ever keep fish again.

The autotimer was still set only because, over the years, they had got used to being woken by the light of the aquarium. Leon angrily pulled the electricity cable out of the plug socket. The light extinguished, and he felt lost.

He sat down on the edge of the bed, buried his head in his hands and tried to find an innocent explanation for what had just happened. But as hard as he tried, he was unable to suppress the certainty that, despite all the doctors' protestations that he had been cured, the past had caught up with him again.

His illness had come back.

2

'. . . you have to speak into it.'

'Into what?'

'For heaven's sake – into the telephone, of course!'

The older man on the tape sounded impatient; it clearly wasn't the first time he had tried to explain to his wife how to record an answerphone message. The line crackled, then it seemed that Leon's mother had brought the receiver into the correct position.

'You have reached the home of Klaus and Maria Nader,' she said, sounding like someone who was doing a bad imitation of a satnav.

Please turn around at the next available opportunity.

'Unfortunately we're not here right now.'

'Speak for yourself,' interjected his father drily from the background.

Even though Leon wasn't in the mood, having felt

21

sick and numb all morning, he couldn't help but chuckle. His adoptive parents didn't miss a single opportunity to act like the old couple on the balcony in *The Muppet Show*. With or without an audience, at home or out in public, barely a sentence from one of them failed to draw commentary from the other. Unwitting onlookers often thought they were witnessing the final scenes of a marriage in its death throes. But that couldn't have been further from the truth.

'And we won't be able to return your call for a while, either, because we're on a cruise,' explained Maria on the tape.

'Why don't you just say where any potential thieves can find the house keys while you're at it?'

'And what would they take? Your Caracho railway?'

Leon smiled.

His mother knew, of course, that the brand was Carrera; she said it wrong on purpose to annoy Klaus. The racing circuit in the loft was his pride and joy. Klaus Nader had always played with it at Christmas, while Leon had only been allowed to watch. At most now and again he had been permitted to put back one of the race cars that had fallen off, while his old man operated the speed control with his eyes glistening. It was a father-and-son classic.

Klaus had more time for his hobby now that the arthritis in his knuckle had rendered him unable to stay in his job as a waiter, much to Maria's chagrin, who now had to 'put up with the old dog' at home all day.

God, I miss them, thought Leon wistfully. He would have given anything to be able to talk to them in person right now. Once again it was far too long since they had last seen each other.

He closed his eyes and longed to be back at the head of the narrow wooden table in the kitchen, the best seat in the Naders' end-of-terrace house for watching their affectionate bickering. Leon could picture his father clearly: his shirt-sleeves rolled up, his broad elbows on the table as he rubbed his chin thoughtfully, waiting for the scrambled eggs that his wife was preparing for him.

If it takes any longer I'm going to need another shave already.

Good idea, and why don't you do your back while you're at it?

Are you trying to imply I have a hairy back?

Of course not. Just like you don't have a double chin.

What are you talking about? I just have a few wrinkles on my neck, not a double chin.

That's what I said.

'Our son bought us the cruise as a present,' Maria announced proudly on the answerphone.

'He's such a good boy,' murmured Klaus, quoting

one of Maria's favourite commentaries, which she always had at the ready whenever someone mentioned her son.

'He sure is. And there's no need to roll your eyes like that, you old fool—'

A beeping tone then accomplished something that Klaus Nader only rarely managed. It silenced Maria, reminding Leon of the reason for his call.

'Er, Mama, Papa?' he said, feeling flustered. 'Nice message. I'm just calling because I . . .'

. . . *wanted to ask if Natalie has been in touch with you?*

It had been the same for his parents as it had for him. They'd fallen in love with Natalie the very second they met her.

'Call me shallow,' his father had said, taking him to the side briefly after Natalie had left the garden that summer afternoon to help Maria with the salad in the kitchen, 'but if the contents are even half as beautiful as the packaging with this woman, then you'll be even more of a loon than the idiot who messed up the fifty-euro question on *Who Wants to Be a Millionaire?* yesterday if you ever let her go.'

The affection was mutual, for Natalie had doted on the cranky couple. Especially Maria, which was astonishing when you thought about it, because the two women could hardly be more different.

Natalie wanted to pursue her career as a photographer

and travel the world as a celebrated artist, while Maria was a housewife who saw the legacy she would bequeath to the world in Leon, not in a retrospective at the Guggenheim Museum. She wore her apron as proudly as Natalie did her stilettos. And while Natalie Lené had grown up in a twenty-room villa, Maria Nader had spent her childhood literally on the street, in a motorhome with a retractable awning and a chemical toilet.

The thing that united these two very different women was not their past or their plans for the future, but the fact that both were judged incorrectly by those around them. Natalie wasn't a superficial bimbo any more than Maria was a simple-minded housewife. They were just two people on the same wavelength; it was up to other people if they wanted to waste their valuable time on earth wondering how such an affinity was possible.

They trusted one another, and so it was very possible that Natalie had turned to Maria in her moment of need. But despite this, Leon had made the phone call without holding out any great hopes, and only now, a day after her hurried departure.

Yesterday he had spent hours waiting for a call that would put his mind at rest, and the countless times he had dialled Natalie's mobile number he had only reached the voicemail.

Today, still not having received a sign of life from

her, he was tentatively beginning to contact people he could trust. People Natalie might confide in.

But he had stumbled into a dead end. His parents were away. On the high seas. Unreachable.

Like Natalie.

Leon realised that he had said nothing for too long, that for the last few seconds the answerphone would have picked up only his breathing, if that. Feeling dazed, he hung up without saying goodbye.

If his parents listened to the abrupt message after their return, they would be sure to call him back right away.

But Leon doubted they could ever feel as distressed as he did right now.

He didn't know what had happened to Natalie, or why she had left him so hurriedly. Leon knew only one thing: whatever his parents might think, he had never given them a cruise as a present.

3

'Did I wake you?'

'Does size matter?' grumbled the voice at the other end. 'Of course you woke me, you idiot.'

'I'm sorry,' Leon apologised to Anouka.

She was Natalie's best friend and, for that reason, the second person on the list of trusted confidants to contact. It was just before nine in the morning, but Anouka was known for being a night owl, and never made an appearance in the gallery before noon. He was sure to have torn her from a deep sleep. Or from the arms of one of the numerous lovers she regularly picked up in the clubs of the city.

Leon couldn't totally understand her success with men, but then again beauty was known to lie in the eye of the beholder. The men drawn to Natalie's svelte girlish body, her long dark hair and melancholic gaze had very little in common with the muscle-bound, hairy-chested and – at first glance – somewhat jaded men who tended to ogle Anouka's artificially enhanced breasts in karaoke bars.

'You sound strange,' Anouka commented. He heard the rustle of bed-sheets, then the sound of bare feet padding across parquet flooring.

'Have you taken something?'

'Don't be ridiculous.'

'Has something happened?'

Leon hesitated. 'I . . . I was hoping you might be able to tell me.'

'Eh?'

'Is Natalie with you?'

'Why would you think that?'

Leon felt sure he could hear water gurgling, and if he knew Natalie's best friend as well as he thought he did, she was squatting on the toilet right now and urinating unashamedly while he was on the line.

'It's complicated. I'm kind of out of sorts, but I don't want to talk about it now, OK?'

'You don't want to talk about it but you called me in the middle of the night?' Anouka managed to inject both amusement and annoyance into her tone at the same time. The sound of a toilet flushing thundered down the line.

'Natalie left the apartment yesterday, and I haven't been able to reach her since,' explained Leon, turning towards the living-room door. He had been pacing up and down between the sofa and the window while talking, but his throat was beginning to tickle, so he decided to get a glass of water from the kitchen.

'Did you have an argument?' asked Anouka.

'I don't know.'

'You don't know whether or not you had an argument?'

I don't even know if it might have been something much worse than a harmless argument, but you would never understand that.

'This must sound really strange, I know, but could you please do me a favour and tell her to call me if you see her in the gallery today?'

Natalie and Anouka had shared first a room and then an apartment during art college. Long before Natalie met Leon, the two women had pledged to realise their dream of opening their own photography gallery in the old town. A space where they would exhibit their own pictures, along with those of other young artists. About a year ago they had put the dream into action and, following the first few press reviews, the gallery had got off to a great start.

'I can't,' said Anouka.

'You can't what?'

'Ask her to call you.'

'Sorry?'

He knew Anouka had hated him ever since Natalie moved out of their apartment together to live with him. She saw him as a bourgeois stiff, because his work as an architect was commercial rather than artistic. On the rare occasions when they met up, they exchanged the bare minimum of small talk, and the aversion had been mutual ever since Leon found out that Anouka had begged her girlfriend not to get into a relationship with him. But despite all the antipathy, until today she had never acted in a hostile way towards him, at least not openly.

'You don't want to give her my message?'

'No, I *can't*, because it's likely I won't see her.'

'What's that supposed to mean?'

'It means your darling Natalie hasn't come to work for the last two weeks. I'm running the gallery all by myself.'

Stunned, as though Anouka had just dealt him a blow to the head, he came to an abrupt halt in the hallway and stared at the magnetic board fastened to the closed kitchen door at head height. Natalie and he used to leave each other affectionate, playful messages on it, depending on who left the house first in the morning. But the last one (*Sweetheart, did we have sex last night? Sorry if I snored. Nat*) had been months ago, and now there was just a notice from the building administration under the magnet, announcing to residents that the renovation of the stairway would begin in a few days' time. (*Be prepared for long waits for the lift!*)

'But Natalie told me you two were working on a big exhibition?'

Star Children.

An exhibition of images as moving as they were disturbing, on the subject of miscarriages and stillbirths.

That, after all, was why Natalie had been leaving early in the morning and coming back late at night.

Just like the day before yesterday!

He had waited for her in the dining room with a bottle of conciliatory wine, eventually opening it as the evening turned to night. Once it was empty, he had fallen into bed drunk, not even noticing how or when Natalie arrived home.

'She told me you guys were working flat out to get everything ready in time.'

'Flat out is right. But I'm doing it all by myself, Leon. I've got no idea what's going on with her. I know she can be a bit unreliable at times, but not calling me back one single time even though I've left dozens of messages on her phone, that's a bit much even for her. I mean, the exhibition was her idea, but perhaps it was too soon.'

No, I don't believe that.

After the miscarriage last summer, Natalie had been devastated, but she got over it with astonishing speed. Perhaps because it happened in the tenth week, together with her period, meaning that a scrape wasn't necessary.

31

A star child.

He had been so happy when her period didn't come. She hadn't told him about the first signs – the soreness in her breasts, the sensitivity to smell first thing in the morning – from fear it could turn out to be a false alarm. But then she bought a test, and those few days after the positive result were the most wonderful of his life.

Then came the morning when she discovered the blood in her pants, and their plans evaporated into thin air, along with the joyful anticipation. It was awful, but somehow, after a short, intensive period of grief, the incident ended up bringing them even closer together. If he hadn't had this feeling, he wouldn't have proposed to her two months ago.

And she had said yes!

The wedding was rather unorthodox; without any witnesses, a photographer or flower girls. They had simply picked the first available appointment at the registry office. Many of their friends reacted with surprise, and some were even indignant, but why shouldn't they get married in exactly the same way as they fell in love: head over heels?

'She was over the worst of it,' said Leon, more to himself than Anouka.

Remembering that he wanted a glass of water, he opened the kitchen door, then began to cough.

Something in the air was making it almost

impossible to enter the room. It felt like thick smoke, but the substance irritating his throat and forcing tears to his eyes in a matter of seconds was completely invisible.

'What did you say?' asked Anouka.

'Nothing,' he spluttered, rushing over to the kitchen window with his hand pressed against his mouth. He flung it open and sucked the cold, clear air into his lungs with relief.

'Anyway, Leon. Whatever's going on at home with you two doesn't really have anything to do with me. I was actually hoping that *you* might call to explain why Natalie's been so rattled recently.'

Leon rubbed his eyes, turning round and searching for the source of the irritant. His gaze fell on the microwave, the neon display of which was blinking.

'I mean, she decides to give up now, of all the moments she could choose. We're still in the beginning stages, we made a profit for the very first time last month, and now Natalie throws in the towel. I just don't get it.'

Nor do I, thought Leon, opening the microwave and starting to cough again. He had found the origin of the acrid smell.

'Is everything OK?' asked Anouka.

No. Nothing, nothing at all, is OK.

With his fingertips, he reached for the trainers in the microwave, but was unable to lift them. The

33

rubber soles had melted on to the microwave plate, and the sight awakened a memory of a time that Leon had so far regarded to be the worst in his life.

Without saying goodbye, he hung up on Anouka and hurried out of the kitchen, along the hallway and into his study. He had to lift up the cardboard model of the children's hospital, which the architectural firm had been planning to enter into the competition for the new build, in order to open the topmost desk drawer. After rummaging around for a while, he found the worn-out looking notebook that he had once used to record important phone numbers. He hoped the number hadn't changed. After all, it was over fifteen years since he last dialled it.

It rang for what felt like an eternity, before someone picked up.

'Dr Volwarth?'

'Speaking. Who is this?'

'It's me. Leon Nader. I think it's started again.'

4

'Thank you for coming so quickly.'

Dr Samuel Volwarth acknowledged Leon's conversation opener with an indulgent smile and made himself comfortable on the sofa. 'I don't normally do house calls, but I have to admit, you made me curious. Yet again.'

Leon had reached the psychiatrist just as he was about to set off on a trip. Dr Volwarth was due to depart for a congress in Tokyo and had made a detour on his way to the airport to pay a flying visit to his former patient.

Now they were sat in the living room while the taxi outside waited on double yellow lines. But despite this, Volwarth looked completely relaxed and composed, just as Leon remembered him. It was a peculiar feeling to be sitting opposite him again, after such a long time.

The psychiatrist didn't look to have aged by even a day. As before, his hair was long and tied in a grey ponytail. It seemed he was still making the greatest effort to be different. But his appearance, despite being scandalous to Leon back in his childhood, now just looked extrovert: Volwarth's leather trousers, his cowboy boots, the swallow tattoo on his neck. Searching for signs of the passing of time, Leon could only find them in the details: the corners of his mouth drooping a little lower, the rings under his eyes a shade darker. And the doctor had replaced his pearl earring with a discreet silver stud.

'It's been a hell of a long time, hasn't it? Almost an entire beach must have passed through the hourglass since we last saw each other.'

Leon nodded. It was seventeen years since his concerned parents had driven him to Volwarth's private clinic for the first time.

Back then, however, he still hadn't called Klaus and Maria his *parents*. In the first years after the accident, it would have felt like a betrayal of his biological parents, who he'd lost at the age of ten. A depressed, suicidal alcoholic had intentionally driven down the wrong slip road of the motorway. The head-on collision claimed three victims. Only two passengers survived: Leon, who even now could remember that he and his sister were singing along to 'Yellow Submarine' on the radio when the headlights suddenly appeared ahead of them; and the wrong-way driver, who came out of it with just a broken collarbone. An ironic twist of fate that only the Devil could find amusing.

The days after Leon had woken up in hospital as an orphan felt like living under a diving bell. He listened to the doctors' diagnoses, the recommendations of the child psychologists and the words of the woman from the youth welfare office, but he didn't understand them. The lips of those who examined him, cared for him and – in the end – wanted to offload him to replacement parents, had moved and produced noise but no meaning.

'It's a lovely place you have here,' said the psychiatrist now, almost two decades later, his gaze fixed on the stuccoed ceiling. 'An old build with a lift and parquet floor. South-facing balcony, and I guess around four bedrooms. It can't have been easy to find something like that in this neighbourhood.'

'Three bedrooms. But yes, it was definitely the proverbial needle in the haystack.'

Natalie had stumbled across the rental notice by chance while out for a walk and had written to the owner without holding out any great hopes. They even thought it might be a hoax, because a choice piece of property like this was more likely to be advertised in the glossy catalogues of the luxury estate agents than on the post of a street lamp.

They'd spent a whole year on the waiting list and

had to submit one guarantee after another before finally being accepted by the building management. Even today Leon still didn't know what tipped the balance in their favour, making them come out ahead of a host of other applicants. Such a desirable and far-from-cheap apartment would normally only be granted to tenants with a fixed income. Not to two freelancers with uncertain commission prospects.

'Did you know that I recently spoke about your case again at a symposium?' the psychiatrist suddenly asked.

Volwarth seemed to be observing Leon's every reaction, and – not for the first time since the doctor walked into the apartment – Leon felt like he was back in the therapy sessions that had defined a significant part of his childhood. While other boys were heading out to the Baggersee, playing football in the gravel pit or making a treehouse in the garden, this man had been cabling him up, plugging him into a computer and rummaging around in his soul with his never-ending questions.

'So what was the catalyst that made you want to see me?'

Leon stood up. 'That's what I'd like to show you.'

He turned the television on with the remote control. The ancient video recorder underneath, however, he had to operate manually. He had hauled it up from the cellar just an hour before, given it a quick dust and connected it to the flatscreen monitor. It was a miracle the clunky monstrosity still worked. The spooling VHS tape crackled with every turn like a badly oiled cog.

'You kept our old tapes?' asked Volwarth in astonishment as he saw the first images appear on the screen. He had given them to Leon at their last session, as a parting gift from the successfully completed therapy.

'Well, would you look at that.'

Volwarth had stood up right next to Leon, his gaze fixed on the screen.

The grainy, slightly yellowed images showed Leon's eleven-year-old face in close-up. Back then he had still been chubby-cheeked and a little dumpy, not anywhere near as slim as he was today. On the recording, he was sat bolt upright in his pyjamas on the edge of a bed in a child's room. The bed-sheets were those of a popular football team, and a poster of Michael Jackson had been tacked on to the wardrobe in the background. He hadn't chosen either of them. Nor the bed, the room or the adoptive parents into whose care he had been passed. They were already the second couple to try with him. But they were the first to enlist a doctor to get to the bottom of his problems.

'Do you know what we're planning to do tonight, Leon?' asked Volwarth on the tape. Even his voice sounded just the same as it did today. The psychiatrist was standing out of sight behind the camera, into which little Leon was blinking nervously. His eyes were red-rimmed and he looked exhausted, because he had slept only a few minutes for the third night in a row. But he nodded.

'It's an experiment that we haven't yet carried out with a child of your age. It's completely harmless, nothing will happen to you. I just want you to know this: nothing will happen against your will here. You can tell me if you'd prefer not to do it after all.'

'No, it's OK. But it won't hurt, will it?'

'No,' laughed Dr Volwarth good-naturedly. 'It might pinch a little when you lie down, but we've cushioned everything well.'

With these words, the psychiatrist appeared in the picture. His back obscured the view for a brief moment, then Volwarth could be seen trying to fasten something to the boy's head. When he stepped aside again, Leon was wearing a shining metal ring that ran around his forehead, with a fist-sized object attached to it that was vaguely reminiscent of a miner's lamp.

'The thing on your head is a radio-controlled sleep camera,' explained Volwarth in a calm voice.

'And it films everything I do while I'm dreaming?'

'Yes, it's motion-activated, which means it comes on as soon as you get up. We've made an exception this time and left off the electrodes that measure your brainwaves and muscle and eye movement. There are no cables, so you can move around freely. There's just one thing I want you to do for me.'

'What?'

'This is the only device like this we have in the institute, and it was very expensive. So please don't take a shower with it on.'

Leon smiled, but his eyes looked sad. 'I don't know what I do when I'm asleep, though. I can never remember.'

'That's exactly why you're going to wear this sleep camera tonight.'

'And what if I do something bad again?'

Volwarth frowned. 'What do you mean *again*? We've spoken about this at length, Leon. You're a sleepwalker. There are thousands of sleepwalkers in this country alone, it's nothing bad.'

'So then why did the Molls want me to leave?'

Watching it now, years after he had said these words for the first time, Leon winced. His stomach started to cramp up. *Moll*.

Too many unbidden memories were linked with this name. Today he knew that it hadn't been his first foster parents' fault. Leon understood why they wanted to be rid of him, even if, at the time, he felt like an unwanted pet brought back to the animal home for not being house-trained.

'Frau Moll thought I was a murderer. She screamed it in my face.'

'Because your foster mother was scared. You know yourself what she saw. It would have scared the heck out of you too, right?'

'I guess so.'

'You see, it's just a completely normal reaction. When someone sleepwalks, to others they look like a ghost. But it's not dangerous.'

'So why did I have a knife in my hand?'

As I stood there in the children's bedroom. Over her son's bed.

To this day it still wasn't clear if he really wanted to hurt nine-year-old Adrian that night. How Leon got into his bedroom was a complete mystery, because to get there he had to go down one floor, and the designer stairs in the Molls' house didn't have a banister, which made them a challenge even awake. But the biggest puzzle was the bread knife Adrian's mother caught the sleepwalking Leon with. He had been holding it in both hands, like a dagger, above the chest of the sleeping child. The knife wasn't from the Molls' kitchen, and Leon hadn't been able to explain how it came into his possession. This put as much fear into him as the question of what would have happened if Frau Moll hadn't been woken by the creaking floorboards and gone to check what was happening. Adrian himself had been completely unaware of both the sleeping visitor and the impending danger.

'Believe me, Leon. You're not a bad person,' Volwarth was saying on the tape. In spite of the bad picture quality, Leon could see in his own eyes that he didn't believe the doctor. Which was hardly a surprise.

The very next morning the Molls had informed the welfare office that they could no longer have him in their house. After a few days in the home he found a new place to stay with the Naders: a sweet-natured, childless couple who wanted a child much too desperately to be scared off by Leon's history. They did the right thing and obtained the best possible psychiatric treatment for him with Dr Volwarth, even though they couldn't really afford the expensive examinations, like the video analysis that Leon had dug out again now.

'With the help of that camera on your head, we'll be able to prove that there's a harmless explanation for everything,' said the young Dr Volwarth on the tape.

'Even for this?' The eleven-year-old leaned over and pulled a plastic bag out from under the bed, holding it up to the camera.

'Oh God,' exclaimed Volwarth as the child pulled an indefinable clump out of the bag and presented it to the camera.

'What the hell is that?'

5

Without waiting to hear the answer he had given the doctor back then, Leon stopped the video and gestured for Dr Volwarth to sit on the sofa.

'It's like it was yesterday,' said the psychiatrist with a far-away smile as he sank back down into the leather upholstery.

For him the images from the past seemed to wake pleasant memories, which was certainly not the case for Leon.

'You gave me a real shock back then, Leon. For a second I was genuinely scared that you were about to show me a dead animal.'

'No,' said Leon, reaching under the coffee table for the shoebox he had put there. He opened the lid and showed his guest the contents. 'Luckily, it wasn't an animal.'

'You kept *these* too?' asked Volwarth.

Leon shook his head. 'They're not the same trainers. I found them in my microwave this morning.'

'Today?'

Volwarth leaned over, looking intrigued.

'Yes. This morning. The day after my wife left me.'

The psychiatrist reached for the stud in his earlobe and played with it for a moment.

'You're married,' he asked after a brief pause.

The question surprised Leon.

'Yes. Why?'

'You're not wearing a ring,' explained Volwarth.

'Sorry?'

Leon touched the ring finger on his left hand (Natalie had suggested they wore them on the side of their hearts, even though in Germany it was traditional to wear them on the right) and, confused, registered only the indent in his skin left behind by the ring.

'I must have taken it off in the bathroom,' he murmured, even though that was practically impossible. It was much too tight and could barely be moved even with oil or soap. Leon had been planning to take it to the jeweller's.

Volwarth fixed him with a long analytical stare, then asked: 'Do you want to have children?'

'Yes, definitely. Natalie stopped taking the pill the day we moved in here, about a year ago now.'

'But she left you anyway?'

'It looks that way.'

Leon summarised the peculiar events for Dr Volwarth, who became increasingly agitated as the story progressed, before clapping his hands together and cutting Leon off: 'No matter what you say, I don't believe you did anything to your wife in your sleep.'

'But we can't rule it out.'

Volwarth made an appeasing hand gesture and clicked his tongue. 'Theoretically, sure. In the decades that I've been researching and treating parasomnias, I've encountered almost everything: people who clean their apartments in the deep-sleep phase, sleepwalkers who have coherent conversations with their partners and even answer questions. I had patients who did washing in the night and even operated complicated devices. In one case a marketing manager typed entire presentations into his computer and sent them by email to his co-workers. Another got into the car while asleep and drove twenty-three kilometres to the neighbouring town . . .'

'. . . to stab his mother-in-law with a kitchen knife,' continued Leon.

Volwarth grimaced regretfully. 'Unfortunately, yes. The Kenneth Parks case was all over the press, and it wasn't the invention of some horror film director.'

'So there are people who become violent in their sleep,' persisted Leon.

'Yes, but that applies to less than one in a thousand sleepwalkers.'

'And what makes you so sure I'm not one of them?'

Volwarth's expression turned thoughtful, nodding as though Leon was a student who had asked a clever question.

'My experience tells me. And the results of my studies. As you know, somnambulism is one of the least-researched phenomena in medicine. But in recent years my clinic has made some ground-breaking discoveries. Starting with the fact that the very definition "sleepwalking" is flawed. Sure, the night-time activities mostly occur in the deep-sleep phase, but strictly speaking the so-called sleepwalker isn't actually asleep. He is in another, barely researched stage of consciousness between being asleep and awake. I call it the third stage.'

Leon tugged nervously at the skin over his Adam's apple. Volwarth's descriptions reminded him of his own sleep paralysis, from which he always struggled to wake.

'In long-term studies, where we put the entire family under clinical observation, we were able to find out that the sleepwalkers' violence is primarily directed towards loved ones.'

'There you go!' Leon clapped his hands together. 'Now you yourself are saying that—'

'But . . .' Volwarth raised his index finger '. . .

there are always warning signs. Had Natalie ever complained that you were rough with her in your sleep?'

'No.'

'Did you ever strangle or hit her in the night?'

'I don't know.'

'Believe me, you would know if you had. Of course you can't remember your night-time activity the next morning, but your wife would certainly have told you. Sleepwalkers don't just tear their partners' finger-nails out from one night to the next, or punch their teeth in. It begins gradually.'

'But I saw it,' retorted Leon.

'What exactly did you see?'

'Her bruised eye,' answered Leon with agitation. 'I already told you about Natalie's injuries.'

'But you also told me that you had just woken up from a horrible nightmare involving a cockroach.'

'What's your point?' asked Leon, feeling rattled.

The psychiatrist leaned forwards on the sofa. 'It was dark. Could it perhaps have just been eye make-up, which in your half-asleep state you confused with a black eye?'

'I don't think so, no. And that wouldn't explain her thumbnail, either.'

Or the broken tooth.

'And she was limping.'

'Your wife was carrying a heavy suitcase. Even I

48

was limping earlier when I had to haul mine to the taxi.'

'So how do you explain this?'

Leon waved the warped shoes around, like a piece of evidence in a courtroom. This was exactly how the pair looked that he had put in the oven at his foster parents' house while sleepwalking, just a few days after he arrived there.

A teasing smile danced on the doctor's lips. His gaze wandered to the empty wine bottle on the sideboard.

'Were you drinking alone?'

'Yes, but—'

'The whole bottle?'

Leon sighed, irritated at himself for not having cleared it away. 'My wife was late coming home. I opened the bottle anyway and I guess I lost track of how much I was drinking.'

'And you can't remember what happened after that, right? You don't know how you got undressed and into bed. You didn't notice when Natalie came home. And maybe you also forgot what you did to your trainers?'

Leon shook his head. 'Why would I nuke my trainers in the microwave while I was drunk?'

'Well, why would you hit your wife?'

Dr Volwarth looked at the clock and repeated what he had said in the video recording: 'I'm sure there's a

49

harmless explanation for all of this. It's possible that Natalie came home late, got mad because you were drunk, and went to stay with her best friend for a few days.'

'I already called her.'

'Well, maybe she's gone to a hotel. The problems in your relationship didn't appear overnight, am I correct?'

Leon nodded absent-mindedly.

'Is it because of the miscarriage?'

The question hit Leon like a slap in the face.

'How do you know about that?' he asked, stunned.

'It was a shot in the dark. You told me you've been trying for a baby for almost a year now. But I don't see any baby books, or catalogues for changing tables and prams on the coffee table, not even the slightest sign of nesting.'

Leon nodded pensively, feeling strangely exposed.

When they managed to secure their dream apartment, they saw it as a good omen for the future. But things had changed after the miscarriage.

'And how are things going professionally?' was Dr Volwarth's next question.

'Natalie just opened a gallery with her best friend,' answered Leon, happy to change the subject.

'I meant with you.'

'Oh, right. Everything's great there too, technically.'

'And non-technically?'

'We're in the middle of a bid for a big project. Sven and I—'

'Who is Sven?'

'Sven Berger, my best friend and co-owner of the practice. He was the one who pulled in this big potential commission. A children's hospital. Our first designs went down really well, and we have a good chance of winning the commission. I just need to make a few changes and submit the scale model by Thursday at the latest.'

Volwarth looked at the time again. 'That's in a few days' time. So you're not just under extreme stress personally, but professionally too.' He stood up.

'Yes. I mean . . . no. That's not the problem.' Leon, who had stood now too, knew what the psychiatrist was getting at. He had suffered from sleep disturbances even before the car accident, but they had got worse afterwards. It was only when he found a caring home with the Naders that the emotional pressure started to recede. His subconscious had finally been able to find some peace. The stronger the love for his foster parents became, the less reason he had to run from his fears in the night. That was Volwarth's theory, who back then had seemed almost sad that Leon's violent outburst at the Molls had not repeated itself. The trainers had been the last act of destruction, and they hadn't even been living things.

'How can you be so sure?' Leon persisted as they walked out of the living room. 'I mean, my behaviour was strange even as a child.'

'Strange, but not violent, Leon. Countless sessions, dozens of recordings, and we weren't able to document a single violent attack.'

'Maybe there's nothing on the tapes because we stopped the experiment too soon.'

Volwarth shook his head and, in a familiar gesture, laid his hand on Leon's shoulder. 'We didn't see anything because there was nothing to see; we knew that even before we put the sleep camera on your head.'

'Oh really? So why did you do it?'

'Because I didn't want to cure your somnambulism, but your psychosis. That's what made your case so interesting: you convinced yourself you were going to do something evil in your sleep. You were so scared that in the end you didn't want to go to sleep. And this fear of going to sleep, also known as hypnophobia, was what I wanted to take away from you with those tapes. Recordings that, when all is said and done, proved the only person you're a danger to is yourself, like if you bump into the corner of a table in your sleep or stumble over something. If anything, you probably would have injured yourself with that knife.'

He scrutinised Leon's face as though searching for

a sign that he had got through. Then he sighed. 'To me it sounds like you're going through an emotional endurance test right now. And just like all those years ago, when everything got back on the right track after you were taken in by the right people, things will figure themselves out once the stress has abated a little.'

Leon wanted to interject, but Volwarth didn't give him the opportunity.

'I have a suggestion for you: complete your work for the bid, submit the model, give your wife a few days of space, and once things have calmed down a bit, come into my lab and we'll plug you in again and have a more detailed look if that would put your mind at rest. OK?'

Volwarth took a prescription pad from the back pocket of his leather trousers and asked to borrow a pen. Leon moved to hand him his fountain pen from the telephone table, but it wasn't there, even though he was sure he'd seen it just recently.

'No problem.' Volwarth pulled a biro from his jacket pocket, scribbled a few indecipherable words, then tore off the slip of paper and handed it to Leon.

'What's this?'

'A gentle sedative. It's based on a herbal remedy and helps to provide a dreamless sleep. The dose I've prescribed should last you until I'm back in the country again.'

'Nocturnalon,' Leon read out loud.

Once the psychiatrist was gone, Leon suddenly felt so tired it was as though he'd already taken a whole packet of it.

6

'Do it!'

The sex was like it always was. Wild, unrestrained and of an intensity that would be embarrassing to him as soon as he could think straight again. But right now orgasm was still a myriad of kicks, bites and screams of lust away. Right now Leon was still relishing whispering all the frivolous abuse into Natalie's ear that he knew turned her on so much.

Bitch. Slut.

Normally she just repeated the insults. As if she had earned them.

Because I've been a naughty girl.

But today she threw him off his rhythm with an unexpected request.

'Come on, do it!'

Leon grabbed at her breasts, pulling her closer.

'No, not like that.'

He slowed down.

'How?'

She reached for his hand and pulled it to her face.

'Hit me,' she gasped beneath him.

Leon propped himself up with his hands either side of her head, in confusion.

'Do it. Please.'

Natalie grabbed his ass and pulled him deeper inside her.

Hit you?

'I don't understand. How—'

'What is there not to understand?' It was another voice. He looked to the right and froze in shock as he recognised his mother sitting on the chair next to the bed. 'The horny slut wants it harder.' She grinned wantonly. 'It's not like you have to reach straight for the whip like your father. A slap will do for now.'

Leon felt his penis go limp inside Natalie.

What's going on?

'It'll figure itself out. It does in most cases.'

The words were coming from his wife's mouth, but Natalie was suddenly speaking with the grating voice of an old man. It took a while before Leon recognised the officer he had spoken to after saying goodbye to Dr Volwarth yesterday, when he had called the police station to file a missing person's report.

'With adults we don't tend to start looking into it until fourteen days after the disappearance.'

Leon's mother, too, was now speaking in the voice of the detective as she said: 'Just wait for a while, then give the whore a good hiding if she turns up.'

No! Leon wanted to scream, but he couldn't utter a single sound.

He tried to disentangle himself from Natalie, but the more he tried, the weaker he became. She reached for his hand and pressed his fingers into a fist. He tried to wriggle free, but couldn't, it was as though his joints had been locked. Leon felt Natalie grab him by the wrist, spurred on by the cheers of encouragement from his mother. Then she smiled and opened her mouth, inside which a living thing was moving around.

Morphet!

The cockroach's feelers came darting out from between her lips like the tongue of a snake. And Natalie rammed Leon's fist into her face.

There was a crunching sound, as though he had kicked in a rotten old door. At the same time he heard a dull echo.

'Bull's-eye,' laughed Natalie, spitting out a piece of her front tooth. As she did so, Morphet crawled from her mouth and scuttled across her cheek towards her eye.

Oh God, screamed Leon silently, unable to stop

it from happening. Powerless to stop her, he let Natalie use his own fist to beat herself with again. This time on her open eye, where the cockroach had positioned itself, its pincers about to bore into her pupil.

'Hit me. I deserve it.'

Natalie magnified the force of the punches by jerking her head forward just before impact. There was a popping sound like an exploding air balloon as Leon's fist crushed her eyeball.

Then another sound was reverberating in his head, high and sonorous. Leon sat up in shock. He blindly fumbled around for the cordless telephone on his nightstand, surprised that it wasn't on the unit in the hallway where he normally put it before going to bed so that the ancient thing could charge overnight. Part of his consciousness was still imprisoned in the nightmare, but the other part registered the familiar number on the vibrating display.

'Where the hell are you?' said Sven. 'We were supposed to go through the presentation!'

His best friend was really mad, that was clear from the tiny pauses scattered between his words.

When he was younger Sven's stutter had been much more pronounced, and Leon was the only one in their class who hadn't bullied him for it. Their deep bond of friendship, much more than a mere working relationship, was based primarily on a foundation of respect that had been obvious even at the tender age of fourteen. Leon accepted Sven's speech impediment, and Sven didn't see him as an exotic orphan like many of their other classmates did. To this day Sven believed that it was thanks to Leon's friendship and the increased confidence it gave him that he was finally able to overcome the stuttering. Nowadays it was only noticeable to those who knew him, and then only when he was very worked up. Leon, however, felt certain that it was much more down to the speech therapist whose exercises Sven still followed even now.

'I, I . . . oh damn.' Leon looked at the alarm clock on his nightstand; the thing must have stopped, because it was showing 4 a.m., and Sven would never call him in the middle of the night.

'Shit.'

'Yes, exactly. I've been waiting for you in the office for an hour now. Where are you?'

'Sorry, I overslept.'

'Overslept?' asked Sven in disbelief. 'We were planning to go through the alterations. It's gone six in the evening!'

'What?'

That was impossible. Leon had gone to bed very early last night because of a persistent headache making it impossible for him to carry on working. He didn't take one of the sleeping tablets that Volwarth had prescribed. He didn't even leave the house to pick up the prescription, and it was impossible that he could have slept that long. Although the headache had subsided, he still felt numb and woozy.

'I think I must be coming down with something,' he mumbled into the receiver.

'Don't get sick on me, Leon. Don't slack off when we're on the home stretch.'

'I won't, don't worry. The model will be ready.'

'Man, this thing with Natalie really seems to have thrown you for a loop.'

'Natalie?'

Leon sat up straight in shock.

How does he know about that?

'Yes. Has she turned up yet?'

'No,' said Leon in confusion.

He pushed the bed-sheet off and noticed to his surprise that he was only wearing boxer shorts. He was sure he remembered having fallen into bed fully clothed, exhausted.

Did I get drunk again? For God's sake, what else can't I remember?

A ringing sound, similar to the one in the dream, made Leon jump. He stood up.

'Hang on, I have to answer the front door.'

He padded barefoot into the hallway. Before he opened the door, he looked through the peephole. Relief flooded through him.

Thank God.

At least his memory hadn't let him down with this. He had spent ages searching on the internet yesterday before finally finding what he was looking for, and, as promised, the company was delivering the very next day.

'Just a moment,' called Leon through the closed door. He grabbed a coat from the cloakroom before opening the door to the delivery guy.

The man, who was around Leon's age, wore a uniform that was threadbare at the knees and elbows, the brown of which matched his closely shorn hair. The name badge above the company logo (*United Deliveries – We Love What We Do*) declared him to be Jonas K., although Jonas K. didn't appear to identify with the logo particularly. He was chewing gum listlessly and listening to music on clunky headphones.

While Leon awkwardly scribbled his signature on a clipboard, he promised Sven he would bring the new designs into the office that evening. 'I've arranged the lifts around the atrium to save space. And there's a show-stopper that the clinic management are going to love.'

He was just about to close the door when the courier took off his headphones abruptly and said, 'Excuse me, I have a problem.'

'Sorry?'

'Could I use your toilet quickly?'

'What?'

'Your toilet. You do have one, don't you?'

Leon blinked nervously; the question was too much for him right now. A reasonable request that was just as difficult to grant as it was to refuse.

He took a closer look at the man. Now that he had stopped chewing gum, he looked a lot more intelligent. A high forehead, alert eyes, his nose a little too big in relation to the rest, albeit not damaging the overall impression any more than the missing left earlobe, which only became noticeable now he'd taken off the headphones.

Leon stepped to the side to let the uninvited guest pass.

'Thank you, that's very kind. I have diarrhoea, you see.'

'Excuse me?'

Leon thought he must have misheard, but the man's expression didn't change. It was only after a few moments that his trembling lower lip betrayed him. 'Oh man, you should take a look at your face in the mirror,' he choked, exploding with laughter. 'You look as though you just shit your own pants.'

Now the courier was laughing manically at his own absurd joke, while Leon struggled to bring his expression back under control.

Has everyone here gone crazy?

'No harm meant, mate, but I have to keep my spirits up with this tedious job somehow.' With a chuckle, the joker put his headphones back on and turned on his heel.

'Who was that?' asked Sven, once Leon had closed the door.

'Just some weirdo. Where was I?'

He looked through the peephole, but the courier had disappeared.

'You were telling me about the show-stopper you've built into the presentation.'

'So I was. An underground tunnel system, connecting the most important wings of the hospital. But not just for pedestrians, as is usually the case: for emergency vehicles too.'

'Which means we've solved the radiology problem and patient transport,' said Sven with delight. Their first designs had been criticised for the location of the diagnosis centre – it was too out of the way. An inevitable problem arising from the rambling hospital grounds. 'And we can keep the basic concept.'

'Yes. Let's just hope they accept the enormous additional costs.'

With the telephone clamped between his chin and collarbone, Leon carried the package in both hands along the hallway to his study, pushing the door open with his foot.

'As I already said, I like it a lot,' said Sven. 'But

we still need to discuss it in detail. You're coming to the party with me, right?'

'Yes, of course,' answered Leon tonelessly, not paying attention. His feeling of elation at Sven's approval had evaporated the second he walked into the study.

With his gaze fixed on the empty desk, he said softly, 'But please give me a bit more time.'

What the hell is happening here?

The scale model, the one he had been working on day and night for the last few weeks, was no longer where he had left it.

7

'Natalie? Please just call me back, will you? I'm out of my mind with worry.'

With the telephone to his ear, Leon flung open one door after another: bedroom, hallway, kitchen, lounge-diner. A fleeting glance was enough. For an object the size of a suitcase, there were very few possible hiding places even in their large apartment, and Leon was unable to find it in any of them. The model had completely vanished.

Leon couldn't make sense of it. The cardboard model had been on the desk, there and nowhere else. Besides that, it was much too bulky to move around. He had been dreading carrying the cumbersome thing into the office by himself. If he had sleepwalked with it, he wouldn't have had a free hand to close the door behind him afterwards.

But it was ajar, he thought, ending his one-sided

conversation with Natalie's voicemail. As with the previous attempts to call her, the voicemail had kicked in after ten rings.

He went into the bathroom and pushed the shower curtain aside, but of course he didn't find the model of the hospital there, nor on the balcony overlooking the courtyard or on top of the wardrobe. He even looked outside the front door. By now he was doubting his sanity so much that he checked every room a second time, starting with Natalie's most holy place: her dark room.

The windowless, tiled room at the far end of the T-shaped hallway had originally been intended as a guest bathroom; now it housed a small laboratory bench and ventilation system, several fixed sinks and a lockable chemicals cupboard next to the washbasin. Natalie had created an additional partition behind the door, using a light-excluding theatre curtain, beyond which Leon had ventured three times at most since they moved in. The dark room was Natalie's territory, a foreign land for which he had no entry visa.

Again, he felt like an intruder, like he was doing something wrong.

He pressed the switch next to the partition, and the red lamp bathed the room in hazy light.

Hidden away somewhere, so that it couldn't be turned on by accident, was the switch for the conventional ceiling light. But Leon wasn't in the mood to search for it, and the lamp gave enough light anyway.

Nothing stood out, apart from a disturbing black-and-white photograph that Natalie had clipped to a washing line. The picture showed her face on a stranger's torso – that of a naked, pregnant woman. It was obviously a montage, but a very good one, because it was impossible to make out a single flaw in the transition from neck to chest.

Natalie must have created the image for the exhibition that Anouka was now working on alone.

Star Children.

Leon looked around more carefully this time, noticing prints of other, slightly modified motifs of the pregnant woman, still swimming in the fixing baths.

He took a step closer.

The smell of the developer was almost impossible to bear, but he didn't know how to turn on the ventilation system. Leon's eyes filled with tears. One of the pictures floating under the red light, as though in a pool of blood, became more blurred every time he blinked.

That's impossible.

Leon wanted to turn away, but the pornographic brutality of the image had an almost magnetic allure. He leaned forward, feeling his stomach flip like he was on a rollercoaster just before it plunged into the abyss for the first time.

This can't be real.

It wasn't so much the manipulated image that shocked him, which was of Natalie, her eyes closed, ramming a broken bottle neck into her rounded belly; it was the object swimming in the fixing bath: a string of artificial pearls. And there was no doubt who it belonged to.

Natalie's name was on the pink identity bracelet, the good-luck charm, the one that had been swinging from her mobile phone as she ran from the apartment.

8

When asked how they met, Leon and Natalie tended to keep quiet and just smile. Sometimes they told the truth, joining in with the questioner's laughter as though to confirm they were joking. But they really had met for the first time in a brothel, and it had been La Fola, one of the most renowned in the city.

At the time neither of them believed the other's explanation as to what had brought them there. He had been on a stag night, while she was looking for inspiration for her final project at art college, entitled 'The Naked Society'.

The music was as loud as in a nightclub, meaning that Leon had to lean in close to Natalie to read her words from her lips. They were marked by the gentle impressions of her front teeth and a little torn at the corners of her mouth, but that didn't stop her from grinning broadly at much of his conversation. Even the parts that weren't funny in the slightest.

'I hate photos,' he had admitted to her hours later, after he had parted company with his friends. They had gone for a walk together, without giving so much as a glance at the window displays of the over-expensive boutiques along the boulevard. 'Especially photos of myself. I'm not very photogenic.'

As proof, he presented his ID photo.

'The photographer obviously didn't like you,' she said, and even though he laughed at the observation, Leon knew she hadn't meant it as a joke.

Natalie opened her handbag and pulled out a Polaroid camera.

Before he could protest, she had pressed the button. While waving the print around like a fan, she explained her theory to him: 'The greater the love of the photographer for their subject, the better the picture.'

Leon stared speechless at the photograph in his hands.

'And do you like yourself?' she asked.

'Much more than in real life,' he admitted, feeling a bit dazed.

A little later they kissed.

How can something that began so perfectly end so terribly? thought Leon as he sat there in his study, only a few weeks after their third anniversary, opening the package that had just arrived.

At first glance the order seemed complete: an elastic headband, two motion sensors, Velcro tape, cable, batteries, a USB stick.

And of course the radio-controlled camera.

Admittedly it didn't look exactly the same as the model he had picked online, but it wasn't the first time the shop had delivered the wrong thing. And in this case it was to Leon's advantage, for the camera had a higher resolution than the one he had actually ordered.

He carried everything into the bedroom, where he had already started up the laptop on the bureau. A hypnophobia forum online had ended up being a real treasure trove of information. Leon was clearly not the only person wanting to film himself in his sleep.

As he fastened the camera to the headband with the Velcro tape, he felt himself starting to get sleepy. *But I already slept for an eternity, damn it. What's wrong with me?*

His desire to sleep increased with the speed of the progress bar on the screen as the camera's software installed on the computer.

He then had to carry out a function test by lying motionless on the bed, which was astonishingly difficult despite his tiredness. His nerves were jangling.

After just a minute he sat back up again to check whether the motion sensors had sent a radio impulse to the component in the USB slot of the laptop, activating the filming function.

Bingo.

The green LED lamp of the USB stick blinked in rhythm with his heartbeat, showing Leon the recording status. When he took the headband off again and laid it next to him on the pillow, the colour changed from green to red. The recording stopped as soon as the camera went into standby mode.

Leon stood up and went over to the bureau. Moving the mouse nervously, he opened the video player's display window. The brief recording was just one megabyte in size and started immediately as he clicked.

Leon stared at what his head movements had managed to capture, overcome by a confusing sensation, similar to the one he'd had when he heard a recording of his voice for the first time. He saw his bed-sheets, followed the camera panning over the wardrobe to the monitor, which was flickering feverishly on the recording, and felt like a stranger in his home.

So as not to be woken by the sun rising, he lowered the blinds and pulled the curtains. The camera had an infrared recording function and a low-light amplifier that was considerably more sensitive than the bulky thing Dr Volwarth had attached to him all those years ago.

Despite the jeans and thick sweatshirt he had on, he was cold with fatigue, and contemplated taking a bath to help him sleep. But he was afraid nothing would stop the thoughts exploding in his mind. Eventually, he drank a glass of red wine and pulled on a thick pair of socks with soles of rubberised dots. Then he put on the headband with the camera, laid down in bed, and waited for his eyes to close.

9

Leon had always been the kind of person who brooded over things. While Natalie could simply turn over and fall asleep even after a heated argument, he would often lie awake for hours on end, staring at the ceiling and trying to get to the bottom of things.

He could still remember clearly the last time he found himself in a similar, almost schizophrenic state of limbo, in which his body was screaming for sleep but his mind for answers. It had been after that unfortunate dinner when he met Natalie's parents for the first time.

Leon had arrived alone in the expensive Italian restaurant, where the walls looked like the event pages of a society magazine: every centimetre adorned with pictures of politicians, singers, actors, artists. All of them grinning broadly, arm in arm with the owner as though he were their best friend and not just a clever businessman primarily interested in gratifying his own vanity.

Leon felt uncomfortable from the start. Not because of the ambience, but because he was a coward who had disowned his own parents. Unlike Hector, Natalie's father, Klaus Nader couldn't afford Savile Row suits, not on his waiter's salary. He would choose wine not by taste but by price, if at all. And if presented with a wine list dominated by expensive bottles, his likely response would be to ask for a menu where the prices weren't given in Turkish lira.

And what would they have talked about? Certainly not about whether it was better to winter in Florida or Mauritius to flee the awful weather. Maria Nader was just happy if the tram tracks didn't freeze up in January, and she was more likely to worry about whether the special offer from the newspaper supplement would still be available the next day than whether seat 4C in first class with Emirates was the best around. His adoptive parents, who had adopted him shortly before his sixteenth birthday, had travelled first class just once. And that had been by train, and only because they got into the wrong carriage by mistake.

Yet the evening didn't get off to the stilted beginning Leon had feared. Hector and Silvia Lené might look like they had just jumped out of the pages of a brochure for luxury retirement properties – healthy, dripping with jewellery, suntanned and full of energy, albeit still unmistakably in the autumn of their lives – but Hector relaxed the atmosphere with some humorous and witty anecdotes, which surprisingly weren't about financial investments or second homes, nor about his passion for collecting classic cars. He even complained about the steep prices in the restaurant, rolling his eyes at the small portions, and Leon became increasingly ashamed at having made a cheap excuse for his parents' absence. In all likelihood everyone would have got on well; he was probably the only snob at this table, one who had failed to stand by the people who loved him unconditionally. Even though the Naders didn't share Leon's interest in architecture and had never been to university, they had sacrificed a car, holidays and other comforts just to finance his studies.

He felt sick as he realised how badly he had acted, how great was his betrayal. Leon could try to convince himself that he just wanted to spare his parents the embarrassment of having to pick up the cheque (their pride would have prevented them from yielding to their son), but in truth he knew he was ashamed of his background and that this was why he'd made a cheap excuse as to why Mum and Dad were unfortunately feeling under the weather today.

He had decided to make up for his mistake and quickly suggest an invitation in return, when something happened to make it crystal clear there would be no further meeting. Not with his parents. Not with him. Never again.

It happened in the toilets. Leon was standing at the urinal when Hector walked in and positioned himself at the next basin, humming cheerfully. Leon was trying to hit the sticker of a fly attached to the urinal as a target, when Hector addressed him: 'She likes it dirty.'

'Excuse me?'

Hector winked at him and unzipped his fly. 'I know I shouldn't say that, as her father. But as men we can speak openly, right? You're not a prude or something, are you?'

'No, of course not,' said Leon, trying to force a smile. He glanced over only briefly, and his gaze inadvertently landed on the hand of his future father-in-law, whose member was either half erect or unusually large. The stream splattering down on to the enamel was correspondingly loud and intense.

'Good, I'm glad to hear it. Because I wouldn't marry my daughter off to some uptight faggot. She needs a proper stallion.'

'Sorry?'

'She gets it from her mother. You might not think it, to look at her now. But under the slap, Silvia's still the same exhibitionist hussy whose virginity I took over forty years ago.'

Leon's fake smile began to choke him. He was still hoping that Hector would cry out 'I had you going there for a minute!' and clout him on the shoulder with his massive paw. But Natalie's father was deadly serious.

'Like mother, like daughter. It's no secret that Natalie was unbelievably horny even from an early age. And so blatant about it. She always left her bedroom door open when her boyfriends stayed the night. And there were more than a few!'

Hector laughed and shook himself off. 'I didn't want to see it, Leon. But Natalie made it impossible for me not to. That's how I know what she gets off on. Handcuffs, collars. Pulled really tight, like on a mangy dog.'

He pulled his zipper up, then, noticing Leon's amazement, gave him a questioning look.

'Hey, this stays between us, OK? I mean, we are family now, aren't we?'

'Of course,' Leon stuttered, and didn't say a word for the rest of the dinner. He felt even more ashamed than before; at the beginning of the meal he had genuinely regretted that his own father wasn't as worldly, well read or cultured as Hector. At the end he was furious he didn't give Hector a piece of his mind and take a swing for him when, as Hector said goodbye, he let his hand rest on Natalie's behind for a brief moment. And Leon hated himself because he knew he would never work up the courage to tell Natalie about the conversation in the men's room, because that would not only have poisoned her love for her father, but possibly her love for him too.

And I can't risk that. I can't risk losing you, thought Leon now, years later.

With the thought, the memory of that awful dinner began to fade.

He opened his eyes, and the nightmare was over.

10

When he sat up in bed, Leon didn't know where he was. Normally the light from the aquarium woke him. Today the darkness around him was so intense that he lost his sense of orientation.

For the first few seconds he thought he was imprisoned in another sleep paralysis and was dreaming his fruitless attempts to reach out for a light source. Wherever he stretched out his hand, he grasped into nothingness.

Natalie, where are you? was his first clear thought as he realised he was lying in bed alone.

And why do the bed-sheets feel so strange?

He traced his fingers over the cotton, missing the warm imprint of her body as she slept. Where was her familiar scent, that mix of fresh hay and green tea he could usually smell even hours after she had got up?

In that moment all he could smell was his own stale breath, and the sheet felt unusually smooth.

And numb.

Exactly. *Numb.* That was the right word.

Leon clawed his fingers into the sheet, made a fist, and as his eyes slowly became accustomed to the scant light in the bedroom, he remembered why he had woken alone.

And why, hovering a short distance away, a little red light was blinking.

With a start, he sat up and rubbed his eyes.

The computer. The recording.

Leon reached his hand up to his forehead, but the camera wasn't there.

Was it just a dream after all? But if so, then why is the USB stick blinking?

He rolled to the left, grappling around on the nightstand until he found the switch for his reading lamp. When he turned it on, he screamed out.

It was a brief, involuntary reflex that he would have been ashamed of in Natalie's company, but he couldn't remember ever having been so shocked in his life.

Not when, at the age of eleven, he was awoken by the screams of Adrian's mother as he stood there with the knife in his hand next to the child's bed. Nor when he first saw himself sleepwalk in Dr Volwarth's practice.

None of his therapy sessions had ever been as disturbing as this moment, as he looked at his own hands to find they were covered in pale-green latex gloves.

What in God's name . . .?

In the light of the reading lamp, he stared at his fingers like a lunatic realising in a rare moment of clarity that he had just committed a crime.

That's why the sheet felt numb!

That's why my hands feel like they don't belong to my body.

Repulsed, he tore off the surgical gloves and threw them next to the bed. The elastic had clung so tightly to his wrists that his fingertips were shrivelled as though he had spent too long in the bath.

He pushed back the bedcovers and crawled out of bed. He was even colder than he had been before going to sleep, and felt like he hadn't slept for even a second, but a glance at his clock on the nightstand revealed the truth: fourteen hours had passed.

What happened in that time?

On the way over to his laptop Leon stumbled upon the headband with the camera attached to it. It was lying on the floor next to the wardrobe, and he resisted his first impulse to pick it up and put it back on.

An alarming thought shot into his mind: *This is a crime scene, you can't touch anything.*

Look, but don't touch!

Leon brushed a few carelessly discarded items of clothing from the chair and sat down on the heavy metal stool in front of the bureau. He opened the laptop and was blinded by the light of the monitor. Squinting, he opened the software. His fingers felt uncomfortably dry on the keyboard – they were still covered with the remains of talcum powder from the gloves.

His right eyelid began to twitch, a reflex Leon was unable to control. He guided the cursor of the mouse towards the replay button, then, after a few seconds of hesitation, clicked on it.

An input field popped up, requesting the password Leon had set up yesterday. He entered four digits, and the recording began. At first all he saw was shadows, which made him feel a little calmer. Despite his exhaustion, his body had clearly gone through several dream and deep-sleep phases, tossing and turning so restlessly in bed that the motion-activated camera was triggered. In the images, which had that typical greyish-green and slightly grainy look of those produced by a night-vision camera, he was able to make out how he trampled the blanket to the foot of the bed then pulled it up again, and how he gripped the big pillow like a life jacket, only to push it away a few minutes later.

As the camera only recorded while he was moving,

during the first two hours of sleep it hadn't even captured ten minutes, and Leon began to hope that his nocturnal activity would be equally unspectacular to the end of the video film – that is, until the timer in the lower right-hand corner of the picture came to the 127th minute.

It began harmlessly. Even though Leon had expected these images, they were still a shock.

Suddenly, with a jolt, the perspective changed. He had sat up in his sleep, and now he was looking around. Slowly, as though he was seeing the room for the first time and wanted to commit every detail of it to his memory, the camera wandered from left to right. If the images before were unclear and flickering, now it was as though the camera was mounted on a tripod.

Like a robot, thought Leon, remembering that steady, mechanical movements were typical of sleepwalkers. Most roamed around like lifeless shells pulled by an invisible cord, and Leon was sure that the sight of them often awoke comparisons with zombies and the undead. His own movements, too, seemed like they were being steered by some unknown hand.

He recoiled in shock at the sight of himself, blurred by the camera shadows, as he walked in profile past the wall mirror next to the door. With the camera on his head, his appearance was reminiscent of the awful photographs of apes in animal laboratories when their skulls were opened up to measure their brain activity. Except that, unlike those poor creatures, he was not jammed into a clamp, but able to move around freely, albeit unconsciously.

The monitor went dark for a moment, then, two steps later, he was on Natalie's side of the bed, as he could see from all the photographs about underground bunker worlds that lay on her nightstand.

Leon turned round and compared the image with how things looked now. The photographs were still in the same place, exactly as in the video.

But the drawer is open!

Just as he turned back to the monitor, Leon's right hand wandered into the camera's field of vision. Holding his breath, he watched himself open Natalie's drawer and take out a pair of latex gloves.

Why in God's name did she have something like that in her nightstand?

Leon leaned forwards and grabbed the monitor with both hands as though he wanted to shake it. If someone had rung the doorbell right then, he wouldn't have heard it. They would have needed to set off a firework right next to his ear to tear his attention from the screen.

He wasn't sure if his brain was consciously slowing down the sequence of images, or if he really was pulling the gloves on as slowly and deliberately as the recording showed.

Leon tried to change the volume. Then he realised that, in his agitated state the day before, he had completely forgotten to activate the microphone software. So he was hearing the creak and snap of the gloves only in his imagination. Besides that, the recording was completely silent. No footsteps, no breathing, no rustling as he shuffled his way across the bedroom.

Where am I going?

Keeping his gaze fixed on the monitor, Leon reached down to touch the slipper socks on his feet, giving a start when his touch dislodged some dried earth from the bobbled soles.

Where have I been?

Leon watched himself march slowly but purposefully towards the wardrobe from which Natalie had been pulling her clothes in tears that unforgettable morning. Instead of opening it, as Leon expected himself to do, he paused, motionless, in front of it. For so long, in fact, that the recording stopped. But then the pictures jolted back, with a quick pan upwards to the bedroom ceiling, and Leon walked into the gap between the bureau and the wardrobe.

He watched as, with a force he would have never thought himself capable of even in his conscious state, he pushed the old wardrobe to the side in his sleep.

But why?

Leon stopped the recording and looked at the

wardrobe to his left. It was the only piece of furniture they had inherited from the previous owner, because Natalie had thought it so beautiful – now it looked like a threatening monolith, exerting an air of danger.

He stood up from the chair, his knees trembling.

He couldn't even begin to imagine how he had moved this heavy monstrosity in the night. Leon knelt down and felt the scrape marks on the parquet floor. They were neither slight nor new. Completely the opposite: deep grooves had been cut into the wood like train tracks, as though the wardrobe had frequently been moved back and forth over a long period of time.

Leon stood up once more.

Like on the recording, he pressed both hands against the side of the wardrobe, took a deep breath and pushed against it with all his strength. At first it refused to budge even a millimetre, but on the second try it moved with astonishing ease.

On the first attempt, admittedly, Leon had given himself a splinter when his hands slipped, and he found himself regretting having taken off the gloves. In the end he didn't need much longer than he had on the video. The wardrobe creaked and groaned, and the parquet floor screeched in protest, but after a few sweat-inducing seconds he had pushed the thing about a metre and a half to the side.

And what now?

Panting, he took a step back – and clapped his hand in front of his mouth.

That's not possible.

In disbelief, Leon stared at the object on the wall he had just exposed.

I must be hallucinating.

But there was no doubt.

Where the wardrobe had been just moments ago was a door that he had never seen before in his life.

11

Do you see that door, there in the wall?
  Only a ghost can hear its call.
Suddenly, the melody was back. The ditty from his childhood – one of many that Leon's biological father had dreamed up to embellish the bedtime stories he invented – was buzzing around in Leon's head like a fly trapped under a glass.
Behind the door lies a hiding place.
But don't go through. Run far, far away.
Even though he had never been into the strong room of a bank, Leon imagined the doors to be just like the one he was currently stretching his hand out towards. It looked like the secure door to a vault containing important documents, money or gold bars.
Ignore this warning and it won't be long before
You lose yourself behind the door.
The metal-clad door was barely a metre-eighty

high, almost his own height, and looked much too heavy and bulky for the doorframe it was riveted to. In place of a door handle were two tilted twist locks that had to be turned in a clockwise direction.

He who crosses the threshold at night
Can never go back, try as hard as he might.

In total confusion Leon placed the palm of his hand against the mysterious door. He had expected to hear a humming in his head, to see blurry, shadowy pictures dancing in front of his eyes, to perceive colours with more intensity or at least to smell some disturbing scent – something that would signal he was starting to lose his mind. But it seemed he wasn't yet teetering on the threshold between insanity and reality. He didn't even have a bad taste in his mouth. Everything he saw and felt, every one of these sensations was undeniably real: the cool door, the digits of the locking mechanism, worn out from frequent use . . . *this damn door in my bedroom!*

Behind the wardrobe.

It exists. It isn't a dream.

Or is it?

Leon turned round and looked towards the bed in fear that he would see himself sleeping there, but the sheet was crumpled and the mattress empty. His gaze fell on the camera at his feet, which must have fallen off while he was sleepwalking, and he was reminded of the video. With two quick paces, Leon was back at the laptop and he pressed play again. The sensation of watching a stranger intensified; he almost felt like a voyeur, slightly ashamed and fearfully anticipating what would happen next.

On the monitor Leon watched himself standing in front of the newly exposed door for some time, as if rooted to the spot. As he did nothing but breathe for minutes on end, he decided to speed up the replay, making his reflected persona on the monitor look like a flagpole swaying in the wind. Only after another ten minutes of the video did Leon change his position, and from then on everything happened very quickly. It was over so suddenly that he didn't manage to press pause in time, and he had to rewind it to see it again.

That's unbelievable, he thought. Even watching it again, the events on the laptop monitor lost none of their morbid, schizophrenic fascination.

Initially, it seemed like he was about to make his way back to the bed, for on the recording Leon had turned round. But he glanced up at the bedroom ceiling, then spun back round so quickly that the picture went blurry.

Once the camera's image correction program started functioning again, Leon was already done with the first of the two twist wheels. With practised hand movements, he moved the second into different positions; it all took no longer than a second or two.

Then the heavy door seemed to snap open of its own accord, only a few centimetres, but enough for Leon to be able to reach both his hands into the gap and pull it open.

What's behind it? The question shot into his mind as he kept his gaze fixed on the laptop screen, trying not to miss a single detail.

Unfortunately, from that moment on there weren't many more images. Everything in Leon was screaming out to discover what lay behind the door; the door that shouldn't really even exist. At the same time, as he watched himself sleepwalking over the threshold, he felt afraid of himself in a way he had never experienced before.

Where am I going? What's behind the door?

As Leon stepped through the door in his sleep, he didn't duck down enough to prevent the camera from hitting the doorframe. The device came loose from his head and fell to the floor, where, for just a few seconds, it recorded Leon's back disappearing into the darkness.

Then the film stopped, but Leon still couldn't pull his gaze from the computer.

As though hypnotised, he stared at the monitor until the screensaver eventually washed away the black video window before his watering eyes.

Only then did he stir, getting up and walking slowly back to the door in the wall.

'OK, let's think about this rationally,' he said to himself, intertwining his fingers to stop them from trembling. 'If you're not asleep, and you haven't lost your mind, the door must be real. And if it's real . . .'

. . . *it must be possible to open it again.*

He didn't have the strength to utter this last thought out loud.

It didn't take long for an even greater fear to rise up in him, above the realisation that he was leading a double life played out behind closed doors: it was that, in his conscious state, it would be impossible to repeat the movements he had made in his sleep.

In the video he hadn't hesitated for a second, determinedly turning the wheel locks into the necessary positions. Clearly he knew the combination in his sleep.

But *only* in his sleep.

Here and now, he didn't have the slightest idea of what he needed to do to open the locks.

12

'A second entrance?'

At the beginning of the telephone conversation the man with the brash voice had sounded merely impatient, but now Benedict Bauer was clearly annoyed. 'What the hell gives you that idea, Herr Nader?'

Leon had prepared a white lie in advance before calling the building custodian. 'We're thinking about renovating our bedroom, and behind the wardrobe there are some markings that I can't find an explanation for.'

One floor above, Michael Tareski was just beginning his daily piano practice. The chemist had discovered his musical passion late in life, and spent at least an hour a day practising the scales.

'I wouldn't want to drill or hammer in a nail in the wrong place,' said Leon, continuing to fib. 'Is it possible that there's something concealed behind the wallpaper?'

'I've got no idea what you're talking about. I gave you the plans when you moved in, remember?'

'Yes, I know,' agreed Leon. At this moment he was sat at his desk in front of the floor plans, which had been included with the rental contract. He'd had to fight for them; originally the custodian did not want to hand them over, presumably to make it more difficult to check the calculation of the rent in the contract against the measurements of the apartment.

'There's no further entrance indicated on my plans . . .'

'There you go then.'

'But perhaps they're not . . .'

'Not complete? Are you implying that we carry out shoddy work?'

'No, of course not . . .'

'But?'

Leon closed his eyes and took a deep breath.

But there's a door behind the wardrobe in my bedroom, and I have no idea what it's doing there.

The clumsy piano-playing above his head was getting louder. Leon looked up at the ceiling.

'I really don't mean to cause any trouble, Herr Bauer . . .'

'Good, then I suggest we end this conversation now, otherwise I'm going to miss my train.'

'Yes, of course. Just one last question: is it possible

the last tenant changed something without informing you?'

'Rebecca Stahl?' The custodian laughed spitefully. 'I very much doubt it.'

'What makes you so sure?'

'The last tenant was blind. She couldn't even manage to operate the lift, let alone build a new entrance to her bedroom.'

'OK, I see,' said Leon, his tone as flat as his emotions. If he hadn't been sitting down, he would have looked around for a chair.

'Please forgive the interruption,' he said, and was about to hang up when Bauer bluntly asked if something was going on with him.

'You're behaving more and more strangely, Herr Nader. And to be honest the apartment is much too sought-after to be wasted on eccentric tenants.'

'What do you mean by eccentric?'

'You've been causing trouble ever since you moved in. First you insisted on being given the floor plans . . .'

'I'm an architect. Those kind of things interest me.'

'Then you bombard me with emails asking to speak to the owner.'

'For the same reason. I've admired the work of Professor von Boyten, who died far too young, ever since my student days, and I would have liked to speak to the son about his genius father . . .'

'Yes, but he didn't want to speak to you. Siegfried von Boyten has never wanted contact with any of his tenants,' said Bauer, letting the second half of his sentence – *and especially not with you* – hang unspoken in the air.

In the background, Leon heard a train station tannoy announcement.

'If you don't change your behaviour, Herr Nader, then I'll have no choice but to dissolve our contract.'

'My behaviour? What's that supposed to mean? Is it against the law to call up the custodian now or something?'

'No. But running around naked in the hallways and frightening other tenants is.'

'I beg your pardon?' asked Leon in confusion, before it occurred to him what the custodian was talking about.

'Oh, I see . . .' he added, not sure what he should say next. *It was only because I was running after my beaten-up wife, because I wanted to stop her leaving me.*

'Spare me the excuses. Instead, turn your attention to clearing all the bicycles, shoes and other objects out of the hallway by the day after tomorrow,' barked Bauer into the phone by way of goodbye.

'Why?'

'Because the renovations on the staircase begin the day after tomorrow. Maybe you would do better to

97

read the notices instead of studying your floor plans, Herr Nader.'

With that he hung up.

At the same time the piano-playing on the floor above died away too.

13

It was a while before Leon dared go back into the bedroom. And yet he didn't know what would be worse: standing in front of the closed metal door in the wall again, or finding the wardrobe in the same position as before, as if it had never been moved.

He delayed the moment by going into the kitchen. Leon hadn't eaten or drunk anything for a long time now, but he was so nervous that he didn't feel hungry or thirsty, even though his stomach was gurgling relentlessly like a central-heating pipe. He wanted to make some tea to calm it down a little, but couldn't find the kettle, which left him wondering why Natalie would bother taking that old, lime-scaled thing.

Once he had taken a drink of water from the tap, his bladder started to press, and he went to the bathroom to relieve himself. Washing his hands, he looked at his face in the mirror. His eyes looked as though he had conjunctivitis. A multitude of burst blood vessels had turned the whites red, providing a strange contrast to the dark shadows beneath them.

He let the water run cold, then splashed some from the basin on to his face. But the enlivening effect he sought failed to materialise, so he leaned over and held his head under the tap.

To begin with he kept his eyes closed, and when he opened them he got such a shock that he jerked his head up, banging his forehead against the tap.

Damn it, what does this mean?

The water had washed a tuft of hair from his scalp, but that wasn't what was unsettling him. When he was under emotional stress, he always tended to lose a little hair, but it was just a temporary problem. This time, though, something else had come away with the hair, and it was turning the water into a brown sludge.

Horrified, he ran both his hands through his hair, then stared at his smeared palms.

How can that be possible?

He had had a shower yesterday, and now his hair was as dirty as the fur of a dog that had been rolling around on the floor. And it smelled like it, too.

He held a finger in front of his nose and breathed in, and for an instant the smell transported him into a mouldy cellar.

Where have I been?

Leon stared at his dirty hands, remembering the earth he had noticed on his socks earlier.

He gave a start and ran back into the bedroom. The mysterious door was still there, the wardrobe pushed aside, and now that he had switched on the ceiling light he could see the specks of dirt he had left on the parquet floor during his nocturnal expedition.

He sat down at the laptop and started the recording from the beginning again. On the very first replay he noticed a peculiarity that he had registered before but not given much thought to: the panning of the camera up. It happened twice. The first time before he heaved the wardrobe to the side in his sleep. The second was just before he opened the mysterious door.

Why do I keep looking up?

Leon stood and went over to the approximate spot where he had also stopped on the recording, half a metre from the vault door. Then he craned his head backwards.

At first glance he couldn't make out anything unusual; that is, if you didn't count the hairline fracture that ran across the white-washed plaster. Leon noticed it now for the first time, but for a building of this age such things weren't unusual. It snaked like a crack in the shell of a hard-boiled egg over to a hook in the ceiling. An ugly chandelier had once hung from the hook, a heavy monstrosity that they had got rid of the day they moved in.

The hook, however, had remained, because Natalie wanted to hang an indoor plant or some other decorative object on it to make the room more homely. Directly next to it was a shell-shaped lampshade made of frosted glass, concealing a bulb. For ages he had wanted to replace the shade with a new one that gave out warmer light. Now the sight of it irritated him, even though he couldn't have said why at first look. It was only once he was at the foot of the bed, directly beneath the light, that Leon realised what was bothering him.

He thought it was a speck of dust, then he thought the black fleck inside the glass lamp was a dead insect that had crept through a gap, unseen by the naked eye, and never found its way out again.

In under a minute he had hauled a stepladder out of the small storage space and into the bedroom. Leon placed it under the lamp. He had to leave the room for a second time to fetch his toolbox from the study, then, armed with a screwdriver, he climbed the steps.

Even up close he couldn't make out what was inside the shell. From his new vantage point, standing at the top of the ladder, the glass cover, curved like an eyeball, seemed a lot bigger. And heavier.

Carefully, so the shade didn't fall on him, he began

loosening the four thick screws holding the lamp to the ceiling. As he did so, he noticed signs of wear and tear on the screw-heads. One screw was quite loose, while the last initially refused to budge at all. Only with a great deal of force did he manage to unscrew it, and then Leon made a grave mistake, letting the screwdriver slip from his grasp, and, as he tried to grab it, he began to teeter. So as not to follow suit behind the tool, he had to let go of the lamp, which meant its entire weight hung on only the last screw. Of course, it didn't hold for long.

The shade lurched to the side, wrenching out the screw, and fell, shattering as it hit the floor.

Shit.

Cursing, Leon climbed down from the ladder and knelt on the parquet to search the shards for the contents of the shell. But given that he didn't know what he was looking for, he didn't hold out great hopes of finding it.

He needed to gather up the shards anyway, piece by piece, and as carefully and thoroughly as possible so that he wouldn't cut himself later. Luckily, the shade had broken into several large pieces, of which two had shot so far under the bed that Leon decided to leave them there. The other pieces he stacked on top of one another like fruit bowls, with the intention of fetching a plastic bag and the vacuum cleaner. But he didn't get to that, instead picking up the smallest shard, carefully and with his fingertips, for this piece had the sharpest edges.

What in God's name . . .?

He turned the shard over and looked at the object, curved like a contact lens and filed off at the edges, still clinging to the glass from its underside.

What is it?

Morphet shot into Leon's mind. The thing had a surface structure and consistency that wasn't unlike the cockroach's shell, albeit a different colour. At close proximity it was clear that it came from a human hand. Dry blood crusted the underside of the keratin plate.

'A fingernail?' whispered Leon, hoping he was wrong. It was painted a mud-like colour and had been extracted almost completely intact. But there could be no doubt as to whose thumb it once belonged to.

14

Volwarth had once compared the subconscious to the deep sea. The further down you go, the greater the danger of being crushed by its strength, and if you surface again too quickly, your head could explode.

Leon looked at the torn-off thumbnail, sensing that he was only at the beginning of a long dive. He had put his head under the water just once, and already he had made unimaginable discoveries, of which the door in the wall behind the wardrobe was definitely the most disturbing.

He turned the nail over, from lacquered, manicured surface to its underside, which until recently had still been united with his wife's thumb. At the sight of the encrusted blood underneath, the thought of how much pain Natalie must have suffered made him close his eyes and take a deep breath.

He looked at the nail again, and only now, on the second glance, did he notice the details. On the underside blood had crusted, but lower down, barely visible to the naked eye, the surface seemed a little too even.

Leon opened his toolbox and took out a halogen torch. Not able to see much more even with that, he reached for a Swiss pocket knife, which contained a little magnifying glass. The magnification wasn't perfect, but it was enough to be able to make out punctures on the nail. With a tiny object, someone had scratched a series of numbers into the encrusted blood.

'*One, two, zero ...*' whispered Leon. He broke out in a cold sweat and his heart seemed to stop for a second, his neck and calf muscles cramping up as if he was preparing to take flight. The final number – a four – a little offset and barely decipherable in the second row, completed his birth date: the twelfth of April.

Slowly, but with his pulse racing, he turned to the door in the wall.

Is it possible that . . .

He stood up to check his suspicion. It suddenly felt a lot warmer than it had a few minutes ago, even though the heating in the bedroom had been turned down to the lowest setting, because Natalie preferred to sleep with an open window and temperature of sixteen degrees. Leon, on the other hand, needed absolute quiet at night and insisted on closed windows and doors, even though there wasn't much street noise in this neighbourhood anyway. Turning down the heating had been their compromise.

Abrupt sadness eclipsed his tense, fearful nervousness as he stood before the vault door, the thumbnail clasped in his fist. He tried with all his might to suppress thoughts of Natalie, but the tighter he balled his fist, the stronger his conviction became that he might never again get the opportunity to squabble with his wife over the temperature in the bedroom.

A relationship is a battle, his mother had once said to him, meaning it in a positive sense. *It's not fighting that poisons a marriage, but indifference.*

'I hope you were right,' said Leon, continuing his whispered monologue as he moved the uppermost of the two wheel locks on the door. Because based on how things looked right now, it was not indifference, but a brutal fight that had torn Natalie and him apart.

A fight to the death?

Leon turned in a clockwise direction until the '1' was beneath the marking arrow above the cogwheel. At once he felt the locking mechanism react to the position into which he had turned the wheel. The click that swiftly followed as he turned the wheel to '2' confirmed his theory. And once Leon had turned the second wheel to the numbers '0' and '4', forming the month of his birth date, the same thing happened that he had witnessed on the video recording: *click!*

The vault door sprang open.

Leon's initial reaction was irrational. He looked around the bedroom, as if for any witnesses to this unbelievable event. Once he had assured himself that he was still alone, he stretched his fingers out, worried that they would be crushed the very second he laid them in the gap around the door.

I can't believe I'm really doing this.

It moved more easily than he expected for a door of its weight, as the hinges were well greased. As soon as he had it completely open, the air turned colder, and this time it wasn't his overwrought psyche playing tricks on him. Cool air was streaming into the bedroom through the dark opening in the wall.

It was stale and smelled of paint, reminding him of the tool cellar where his father had always built the Carrera track at Christmas. And it also smelled like the dirt he had washed out of his hair earlier. Leon squinted and tilted his head to the side, but even as he moved closer, he could only make out the black-painted walls of a small room that didn't seem to have any floor.

It was as though he had opened the portal to a black hole.

He reached for the torch again and, keeping his

distance from the door, shone it into the darkness. It wasn't a wise decision.

For beyond the threshold there really was no floor, just an abyss, *opening up like the jaws of a beast of prey*, as Leon suddenly thought. He even thought he could make out the teeth, stretching back into the neck of this supernatural being. In reality they were just the rungs of a ladder set into the brickwork, leading deeper and deeper down into the darkness.

Out of fear that an ill-advised movement might make him lose balance, Leon knelt and shone the torch down into the shaft, which was spherical. The beam became thinner and thinner, not reaching the bottom. The walls were rough and uneven, and here and there black-painted bricks jutted out of the chute, which became increasingly narrow as it stretched down.

And I climbed down this in the night?

Leon thought back to the self-assuredness he had observed in his sleepwalking self. The schizophrenic feeling of being in another body during his conscious state intensified.

His knees trembling, he stood up and made the decision to sort through the facts calmly before going any further.

There must be a logical explanation for all of this. For Natalie's injuries. The trainers. The thumbnail. *For the door.*

Dr Volwarth had said that he was fine. That he wasn't violent. But Dr Volwarth had seen neither the video nor the shaft, opening up in his bedroom like a portal to another world.

A shaft, from which cold cellar air was still streaming.

Along with a noise that Leon had heard many times in his life, and which was getting louder every second.

That's impossible, he thought, creeping back towards the vault door. Once again he directed the beam of the torchlight down into the abyss, which wasn't actually necessary, because the classical melody had its own light source: a display that was blinking in rhythm with the tinkling sound.

'Natalie,' cried Leon, pressing his hand over his mouth.

His wife's mobile phone, which she had been holding when she left the house a few days ago, lay at the foot of the shaft and was ringing non-stop.

15

In the end it happened despite all his attempts to prevent it. He fell.

Leon had, however, been sensible enough to pull on the work overalls he wore for site visits. His fingers, gripping the metal rungs, were clad in his work gloves, and thanks to the thick rubber soles on his steel-capped boots, his feet were sure not to slip.

He had attached the torch to the tool belt of his overalls so that it shone straight down, even though as he climbed he was avoiding looking into the depths. Step by step, rung by rung, he fumbled his way down towards the mobile phone, which had stopped ringing as soon as he crossed the threshold of the door.

It wasn't long before he had descended more than halfway. Even though it was getting cooler with every metre, beads of sweat were gathering on his forehead.

He tried to ignore it, but it got worse so he stopped to wipe the back of his hands across his eyes.

It happened as he was descending the last third. By now Leon had developed a method; he knew how far down to stretch his right leg to reach the next rung, how far he had to go before his foot would reach the step and he was able to release his left hand and bring it down so that it could grip the next rung, after which this succession of movements could be repeated with his left leg and right hand. Leon felt sure he could do the last few metres with his eyes closed if he needed to, and it was this mistaken belief that was his downfall.

Several things happened at once: Leon heard a light knocking that seemed to be coming from his apartment's front door above, just as his foot stepped into nothingness. For the first time the space between the rungs had changed, if only slightly. He didn't have a foothold, and then the phone beneath him began to ring again.

With the unmistakable classical ringtone that Natalie had only recently picked, except this time much louder.

Leon gave such a start that he released his right hand – too quickly. He literally jumped down to the next rung. And by chance this one had been either badly made, weakened by age or, for some reason or other, not securely fastened to the wall. As soon as Leon's foot landed on it, he knew the rung wouldn't hold his weight. By then it was too late.

He just had time to grip one hand around the metal strut, cushioning his fall a little. But he still ended up swinging to the side like a window shutter and banging his hip against a protruding brick, causing his torch to come loose from the belt and fall. He didn't hear the glass shatter because of the phone ringing, but the fact that the beam of light was immediately extinguished spoke for itself.

'Shit!' cried Leon into the darkness. Only the weakly flickering phone display was still casting light across the floor, like a glow worm.

It took him almost as long to descend the last section as it had the whole preceding stretch, because he didn't want to make another mistake. By the time he finally felt solid ground under his feet, the telephone had long since gone silent, as had the knocking on the apartment door, and it took Leon a while to find the phone on the dry floor, which was covered by a thick blanket of dust.

In the process he stirred up so much dirt that he sneezed, which down here sounded like a small explosion. The sound was reflected by the brickwork, then amplified and sent back as a dull echo. With these acoustics, no wonder the ringing of the phone had been so loud. Even a gentle cough sounded like the crack of a whip.

Where in God's name am I?

Leon snapped the mobile open and gasped for air. When he saw the photo used as the background, he knew he was holding Natalie's phone in his hands. It was a portrait of her, one of those typical snapshots that people take of themselves, head thrown back, mouth stretched into a broad smile, all in hope that the outstretched hand was at such an angle that the camera wouldn't cut off the forehead or only capture the upper body.

First the identity bracelet in the fixing bath. Now the mobile phone down here. Natalie, what happened?

Leon erased the message announcing sixteen missed calls and several voicemails. Most were from him. The other incoming calls, including the last, had been dialled from a withheld number.

For a mobile phone, the illumination from the display was surprisingly strong, but it wasn't enough to give him a good look at this mysterious place. In spite of the anxiety gripping him, Leon tried to approach things systematically. He imagined the floor of the shaft as a clockface, and made a mark in the dust directly in front of the wall, as twelve o'clock. Using it as a starting point, he groped his way along the brickwork, until, after a three-quarter-turn to around nine o'clock, he stumbled into another rung. At first glance it didn't seem to serve any purpose, for he couldn't make out any further struts above it. So it wasn't another way up.

Leon put the mobile in the breast pocket of his overalls and gave the strut a shake. It moved, and for a second he thought he had pulled it off the wall, but the weight in his hands was too heavy for that. As he heard a creaking sound, he realised he had just found another door.

This was made of plywood, not metal like the one above, and so was much easier to move. Thanks also to it being not much bigger than the door to a dog kennel, as Leon could see when he shone the mobile on it again.

He held his arm out in front of him as far as possible to illuminate the tunnel beyond the newly discovered opening. Given that the entrance was small, he imagined the passageway would be the same, but when he shone the phone up, the light met no resistance – if he could squeeze through the gateway he would be able to stand up in the room beyond it.

But do I want to?

Leon looked up the shaft to the light from his bedroom, feeling as though he had been buried alive, with only weak signals from the outside world making their way through.

He stood up and shook the rungs of the ladder – apart from the one on which he had lost his balance, they were firmly attached to the brickwork. So he shouldn't have any problems getting back up, as long as he didn't get lost down here.

And it seems I know the way even in my sleep.

The voice of reason inside his head was screaming at him to climb back up and fetch help. But what if something awful had happened down here? Something he had been involved in?

Something I'm responsible for?

Leon knew that feeling, and he couldn't ignore it any more. Much like the flu, it had begun with symptoms that could be suppressed at first, but which ultimately end up seizing the entire body in an iron grip: he was afraid. Afraid of a real person who was lurking down here and who he had never before encountered in his life, even though they had always been in close proximity. He was afraid of himself. Of his other, sleeping self.

For this reason, ironically it ended up being the voice of cowardice that stopped him from contacting the building management, Sven, Dr Volwarth or even the police.

Leon wanted to find out what was waiting for him down here before he fetched back-up. And as he crept head first through the narrow entrance into the darkness, he was already fearing the worst.

16

It was the barely noticeable smell of fresh washing that made Leon come to an abrupt halt. From one second to the next, he was no longer in the world between worlds that he had stepped into through his wardrobe but back in his childhood.

He had been ten years old at the time, his surname still Wieler, when his biological father Roman first told him about the Ghosts of the Twelve Nights. Sarah Wieler had rebuked her husband considerably for this after finding out. She was of the opinion that such horror stories were not for children of Leon's age, that they would only make his night terrors worse. And she was right. That same night Leon had nightmares about the ghosts being in his wardrobe, and of the misfortune they had already brought upon many a family.

'Do you know why your mama doesn't do any

washing between Christmas and New Year?' Roman had asked, by way of beginning the story. Leon had instinctively grabbed his father's hand, as if in fear that the answer alone could cause him to stumble.

Whenever he thought back to that day, as he did now, on all fours in the darkness, every detail of that Sunday stroll came rushing back: the cold wind in his face, the snow under his boots, their gloved, interlinked fingers, the Christmas decorations in the windows of the neighbouring houses.

'I'm guessing you've never heard about the Ghosts of the Twelve Nights, have you? They hide themselves away all year, and there's just one time when they dare to venture out. And that time is coming. The Twelve Nights; that's what we call the time between Christmas and New Year.'

'What do the ghosts do?' Leon wanted to know.

His father nodded as though he had asked a particularly clever question.

'They are the opposite of guardian angels. Misfortune befalls the houses they live in. And during these days they are on the search for new families.'

'Will they come to us, too?'

'Only if we use the washing machine. Not many people know this, but these ghosts need wet washing to survive. They creep into the wet bed-sheets, into your socks or trousers, and once everything is dry they cling there for a year.'

To this day Leon still didn't know where in the world this superstition came from, but in the days that followed that walk he had scrupulously made sure his clothes didn't go anywhere near the laundry. And he was horrified when, on New Year's Eve, he found his older sister's blouses hanging on the washing line. She had laughed at him when he begged her to remove the wet shirts from the house immediately. From that day on he lived in the irrational certainty of a ten-year-old convinced his bedroom had been seized by evil spirits. His parents' attempts to reassure him were all in vain.

It was months before he stopped insisting his mother check under the bed or in the wardrobe after turning out the lights, to see if a ghost might be hiding there. The night of the seventh of May was the first that Leon no longer gave any thought to the Twelve Nights, having calmed down by then. He could remember the date so precisely because it was the night before the accident.

Fate?

Leon was shivering with cold; because of his rigid stance on the hard ground it had penetrated his limbs. He shook himself free from his memory-filled paralysis. Ever since the accident he had refused to do washing between Christmas and New Year. This made it all the more disturbing to him that here, of all places, he was confronted with the scent of softener and detergent. Whoever was responsible for it clearly didn't know the legend of the Twelve Nights.

Or they are ignoring it.

Leon activated the display of the mobile again, for the screensaver had vanished into the darkness, and saw that he didn't need to crawl any longer. The subtle scent of washing had disappeared too, or maybe Leon just couldn't smell it any more on account of the fact that his senses were focused on figuring out his new surroundings.

The passageway stretching out in front of him looked like a mining tunnel that had been carved into the rock with some blunt device. Pitch-black, uneven walls made a channel of varying size. Even over his head the height kept changing, and he had to stretch his hand out to prevent himself from banging into a sharp edge.

The ground beneath his feet felt strange. As Leon walked along, it gave a little like a forest path and when he knelt down, he was able to dislodge some earth. The path sloped downwards, intensifying the unsettling sensation of approaching an underworld that it would be better not to enter.

The tension mounted with every step, and became so intense he was convinced he could feel a subtle vibration spreading through his whole body. He wasn't claustrophobic, but right now he could easily imagine how it felt to be one of those people who avoid enclosed spaces. Whenever the light on the mobile cut out, and he found himself in complete darkness for a split second, it was as though the blackness hit him in the face. He could feel his heart hammering in his chest and the blood rushing in his veins, and his mouth become dry.

'Natalie?' he called tentatively. He had made it to the end of the passageway and found himself before a fork in the path. Calling his wife's name probably had an equally slim chance of success as trying to navigate the tunnel system down here by himself. But what else was he supposed to do? Go back upstairs? Call Volwarth? Or the building management?

He came to the conclusion that this probably wasn't as bad an idea as he had initially thought. At least he now had proof of a second entrance to his bedroom, one that for some reason hadn't been included in the floor plans.

But who put it there? And why? And what was Natalie's phone doing down here?

Leon shone the light to the right, into the shorter part of the fork. After just a few steps the path ended at a wall on which hung a warning sign: 'DANGER' was written in old-fashioned script, directly above an image of a lightning bolt as warning of high voltage.

Leon decided to contact Dr Volwarth before doing anything else; this would give him a witness who could testify that he wasn't hallucinating. But then he realised the psychiatrist would be on the plane now, well on his way to Tokyo.

He still wanted to turn back, out of fear of getting lost down here. Who knew how many forks might be lying ahead? He had stumbled into a labyrinth. After all, the architect of the building, Albert von Boyten, had also been known as a landscape artist, whose artfully created mazes attracted international renown. Did he give this building a maze too, albeit one made of stone rather than tall hedges?

Leon called his wife's name again before he turned to leave, but then something happened that stopped him from heading back: he suddenly realised that he had been mistaken. The vibration that he had put down to a trick of the senses was real. It existed – and not inside, but outside his body, and now he could not just feel it, but *hear* it too.

Leon tilted his head to the side and took a step towards the sound – the longer of the forked paths. The light of the phone's display had a greenish tinge, which made it even harder to see. If Leon wasn't mistaken, the walls in this part of the tunnel were smooth and even.

He put his hands out to touch the sides, tentatively, as though he might be electrocuted: to his left, he felt an even surface. To his right, the brickwork was clad with some coarse material.

With every step, the background noise became louder. Leon suspected that an inaudible, deep bass was causing the regular vibrations coming from the walls.

And what the hell is . . . that?

He had only gone a few metres before he stumbled upon a door handle.

Leon held the mobile up, and discovered he was right. There really was a door built into the right-hand side of the passageway – all the more disturbing was how incredibly normal it looked.

He pressed down on the handle, which was astonishingly warm to the touch, and expected to hear a creaking or squeaking, but the door opened almost silently. In the very same breath, the sounds around Leon died down and the vibrations ebbed away.

Clearly the door was used often, for the hinges were well oiled.

The room he entered was barely bigger than Natalie's dark room, and reminded him of the plywood crates every tenant had been given as cellar space, and which you needed to put your bicycle into upended so that it fit.

Leon's next thought was that he had stumbled into some homeless person's night-time shelter. The light from the mobile revealed a threadbare mattress on the floor, a half-opened removal box and several plastic bags, the contents of which he was reluctant to investigate. Judging by the smell, they contained rotting food products and other household waste.

Leon's foot became entangled with a scrunched-up sheet. As he bent down to remove it, he saw the box was full of objects, one of which he recognised.

But that's impossible . . .

He reached for the kettle that he had been searching for earlier in his kitchen. To Leon's astonishment, it was full to the first marker, as though it had been used down here not so long ago.

But that doesn't make any sense.

Leon looked around for a power point. Right next to the door, he saw a multi socket in the wall. A small, familiar-looking table lamp had been plugged into it. It was a cheap one, without a shade or base, nothing more than a bulb attached to a pliable stem. Unless he was mistaken, Natalie had used it in her flat-share as a bedside lamp, and had never unpacked it from the box after they moved in together.

He flipped on the switch. The bulb lit up, if only weakly, a scene that made Leon doubt his sanity more and more.

To his right, next to the door, there was an old garden chair with a rusted frame. The seat had been covered with the catalogue from an electronics store, under which there was a cigar-shaped bulge.

Leon formed his index finger and thumb into a pincer and pulled the catalogue from the chair, revealing a pile of white paper, the kind he used in his study for architectural drawings. And on the top, right in the middle of a sheet, was the *fountain pen*! The graduation present from his adoptive father which he had been looking for on the telephone table so that Volwarth could make out the prescription. Speechless, Leon stared at the golden pen, its nib pointing at him like a compass needle. He picked it up, revealing a column of figures noted carefully on the paper, which until then had been hidden by the pen.

Guessing it to be a phone number, Leon tapped it into Natalie's mobile so he could look it up later, but before he had entered the last digit he froze in shock. Natalie's phone had recognised the number. It was saved as a contact, and Leon was just as unable to explain this as he was the circumstances that led him down into this hiding place.

Dr Volwarth?

What was his psychiatrist's number doing in his wife's mobile phone?

Clueless, he stared at the carefully input address details.

He and Natalie had talked many times about the sleep disturbances of his childhood, and he was sure to have mentioned the name of the doctor who had treated him back then, but that still didn't explain why she would have the address of Dr Volwarth's practice, his email address and even an emergency telephone number.

Were the two of them in contact?

Under normal circumstances he would have looked for a logical, harmless explanation. But, down here, things were neither normal nor logical.

And they certainly aren't harmless.

He studied the hiding place more closely in the light of the lamp. He paused. Held his breath, tried to stay calm. And looked at the floor again.

What he thought was a bed-sheet, the thing he had stumbled over . . . was in fact something much worse.

He leaned over and grabbed at the material, which felt soft, as though it had just been washed – then he saw the rust-coloured flecks that had seeped into the cotton's flower design where the smooth material became ruffled.

Leon closed his eyes, and the image of Natalie kneeling in front of the wardrobe and cramming her things into the suitcase shot back into his mind. The memory of her flight from the apartment had imprinted itself in his head like a tyre track in wet concrete. He felt sure he would be able to recall every detail of this scene, again and again, to the very end of his life, even the insignificant things – for example, what top Natalie had been wearing: the flower-patterned one with the ruffled sleeves.

Natalie? Where are you?

Leon was about to bury his face in the material, to inhale his wife's scent, insofar as it was still present and not overpowered by other smells (*cellar, blood, fear*) – but then the light went out.

There was a soft *clink*, indicating that the lamp's bulb had blown, and this, combined with the unexpected plunge into darkness, startled Leon so much that he dropped the phone.

He fumbled around on the dusty floor for it. The oppressive fear that he would never find his way out of this underworld again was almost overpowering him when, there in the darkness, something brushed against Leon.

17

Leon yelled out, jumping at the sound of his own voice. He hit out at his trouser leg where he had felt as though someone was trying to grab hold of him. As he did, his fingers touched the mobile he thought he had lost. He clasped his fingers tightly around it as though it were a dumbbell.

The battery made a beeping sound to announce that it was now at under 20 per cent as he activated the display for the umpteenth time, convinced that it would light up a grotesque face with bleeding eyes. He was expecting a wide-open jaw and fangs just centimetres away from his face, ready to bite, chew, swallow.

But all he saw was the open door.

I have to get out of here!

Leon pulled himself to his feet and stumbled out of the room. Without stopping to think, he ran in the wrong direction, away from the fork that would have led him back to the ladder.

After a few metres he stumbled into a stone ledge and stopped to look around, but there was nothing but the impenetrable blackness of the passageway. Leon's thoughts were racing as quickly as his pulse. He needed to get back upstairs fast, without having to pass the room again. Only now did he realise he still had the blood-smeared blouse in his hands. His fingers had cramped up around the material. He stuffed it into his overalls, then talked himself into going back the way he had come. If he didn't, the danger of getting lost would be too great. And if there really was something down here lying in wait for him, it could be anywhere; it wouldn't necessarily be waiting in that room to jump out at him.

Then there was a rustling sound. Right next to him.

It's just some animal. A rat, perhaps. Or Morphet, he tried to reassure himself, but in vain. His survival instinct was stronger than his sense of reason.

Leon edged away, turned and ran, crashing into a wall and completely losing his sense of orientation. The only thing he had to go on was the rustling behind his back, which had now become a loud scraping, one he wanted to get as far away from as possible. But the noise grew louder the further he stumbled along the passageway, the contours of which he was only able to guess at in the weak gleam coming from the mobile.

Suddenly, a jolting pain shot through his shoulder, forcing him to stop. He looked at the thing he had run into, and recognised the metal rungs in the wall. It vibrated like a tuning fork as he grabbed it. Then he heard the rustling sound behind him again, louder and nearer, and in that second Leon realised there were two different sounds hunting him. They were coming from different directions. As they slowly made their way towards him, a metallic scraping sound droned above his head, albeit from a considerable distance. To Leon, it seemed less alive and therefore less dangerous.

Once he had discovered a second rung in the brick-work at head height, he didn't hesitate for one more second.

He made his way upwards hand over hand, and this time it was the ascent that would lead him into the unknown.

18

Rung by rung, Leon climbed towards the din, and rung by rung he became increasingly unsure that he had made the right decision. It wasn't just the droning, scraping and stamping – the vibrations, too, were becoming stronger.

But the irrational fear of what was behind him and the hope of escaping this labyrinth of darkness drove him on.

The way up seemed instinctively more promising than staying down there in the cellar.

His arms were sore and becoming heavier with every bar he grasped, but he forced himself to keep up the pace and even quicken it. Then, sooner than expected, he collided with the top of the shaft.

In shock, he almost let go of the last rung. He didn't even want to think about what could have happened if he had fallen backwards into the darkness.

If the shaft was as deep as the one he had discovered behind his wardrobe, he would have broken his spine or neck. Probably both.

And if the obstacle he had crashed into above had not given way a little, the collision would have been much more painful.

Slowly, Leon stretched his left hand upwards, but the trapdoor on top of the shaft was very heavy. He hunched his back and climbed further up to try to lift it with his shoulders. He braced himself against it, feeling like he was carrying a sack of coals on his back. In reality, he was opening a trapdoor, which tipped to the side with a clatter as Leon climbed up into a room.

Visibly, there was no great change. Wherever he was, he was still in almost complete darkness. He could see just two soft LED lights hovering at the end of the room, reminding him of the lights on the USB stick of his laptop.

Leon, wheezing now, lay flat on his stomach on the floor. It was pleasantly cool.

Then he smelled the scent he had caught just a whiff of in the labyrinth, and all of a sudden he knew where he was and what had caused the vibrating noise. The noise that had stopped briefly at the moment he opened the trapdoor, and which was now shaking the floor again just as loudly as before.

Leon propped himself on all fours, crept over the

132

cold tiles to the wall and pulled himself up to a standing position. He took Natalie's mobile from his overalls and, shining the light around the room, confirmed his suspicion: he was in a bathroom, a completely normal one.

To his right was a washbasin, next to it a bathtub, and inside that an open and fully laden clothes horse. Between the washbasin and the tub, a bulky washing machine was just finishing its spin cycle.

Leon was wondering who it belonged to, and whose apartment he had unintentionally stumbled into, when outside the bathroom the hallway light went on.

19

'Where are you, my darling?'

Ivana Helsing stood in the doorway in her dressing gown, both hands on her bony hips, sweeping her gaze around the bathroom.

'Have you hidden yourself away in here?'

She hadn't noticed the hole in her bathroom floor (*at least, not yet*), for Leon had just managed to shut the trapdoor in time and pull the rug over it. His neighbour must have heard the noise, even if it had been drowned out to a great extent by the roar of the washing machine. The hiding place he had found was so poor that Leon expected to be discovered at any second. He had jumped into the bathtub almost as Ivana walked into the bathroom, and now stood on trembling legs between the wall and the clothes horse. He had pulled the shower curtain hastily across, and even this seemed to have escaped the old woman's attention. Clearly she was more interested in where her cat was hiding.

'Alba, where are you this time?'

Peeping around the shower curtain, Leon shot a quick glance at the mirror over the sink, and saw Ivana pulling a little metal box from the pocket of her dressing gown.

'Come on, my darling,' she called, shaking the dry cat food. 'I have some delicious treats here for you.'

She positioned herself next to the washing machine.

'Alba? Can you hear me?'

She rattled the box again, but the animal showed no sign of revealing itself. She put the box back into her pocket.

Leon watched Ivana walk over to the mirror and take off her glasses. Then she blinked, as though she had a speck of dust in her eye. She seemed to be fighting back tears.

'She's just like you, Richard,' she whispered, barely audible now. 'She always leaves me alone.'

Leon's senses were stretched to breaking point. He was stood in an uncomfortable position, one hand pressed against the wall, the other stopping the clothes horse from falling over. He was breathing shallowly and trying not to make any noise, but as soon as this next thought occurred to him (*Hopefully I won't need to sneeze!*), he felt a prickling sensation in his nose.

Ivana was studying her face in the mirror. She massaged the sizeable bags under her eyes, shook her head and pulled her wrinkled skin down over her jaw. Then she checked her hair, which was grey but still thick, but she didn't seem satisfied even with that.

'Everyone leaves me,' she whispered, turning the tap on. 'They always do.'

Leon felt the muscles in his back tensing up. He wouldn't be able to hold this position much longer, but how could he explain himself if a careless movement revealed his presence?

He could only hope that Ivana would hurry up. But she seemed unwilling to do him this favour, because she began to take her clothes off – even though there wasn't very much that she could take off.

First she pulled the dressing gown down over her drooping, slightly forward-curving shoulders. As she was wearing neither a top nor a bra, Leon could see her breasts in the mirror. They were saturated with liver spots and hung over her ribs like half-deflated air balloons.

Leon felt ashamed for this unwitting, intimate insight his neighbour had granted him. And yet he couldn't bring himself to turn away; not even when Ivana Helsing lifted up her varicose-vein-covered legs, one after the other, to take off her nude-coloured pants.

Leon had never before seen a naked woman of this age (he was guessing she was in her late seventies), but it was not her nakedness that had seized his attention, it was the tattoo on her back: two blue snakes wound themselves around her spine like a DNA helix, their heads turned towards each other on her bony shoulders, the sharp tongues knotting together into a kiss on her neck.

Ivana began to wash herself with a flannel, first her face, then her neck, and finally her breasts, and as she did so Leon's nose itched more and more. The smell of clean washing made him think back to the legend of the Twelve Nights for a moment, which made the bizarre situation even more real. All of a sudden, Ivana began to sob loudly, and she threw the wet flannel against the mirror in anger.

'You piece of shit,' she cried out. Then she grabbed her dressing gown again and shuffled out of the bathroom without turning off the light.

Leon's urge to sneeze disappeared with Ivana. He waited a while. Only when he heard the TV being switched on in the living room did he finally dare to leave his hiding place.

The apartment was laid out just like his: the corridor beyond the bathroom went left into the living room; on the right-hand side to the hallway, and the front door leading out into the stairwell just a few steps away. But there was a problem. Unlike his apartment, just one floor above, this one hadn't been renovated for years. This was evident not just from the yellowing wallpaper and partially loose skirting boards, but also from the floorboards that creaked loudly with every movement.

Hoping that the TV would be just as good an acoustic distraction as the washing machine, Leon crept out to the front door, and he probably would have made it past her unnoticed, had the telephone not rung.

The green phone with its old-fashioned rotary dial was right next to him, on a crocheted coaster, on the edge of a teak commode.

Looking around in desperation, Leon hesitated, before diving into the small room by the front door, which in his flat would have been his study. Down here the door had been removed, and the room was completely empty apart from a small removals box.

There's nowhere I can hide, he thought, as the phone stopped ringing. And as he heard the shocked voice of Ivana Helsing behind him.

20

'Herr Nader?'

Leon whipped round and saw a nervous-looking woman standing opposite him, fiddling anxiously with the belt of her dressing gown. Her glasses were a little foggy and her face was still wet from her tears. She was wearing polka-dot slippers, the joints of her knobbly toes pressing into the material.

Leon felt there was only one way he could get away with this.

'What are you doing here, Frau Helsing?'

'Me?' she asked in astonishment. She smiled nervously.

'Yes, what are you doing in my apartment?'

'In *your* apartment?' Her smile took on a tortured look.

Leon could almost feel her inner conflict. On the one hand, she knew him as her pleasant, unassuming neighbour. But on the other hand, she was afraid of finding out why he had suddenly appeared out of nowhere and was talking nonsense. And in that get-up! After all, he was standing before her in dusty overalls, his hair dripping with sweat and plastered to his face, his hands covered in dirt.

Leon's thoughts raced. Simply telling the truth (*I found a door behind my wardrobe through which I climb down into a shaft when I'm sleepwalking, and I got lost and ended up in your bathroom*) certainly wouldn't be of much help in defusing the situation.

If he said that, of course, he would need to prove it and show her the hatch in her bathroom. But until he knew what he had unleashed down there in the labyrinth (that was what he had christened the world behind the walls), he didn't want to confide in anyone else.

'Can I help you in some way, Frau Helsing?' said Leon, continuing his charade, then he glanced into the empty room on the left and feigned a surprised expression. 'Wait a moment, I . . .'

He inspected his surroundings like an actor stepping into unknown territory. Then he held his hand up in front of his mouth. 'My God, I . . . I . . . Oh, this is very embarrassing. I'm afraid that I've . . .'

'You've . . . what?'

'Got lost.'

'Excuse me?'

'Yes, I went downstairs to fetch the post and when I came back up the steps I was lost in thought. Your front door was open, and I must have thought I was already on the third floor, because I left my front door ajar too. Frau Helsing, I don't know what to say . . .'

He let the last sentence hang in the air, searching the old woman's face for a sign that she had bought his cock and bull story.

'My front door was open?' asked Ivana, not one jot less suspicious.

'Yes, I know how it sounds, but I'm working on a big project right now, a commission I have to finish in the next few days, and whenever I think about some of the problems with it, it's like I'm in another world.'

Leon began to sweat; he was aware that his story, like every good lie, had truth at the heart of it.

Ivana Helsing shook her head in disbelief and stepped sideways to look past him to the front door. Her expression darkened when she saw the chain was on.

Damn it.

'I don't believe it . . .' she said softly.

'I know it sounds crazy, but—'

'I don't believe this has happened yet again.'

'Again?' Now it was Leon's turn to be confused.

Ivana sighed and rubbed one of her eyes, without

141

taking off her glasses. 'I've already spoken to my doctor about my forgetfulness, you see. He says it's nothing to worry about, not Alzheimer's or dementia or anything like that. Just the normal deterioration of the body as the years pass.' She shook her head again. 'But it scares me, Leon. I forget the simplest things. Like to drink enough water, for example. I should drink much more. And at night I sometimes leave the TV on. And Alba is always dashing past me through the door. You didn't see her, by any chance, did you?'

'No,' said Leon. 'But don't worry. Forgetfulness isn't necessarily connected to age,' he added, trying to ease the situation. 'I mean, which of us is in the wrong apartment right now?'

She couldn't help but laugh, and at once much of the tension fell away.

'I'm really very sorry, and I promise it won't happen again, Frau Helsing.'

'Wait a moment, please,' she called as he turned to go.

'Yes?'

'I've just put some tea on.' Shyly, she gestured towards the living room behind her. 'Won't you keep me company just a little, now that you're here?'

She reached for his hand, seemingly unbothered by the dirt. 'Please stay just a little.'

'That's really very sweet of you,' Leon protested,

'but as I said, I'm right in the middle of this pitch for an architectural project, and I . . .'

As he shook her hand, his gaze fell on a set of armchairs grouped around an open fire in the living room. Over the fireplace hung an immense oil painting.

He stopped.

'Is something wrong?' asked Ivana, nervous again, turning to follow the direction of Leon's rigid gaze.

'Yes,' he said absent-mindedly, letting go of her hand and walking into the sitting room, intrigued.

'What's wrong? Are you feeling unwell?'

'Excuse me?' Leon blinked. 'Oh, no, nothing's wrong. I'm just wondering about . . . this picture.'

He pointed above the fireplace, suddenly feeling dazed again.

'Yes, what about it?'

'The man, the portrait, isn't that . . .?'

'Albert von Boyten? Yes.'

'You knew the architect who designed this building?' Leon turned to look at her.

'Yes,' smiled Ivana, a little mischievously this time, and all at once the spark she must have had in her younger years was reignited. 'For many years I was his lover.'

21

Leon sat opposite her on a chair from which, moments ago, he had cleared a pile of women's magazines and crossword books, setting them on the coffee table.

Ivana sat bolt upright, without touching the chair's backrest and taking care that the hem of her dressing gown didn't come over her pressed-together knees.

'I'm really sorry about your wife, by the way,' she said as she poured Leon a cup of the steaming tea.

He tensed.

'It's the building, you know. If you'd spoken to me before you moved in, I would have warned you.'

'About what?'

She put the teapot back on a coaster and interlaced her fingers on her lap, the tips of her thumbs drumming against one another and reminding Leon of the heads of the kissing snakes on her back.

'It has eyes, you know. The house, I mean. Don't

you often feel as though you're being watched? Sometimes I wake up in the night and feel like there's someone sat on my bed. I turn the light on, and of course there's never anyone there, but I just can't get rid of the feeling. Sometimes I even look in the cupboard, such a silly goose, and can only go back to sleep again once I've assured myself that there's no one there.'

She shook her head as she spoke – as older people have a tendency to do without realising – and Leon hoped that it wasn't an early sign of Parkinson's.

'My God, you must think I'm a crazy old bat.'

'No, not in the slightest,' replied Leon, anxiously recalling how he had spied on her in the bathroom just a few minutes ago. Then he remembered the clothes horse, the wet sheets hanging on it, the Twelve Nights they were currently in, and the ghosts that were on the hunt for a new home.

He took a sip of tea and tried to concentrate on the pleasant subtle taste in an attempt to bring his thoughts back to reality.

'My doctor says it's all in my imagination and that it stems from the fear of loss I've had since Richard moved out.'

'Richard?'

'My husband. One day he just packed his bags and left, without even saying goodbye.'

Ivana had Leon's undivided attention again; she

didn't even need to mention the direct parallels with Natalie's hasty departure.

'Do you know why he left?'

'It's this house. Albert von Boyten wanted to make some kind of artistic commune, open to friends and family who would be able to live here rent-free. That's the only reason why I, a penniless artist, was able to get this apartment in the first place. I could never have afforded the rent in this neighbourhood on two painting sales a month and my part-time job as a nurse. He even let me stay after we had ended our open relationship and I was no longer his muse.'

Leon pointed at the painting over the fire. 'Did you paint that?'

'Yes. When we were still in our wild phase. Albert had a lot of women, and I didn't mind. I don't know a single artist who doesn't have a colourful sex life. And if not actively, then certainly in their head. Even Richard, a theatre director, who I met at one of Albert's parties, wasn't bothered by my relationship with Albert. For a while, after we moved in here together, we even had a *ménage à trois* going on.'

Ivana smiled in the same mischievous way as before, when she'd told Leon about her relationship with von Boyten.

'Clearly your benefactor had a soft spot for creative types,' said Leon.

'Oh yes. In his will he actually stipulated a quorum for artists to be granted apartments in the building.'

Leon nodded. That explained why Natalie and he had been approved.

'The house was supposed to be a creative oasis. But in the end it only brought him bad luck.'

She took off her glasses, which were slightly too large for her head, and chewed at the arms. 'Just like it has to all its tenants.'

Leon raised his eyebrows. 'What do you mean by that?'

'The pretty woman who used to live in your apartment, for example. She fell into the lift shaft and died. That set off an endless chain of tragic events.'

Leon nodded, thinking back to the cynical-sounding words of the building manager on the phone.

The last tenant was blind. She couldn't even manage to operate the lift, let alone build a new entrance to her bedroom.

'I'm no statistician, but over the years I've lived here now, an unusual number of tenants have died unnatural or at least premature deaths. Some committed suicide or were taken into psychiatric clinics – like Albert.'

'Von Boyten?'

She nodded. 'The biographies all say that Albert retreated to some unknown place in order to meditate, in keeping with his eccentric nature. It wasn't a voluntary exile, though, but a private psychiatric asylum. He died there some years ago, mentally deranged.'

'And his son inherited the house?'

'Exactly. But it didn't make him happy either.'

'What happened?'

Ivana hesitated. It looked as though she was wrangling with herself as to whether she was able to share this secret.

'No one knows exactly. His apartment was locked and shuttered from the inside. All his possessions – his money, clothes and documents – were still there. The only thing missing and which never appeared again was him. It was as though his own apartment had swallowed him up.'

No wonder the building manager didn't want to put us in contact. It's not even possible.

'Which apartment did Siegfried live in?' asked Leon, even though he was pretty sure he knew the answer.

'I really don't mean to scare you with my stories, Leon. But it was on the third floor, your apartment. As I said, I would have warned you against it had you come to me before signing the contract.'

Ivana craned her head upwards and gestured at the ceiling. 'Can you hear that?'

He shook his head, but then he heard the scales, much more muffled down here than in his apartment.

'Tareski will be the next one to lose his mind, I

fear. He keeps practising the same piece over and over again. That's not normal, is it?'

Leon shrugged his shoulders. After everything he had experienced in the last few hours, he was certainly in no position to differentiate between normal and irrational behaviour.

'And then there's the Falconis on the first floor,' Ivana continued.

'What about them?'

'Have you ever noticed that the two of them are obsessed with keeping their door closed whenever someone walks by? And if you ring the bell they poke their heads out of the smallest gap possible, so you can't see in. I recently made the mistake of accepting some post for them, a heavy package that I carried downstairs all by myself. Do you think they thanked me?' Ivana Helsing stirred her tea energetically. 'They didn't even open the door. I was just expected to put the package down and disappear again.'

'That's strange.'

'Yes, isn't it just? I'd love to know what they have to hide. Sometimes I think . . . Oh, never mind.'

She waved her hand and gave an embarrassed smile.

'What?' asked Leon.

'It's not worth mentioning. I'm an old tattletale, anyway. Would you like some more tea?'

She reached for the pot.

'No, thank you very much, though.' Leon went to look at his watch and saw to his surprise that it was no longer on his wrist. While he was still thinking about whether he had taken it off or lost it, Natalie's phone beeped in his pocket, muffled by the blood-soaked blouse that he had stuffed into his overalls. The warning signal for the steadily dying battery acted like a wake-up call.

'Thank you very much for the tea, Frau Helsing, and sorry again for my rather abrupt entrance here, but I really must go now.'

'Of course, I understand,' said Ivana, a trace of melancholy in her voice, as though she didn't often have someone to talk to, let alone someone who actually listened. 'Please don't let me keep you.'

She accompanied him to the door, where she looked in amazement at the chain again, and Leon almost thought she was going to ask him why he hadn't realised he was in the wrong apartment as soon as he secured it. After all, a women's quilted jacket was hanging on the inside; but Ivana just said softly, 'Leon, could you do me a favour?'

'Yes?'

'You seem to be a good man. Don't make the same mistakes I did.'

'I'm not sure I follow.'

She glanced quickly through the spy hole, before adding quietly: 'This house is like a magnet. It holds on to you with all its might. And the longer you stay, the harder it is to get away.'

'Oh, I'm sure you don't really believe that,' said Leon, with a forced laugh.

'Only very few have the strength of will to get out. Like Richard. Like your wife.'

'You don't know anything about Natalie and me,' exclaimed Leon, a little more brusquely than he had intended.

Ivana opened the door and checked to see if anyone was in the stairwell. Then she whispered to him, with a conspiratorial look on her face: 'That may be true, but I'm too old to mince my words, so I'll be straight with you. Don't make the same mistake I did. Don't wait for her to come back – go after her.'

'You're saying I should move out?'

Ivana gave him a meaningful look. 'First the nightmares, then they come true, Leon. Get out of here while you still can. If you stay too long, the house will change you, and the evil in you will come out.'

She grabbed his hand and came so close that he could see the fine hairs on her top lip and feel her warm, stale breath on his face as she bid him farewell with this mysterious prophecy: 'First the nightmares, then the reality. Don't wait too long, otherwise you won't be able to fight it.'

22

As Leon climbed the steps to his apartment, he was thinking about what he needed to do not to lose his mind completely. But he didn't have much time to deliberate. As he went around the corner between floors in the stairwell, he heard someone calling out his name.

'Herr Nader?'

Leon looked up and took the last flight at a slower pace. The man standing in front of his apartment door had an intimidating look about him, and Leon wasn't sure if it was down to his bulky physique, the Gestapo-like coat or his self-assertive tone. As so often with men who were losing their hair, the age of the stranger was hard to guess, but he looked to be in an age bracket in which a receding hairline was no longer a disadvantage in the attraction stakes, certainly closer to forty than thirty.

'Leon Nader?'

'Yes, that's me,' answered Leon with a nod as he took the last step.

The stranger sighed in a way that could only be interpreted as *finally*, then pulled out his identification badge.

'Kroeger, Criminal Investigation Department,' he said, stretching out his hand. In the dim light of the hallway, Leon didn't have to worry about the policeman seeing how dirty his hands were, but he still felt sick with nerves. After all the inexplicable events, the last person he wanted around was a cop. He had just been thinking about calling Sven. He needed an ally, a friend at his side. Not someone whose job it was to uncover the darkest of secrets and pull them into the light of day to the disadvantage of their owner.

'Is something wrong?'

'Are you just coming home from work?' asked the policeman, as if he hadn't heard Leon's question.

'Yes … I mean, no.'

Leon brushed his sweaty hair from his forehead, then gestured at his overalls and worker's boots.

'I'm renovating,' he said, hoping this would explain his deranged appearance.

The policeman looked at him, his eyes containing a variety of green tones, reminiscent of camouflage fabric. Leon avoided his gaze.

'I tried to find you an hour ago, but you didn't answer the door. Your bell's broken.' As proof, Kroeger pressed the brass button next to the door, and he was right. No sound came from inside the apartment.

'I went out to get a bite to eat and decided to try my luck a second time.'

'Was that you knocking earlier?' asked Leon, remembering the sound he had heard when he was clambering down into the shaft. He regretted his unguarded observation at once.

'If you heard it, then why didn't you come to the door?' Kroeger looked him up and down with suspicion.

'I wasn't feeling well. I was on the toilet.'

The detective instinctively took a step back and wiped his hand on his coat, obviously regretting having shaken hands with someone who was potentially contagious.

'You do DIY while you're feeling unwell?'

'No, I . . . well, it came on quickly. I felt sick all of a sudden. That's why I stopped.'

'I see,' said Kroeger, although his face said that he didn't.

'What did you want to speak to me about?' asked Leon, trying to take back the upper hand in the conversation. He felt a little dazed again, as if he had been drinking, and his tongue seemed to get heavier with every word he said.

'I want to show you something,' declared the policeman.

Show?

'Perhaps it would be better if we could . . .'

'What?' Leon looked at the door as the detective jerked his chin towards it.

'Oh, right. Yes, of course.'

As he realised what Kroeger was getting at, he abruptly became aware of the next problem. 'I'm afraid I can't ask you in,' he said, patting his empty pockets under the policeman's suspicious gaze. 'I forgot my key.'

Am I slurring?

His own voice suddenly sounded foreign to him.

'You've locked yourself out?'

'Yes, I just wanted to fetch the post . . .'

Inside the apartment, the telephone began to ring.

'After you were in the bathroom and decided to stop renovating?'

'Yes,' confirmed Leon flatly.

The detective looked amused.

'Then it seems like today just isn't your day, huh?'

You could put it like that . . .

'Man, oh man. I think you really are a little out of sorts. Not only did you forget your key, but . . .'

The detective put his foot against the door, and the ringing from the telephone became louder.

'. . . you also forgot to lock up.'

The door opened with a creaking sound, although it could just as easily have come from Leon's throat.

'But that's impossible,' he exclaimed, making yet another blunder.

'Why?'

Because I checked it was locked yesterday before going to bed, and have only left the apartment since then through my wardrobe.

As they walked in, he heard his own voice coming from the answering machine in the hallway: '. . . reached the home of Natalie and Leon Nader. Please leave a message after the tone.'

A moment later they could hear the dulcet tones of a young woman speaking with exaggerated politeness on the tape: 'This is a message for Herr Nader from Geraldine Neuss at Bindner Jewellers. Please excuse the interruption during the holidays, but we just wanted to let you know your wedding ring is ready to be collected and hopefully won't be quite so tight any more.'

There were two beeps, then the connection was broken. Leon grasped the ring finger of his left hand, no longer feeling even the imprint on his skin. It had disappeared, along with any recollection of having taken the ring in to be adjusted.

'Are you OK?' asked Kroeger, and Leon realised he was standing there staring straight through the detective.

He was suddenly overcome by the urge to confide in somebody, and perhaps it wouldn't be so wrong to speak to a policeman, even if he would immediately become a suspect if he showed Kroeger the entrance to the tunnel system. Maybe Natalie had got lost in there and needed help? If that were the case, it would be negligent of him to hesitate too long purely out of fear of incriminating himself.

'Why don't we sit down in the living room?' suggested Leon, unsure as to whether he should open the door to his bedroom in the man's presence.

What if he hadn't committed a crime after all? What if everything sorted itself out and Natalie came through the door laughing in the next moment?

Oh, really? And what would she say? 'Sweetheart, did you find my mobile down in the shaft? I must have lost it when I tore off my thumbnail.'

Leon shook his head, incapable of finding any explanation that would put his world back into place.

'Excuse me?' asked Kroeger, looking around the living room.

'I didn't say anything.'

'Yes, you did. You mumbled someone's name, I think.'

Shit, now I don't even notice when I'm thinking out loud any more.

'You must have misheard.'

'Hmm.' The inspector nodded ponderously. 'I

157

could have sworn you said "Natalie". Is your wife at home?'

'No.'

'Where can I reach her?'

Leon hesitated, then decided to tell the truth; it was already on record, after all.

'I have no idea. She hasn't come home for the last few days, that's why I called the police.'

'I wasn't aware of a missing person's report.'

'The officer said that with adults you have to wait at least fourteen days, unless there are unusual circumstances.'

Kroeger nodded again. 'That's correct. Otherwise we would waste all our time with marital crises.'

He stepped towards the mantelpiece and picked up a silver frame. 'This is a nice photo.'

'Yes. Natalie took that one.'

On the day we met.

'I only see pictures of you here,' said the detective in surprise. 'None of your wife.'

'Hazard of the job. Natalie is a photographer, she prefers to be behind the camera.'

'Hmm.'

Practically able to feel the policeman's mounting suspicion, Leon decided to find out the reason for his visit before saying anything else.

'What exactly did you want to show me?'

'This.'

Kroeger pulled a mobile phone from the pocket of his leather coat and handed it to Leon.

'Where did you get this?' asked Leon, immediately recognising it as his own. He wondered why he hadn't noticed it was missing.

'We seized it.'

Seized it?

'When?'

Kroeger posed an unexpected counter-question. 'Is everything OK with your eye, Herr Nader?'

'Sorry?'

'You keep blinking. And you're avoiding making eye contact.'

'I have nothing to hide,' lied Leon, changing the subject quickly by pointing at the phone. 'Where did you find it?'

'Given that it's part of a criminal investigation, I'm not able to say for investigatory reasons.'

A criminal investigation?

'Your contact details weren't saved, so it took a while before we were able to identify you as the owner via the network provider.'

Investigatory reasons?

Leon gripped the edge of the dining table. His nausea was growing by the second.

'Thank you for going to the trouble,' he murmured flatly. The phone lay in his hand like a foreign body. It had only 10 per cent charge left. As soon as he keyed in the pin code, a ringing sounded out. It wasn't coming from his hand, but the breast pocket of his overalls.

'You have another mobile?' asked Kroeger in confusion.

'What? Erm, yes.'

'Don't you want to answer it?'

'It's not important.' He shook his head.

He might be able to explain having Natalie's mobile in his possession, but if he pulled it out of his pocket together with the blood-soaked blouse, it would be another matter . . .

'Right then!' Kroeger was now stood next to him at the dining table, no longer interested in the frame on the mantelpiece. He waited for what seemed a painfully long time, until the phone had stopped ringing, before continuing.

'As I'm sure you can imagine, the police have better things to do than act as delivery boys. I'm not here to give you your phone back, but because we stumbled across some strange content while evaluating your saved data.'

'Content?'

'Pictures, to be precise. Open the photo gallery.'

Leon did as he was told, and the first image was like a stab to the heart. Casual acquaintances would hardly have recognised him and Natalie on the photograph, because they were both in disguise. He looked like an old man: with a walking stick, hunched back, a double chin and a red, alcoholic's nose. She was dressed as a beggar and also looked years older. Her masquerade was deceptively real; only her broad smile exposed her true identity.

'We took that at Halloween, just before leaving for a fancy dress party,' explained Leon.

Alongside her studies, Natalie had trained as a make-up artist, and that evening she had created a genuine masterpiece. He thought back wistfully to the preparations. His favourite part had been the almost intimate caresses as she applied the make-up, the tender brush-strokes on the cheek, the stroking movements on the eyelids; her dark eyes and lightly parted mouth so close to his own lips.

'Lovely,' Kroeger said drily. 'But let's skip the first twenty snapshots. I'm not interested in how you spend your free time, but more in this.' The detective gave him the mobile back once he had scrolled down to the final pictures in the folder. Leon's eyes widened.

'That's private,' he said, his voice cracking.

'I know. But believe me, I wouldn't be here if it were merely a matter of your sexual preferences.'

The badly lit photo had been shot without the flash and showed Natalie sitting by the upholstered bed-head of their double bed. She was cross-legged, with her arms stretched wide above her head like someone bound to a cross, which in a way she was, for her wrists were in leather handcuffs, attached to the bed-posts with chains. She was wearing a man's vest ripped at the collar bone, which revealed more than it concealed, for her breasts were either wet or soaked with sweat. Either way, her erect nipples were plain to see despite the poor quality of the image.

Leon felt ashamed, a new feeling after all the worry, fear and panic he had suffered in the last hours. But the problem was not that Kroeger had trespassed into their intimate sphere and now knew about his wife's most secret sexual fantasies. The problem was that Leon had never seen this picture before. Nor all the others that Kroeger was about to show him.

At the behest of the policeman, he opened the next three images, each one worse than the last.

On the first, Natalie was completely naked, a rubber ball in her mouth. On the next, her eyes seemed about to pop out of their sockets, so tight was the dog's collar around her neck. But the real shock came from the last photo in the unknown series, taken three days ago, at 3.04 in the morning.

When I was sleeping . . .

If it had been possible – with some effort – to interpret Natalie's facial expression as sexual arousal before, then on this her eyes were filled with raw pain. She was bleeding from her closed mouth, her right eye was swollen, and if Leon wasn't mistaken, her thumb was injured too.

'Is there something you can tell me about this?' asked Kroeger.

'Only that it has nothing to do with you.'

'We'll see about that.'

'What's that supposed to mean?' asked Leon, now certain he would not be showing this man the door to the labyrinth under any circumstances. Too great was his fear of finding out what he was capable of.

What have I done to Natalie?

'You can take whatever pictures you want,' said Kroeger. 'As far as I'm concerned you can hang from the ceiling fan by your knotted balls. As I've already mentioned, Herr Nader, the police aren't there to get mixed up in marital issues. But you don't need to be investigator of the month to figure out that something's not right here. Your wife disappeared shortly after these photographs were taken.'

Leon tapped his thumb on the now-dead mobile display and asked, 'Would I have phoned the police if I had done something that was against the law?'

Kroeger laughed throatily and turned to leave. 'You wouldn't believe how stupid most of the criminals we deal with are.'

Leon followed him into the hallway, becoming anxious when the policeman went in the wrong direction, towards the bedroom, the door of which stood ajar.

'This is the way out,' said Leon, a little too insist-ently. The detective stopped abruptly.

'Are you trying to get rid of me?'

'No. I just don't want you to go the wrong way.'

Kroeger looked Leon right in the eyes, frowning, then turned back.

'OK then . . .' he said in a threatening tone, reaching inside his coat. Leon felt sure Kroeger was about to pull out a pair of handcuffs or a weapon, but it was just a wallet.

'For the moment you seem to have a clean record, Herr Nader. So see my visit as a warning. As of now, we have the special circumstances we need to take your missing person's report seriously. And while we look for your wife, I'll be keeping an eye on you.'

He handed Leon his card.

'Please do yourself a favour, and call me as soon as you have something to say.'

23

'Sven? Where are you? If you get this message, please call me back as soon as you can. I need your help.' Leon cut the connection with his friend's voicemail and turned his landline phone over in his hands thoughtfully. Before him on the desk in his office lay the discoveries from the shaft: Natalie's blouse and mobile phone. The latter was charging before the battery died completely.

The police detective had taken Leon's mobile phone with him, saying that he wasn't yet able to release it on account of the fact that it was potentially evidence. Leon wasn't sure if that was legal, but he had only protested half-heartedly. An argument with Kroeger wouldn't have gained him anything, and would only have made the policeman more suspicious.

Damn it, Sven. Why aren't you picking up?

Normally his friend was always contactable,

especially at times like these, when it was all or nothing in the final stages of a pitch.

Leon sat at the desk and reached for Natalie's phone. Since Kroeger left, he had already checked it. But with the exception of Dr Volwarth's contact details, he hadn't found any other entries, pictures or dates that seemed suspicious.

Many of the names in her contacts were, admittedly, unknown to him, but that wasn't surprising given that Natalie had friends from her student days saved there, many of whom Leon hadn't met or only briefly, and to whose names he wouldn't have been able to put a face.

And yet he still had a strange feeling as he opened the list of missed calls and saw an unusually long number at the top.

Who called Natalie while Kroeger was grilling me?

Leon pressed to return the call. A large part of him wanted to hang up at the dial tone. But on the other hand, if someone on the other end had information about Natalie, he desperately wanted them to pick up.

It was a while before he heard a noisy ringing, which sounded like the dial tone of a foreign line.

'Hello?' Leon heard a man answer. The voice sounded tired, but despite some interference from what sounded a little like a vacuum cleaner in the background, it was clear and easy to make out.

'Hello?' asked Leon hesitantly.

'Yes, who am I speaking to?'

Recognising the voice now, Leon jumped up from his seat as though he had been electrocuted.

'Dr Volwarth?' he asked in bewilderment.

'Yes, speaking.'

Leon's first impulse was to hang up, but it was already too late for that, because the psychiatrist had recognised his voice too.

'Leon? Leon, is that you?'

'Yes,' croaked Leon after a brief pause, in which he tried in vain to collect his wits. 'Why are you, I mean, how . . .? I thought you were on your way to Tokyo?' he stammered.

'And that's exactly where you're reaching me right now. On my seat in the plane.'

'You've been flying for over twenty-four hours?'

'What's this about, Leon? Don't you watch the news? The snow closed all the airports and our departure was delayed until this morning.'

Leon went over to the window and pulled the curtains apart. It was dark outside in the courtyard, but he could see thick peaks of snow on top of the rubbish bins.

'How did you get this number?' Volwarth asked.

'I pressed redial.'

'But how? I didn't call you.'

'Not me, no. You called my wife.'

'What? No, that's not possible. I don't know your wife.'

'Oh no?' asked Leon, feeling rage surge within him. 'So why is your name in her contacts list? And why did you try to call Natalie exactly twelve minutes ago on her mobile?'

'Just a moment.' Volwarth now sounded as confused as Leon had at the beginning of their conversation. 'What did you say your wife's name was?'

'Natalie.'

'My God . . .'

'Why, what is it?'

After a brief pause, in which the background noise from the aeroplane cabin became louder, Leon was able to hear the muffled sounds of the psychiatrist moving in his seat, then Volwarth spoke in a quiet but urgent tone: 'Listen, that clears up a few things, Leon. But I have to end this call immediately.'

'What's *that* supposed to mean?'

'That I can't help you any further.'

'What? But you're my doctor. I confided in you that my wife has disappeared and that I'm scared I have something to do with it, that my illness might have come back. And now even the police think I'm violent, and they showed me these horrific pictures they found on my mobile. Shot in our bedroom, a place where a void opens up, literally. Dr Volwarth, don't you think that, as my psychiatrist, you're duty-bound to help me in this situation?'

'Yes, you're right. And I wish I could.'

Could?

'Who the hell is stopping you?'

'Doctor–patient confidentiality.'

Leon choked as if Volwarth's last sentence had been forced down his throat. 'Just a moment, are you implying that Natalie is your patient too?'

'I really have to go now,' said the psychiatrist evasively, but Leon wasn't going to be shaken off that easily.

'What are you treating her for?'

'Please, I've already said too much.'

'She introduced herself with a different name, didn't she?'

'Leon . . .'

'I'd hazard a guess it was under Lené, her maiden name. Is that correct?'

'We're about to land, so we have to turn off all electronic devices. Goodbye.'

'You bastard!' bellowed Leon into the phone. 'What do you know about my wife? What's happened to her?'

'I have no idea what you're talking about, Leon. But it was really lovely to see you again after such a long time. Once again, congratulations on your wonderful apartment.'

What's that supposed to mean?

'I'm terrified that I'm losing my mind, and you spout this small talk? Please, Dr Volwarth, if you know something—'

'I just hope your fireplace starts working again soon, especially as it gets so cold over New Year.'

There was a crackle on the line, then the connection went dead.

24

Leon's rage had subsided, and a tense, all-consuming anxiety had won back the upper hand in his emotions.

He stood in the living room in front of the mantelpiece, in exactly the spot where the detective had stood searching in vain for photos of Natalie, and heard Volwarth's words replay in his mind: *I just hope your fireplace starts working again soon . . .*

Leon shook his head in a barely perceptible manner, like Ivana Helsing had done earlier while talking in her apartment. Then he kneeled on the protective brass fender in front of the fireplace. They hadn't used the open fire once since they moved in, because the chimney didn't work properly and there was a danger of carbon monoxide poisoning if they burned so much as a single log. It was an irritating problem that the building management had promised to deal with, but so far nothing had been done.

As a temporary measure, Leon and Natalie had installed a smoke-free ethanol heater. Artificial, plastic logs lay over a fuel chamber, creating an astonishingly genuine-looking and even warming light play.

'Our Las Vegas fireplace,' Natalie had joked. Like Leon, she tended to prefer more natural materials. 'Kitsch, but kind of cool.'

Thinking back to that day made Leon sad. Only a few weeks later, Natalie's laugh was just a memory of a time that was probably irrevocably lost.

And now?

After Volwarth had hung up, Leon had stood in his study as if nailed to the floor, wishing there were a lid on top of his skull so he could reach in and stop the carousel of his thoughts.

How does Volwarth know the fire's not working? was no longer the most burning question in his mind.

Only Natalie could have told him, but that was of marginal importance right now. Much more decisive was the fact that the psychiatrist had rudely ended their conversation with this very refrain, and there could be only one explanation for that.

Volwarth wanted to give me a clue without damaging his professional integrity.

'Come on, then,' said Leon to himself.

He removed the artificial pile of wood from the fireplace, then the pot with the fuel, and lit a match. The flame revealed the sooty, cracked inner wall of the fireplace, and as Leon poked his head into the opening, he couldn't help but think about the fairy tale of Hansel and Gretel, when the evil witch burns in her own oven after Gretel deviously lures her in there. His nerves were stretched to breaking point, and he looked behind him to make sure he was alone and that no one was standing there watching him.

It has eyes, you know. The house, I mean. He thought back to the cryptic words of the old Helsing woman, who was probably sat in front of her fireplace right this second, one storey down, talking to herself.

Once the first match had burned away between his fingers without him having seen anything, he lit another and tried to approach things in a more systematic way.

Thick, grimy soot – harking back to the days when tenants were lucky enough to have an intact chimney – covered his finger as Leon fumbled his hand around the base, centimetre by centimetre, in the hope of finding some hollow, groove or other feature that would suggest a hiding place.

Once he had checked the base and the walls of the fireplace, in vain, he moved to the chimney's smoke flap, which sealed the vent and, strangely, he couldn't open by hand.

Leon had to use the tongs to open it from the inside, and almost as soon as he had, after considerable effort, the obstruction that had been blocking the vent fell to the floor.

What in God's name . . .?

He flinched back from the small package as though it were a venomous snake. After a moment of shock, he bent over to pick up the object, which was wrapped in a plastic bag. It felt like a heavy book. Old, grey soot rose up towards him. Once he had taken off the wrapping, he realised that Dr Volwarth had led him to probably the most intimate document that Natalie had ever created.

Her diary wasn't very big, containing at most a hundred pages which had been bound into a rigid book. She'd only written on some of the pages, as Leon had established after wiping the soot from his fingers and sitting on a chair to inspect his find.

For the most part, the handwritten entries consisted of just one or two sentences, illustrated here and there with a drawing or photo.

Leon felt even more guilt than he had when searching Natalie's photography lab. By reading her diary entries, he was crossing yet another line, trespassing into forbidden territory.

Should I leave him? Natalie had asked her diary. The entry, made in her familiar, florid handwriting, was dated 28 February, just two months after they moved in.

> I thought we were soul mates. But sometimes I
> don't even recognise him. It's almost as though he
> has two faces.

Leon's throat began to tighten and the tips of his fingers became numb. He flicked through a few insignificant entries about problems or successes in the gallery, and her father's approaching birthday – the fact that she didn't know what to buy him.

Then, at the beginning of June, he found a photograph. There could be no doubt as to what it meant, but Leon spent several tortured seconds trying to find another explanation to the one that was so obvious. But all his efforts were in vain.

The fact that he had never seen the ultrasound picture before was like a blow to the gut, and Natalie's entry made it even worse.

> What should I do? I don't want to keep it. I CAN'T keep it.

'Tell me it isn't true,' said Leon, barely managing to get the words out. It felt like his throat had been sealed shut. He flicked further on, page by page, with every entry getting more nervous of finding the words he was expecting. Then he found them, dated two weeks later, just before the end of the first trimester.

Leon's eyes filled with tears.

The appointment in the clinic was awful. I only hope that Leon never discovers the truth.

'No!'

Something shattered inside him, something that would never be whole again.

'But why?' he whispered.

We wanted that baby so much.

At that moment he wished Dr Volwarth had kept his oath of confidentiality. He would never have wanted to find out this truth. He had been hoping the psychiatrist had some information that could have brought Natalie back. But now Leon felt further away from her than ever before.

It was the right decision not to tell him. Things are getting worse and worse with him, said an entry some weeks later. He felt just as agitated and shaky as Natalie's handwriting.

Her writing seemed rushed, fragile. No longer neat and artistic as he knew it to be from the notes she had so often left him on the fridge.

But that had been before, and *before* was clearly over.

I'm afraid, Natalie had written on one of the last pages, underlining the most terrible word in the sentence twice. *He's* hurting *me so much. It was all a terrible mistake. I have to leave him.*

'Our marriage? Me? The baby? Everything a mistake?'

Leon closed first the diary and then his eyes.

See nothing. Feel nothing. Forget everything.

'Am I responsible for what's happened to her?'

From the abortion to her disappearance?

Leon knew he was behaving oddly, sitting there having a conversation with the diary in his hand, but he couldn't help it.

'What did I do?'

Almost as soon as he had spoken the words out loud, he felt unbelievably tired, and this made him realise two things: firstly, he didn't have the strength for any more discoveries; he would lose his mind completely if he stayed in this apartment alone any longer, if in fact it hadn't happened already.

And he had asked the wrong question. The decisive factor was not what he had done in the past, but what he would do from now on that could damage himself or others.

I can't go to sleep, he thought, going into the bathroom to splash his face with cold water. *Not until I know the whole truth.*

He made a decision, the start of which entailed checking the front door to make sure he had secured it properly after Kroeger's departure. Normally he left the key in the lock when he was at home, but this time he took it out to keep on his person.

Leon knew how laughable these security precautions were in a building with doors hidden behind wardrobes, but he still checked the windows and searched every single room before sitting down in his living room and calling for help.

25

'Where the hell have you been hiding?' snarled Sven, his voice low and dangerous, as if he was only managing to hold back with a great deal of effort.

'I wanted to ask you exactly the same thing, I've tried to get hold of you several times already.'

'Well, you could have saved yourself the effort if you'd come to the party with me like we planned.'

By the fact that Sven spoke haltingly, Leon could tell how worked up his friend and business partner was. He had only heard him stutter this much once in recent times, and that was the day his mother had died.

'Which party?' asked Leon.

'Are you kidding me? Professor Adomeit? The executive director of the hospital consortium? The man with the sack of money and the golden fountain pen ready to sign our contract?'

Oh Christ, the birthday celebration for Adomeit's fiftieth.

Leon's hand rose to his forehead.

'I drove the four hundred kilometres to his holiday home out by the lake completely by myself.'

'I'm sorry, I totally forgot.'

'So I noticed,' said Sven, with a prolonged 'n'. Alongside 'd', this was the consonant that gave him the most difficulties.

'The idea with the tunnel connecting the hospital buildings was a hit, by the way!'

Leon closed his eyes. He had completely forgotten the fact that the model had disappeared from his study.

'Great, thank you. Why is it so quiet there?' asked Leon, who couldn't hear music, the clink of glasses, or any of the other usual sounds that accompany parties.

'Because I'm freezing my arse off on the veranda by the lake. It's too loud inside to take calls.'

As proof, Leon suddenly heard the rhythmic sound of the bass, as though someone had just opened the door to a club. Just as quickly, it stopped again.

'Where have you been? I tried your mobile a dozen times.'

'The police seized it.'

'What?'

Leon didn't know where to start. Ideally he would have liked to tell his friend about the door and the labyrinth, the thumbnail and the bloody blouse, but he couldn't do that on the telephone – and especially not while Sven was at a party.

Leon summarised the events of the last few days as briefly as he could, omitting the details that would cast doubt on his sanity.

Once he had finished, Sven's voice sounded even shakier than before, and Leon wasn't sure if it was exclusively down to the cold. 'So you're telling me your wife ran into the street in a distraught state, and you're scared you might have hurt her in some way?'

'Yes. And I'm afraid there's proof.'

'Sorry?' said Sven. 'The line is bad. What was the last thing you said?'

'There's proof.'

'The photos on your phone?'

'Not just that.'

'I'm not understanding any of this,' said Sven after a thoughtful pause.

Believe me, neither am I.

'Didn't you tell me during our last phone conversation that Natalie said she needed some space and that she was going to take some time for herself?'

'What? No, what gives you that idea?'

'Look, I'm not mad, you know,' protested Sven. 'You told me about the card she left you.'

'What card?'

'The one she pinned on your kitchen door before she went.'

All of a sudden Leon felt like his muscles had frozen. It took all of his strength of will to order his legs to carry him into the hallway.

'You must be mistaken,' he said to Sven, even though the proof was right in front of his eyes. Next to the newsletter from the building management, there was a postcard with an orange and yellow flower motif. Carefully, as though it might turn into dust, he freed it from the magnet and flipped it over.

Dearest Leon, began the brief note, composed by Natalie in her unmistakable handwriting. The postcard in his hand was shaking so much that he had trouble deciphering the lines that followed.

> I need some space. I can't tell you any more than
> that, I'm afraid, just that I need to take a few days
> to figure out where we go from here. Don't worry.
> I'll be in touch as soon as I'm strong enough.
> Your Natalie

No postage stamp, no watermark. And yet here it was. In his apartment. In his hands.

Without realising, Leon had let his hand holding the phone fall to his side, and once he put the handset to his ear again he heard an engaged tone. Thinking he had lost the connection to Sven, he pressed redial, in the process answering a new incoming call.

'United Deliveries, Customer Service, good morning . . .'

'Who?' asked Leon, utterly confused.

'We would like to apologise for the inconvenience, Herr Nader.'

Leon was about to hang up on the woman with the impersonal sing-song voice, but then she said, 'We're very sorry, but for some reason your last order seems to have gone missing.'

Leon shook his head in frustration. 'I don't have time to talk right now. And besides, I received everything.'

'Really? Oh, then the mistake must lie with the delivery company. Because we don't have your confirmation of receipt.'

No wonder with that idiot of a courier.

Without saying goodbye, Leon switched back to the call with Sven.

'Are you still there?'

'Yes.'

The background atmosphere had changed now. His friend's voice sounded closer; presumably he was no longer outside and had managed to find a quiet spot in Adomeit's house after all.

'You're right . . .' Leon had gone back into the living room with the postcard and laid it on the dining table next to Natalie's diary. 'There really is a note from her.' He looked at the dappled sunflowers on the front. *Van Gogh. How appropriate. He was also an expert in madness.*

'But I can't remember how it got on to the kitchen door.' His voice started to crack. 'I can't remember so many of the things I do in my sleep.'

'Leon, I—'

'Please, let me finish.'

'No,' Sven cut in. 'Now it's time for you to listen to me, Leon.'

'OK.'

'You know I've never really warmed to Natalie. And I'm saying this to you now as a friend, even at the risk that I might not be one afterwards.'

'What?'

'I don't trust her. She's playing games with you.'

'What do you mean?'

'Just think about how rushed your wedding was. Why do you think she wanted everything to be so quick?'

'But *I* proposed to her.'

'Yes, but you always wanted to have a big wedding. She wanted it to be secretive and really small. Why?'

'That was down to both of us.'

'Really? And did you make a pre-nup in all the rush?'

'What do you mean? She's the one with the rich parents, I'm the charity case.'

'And what about our business, Leon? If we get this commission, it's only the beginning.'

'I don't understand what you're getting at.'

'I'm just listing the facts. You're the one who needs to put two and two together.'

'The facts are that something awful has happened to Natalie. *Before* she left me.'

'You mean the injuries?'

'Yes.'

'They looked terrible, right?'

'Yes.'

'As real as the make-up you guys put on for Halloween?'

Boom. Another blow to the gut.

'You're crazy, Sven,' said Leon listlessly.

'And you're looking at things from too one-sided a viewpoint. Who was it that told me so proudly that Natalie was a genius of transformation? Maybe she's deceiving you.'

'Sven . . .'

'No, trust me. You couldn't hurt a fly. I know you.'

'Perhaps not well enough,' Leon interjected, his voice louder. 'I'm holding a diary in my hands in which she wrote that I was hurting her. And that she was so afraid of me that she *didn't want to keep our child.*'

Beside himself with rage, he flung the book away. It somersaulted across the room, opening up into a 'V' shape and shedding some pages, before crashing into the wall near the door.

He regretted his outburst at once, but he couldn't take it back.

'I'm just trying to help you,' stuttered Sven as Leon bent down to pick up the pages from the parquet floor. There were two drawings and a photo, which he must have missed when going through the diary. He recognised the location in the snapshot, even though this picture was even more dark and shadowy than an ultrasound image.

With great effort, Leon was able to decipher the word, written in old-fashioned script above a picture of a lightning bolt.

DANGER

Before, he had thought he saw it at the end of a tunnel. But now he realised his mistake. The wall on which the warning sign hung wasn't a wall at all, but a door. And on the blurry photo in his hands, it was slightly ajar.

All at once Leon felt so exhausted that he needed to sit on the floor so as not to fall over.

'How long will it take you to get here?' he asked Sven, who by that point had asked several times if his friend was still on the line.

'I've been drinking. I won't be able to leave until tomorrow morning.'

'Please hurry. I have to show you something.'

26

The second descent was even harder than the first, primarily due to the equipment Leon was carrying. This time he didn't want to be reliant on the sketchy background illumination of a mobile phone.

Nor did he want to venture into the labyrinth without protection, for fear that he really had escaped a genuine danger earlier and not just a stray cat. Leon had armed himself with a pocket torch and a crowbar, something that could be used as both a tool and a weapon.

Because he wanted to keep both hands free, he stowed most of it away in his tool belt, which he wore around his hips as he made his way down the ladder for the second time.

But, most importantly, he was now documenting every one of these steps with the head camera. He only hoped the radio signal would be strong enough to reach from the secret passageways of the labyrinth up to the laptop in the bedroom.

For now he was using the built-in miniature head-lamp of the motion-activated camera as a light source. As he descended into the abandoned tunnel with this instrument strapped to his head, he didn't just look like a miner, he felt like one too. This time Leon avoided the falling hazard towards the bottom of the shaft by leaving out the loose rung.

Once at the bottom, he surveyed the remains of his first expedition into the unknown. The sight of the shattered torch on the floor was a warning not to test his luck again. He had escaped unscathed, albeit shell-shocked, the first time. But next time there might be more than just damage to his possessions.

'I'm now going to crawl through a low tunnel,' said Leon, in case the images were too dark for the camera.

He didn't want to leave any room for doubt if anyone looked at the proof later.

Once again Leon got down on all fours, and once again he crept head first through the roughly hewn stone shaft. Surprisingly, even the light didn't make it any easier.

A constrictive pressure descended on his chest, and he couldn't help but think of being buried alive; of people who, after some horrific mistake, wait for rescue and have to ration every breath until the oxygen supply eventually runs out.

No one knows where you are. No one will look for you. Who knows if the passageways here are even stable?

In his visions, he was trapped by stones and debris, his arms broken, with no chance of using the mobile phone.

Leon paused, held his breath and listened to his heart, which refused to settle and was making the pulse in his neck flutter. When he couldn't hold it any longer, he gasped greedily for air, air that smelled of dust, earth and his own sweat.

But not of clean washing . . .

That's what was missing!

Both the droning sound of the washing machine and the smell had vanished. Only the cold remained, but right now Leon was glad about that. His body was seething with tension, and he would use any way of cooling off he could find. Ideally he would have liked to take off his gloves, but he didn't want to risk injuring his hands.

'I'm just reaching a passageway,' said Leon, standing up. 'I'll call it the tube.'

Last time he had only been able to touch the rough walls, but now he saw that the tube was significantly shorter than he remembered.

Leon had almost reached the fork at the end when

he felt a gust of air on his legs, carrying something with it that almost knocked him over. And yet it wasn't a physical object or living being, but a voice.

'Help! Please, I need help . . .'

'Natalie?' shouted Leon. He had recognised his wife's voice instantly, even though it was very faint.

A fleeting waft, no louder than a whisper underwater.

'Natalie, where are you?'

No answer. His call echoed into the labyrinth, the depths of which he didn't know and in which he was at risk of losing himself, in every sense of the word.

'Natalie, don't be afraid.' He was just about to add, *I'm coming to help you*, when he heard more voices.

A man and a woman. At very close proximity. He turned off the light on his headband and held his breath.

Who is that?

The voices, which seemed weirdly familiar, were coming closer.

But from which direction?

The woman's words were too faint to make out, but what he heard was enough to intensify his fear for Natalie.

Are they coming from up ahead?

'Damn it, not again,' he heard the man curse, and Leon turned in the darkness towards the voice.

No, they're coming from behind. Or are they?

'Why weren't you more careful? Hurry up. You have to get it out again somehow.'

There was a crashing sound, and Leon, who by spinning around had lost his bearings, stared into what seemed like a never-ending wall of impenetrable darkness.

He freed the crowbar from his tool belt and held it at head height like a club. Ready to strike.

As exhausted as he was nervous, he grabbed hold of his headband to activate the camera lamp once more. Then something blinded him so completely that he had to shut his eyes.

When he opened them again, a woman was standing right next to him, crying.

27

The shock penetrated Leon's whole body so intensely that he hit out instinctively.

Hard. With all his strength. Without thinking for even a second.

He hit the woman, who had her black hair pulled into a tight ponytail, right between the eyes. He wasn't able to swing far because of the low tunnel, but at least the tip of the crowbar must have ploughed deep into the bone of her skull.

Yet Frau Falconi stood there unmoving, before she spoke: 'Man, I'm not even sure if the damn thing is still in there.'

Staring at the cleft in her face, Leon felt like he was having an out-of-body experience. Then his neighbour from the first floor rolled her tear-filled, red-rimmed eye, the lid of which she was holding with both index fingers to stop herself blinking, and it dawned on him what must have happened.

Frau Falconi's head really was just an arm's length away from him, but she wasn't on his side of the passageway. She was on the other side of the wall! In front of her bathroom mirror!

'Can a contact lens just disappear behind the eye like that?' Leon heard her husband ask. His voice, like his wife's, was muffled.

Leon stretched his arm out and tentatively touched the splinter he had made in the panel on the wall with his crowbar. The glass was at head height, and was roughly as big as a flatscreen TV.

A two-way mirror!

From here Leon had a direct view into his neighbours' bathroom, while Frau Falconi could only see herself in the mirror, which on Leon's side must be strengthened with thick, soundproofed safety glass. His arm was sore from the impact of the crowbar jolting back into his bones. Frau Falconi, on the other hand, had heard and felt nothing, and continued the search for her lost contact lens unperturbed.

'No, the connective tissue stops them from going behind your eye and disappearing into your head,' she answered her husband, who had come into the bathroom.

Like his wife, his Italian roots were unmistakable: thick dark hair, brown eyes and healthy-looking tan skin even in winter. But in contrast to the well-groomed appearance of his wife, the husband was quite scruffy. While she wore a white, figure-hugging blouse, he had on a creased linen shirt hanging down over his pot belly. 'It's always the same with you. We need to talk about something important, and you start messing about.'

'Of course. I'm just poking my eyeball around specifically to annoy you.'

The couple's voices were coming from a small gap directly above the mirror, presumably connected to the bathroom's ventilation system.

Leon noticed a movement in the background, then saw the husband opening a bathroom cabinet and fetching out a brightly coloured sports bag.

'Our money's getting tight, darling.'

'You mean, *my* money.'

Herr Falconi pulled his face into a derogatory grimace behind her back.

'I saw that,' said his wife, without turning round.

Leon, who so far had been fixated on Frau Falconi's tear-stained face, took a step closer to the mirror to get a better look at the man. 'Will you be fetching some more soon?' he asked, fanning through the bundle of notes he had taken from the bag.

'That should be enough for now,' sighed Frau Falconi, who had taken a step away from the sink. Thanks to her fingers, her eye was now so bloodshot barely any white could be seen. Her nose was running too, but she made no move to blow it.

'For now, yes,' said the man, stuffing the money into the back pocket of his trousers.

'But if things carry on like this, soon we won't be able to afford the rent.' He made a fawning bow and feigned an apologetic expression. 'Sorry, I mean of course that *you* won't be able to pay the rent.'

'Let me worry about that,' said Frau Falconi, grabbing a tissue from the box on the basin. She was just about to blow her nose when she stopped abruptly and cocked her head to the side. It was a few moments before Leon heard what had caught her attention.

A soft melody.

No, not a melody. Scales.

Herr Tareski on the fourth floor had begun his piano practice again, and for some reason it was making Frau Falconi smile. She listened for a short while, as though enchanted, then followed her husband out of the bathroom. Leon didn't know what was bothering him more: that he had been plunged back into darkness, into a world between worlds that he understood less and less with every new discovery, or that, shortly before the light went out, he had the feeling Frau Falconi had given him a conspiratorial wink through the mirror.

28

An hour later Leon had switched sides. Now he was no longer standing in the tunnel, but in the bathroom; and it wasn't the Falconis', it was his own.

He took another swing, smashing the crowbar into the mirror again. But unlike down in the labyrinth, the glass here shattered, revealing a concrete wall.

No two-way mirror. Logical.

Leon laughed, close to hysteria.

After all, why would you want to spy on yourself?

And even if he did – was it plausible that he had constructed this world of shadows in his sleep: the wardrobe? The labyrinth? The mirror?

He wheezed, breathless from the fast climb and still exhausted from the fruitless attempts to open the door in the small passageway.

After the Falconis had disappeared, he remained in the darkness for a while, listening for further scraps of conversation. But he couldn't shake his confusion, numbed by the shock of realising that he could spy on his neighbours from down here. At some point (and he didn't know whether minutes or hours had passed) he turned the light on again and made his way to the DANGER sign.

The door was concealed so well that if he hadn't seen it in black and white on the picture from Natalie's diary, he would never have found it in a thousand years.

Leon groped around the wall of the apparent dead end, and didn't find anything to grab hold of. No gap. No edge. No hinge.

Secretly, he had suspected as much.

After all the exertions so far, that would just have been too easy.

He knocked against the wall looking for hollow spaces, hammered the crowbar against the sign, and even searched the surrounding walls and floor for hidden levers. But all in vain. Perhaps a blow-torch or sledgehammer would have come in useful, but against what?

And even if he did succeed in opening this secret door, would he really find Natalie behind it? Her calls had gone silent, just like Tareski's muffled piano playing, and by now Leon was no longer sure if he had even really heard her. He wasn't sure of any of his senses any more.

After the failed attempts to open the door, and feeling close to a mental breakdown, he had sunk down on to the earthy floor and buried his face in his hands.

Here, at the very lowest point of his despair, not knowing what nightmares lay ahead, he had the all-decisive thought: *Let's suppose I have a second, nocturnally active self. And let's assume that in my second consciousness I constructed a parallel world – then the entrance to this world can't be that complicated. Otherwise I wouldn't be able to master it in my sleep!*

Under this premise, everything argued against the idea that the door had to be opened with brute force.

Leon had pulled himself back to his feet and using his thumbs pressed with all his strength on the middle of the sign, as though it were the child-proof lock of a medicine container. At the same time he tried to turn the DANGER sign clockwise with his other hand, something that presumably would have been much easier if he hadn't already bent the edges. But after the third attempt it made an audible click, then suddenly moved to the side.

That had been half an hour ago. Leon had gazed in amazement at the safety lock exposed behind the sign, touching it with his fingers and checking to see if any of the keys on his keychain fit. The euphoria he felt when his front-door key turned in the lock disintegrated as Leon discovered that he hadn't opened the door, just a postcard-sized cover, beneath which lay an electronic input screen. The buttons were inscribed not with numbers, but letters.

Now what?

He had the key but not the code.

Leon tried the first passwords that came to mind: *Natalie, Leon*, their surnames and pet names, and even *Morphet*. All without success.

Then his gaze fell on the inside of the lock's protection plate. On closer inspection, he was able to make out the thin pencil lines, which formed a series of letters. He read:

The violin is the key!

What was that supposed to mean?

My sleepwalking self is making mnemonics I don't recognise in my conscious state!

Leon had reached breaking point. Once again solving one mystery had only brought him another one, and now, standing before the ruins of his bathroom mirror, Leon became aware that he was neither physically nor psychologically able to figure this out alone.

He didn't want to wait any longer for Sven. No, he *couldn't* wait. He needed help.

Immediate help.

Leon hurried out of the bathroom into the hallway, picked up the telephone from the unit and took it into the bedroom. He had left Inspector Kroeger's card there, next to his laptop.

What the hell?

He stared at the keypad of his telephone.

The buttons lit up when pressed, and he could hear an electronic crackle when he put it against his ear and listened hard. But other than that, the line was dead.

But I thought I charged it?

No dial tone. Not even when he tapped in the first few digits.

This can't be happening.

He thought of Natalie's mobile, but couldn't remember where he had put it. Was it still down in the shaft? It wasn't in his pockets, and he couldn't see it anywhere else. So he went to the front door to go downstairs and ask Frau Helsing if he could use her landline, but then found himself confronted by the next problem. He was locked in.

Leon stared at his front door as though entranced, fixated on the lock, which normally contained a key. Then he remembered which lock he had left it in.

Down there. In the labyrinth. Damn it . . .

Leon let out a sigh that became a drawn-out yawn.

I can't. Not again.

But he didn't have a choice. He was unbelievably

exhausted, his eyelids heavy as though they had weights hanging on them, yet it didn't matter. If he wanted to end all this insanity quickly, he had to go down there again.

Into the labyrinth.

But first he went to the bathroom to relieve himself, grateful for the destroyed mirror, which meant he could no longer see his reflection. If he looked only a fraction as bad as he felt, his appearance would scare even him.

While Leon stood there urinating, his gaze fell on the medicine cabinet that Natalie had installed at head height over the toilet. Ever since the trip to Réunion, it had been well-stocked. Alongside aspirin, antibiotics, iodine, flu and diarrhoea remedies, pills for travel sickness, allergies and plasters, Leon also found the high-dosage caffeine tablets that she had taken in the initial phase of the gallery opening so she could work through the night. He swallowed two pills in one go and put the pack in his pocket.

Just don't fall asleep.

Then he readjusted the head camera, activated the lamp and armed himself a third time for his descent into the darkness.

29

Hours later, when Leon opened his eyes, he had no idea where he was.

He sat bolt upright in bed, startled awake by a sound like a squeaking tap. Seeing the make-up brushes on the bureau and the intact ceiling lamp above his head, he wondered why he felt so incredibly relieved.

He stroked his hand across the rumpled sheets, feeling the warmth from a body that must have been lying next to him until moments ago. And then he smelled it: the perfume, that subtle summery scent he had missed so much in his nightmare.

'Natalie?' he called, his voice still thick with sleep.

'Yes, darling?' he heard her answer from the neighbouring room.

Calm, relaxed, cheerful.

Thank God.

The incubus the nightmare had left behind began to lose its intensity.

It was all just in my imagination!

'You won't believe the crazy dream I had,' he called, starting to laugh.

He looked at the wardrobe, which was in its familiar place. In the light of day, it looked much too heavy to be moved without help.

There's no door. No shaft. No transparent mirror.

'I dreamed I discovered a labyrinth behind our bedroom wall while I was sleepwalking,' he said, shaking his head in disbelief at his own words. He made sure there was no USB stick in the laptop on the bureau, then jumped out of bed. He felt well rested and motivated for the first time in ages.

'There were passageways down there, and mirrors through which we could spy on the Falconis. Can you imagine? It was a nightmare, and I was afraid of falling asleep.' Leon heard the toilet being flushed in the bathroom.

'And I filmed myself, like that time when I was a kid. Can you hear me, Natalie?'

'Loud and clear, darling.'

The rushing sound from a tap being turned on swallowed his wife's words.

'It was like in a computer game, completely insane. You had disappeared, and I found all these clues everywhere that led me to a different level or to a new door I needed to look behind. But do you know what the strangest thing was?'

'No, what?'

Leon wrapped his hands around his upper body, shivering. He was naked and, like always, Natalie had turned down the heating before going to bed.

'I can remember all of it, every detail. Normally I forget my dreams as soon as I wake up, but this time I can even remember what I was thinking just before-hand.'

Leon opened the door of the wardrobe to get some clothes out.

My last thought down there, before I fell asleep in front of the secret door with the DANGER *sign, was:* You have to stay awake. Get your front door key, climb back up, fetch help. But for God's sake don't fall asleep.

'I was so scared of what I was capable of while sleepwalking that I wanted to stay awake at all costs. I even took some of your Hello Awake pills from the medicine cabinet.'

'I know,' said Natalie, with a voice that was no longer coming from the bathroom.

Leon clapped his hand over his mouth in shock.

'You just wanted to get your key from the DANGER door, but you suddenly felt so tired you fell asleep right there with the camera on your head, is that right?'

No, please no. Don't let it start all over again.

His wife's voice sounded so clear, as if she was standing right in front of him. But there was nothing there but . . .

. . . the wardrobe!

'Natalie?'

Leon pushed the hangers to the side, as if he genuinely believed his wife could be hiding among the clothes like a child.

'Darling, where are you?'

'Here, I'm here.'

'Where's HERE?'

'I don't know. It's so dark. Please help me!' said Natalie in a voice that sounded more distant now, but its source hadn't changed. It was still coming from right behind the wardrobe.

But that's impossible.

Leon tore out the whole clothing rail, hangers and clothes included. Then he kicked the rear panel until it gave way and fell to the side.

Instead of the vault door that Leon was expecting, he found himself staring at a recently bricked-up section in the wall. The mortar between the bricks was still damp; Leon was able to leave fingerprints behind in the grey sludge.

'Get me out of here,' Natalie pleaded, close to tears now.

Her pleading was like a downpour of icy water.

Leon took a step back, stumbling over the crowbar that he had used to hit the mirror earlier.

But EARLIER was a dream. And NOW is reality, isn't it?

'Leon. Get me out of here before it's too late!'

Natalie's despair was like a baby's crying: impossible to ignore. Guided by his primal instincts, Leon grabbed the crowbar and started raking out the mortar.

'I'm coming,' were the last words he uttered before he managed to get some purchase between the bricks. Quickly, much too quickly, the first small crumbs of brick began to come away from the wall, then shards, then finally a whole brick.

'Hurry. Before you fall asleep again,' he heard Natalie call, and then came the water.

A dark drop bulged out, then it began to gush as though a valve had burst, and before Leon had time to press his hand against the hole in the wall, a fountain shot out. There was so much pressure that more and more bricks broke free, until eventually the entire wall collapsed over Leon.

He tried to scream, but only breathed in cold, dirty-tasting water, which he couldn't cough up because the pressure on his chest was growing and growing. Something pulled him down into the depths, threatening to drown him in its wet embrace.

Leon hit out, thrashing his arms and legs, realised

he was trapped by something, then pushed himself against it with all his strength and finally managed to break through a viscous upper layer with his head. He opened his eyes wide, gasped for air and coughed. And with his attempts to purge the liquid from his windpipe, the dream ended.

30

Leon soon wished he was still in the sleep paralysis from which he had just freed himself.

At least then he wouldn't be lying fully clothed in his bathtub, covered with some liquid that smelled like iron, and a with distant hum in his ear, not knowing whether the red stains came from one of his wounds or from the other, motionless creature that was in the bath with him.

What IS that?

He had touched it with his hand, and felt intense disgust as his fingers sank into the soft body under the water. He had gone through all the harmless explanations in his mind: a sponge, a flannel, a toy, but he couldn't fool himself. The fur had belonged to a living thing once, as had the tubular internal organs that were floating on the surface of the water.

Retching, Leon jumped out of the water, and in

the process became entangled in the entrails, unintentionally pulling the animal over the edge of the bathtub.

Alba?

The dead cat thudded on to the tiles with a dull splat, its lifeless eyes fixed on Leon, the mouth open in a final hiss that seemed to have got stuck in its throat.

Leon, too, opened his mouth, because he had become so nauseated he could no longer breathe through his nose.

The smell of blood was just as intense as the sound of hammering on wood that had been coming from the hallway for a while now. It wasn't the only way that someone was trying to make their presence known at the front door. The impatient visitor was also ringing the doorbell, and it was reverberating through the whole apartment.

I thought it was broken? Leon asked himself, as close to hysteria as to a mental breakdown.

My wife has left me because I've mistreated her; I can no longer tell the difference between dream and reality; I wake up in the bathtub with a dead cat – and now I'm worried about the doorbell?

He shuffled out of the bathroom and crept along the corridor like a burglar: slowly, carefully, taking care not to make a sound. This was practically impossible, as his soaking boots squelched with every step.

On top of that, he was struggling not to lose the left boot, which for some reason was missing its lace.

There was still water in his windpipe, and Leon had to cough. But there was no danger of the person at the door hearing him, given the din they were making already.

Who the hell is it?

Leon looked through the peephole and closed his eyes in relief.

'Thank God,' he said, close to tears with happiness.

The knocking and ringing died away.

'Leon?' asked Sven through the door.

'Yes.'

'What are you playing at? Open up, will you!'

'Just a second.'

Leon patted his pockets and was astonished to feel the bundle of keys that he thought he had left in the lock of the DANGER door in the labyrinth.

How did they get back in my pocket?

It was a struggle to get the key out of his damp pocket, before he opened the door to his friend, who pushed past him into the apartment, gesticulating wildly.

'Leon, I've been outside your door for a quarter of an hour already, and . . . Oh God.' Every trace of rage disappeared from Sven's face as soon as he looked at Leon.

'What in God's name happened to you?' he asked.

At least, that's what Leon presumed Sven *wanted* to ask, because his stuttering was worse than it had been in a long time.

'I'm so glad you're here,' said Leon, turning towards the mirror. Then he understood why Sven was looking at him in such shock. He was still wearing his overalls, but now they were black from being drenched with water, or perhaps because of the blood, and that was not the worst thing about his appearance by far. His face looked as though he had made himself up like a clown and then put his head underwater: black and red make-up was daubed across his forehead and cheeks, down to his chin. Soot-like dirt made his hair stick together in thick strands, standing up erratically or clinging to his skull like algae. His red, inflamed eyes, over deep bags, completed the look of someone who was severely ill, with the worst symptoms still to come.

'I need your help,' croaked Leon, whose voice had failed at the sight of himself.

'Are you having a breakdown?' asked Sven, trying to form short sentences.

'No, it's not the work.' Leon giggled, because the question seemed so absurd to him. 'I haven't done any work since the model disappeared.'

'Disappeared?' Sven stared at him with an expression of rising disbelief.

'Yes. Gone. No longer there. Like Natalie. I told

you. I think our work is down there with her in the labyrinth.'

'Where?'

'In the labyrinth I discovered behind my wardrobe. Come on, I'll show you the door.'

Leon grabbed for Sven's hand, but he pulled away just before their fingers touched.

'You have a fever!'

'No. Yes, possibly. I'm not sure.'

Leon searched in desperation for the right words to explain to Sven the insanity he was imprisoned in. When he didn't find them, he pressed his fists against his temples in despair. 'I don't know what's happening to me. Please, I'm begging you. Let me show you the door.'

For a few moments they stood silently before one another, then Sven nodded hesitantly and sighed. 'OK.'

Leon was relieved. 'Thank you. Really, thank you. Come with me.'

He turned round after every two steps to make sure Sven was really following him. 'Here it is,' he said, once they had entered the bedroom.

'Where?'

'Here . . .'

Leon positioned himself by the side of the wardrobe and braced both hands against it, like a runner stretching his muscles before exercise.

'I just need to push the thing to the side so that—'

Leon stopped in bewilderment. Even though he was pushing with all his strength, the wardrobe refused to budge by even a millimetre.

'Help me?' he asked, but Sven just lifted his hands dismissively.

'I've seen enough.'

His gaze wandered over the chaos Leon had left behind in his bedroom during the last few days: clothes lay strewn wildly, the metal chair in front of the bureau was on its side, the glass shards of the ceiling lamp lay among the crowbar and other work tools from the upended toolbox.

'I think you must be really burned out,' said Sven with a stutter, eyeing the trainers with the melted soles by his feet warily. They lay next to a pair of used latex gloves.

'No,' retorted Leon, more loudly than he had intended. 'It's worse than that. Believe me.'

I can't let him leave again. Not before I've proved it to him.

Leon had let go of the wardrobe and was now down on his knees, peering under the bed.

'What are you looking for?'

'My headband. My head camera. I filmed it all while I was down there.' Leon sat up and gave a tortured grin. 'Of course, God, I'm so stupid. You can see it all yourself. Come on.'

He jumped up and went over to the laptop on the

bureau, which was still turned on, but in energy-saving mode.

'Wait, soon you'll understand what I'm talking about . . .' Leon pressed the escape button multiple times. As the screen came back to life, he turned – and found himself alone in the room.

'Sven?'

No, please no. Don't let him have disappeared too.

He rushed into the hallway, looking frantically in all directions.

'Sven?'

Instead of an answer, he heard the creak of the parquet floor, relatively close by in the stairwell.

'Sven, come back!' he called after his friend, running towards the exit. Rushing to catch Sven at the lift, Leon almost stumbled over him, as he didn't reckon on Sven being ducked down directly behind the front door.

'Hey, watch out. Otherwise you'll break it!'

'Break what?' asked Leon breathlessly. Instead of answering, Sven stepped to the side.

'*Voila!* Our vanished model,' grinned Sven, who was speaking more easily now. He lifted up the cardboard model of the hospital renovation with both hands and carried it past Leon.

'But, but, but, but . . .' Now it was Leon's turn to stutter. 'But that can't be possible.'

'And why not?' asked Sven on his way into the study.

'Where did you get it from?'

Sven had reached the desk and was placing the model in the middle of the work surface. 'Where do you think? I picked it up, remember?' Worry lines appeared on his forehead. 'You haven't forgotten that, have you?'

'Yes,' sighed Leon.

Like so many things.

'I guess I must have been sleepwalking when you came.'

His friend gave him a mocking look.

'Don't be ridiculous. That's impossible. I had a long conversation with you.'

'Well, that can happen in an unconscious state too.'

'You're kidding, right?'

'No. It's unusual, but not all that rare for sleep-walkers to act almost like normal, conscious people,' explained Leon in agitation. As he spoke, his thoughts were crashing together in his mind.

Who knows how often I fall asleep? And if I don't always have the camera on? What else have I done in my sleep that isn't on the tapes?

'Some cook meals for themselves, and by the next morning they've forgotten that they ate a salami pizza in deep sleep and washed up the dishes afterwards,' he continued. 'Others have whole conversations with their partners, go for a walk, turn the TV on or start up their cars.'

And others enter into a gruesome underworld in order to hurt their wives . . .

Leon didn't want to dwell on this last thought.

'There is a simpler answer to all this, partner,' said Sven as he walked out of the study. 'You're just over-worked.'

Leon sighed. 'No. That's not it. I wish it was, but it's not. You have no idea. You don't know what's happening here . . . what happens to *me* when I sleep. I filmed it. Please believe me. Watch the tape.'

Sven groaned, and he sounded almost amused. 'A film?'

'Yes.'

'Of you sleeping?'

'Exactly.'

'And it's on your laptop?'

'In the bedroom. Please.'

For a while the friends didn't say another word, then Sven rolled his eyes like a father who couldn't say no to his son's ridiculous request.

'Fine. But first I need to use your bathroom.'

'What?'

'The toilet. I need to go.'

'No.'

Leon made a step to block his way, but it was too late. His friend had already opened the bathroom door.

'What the . . . Oh God!'

Sven flinched as though he had just been lashed in the face with a whip.

'You're sick,' he whispered. Strangely, when he lowered his voice, the stutter disappeared.

'That wasn't me,' said Leon, pointing at the dead cat on the tiles.

'I mean, it wasn't *the* Leon that *you* know.'

'Get away from me,' exclaimed Sven with a look of disgust on his face, stretching both his arms out to keep Leon at a distance.

'No, you have to stay!'

Leon screamed so loudly that spittle flew from his mouth. He grabbed Sven with both arms to keep him from going by force if necessary, but he was too weak. Sven had no difficulty in freeing himself from his grasp.

'Don't touch me!' he panted, backing towards the exit with his hands balled into fists.

'Please, Sven. I filmed everything. Myself, the shaft, the tunnel. Even the Falconis behind the mirror.'

He begged Sven to stay, to look at the video, but his words just drove his friend from the apartment more quickly.

'You've completely lost your mind,' shouted Sven. These were his last words as he flung open the front door and disappeared from view. Leon could only hear his heavy footsteps hammering down the stairs.

And now? What do I do now?

Leon would have hurried after him, but just the memory of Natalie fleeing into the stairwell only a few days ago under similarly mysterious circumstances – perhaps to disappear from his life for ever – held him back.

He leaned against the door from the inside, exhausted, closing it with his back and beginning to talk to himself again.

'I should get out of here. Ivana was right. It's the building. I have to get out of here.'

He went over to the telephone table and picked up the landline from its unit.

'I have to get out of here.'

When he heard the dial tone, he lost it completely. Leon laughed so hard that his whole body shook.

My key. The model. The dial tone – they're all back.

'Only my sanity is still nowhere to be found.'

Giggling hysterically, he went back into the bedroom to fetch the policeman's card. It was next to the laptop, and at least his memory didn't fail him on that point.

'Hello, Herr Kroeger? Please come and pick me up,' he laughed breathlessly as he dialled the inspector's number. After the fourth digit, he heard an engaged tone and stopped in confusion.

Clearly the blinking light of the USB stick in the laptop had distracted him so much that he had delayed too long dialling the number, and now needed to start again from scratch.

'No. Things can't go on like this,' he said to himself. 'I don't want to see what I recorded.'

During my last sleep phase. After I fell asleep in the tunnel in front of the DANGER *door.*

'I don't want to see it,' repeated Leon in a whisper.

Not while I'm alone, he added in his head.

But then he leaned over to lift up the metal chair and put it in front of the laptop screen.

31

A few minutes later Leon ran back into the bathroom so quickly he almost lost his boot that was missing its lace.

Too late. Damn it. Hopefully I won't be too late.

His wet clothes rubbed against his skin with every movement, but right now that was the least of his worries.

I shouldn't have watched it, he thought, cursing himself mentally. But how could he have resisted the blinking light when it might have signalled the solution to all his problems?

His hopes had been dashed, of course. Even worse than that: the images on the last recording had punished him ruthlessly for his lack of self-control.

If he had interpreted the video correctly, he had much bigger problems than he'd feared. Of the huge volume of material that had now been collected by the hard drive, he had watched only the very last, continuous recording, the first seconds of which were entirely unspectacular: the video had predominantly shown walls, stones and steps, in other words the path that Leon had walked along – from the door with the DANGER sign, out of the shaft and back to his apartment – almost as soon as he had fallen asleep.

The violin is the key!

Leon had been expecting to see himself operate the keypad and open the secret door.

But instead, I did something much worse.

He hadn't even glanced at the secret door at the far end of the dead-end tunnel, but instead went straight back, clambered up into his apartment, and pushed the wardrobe back in front of the opening in the wall. Still sleepwalking, he had then hobbled into the bathroom with strangely wooden movements.

At this point the bathtub wasn't yet filled with bloody water, Alba wasn't yet lying dead on the tiles, and apart from the debris from the destroyed mirror, there was no sign at all of the chaos Leon would unleash in just a few minutes.

Right now Leon was stood exactly on the spot where he had stopped and stared at the ceiling in the video.

Literally.

Directly above the toilet, a cover panel had slipped

to the side, which until now he had always assumed was the casing for the service box of the water thermostat.

Not the first mistake he had made since moving in.

He clambered on to the toilet lid, on which his boots had already left prints, and pushed against the cover above his head. In his hurry he had left the torch in the bedroom, but the bathroom light was enough to illuminate the start of the chimney-like shaft and the rungs leading upwards.

Everything was exactly as he had seen it on the video, with one exception: the piano playing had stopped. While before he had been able to hear the soft but unmistakable sounds of Tareski's scale practice on the film's audio, now nothing but silence came out of the newly discovered exit.

A deathly silence, he thought as he grabbed the first rung above him.

He was tired and weak, and no wonder, for it seemed he had spent the last few hours doing anything but sleeping. The cold, hard edge of the rung didn't trigger his memory as he grabbed it, nor did the musty smell of mould as he struggled his way upwards, but such recollections would have been highly unusual anyway.

Like most sleepwalkers, Leon couldn't remember his nocturnal activities. For that reason he wasn't surprised that the narrow shaft, which was becoming darker over his head by the second, seemed so unfamiliar.

Quickly. Hurry. Don't lose any time. He drove himself on in his head.

Halfway, shortly before the light shining up from below threatened to be extinguished, plunging the bricked walls into darkness, the fingers of his right hand unexpectedly touched a scrap of material.

Leon groped around his knee and found the corresponding rip in his trousers. So far he hadn't noticed that he must have caught his right leg on a sharp edge of the ladder in his sleep. But ruined clothing was the least of his worries; right now it was a matter of life and death.

What have I done?

Unlike when he ended up in Ivana Helsing's apartment, this shaft didn't lead into a bathroom, but a small chamber. The windowless room into which Leon had crept – through an already open floor panel – was in complete darkness, so he could hardly see his hand in front of his face. From the video recording, he knew the room had a square layout and was utterly empty.

Crawling on all fours, he groped around the wooden floor until he found the head camera. He had clearly lost it on his way back.

Leon switched on the camera's lamp and shone it at the path to the door.

He knew he had to go to the right. And he knew he didn't need to be quiet. Tareski wouldn't wake up even if a bomb went off in his apartment.

Leon hung the headband of the camera around his neck and ran along the corridor, flinging the door to the living room open.

'No!' he screamed, as he met the sight before him.

It had looked unreal on the video; not as gruesome, more like an illusion that could be erased simply by deleting the recording. But Tareski's bulging eyes, his foaming mouth and bloated, blue-violet face could not be made to disappear at the touch of a button. The sight of the chemist lying lifelessly in front of his piano on the carpet would haunt Leon for the rest of his life, he was sure of that.

He looked around and noticed a pair of scissors on a side table near the window. He reached out for them, even though they probably wouldn't be of much use now.

On the recording he had crept up behind Tareski as he sat there unsuspectingly at his piano. The chemist's eyes had been closed in concentration, as could be seen in the reflection of the polished, black lacquered surface of the piano. Somewhere between the chamber and the living room, Leon must have loosened his shoelace. A few steps later he had lurched forward swiftly and wrapped it around his victim's neck.

Tareski had gasped for air. His eyes, now dull and lifeless, had been wide open. In reaction he had tried to get his fingers under the noose Leon was using to choke off his air supply. At the same time he had reared up, forcing them away from the piano bench, and tried to turn to see his treacherous attacker, but when he couldn't he concentrated on mere survival, directing all his efforts towards finding a way to breathe again.

At some point, after Leon had tied a knot in the lace and left Tareski to choke in front of his piano, the chemist had managed to get a thumb under the noose. Clearly Leon had only tightened it half-heartedly or – which would be even worse – intentionally left a little leeway so the death throes lasted longer.

'I strangled him,' whispered Leon in devastation, kneeling. Tears rolled down his face, and he felt such intense guilt that for the first time he understood why people took their own lives. He put the scissors at the knot, accidentally knicking Tareski's skin. And it was lucky he did, for otherwise there would have been no pain reflex. Tareski's upper lip trembled slightly, but it was still a sign of life.

Without wasting time feeling for a pulse, Leon began to resuscitate Tareski. He turned the chemist on to his back, applied both hands in pressure-point massage above the heart, and . . .

Three . . . two . . . one.

Nothing!

'Come on!' he shouted, starting over again.

Three . . . two . . . one.

Leon flexed Tareski's neck and pressed his lips on to the chemist's open mouth. Fired by the hope that it might not be too late after all, he expelled the air from his lungs into Tareski's; felt how his upper body swelled and sank down again.

'Come on. Please . . .'

Leon switched back to heart massage, feeling like all his movements were in slow motion. Whenever he rammed down on Tareski's ribs, thoughts shot into his mind like lightning bolts.

Three . . .

It's not just about Natalie. Or Tareski. I'm connected to all the apartments, I can spy on all the neighbours.

Two . . .

I'm a fan of the architect's work, I studied von Boyten.

One . . .

We didn't choose this apartment. It chose us.

Zero.

At the end of the fourth interval, Leon was physically forced backwards. Tareski reared up beneath him, vomiting and wheezing at the same time. And then came the spasms.

Thank God!

Tareski's distorted body shook in a vicious fit of coughing. Leon feared the brought-back-to-life chemist still wasn't getting enough oxygen. Then, between two convulsive attacks, Tareski managed to suck in a stream of air, and the whistling breaths accompanying it were like music to Leon's ears.

'I'm sorry,' said Leon, knowing how inadequate the apology was for what he had done, even if he had been in a state in which he wasn't criminally responsible. Even if his attack hadn't caused any lasting physical damage – from this day on his neighbour would never feel safe again. Not when he went for a walk in the evening. Not when he sat in his car and looked in the rear-view mirror. And certainly not in his apartment, where he had been attacked completely out of the blue.

'I'll fetch help,' said Leon, pretty sure he wasn't getting through to Tareski at all. The poor man may not be fighting for his life any more, but he was still struggling for air, incapable of registering anything. Perhaps he could taste the blood in his mouth from his chewed-up tongue, possibly he could hear his own choking and wheezing, maybe the epileptic pumping of his heart and the blood crashing against his eardrums with the force of a water cannon. But certainly Tareski didn't hear the sound that cut Leon to the quick as he was looking around for a telephone.

That's impossible.

Leon turned back to the piano, in front of which the chemist was still cowering in a fetal posture. He stared at the keys, before which sat no one but which were still moving regardless – creating exactly the notes he had heard so often in the past few months.

But how . . .?

Leon took a step closer and saw the thin cable concealed on the side of the piano and running past his feet, presumably to a power point in the wall.

Bewildered, he looked between the chemist and the electric piano, which had clearly been programmed. The rhythm of the scales was halting and sounded unpractised, and now and again, seemingly by coincidence, there was a discord, as if someone had played a wrong note.

But none of this makes any sense.

Leon leaned over the keys, studying the open sheet music, then looked at Tareski, who by now had struggled up on to all fours and was coughing like a dog – and at that moment he realised, with painful clarity, the code that would open the secret door in the labyrinth.

32

Going back to the labyrinth through Tareski's chamber wasn't an option.

Leon wanted to return, which theoretically would have been possible as soon as he got back to his own apartment. But the secret door in his bedroom was blocked to him now that he could no longer move the wardrobe. This was probably due to the depth of Leon's exhaustion, and his dwindling strength. He would fall asleep again in a matter of seconds if he allowed himself even a moment's rest – but then again his inability to move the wardrobe was just as inexplicable as everything else that had happened to him so far on his search for Natalie, a search that was increasingly becoming a search for himself.

Either way, the consequence remained the same: if he wanted to test his suspicion, Leon would have to choose another entrance to the world between the apartments. And for that, only one possibility remained.

He unlocked the chemist's front door. Tareski was still the worse for wear, but significantly better than before. By now he had managed to get himself on to the couch and wasn't coughing as loudly. Leon didn't know whether his neighbour had recognised him or not, but right now he didn't care.

All that mattered was getting back to the DANGER door in the labyrinth as quickly as possible.

In the stairwell, Leon was met by a dull hammering and the screeching of a chainsaw, which immediately swallowed up the mysterious scales of the piano.

The scent of fresh woodchips hung in the air. Judging by the noise level, the builders were on the ground floor.

My God, has that much time really passed already?

Leon thought back to the notice from the building management. When he last looked at the magnetic board on the kitchen door, the renovation work had still been three days away. And now the workers were here, tearing up the floorboards on the steps.

He wanted to take the lift, but it was stuck on the ground floor, presumably blocked by the builders (*Be prepared for long waits!*). Leon had no patience, so he took the stairs.

Luckily for him, the works on the stairs had not progressed very far, so he was able to get to the second floor unobstructed, where he smoothed his hair with the palm of his hand and a little spit before ringing on the front door.

The din on the ground floor was so loud that he couldn't hear any sounds coming from inside the apartment. Impatient, he dispensed with all politeness and rang the bell repeatedly, until eventually the door edged open and a bony foot appeared in the gap.

'Herr Nader?' asked Ivana Helsing in surprise, once she had managed to open the door fully. She hadn't been able to use her hands, because she was holding a pile of small packages covering the expanse from her belly button to her chin.

'I wasn't expecting you,' she said, bending awkwardly to balance her load on a chair next to the bureau. 'I thought you were the delivery boy I arranged for a pick-up.'

Ivana didn't seem disturbed by Leon's appearance. Even the head camera flapping around his neck failed to draw a reaction. She was a little dishevelled herself, and looked considerably older than during their last encounter. The shadows under her eyes were darker, her skin greyer, and her hair was sticking up at odd angles from her head as if he had woken her.

'eBay,' she said and grinned impishly, glancing at the packages. 'You don't want to know what some people with strange fetishes order from old people like me. Well, you're married to an artist, so I'm sure you're not unfamiliar with such things. And these little packages help me to enjoy my retirement more.'

'Sure,' answered Leon absent-mindedly, not even listening properly to what Ivana was saying. He was distracted by the sound of heavy footsteps stomping down the stairwell from above.

Who could that be?

No one lived above him but Tareski.

'May I come in?' asked Leon nervously.

To his surprise, the old woman hesitated. 'Well, I'm not really prepared for guests right now, you see.'

The heavy footsteps, surely those of a man, came closer.

'I understand. But the builders seem to have damaged my water pipes.'

Ivana's eyebrows knotted together in surprise behind her glasses. 'But I thought they were just working on the steps?'

'Yes. Crazy, isn't it? They can't explain it either. But it's happened somehow, and now I'm without water.'

Leon didn't dare turn round. If the person who was marching down the steps couldn't see him yet, then any moment now they would reach the spot where they would be able to.

'And how can I help you?' asked Ivana.

'I hate to ask, but could I use your toilet?'

The look Ivana was giving him must have been the same one he had given the courier who brought the camera. Except that Leon, unlike that joker, was serious. Deadly serious. He *had* to go to Ivana's bathroom, and as quickly as possible, even if it wasn't to go to the toilet.

'Well, I . . . of course. No problem.'

Ivana moved aside and Leon slipped past her, just as the steps behind him got not only louder, but significantly quicker.

He shut the door hastily. Ideally he would have liked to look through the peephole, but that would only have made his neighbour more nervous.

'It's along there,' she said, showing him what he already knew. 'And please ignore the mess.'

'No problem. This is really very kind of you.'

Leon walked past the room that had previously contained a box and was now completely empty. The carpet billowed under his feet, and with his loose boot he had to take care not to trip.

'She's back now, by the way,' he heard Ivana say as he was about to open the bathroom door.

He whipped round to face her. 'Who?'

The old woman smiled so broadly that he saw the dentures in her upper jaw gleam.

'So you didn't see her?' she asked with a relieved smile.

Leon turned back to the living room, towards which

his neighbour was pointing with her outstretched hand, and suddenly felt like his ribcage was about to break from the sheer force of his pounding heart.

That's impossible.

And yet there she sat. As if nothing had happened to her. As if she had never disappeared.

Full of beans.

'Come here, Alba,' called Ivana, patting her thighs as she did so. But the black cat just swished her tail, not even considering giving up her comfortable position on the armchair in front of the fire again.

33

Exhausted, Leon climbed down as quickly as he could. This time, though, he felt less like the shaft led down into some hidden world between worlds, and much more that it led into his subconscious.

He had locked Ivana's bathroom door, pushed the bath mat to one side and discovered a dull tile beneath, the rear edge of which jutted up a little from the floor. All he had to do was press down on it firmly and the tile came loose from its position, transforming into a lever with which to open the hatch.

With every step he took down into the darkness, the voices in his head became louder, all asking more or less the same question.

Are you still in your right mind? Or is all this just an illusion?

The darker it became, the more unsure Leon was as to whether he was really experiencing all this: *the dead cat, the choking chemist, the secret entrance in the bathroom.*

The cold rungs in his hand.

Once he got to the bottom, Leon put the camera headband back into position and activated the lamp, which once again would be his only light source.

He hadn't bothered closing the hatch door behind him. It would only be a matter of time before old Helsing started to worry and went to check why he hadn't come out of the bathroom.

Leon could only hope that a decent amount of time would pass before she found a way to open the bathroom door from the outside.

He just needed a few minutes to confirm his suspicion.

To open the door with the DANGER *sign.*

To find out what I did in my sleep.

At the end of the passage, he touched the secret door's exposed input screen lightly. He had already tried so many wrong combinations that he was worried the electronic lock would block further attempts.

Leon pulled out the sheet music that he had put in his pocket in Tareski's apartment and smoothed it out.

He felt like he was holding the solution to the puzzle in his hand.

The violin is the key!

The violin key.

His sleepwalking self had heard Tareski's piano playing and created a memory trigger. To open the door, he didn't need to enter a password, but a series of notes.

The ones behind the violin key!

He looked at Tareski's sheet music, and for the first time in his life felt grateful that his adoptive parents had tortured him with trumpet lessons for years when he was a child. Without that the dots and lines would have meant nothing to him.

Voices disturbed Leon's concentration, a murmur at a distance, as soft as the sound of a television in the neighbouring apartment. But they were *voices*, plural, and one of them sounded like Ivana, as though she had fetched help and discovered the hatch in her bathroom.

So quickly?

Leon turned back to the secret door and the sheet music. All of a sudden his biological parents came into his mind. The accident. He wondered why these terrible memories were haunting him now, of all times. Leon stared at the sheet music in his hands, and it felt like a cog in his mind clicked into position, exposing a previously blocked chain of thoughts: *Moll*.

The surname of his first foster parents.

The ones who sent me away. Because, in my sleep, I stood in front of their son's bed with a knife.

Adrian Moll.

A-Moll.

A-H-C-D-E-F-G-A

The voice in Leon's head urging him to be quick quietened down as he pressed the corresponding buttons. When he got to the final 'A', with the noises behind him getting louder and closer, the voices in his head died away completely.

There was a sound as though someone had trodden on a cockroach, and the lock opened.

Leon put his whole body weight against the door, and a gap appeared in the wall as it opened.

It wasn't even half open before he heard the tortured whimper of a woman, and he knew that he had found her.

34

Opaque plastic sheeting, as if from a cold store, obstructed Leon's view of something that, fundamentally, he didn't want to see. He pictured his wife, bound and gagged, in a bare room with concrete walls and blood stains, doubled over in pain on a rusty chair.

He was right about the bound and gagged part. But the rest was even worse than he had imagined.

Leon shoved the sheeting to the side, smelled the sweat and odours of a suffering, sick person, stumbled a step forwards across the wooden floor into a room, and for a moment couldn't understand what he was seeing, for he was in . . .

. . . *my own bedroom?*

Slowly, as though in a trance, he touched the wardrobe to his left, next to a wall. Then he registered the bureau beside it, the metal chair, a few of his clothes strewn over it.

Leon's eyes darted around, searching for an anchor to keep them from the lifeless human being on the mattress. She was half-sitting, half-lying, and illuminated by a lamp on the bedside table next to the big double bed that looked exactly the same as his own. Just like almost everything down here looked like his bedroom. Someone had created the room and it was so perfect at first glance, in the otherwise bare cellar, that for the first few moments Leon had really thought he was in his own apartment.

Now, as soon as he realised it was a copy, he stumbled forwards.

'Natalie!'

It was more a croak than a scream. The shock slowed his breathing, and his movements. Leon felt like the air had transformed into syrup, as though he was only able to fight his way through it like a swimmer.

Over to the bed. To Natalie. To the blood.

She was bound in the same posture as on the photo the detective had shown him. Her arms above her head, chained to the bed-posts, her head bound with a dog collar.

'Darling, sweetheart, Natalie?'

He tried words, caresses, strokes, kisses, but he couldn't get through to her. Natalie was whimpering, but she wasn't conscious. Her head hung slackly, her chin propped against her naked chest. He touched her cheek gently, lifted her head, and a red thread of mucous freed itself from the corner of her mouth, dropping on to her chest. Her breasts were smeared with dirt and blood. The welts on her skin looked as though they had been inflicted by a riding whip.

Leon covered his face with his hands in shock.

This wasn't me. It couldn't be. Or could it?

'Natalie, darling. Did *I* do this?'

He lifted her chin carefully. Her right eye was buried beneath a bruise. With the other, she blinked sluggishly.

'Natalie, darling. Can you hear me?'

Even if his wife had been conscious, she wouldn't have been able to answer him. A black rubber gagging ball was in her mouth. She had bitten into it so hard that Leon feared he wouldn't be able to take it out without breaking even more of her teeth. In the end he managed it.

Next he inspected her ties, but to get the handcuffs off, he would need a key or a bolt cutter.

Leon looked around and reached for the bedside lamp to light under the bed. Then he stopped; there were two defunct spotlights next to a camera tripod.

They don't belong to me. Or do they?

He spotted a low table, covered with black latex film and with a variety of objects on top.

'Hmhmm.'

He looked at Natalie, unsure as to whether she had just groaned his name, and stroked her dull hair.

'Can you hear me?'

No reaction.

Leon promised her that he would be back soon, and went over to the table. He was repulsed by the wild collection of sex toys spread out on it: dildos, whips, lube, chains, various clamps, even a gas mask lay at the ready, along with another pair of handcuffs and keys. He picked them up and returned to Natalie.

I didn't do this. These don't belong to me.

He knelt down next to her and tried first her left wrist and then the other, but the key wouldn't fit, and he was unable to find any others, not even in the drawers of the nightstand, which he tore open one after the other, finding nothing but porno magazines.

'Lon?' he heard Natalie murmur next to him.

Now her groans sounded very much like his name, but beyond that he still couldn't get through to her. Leon suspected she was talking in her sleep and reacting subconsciously to his voice and touch – leaving her alone now would mean sacrificing the fragile connection.

But he didn't have a choice. He had to get help.

As quickly as he could, he hurried through the sheeting back to the secret door, only to encounter the next shock. The door must have been equipped with a fire protection mechanism or something which had pushed it closed automatically and locked it. As on the outside, the inner side of the door had an entry field, but this time the electronic lock didn't react to the a-Moll combination.

Leon tried every other combination of letters he could think of. His name, Natalie's, other musical keys . . . He even typed 'help' in different languages, but all it brought him was an increasing feeling of exhaustion. He yawned, fighting the urge to lie on the floor there and then.

Just briefly. To build up some strength.

If Natalie hadn't called his name again, her voice filled with fear and pain and unmistakably clear this time, he might have given in to the pull threatening to make him sleep.

When he got back to his wife, she opened her uninjured eye.

Her breathing quickened erratically as she recognised him. Her ribcage rose and fell as though she was trying to draw in air before diving underwater.

'Stay calm, darling. I won't hurt you.'

Not any more.

She began to tug at her handcuffs.

'What is it?' he asked, then understood her panicked reaction as he saw the reflection of light in her pupils.

'Don't worry, I'm awake.' He pulled the headband with the camera down over his chin, until it hung slackly around his neck like a necklace.

'I'm not here to film you.'

Or to hurt you.

She didn't seem to believe him, continuing to pull at her handcuffs.

'I'm sorry, I can't open them,' Leon said resignedly. He omitted to mention that he had the same problem with the exit and that she was imprisoned here with him. Nor did he tell her that he was struggling just as much as she was to stay conscious. He would have thought that the horror he was living through right now would have activated his last survival instincts. But, instead, it seemed to have killed them off.

'Please . . . you have to . . .' groaned Natalie.

She was so weak she couldn't even finish her sentence.

'Yes. I know.'

I have to stay awake.

'Please don't . . .'

Leon yawned, hating himself for doing it now of all times. But as inappropriate as it was, he couldn't fight his body's need for sleep any longer without some kind of help.

'I'm so sorry,' he whispered, kissing her on the forehead. 'It will all be over soon.'

As soon as I've found a way out of here. He remembered Ivana and the sound of voices in the shaft, and it gave him hope.

'I'm sure they're already looking for me, Natalie.'

His wife sniffed, a bubble of snot bursting. Then she said something that tore Leon's heart in two.

'. . . hurts so much, you have to . . .'

'I will, darling. I'll stop. I'll never hurt you again.' He felt tears pricking his eyes. 'I'm so sorry. I change when I sleep. I'm no longer myself.' Leon pulled the packet of caffeine pills from his pocket. 'Here, look. These are yours, I'll take them. I'll stay awake until help comes.'

And not sleepwalk any more. I'll never hurt you again.

His mouth was so dry that he struggled to swallow two tablets at once, and when he had finally managed it, Natalie's eye began to twitch. It was less a question of minutes than seconds until she lost consciousness once more.

'You can't . . .' she mumbled again, but this time it sounded less like pleading. Not as though she wanted to ask him something, but instead like she wanted to tell him something.

His gaze wandered to her hand with the ripped-off thumbnail.

What can't I do? Torture you any more?

He didn't dare look her in the face, so great was his fear of seeing the truth.

'You have to . . .'

Stay here? Save you? Is that what you wanted to say?

246

Hope sparked inside him, and he leaned forwards to be able to understand her more clearly.

'Don't worry, sweetheart. I know I can't fall asleep again.'

'NO!'

She reared up in one final, despairing lurch, then sank down again, robbed of all energy.

'*No?* What do you mean?'

That I should fall asleep after all? But that doesn't make any sense.

Natalie's breathing became shallower, her voice still just a whisper, but it shattered Leon with the strength of a hurricane when she said: 'You're wrong, it's exactly the opposite.'

'The opposite? What do you mean, the opposite?' he asked anxiously, then a terrible thought sprang into the car of the rollercoaster, the tracks spiralling through Leon's mind, going up, turning in a loop and shooting into his consciousness at an unbelievable speed:

It's not about the fact that I can't fall asleep.

It's exactly the opposite.

I have to stay . . . like this.

I CAN'T . . . WAKE UP!

35

Wake up.

Just two simple words, but with the impact of an explosion.

The first explosive charges of the looming realisation detonated with painful force within Leon's head.

I can't wake up?

'I don't believe it,' he protested flatly, abruptly recognising how strange his voice sounded. Or had he been slurring the whole time as though he were drugged?

Leon stood up and tried to step away from the bed, but his legs refused to obey him. He was tempted to laugh, but even his lips felt numb. His face was frozen into a mask.

'Are you trying to say I'm dreaming?'

That I'm just imagining all of this? You? The labyrinth? Our conversation?

'No,' cried Natalie in despair.

'No what?' Leon shouted. 'What's happening to me?'

I'm not sleeping. I'm not awake. So what am I?

Natalie tried to answer him, but her lips moved without a sound.

'What am I?' Leon held on to her head, which was sinking downwards.

She needs water. A doctor.

He remembered Volwarth and how he had explained why he didn't believe Leon was capable of being violent during his sleep, and all of a sudden Leon understood what Natalie had been trying to tell him this whole time.

Of course. Volwarth.

Not asleep. Not awake. What am I?

The psychiatrist had given him the answer to this question just a few days ago.

. . . strictly speaking the so-called sleepwalker isn't actually asleep. He is in another, barely researched state of consciousness between being asleep and being awake. I call it the third stage.

A stage in which Leon, as he suddenly understood, was imprisoned. Right now. The psychiatrist had diagnosed it perfectly: *No matter what you say, I don't believe you harmed your wife in your sleep.*

Not in my sleep.

No.

In a conscious, criminally liable state.

Leon grabbed his head with both hands and stared at Natalie, who had plunged once more into another, hopefully pain-free world. He tried to fight the terrible truth: that he wasn't violent when he was sleep-walking.

But when he was awake!

That was when he had planned the architecture of his torture chamber, built doors in the walls and created another world beyond his apartment.

The door behind the wardrobe, the two-way mirror, the blood in the bath . . .

Everything he could remember right now, he had experienced not in a conscious, awake state, but as a sleepwalker.

'That can't be true,' he heard himself say as though from a great distance, but deep inside he knew it was very probably true. Volwarth had told him about similar cases.

In the decades that I've been researching and treating parasomnias, I've encountered almost everything: people who clean their apartments in the deep-sleep phase . . .

Or who crawl along tunnels, climb down into shafts, up ladders.

Sleepwalkers who have coherent conversations with their partners and even answer questions.

For example on the telephone with Natalie's best

friend Anouka, Sven, the police, or over tea with Ivana.

I had patients who did washing in the night and even operated complicated devices.

Complicated devices like a head-mounted camera. Like a laptop in front of which Leon had sat and watched videos, in the mistaken assumption that he was awake. But he hadn't been sleeping either. Everything had really happened, except on a new, third level of consciousness, in the third stage, between being awake and asleep.

I freed Tareski, and opened the secret door. And right now I'm standing in front of my tortured wife. Stroking her hair from her forehead, kissing her dry lips and talking to her. It's while sleepwalking that I reflect on the state I'm in. And it's a state that I can't be permitted to leave. Not yet. Because I become a danger not when I sleepwalk, but when I'm awake.

Leon stared at Natalie, who seemed to be losing consciousness completely, while he was clearly in the process of waking up.

The whole time he had thought he could remember his dreams, but it was exactly the opposite. As a sleepwalker, he had no memory of what he had done in his conscious state.

That's why he couldn't remember the door codes or the postcard on the fridge or the fact that Sven had collected the architectural model. And that's why the policeman had asked him why he wasn't looking him in the eye. That was why Sven had fled, scared. Those two, at least, had noticed his state.

Oh God. No.

Leon saw the open packet of pills he had put on the nightstand.

The more caffeine I took, the more pills I swallowed . . . the sooner I will wake up.

And what will happen then?

Leon began to shiver.

It's all exactly the opposite.

This whole time he had been asking himself whether he was leading a double life in his sleep. Now he didn't know who he was in real life. What would he do once he regained consciousness?

Was he a perpetrator? Or a victim?

Did his presence put Natalie in danger? Or make her safe?

He could feel it wouldn't be much longer now, that he would soon leave the third stage, presumably by falling into a brief intermittent sleep before finally waking up.

As a murderer? Or a rescuer?

Leon knew he couldn't leave these answers to fate. He had to take precautions against the worst of all possibilities, and use the last remaining seconds he had.

He grabbed the handcuffs from the table and

clapped one around his left wrist. Then, with the last of his strength, he dragged himself over to a heating pipe on the wall, approximately five paces from the bed. As he knelt down, he could no longer see Natalie, only hear her vegetative groans.

'Everything's going to be OK,' he called to her as he yawned, longer and deeper than ever before. Then, with the open end of the handcuffs, he chained himself to the pipe.

'I won't hurt you any more.'

He patted at his breast pocket, relieved to feel the fountain pen he had found in the hiding place in the adjoining passageway. Leon wrote a single word on the palm of his right hand, and four numbers on the left.

Finally, he pulled the headband with the camera back onto his head, opened his mouth, placed the handcuff key on his tongue and swallowed it.

Just a few moments later he changed states of consciousness.

36

Leon was awoken by a persistent ringing. For a while the shrill tones had formed part of his dream, the rest of which he could no longer remember just a few seconds after waking up. Natalie had been in it, as had a cellar, vault doors and long, dark passageways, but then the acoustic stimuli had become too intense to be filtered out by his brain. Unable to ignore the ringing of the telephone, Leon had opened his eyes.

How is that possible?

It was pitch black in the room, and he fumbled blindly for the light switch on the nightstand. The smell of clean washing and softener assailed his nose as he turned to the side. For an instant he felt irritated that Natalie had ignored his superstition and changed the bed-sheets during the Twelve Nights. Then he remembered that this was the least of his worries right now.

If the ringing phone in the hallway had been the

cause of him waking, the sight of the empty half of
the bed brought him crashing back to reality.

I'm alone.

'Yes, I'm coming,' he called in irritation as he flung
back the blanket, wondering whether he had drunk
too much or too little yesterday. His voice was hoarse,
his mouth was dry, and his throat felt like he had
been gargling with glass shards.

*Speaking of glass, I really need to repair that ceiling
lamp.*

He looked around for his clothes. Instead of his
jeans and sweatshirt, a pair of blue overalls were
draped over the bureau, and the boots that he only
ever wore on building sites were under the chair.

What the hell are they doing there?

Still drunk from a sleep that seemed to have
depleted rather than increased his energy, he shuffled
into the hallway naked and grabbed the telephone
from the docking station.

'Yes?'

At first all he heard was a static crackle, making
him think his adoptive parents, whom he had sent
on a cruise as a Christmas present, were trying to
call him from the ship. Then a familiar voice said
hesitantly: 'It's me.'

'Sven?'

Leon pushed his hand through his unkempt hair
and wondered why it felt so dirty. Stiff with dirt.

'What are you calling me in the middle of the night for?'

'The night? It's afternoon.'

'What?'

Leon went to the kitchen to get some water.

'Don't be ridiculous.'

He opened the door, causing Natalie's Van Gogh postcard with the sunflower motif to come loose from the magnetic board and fall to the floor.

'I'm not in the mood for jokes,' said Sven, as Leon stood rooted to the spot in front of the fridge.

'That's not possible.'

The green digits of the LED clock on the fridge door blurred in front of his tired eyes, but there could be no doubt that they confirmed Sven's claim: 17.22.

That can't be possible. I can't possibly have slept that long. He ached so much that he felt more like he had just helped someone to move house.

'I'm really sorry,' groaned Leon. 'Did I miss an appointment or something?' He had a vague memory about a client's birthday party.

'Yes, but that's not why I'm calling.'

Even though Sven was speaking slowly, he was struggling with every other word.

'You sound agitated,' said Leon tentatively so as not to insult his friend, who couldn't stand it when people brought up the subject of his speech impediment. 'Has something happened?'

Did we lose the commission?

In the days since Natalie had left him for what seemed like no apparent reason, he had thrown himself into his work. He had sat working on the model day and night and hadn't left the apartment once, not even to go to the office, which was why Sven had come by to pick it up.

'It should be me asking you that. Are you feeling better now?'

'Better?' Leon opened the fridge and reached for the long-life milk. 'Why do you ask?'

'You were completely out of it last time I saw you. I felt guilty about having left you alone afterwards, but the thing with the cat was just too much.'

'When did you see me? What cat? What the hell are you talking about?' He took a slug of milk straight from the carton; while Natalie was taking her ominous 'time out', at least she couldn't have a go at him about this. It was the only advantage of his forced single existence, which he would gladly relinquish if she would just come back.

'I'm talking about yesterday,' stuttered Sven, even more agitated. 'When I brought the model back.'

'Back?'

Leon could only remember Sven having picked it up. Since then he hadn't heard anything from him.

'Yes. Back to your study,' insisted Sven. 'I put it on your desk.'

'If that's supposed to be a joke, it's not funny.'

Leon put the milk back, and as he did so he saw that the palm of his right hand was smeared with ink.

Laptop?

He gaped at his hand as though it didn't belong to him.

When did I scribble the word 'laptop' on myself? And why?

His confusion mounted when he noticed he had also used his left hand as a notepad.

07.05.

He couldn't imagine why he had noted down these numbers, for God knows he didn't need a reminder of this date. It was the day his biological parents had died in the car accident.

'Go and look if you don't believe me,' demanded Sven.

'For what?' asked Leon, still not really present.

'For the model.'

A sense of foreboding rose up in him as he left the kitchen, becoming terrible certainty as he entered his study.

It's started again.

The proof stood before him. In the middle of the desk. The model he had been working on for the last few days was back, covered by Post-its with Sven's suggested adjustments on them.

'Is everything OK?' he heard his partner ask, and answered in the affirmative even though absolutely nothing was OK any more.

'And you dropped it off with me yesterday?' he asked flatly.

'Yes.'

Leon went over to the desk and touched the roof of the accident and emergency department with his index finger.

'I was here? You spoke to me?'

'More or less. You were very incoherent and your mind seemed to be somewhere else.'

Sven's stutter was getting more pronounced. It took twice as long as it normally would for him to get the words out, but that was fine by Leon right now. His brain was working slowly, as though the hand-brake was on, and the slower Sven spoke the more time he had to understand what was going on.

Leon closed his eyes. 'I'm really sorry, I don't think I even know my own name right now.'

'Well, yesterday you certainly didn't. You were a completely different person, Leon.'

I know. I always am when I sleepwalk.

'Don't take this the wrong way, but as your best friend I have to ask.'

'What?'

'Are you on drugs?'

Leon shook his head. 'No, that's not it.'

It's much worse.

Not seeming to believe him, Sven persevered. 'My brother used to take LSD. Whenever he was high, he would get this absent, empty look on his face, and talked in just the same paranoid way as you did yesterday.'

'That may well be, but I swear I'm not taking anything.'

My dark side is something else.

'Then it's really just because Natalie disappeared?'

'Hang on a minute, who said she disappeared?'

'You,' retorted Sven, speaking in a surprisingly loud voice now.

Leon snorted. 'That's ridiculous. She just needed a bit of time to herself. I told you about her card, remember.'

. . . I need some space . . . to figure out where we should go from here . . .

'That's why I'm calling, Leon. Because I don't know what to believe any more. First you tell me Natalie left you after a fight. That you woke up in the morning and she wasn't there.'

'Exactly. You told me to give her some time and distract myself with work.'

'And I thought that was what you were doing. Then you call me at the party and tell me about the injuries you supposedly inflicted on her. And yesterday you completely lose it and tell me you imprisoned her in a labyrinth behind your wardrobe.'

'Whaaat?' Leon laughed in disbelief. 'Now I should be asking *you* if you're on drugs.'

He walked from the study to get something to put on. The apartment had become cold and he was shivering.

'It's not funny, Leon, and to be honest I don't know what worries me more. The way you acted yesterday or the fact that you claim not to be able to remember it.'

'I'm not *claiming*—' Leon corrected Sven on his way into the bedroom, but he didn't manage to finish, for he felt a searing pain in the sole of his foot.

'What's wrong?' Sven asked as he heard Leon cursing.

'Sorry, I trod on something.'

Leon bent down, unable to believe what he had in his hands.

The last time he had worn such a device was many years ago, during the therapy sessions with Dr Volwarth.

'So, anyway, you were completely out of it,' Sven continued, his words accompanied by a gradually surging tinnitus in Leon's ears; a sure sign he had a migraine coming on.

Or worse.

With the headband that he had just found on the

floor, he was holding further proof in his hands that his nocturnal phases had started again.

When did I buy this camera?

The lens of the motion-activated head camera was smudged and a cable hung loose at the side, as though it had been put together in a hurry. By someone who hadn't been concentrating that much, because he was under massive stress.

Or because he wasn't conscious.

'You even wanted to show me a video you supposedly filmed of you looking for Natalie in your sleep.'

A video?

Along with the tinnitus, a surreal, schizophrenic feeling was welling up in Leon. On the one hand, everything Sven was saying seemed to make sense. On the other, it was as though his friend was speaking to him in a foreign language.

He clamped the telephone between his chin and shoulder so that he had both hands free to inspect the headband. If Sven was talking about a video, there must be some kind of replay function.

Leon was just about to go back into the study to start his computer when he remembered the word on his right palm.

Laptop.

There was only one portable computer in the apartment.

'Are you still there?' he heard Sven ask.

Without answering, he went into the bedroom. He pushed the chair to the side and picked up the carefully folded but completely soiled overalls from the desk.

What the hell . . .?

He had expected to find Natalie's laptop beneath them. Not the USB stick attached to it, blinking rhythmically.

Leon opened the laptop and gave a start when, with a gentle hum, it awoke from standby mode.

'Hey, Leon, why have you gone quiet?'

Because I can't find the words. No, more than that. I'm afraid I can't find part of myself.

A replay window for video files had appeared on the screen, and all of a sudden Leon no longer felt cold. His whole body was numb, insensitive to external stimuli.

He balled his right fist, pressed his fingernails hard into his palm, and before he could even ask the question as to whether he should dare do it, he had stretched his hand out and moved the mouse towards PLAY.

'What's wrong with you?' asked Sven anxiously.

Nothing. Nothing's wrong.

The video file didn't start. Instead, an entry field appeared, demanding a password.

Damn it, how am I supposed to be able to remember a password I chose in my sleep?

Leon held his breath in shock. Slowly, he turned the palm of his left hand up and stared at the two pairs of digits, separated by a full stop.

07.05.

'I'll call you back in a minute,' he said to Sven, hanging up. Then he typed the date of the car accident into the laptop.

The replay started at once.

37

At first there was nothing to see but dark flecks, twitching across the screen in various degrees of shadow. Then, as the sound of rattling breaths suddenly strained the loudspeakers, the image became brighter. Threads of light snaked across the picture like the tentacles of a jellyfish.

The contrasts sharpened and the contours of a room became increasingly clear, reminding Leon of his bedroom. The large bed, filmed from the perspective of someone sitting on the floor, certainly looked identical to the one he had woken up in a little earlier.

There was a jolt on the screen, and while the camera focused on a table leg, Leon heard a metallic clanking that sounded like a chain – reminding him of something that he couldn't figure out at first.

Handcuffs?

Then he heard a voice that wasn't his own and

which seemed to be coming from the bed. The person lying on it wasn't visible, but Leon didn't need to see to know who was sobbing his name.

Natalie!

He stared at the monitor with his eyes wide, and suddenly a flood of memories almost knocked him off the chair. It wasn't a dream!

I was there. In the labyrinth. Behind the door. With her.

He vaguely remembered a door behind the wardrobe, the dark passageways and the secret code (a-Moll), and the handcuffs he had used to chain himself to a heating pipe.

To prevent the worst from happening.

Leon felt as though someone had managed to install a dream camera in his head, saving the images he normally forgot right after waking up.

But I wasn't sleeping. And I wasn't awake either.

On the recording, the rasping breaths turned into a choking sound. He instinctively put his hands to his throat, suspecting he knew why it was so raw and why it still hurt to swallow.

The key. Natalie's life insurance policy.

He stared fixedly at the monitor.

The picture began to shake, and he heard a guttural groan. Then the camera tipped down and Leon saw a wave of vomit flow over the worker's boots on his feet.

As he continued to retch on the video, Leon groped his hand over to the overalls next to him on the desk and felt the dried sick on the trouser legs. A quick glance at the boot under the chair confirmed that they were soiled too. And one of them was missing the bootlace.

'No, no!' roared Leon at the laptop, as though he could somehow prevent himself from picking the key out of the pool of vomit.

Please, don't let me do it. Let it stop, he pleaded in his thoughts. But it didn't stop. The recording ran on mercilessly. The image was blurred because the camera was so close to the pipe, but the audio was clearer than ever now.

A handcuff scraped across metal, then clicked loudly, and when the camera abruptly rushed upwards Leon knew he had freed himself from his shackles.

My God.

The sight that revealed itself to him from a standing perspective was exactly as Leon had expected: Natalie lay stretched out on the bed as though on a crucifix, chained with a dog collar. But unlike in his dream, she was fully conscious.

The camera moved closer to her face, so close that Leon could make out the fine pores on her nose and the encrusted blood on her chin covering the small freckle he had kissed so often in these last years. She blinked, blinded by the light of the head camera. Fat tears tumbled down from both the open and the injured eye.

'Leon?' she asked, and the camera image moved up and down affirmatively.

'Leon, I'm so sorry.'

You? You're sorry?

She sounded exhausted and breathless, but not panicked. Like a human being who had come to the end of their journey.

'I didn't mean to betray you.'

'Betray me?' Leon asked the monitor. With tears in his eyes, he touched the crackling surface of the laptop and traced his index finger along his wife's split lip.

'Leon, please. Forgive me.'

'Oh God, darling.'

Of course. Whatever you've done, I'll forgive you, he thought. *All I want is to have you back here with me.*

But his alter ego, down in the labyrinth, didn't seem to want to forgive his victim. A shadow fell across his wife's beaten face.

'Please, please don't . . .'

'No, no more pain . . .'

They both began to speak at the same time.

Natalie was pleading at the camera and Leon at his computer. He prayed that he was in one of his sleep paralyses right now, one from which he could only free himself with loud screams. But unlike usual, he had long realised that this wasn't a dream.

Something golden flashed on the monitor. It was a few moments before Leon recognised the tip of his own fountain pen.

Please . . . No!

'I love you,' they said, almost simultaneously. He, up in his bedroom. She, down in the torture chamber. And while Leon screamed out his despair, Natalie only sounded sad and resigned. He could see in her face that she knew what was awaiting her.

Natalie closed her uninjured eye just before it happened. Just before he rammed the fountain pen into her neck, with such force that almost half its length disappeared.

'*Noooooo!*'

Leon screamed, jumped up, grabbed the metal chair he had been sitting on and threw it across the room against the wall mirror. Cracks spread across the glass like a spider's web, then jagged-edged splinters came away, falling to the floor. At the same time, four hundred litres of water gushed onto the bedroom floor. The metal chair had rebounded from the wall into Natalie's aquarium, smashing a section of the glass panes.

Please no. Don't let it be true.

In tears, Leon buried his face in his hands, biting his fingers so hard that the pain would have ripped him out of the dream if it had been one. But it was real. The fountain pen in Natalie's neck, her punctured windpipe, her choked wheezing, the whistle with every breath that became first longer, then quieter, her slowly twitching body, her head slumping forwards. And the unbearable silence that set in, still far from being the end of the recording.

Leon continued to look through his fingers, covering his eyes, unable to bear the sight for longer than a second at a time. The monitor picture with Natalie's motionless body in the centre shook and blurred, but this time it wasn't down to the recording. Leon's eyes had transformed into torrents, and his body was shaking convulsively.

He wiped his tears away with the back of his hand, and as he did so his gaze fell on the business card next to the computer.

Kroeger?

Leon had never seen the card before, never heard the name, and didn't know what it was doing there, but the embossed signet on the front told him what he had to do next.

The police! I have to call the police!

To use the telephone, he needed both hands. He was in shock, and so overwhelmed that he had even forgotten the number of the emergency services. By the time he remembered, there was a dramatic change on the screen.

His alter ego in the torture dungeon seemed to have finally had his fill of the sight of Natalie's motionless body, and moved just as the camera started to go into standby mode. The image flickered back on.

What now? What am I going to do now?

The camera panned left behind the bed to the spotlight and table, which Leon had a vague memory of. The sex toys spread out on it also seemed eerily familiar.

'I'm sorry,' he sobbed.

What have I done? And why?

He didn't understand why she had asked for his forgiveness. And he was unable to believe what happened next.

Just as at the entrance, there was plastic sheeting hanging from the ceiling at the far side of the room. It parted in front of the camera as though moved by some invisible hand, exposing a door. Just one kick with his boot and it sprang open.

There's a second exit? I could have just gone to fetch help?

Leon's despair had reached a new level that usually only suicidal people reach. The telephone in his hand had been forgotten for now.

Where am I going?

Behind the door some steps, steep like a fire ladder, headed upwards in a zigzag pattern. Leon heard himself panting after just the first few steps.

He didn't want to watch any more. He wanted this to be the end. Over. Finished. Like the rest of his life.

But his sleepwalking self was nowhere near finished. Step by step, he climbed up. Step by step, his breathing on the tape became more laboured, and even in the bedroom an invisible clamp tightened around Leon's ribcage.

What else have I done?

Once he got to the top of the steps, the picture became blurry again, just as at the beginning of the recording. Leon leaned towards the flickering monitor, so close that the picture before him resolved into individual dots.

The spotlight of the head camera focused on something that looked like a chipboard panel. Leon saw himself stretch his hand out and press the panel inwards.

On the video, another secret door opened.

At the same time Leon felt a gust of cold air at the back of his neck, and a shadow wandered across the screen. Then he suddenly heard everything in duplicate.

The creak of the secret door opening.

The crunch of the boots on the glass shards.

And even though there could only be one possible explanation for this, it took Leon far too long to react.

He stared at the screen, paralysed by the sight of a young man's back, a man who was staring at a laptop monitor, not wanting to believe that he wasn't watching a stranger.

But himself.

He didn't want to believe that he wasn't watching a recording. But the present.

Late, much too late, he turned to the hole in the wall from which until just a moment ago his splintered bedroom mirror had been hanging, where a man was now standing in a puddle on the flooded parquet floor. He was around the same height as Leon, of a similar stature. With brown hair, blue overalls, a sweatshirt and a pair of worker's boots, the right one of which was missing its bootlace.

The stranger had on a headband with a camera attached to it, the lamp of which was shining right into Leon's eyes. As a result, he was unable to see the man's face as he ran forward, as quick as lightning, to tear Leon into a maelstrom of pain. And a whole new dimension of darkness.

38

Like sleep, the process of waking up is an under-researched medical mystery. So as not to be woken by each and every noise, the brain restricts the intensity of external stimuli. However, it isn't in a permanently muffled state. Several times per hour, it shifts for a few moments into a near-conscious mode. In this brief phase the brain stretches its feelers into the world outside the dream, like a submarine does its periscope, to check if it would be advisable to change the state of consciousness, for example if the sleeping person is in danger.

Generally speaking, outside the near-conscious sleep stage only very strong stimuli are able to wake the person from sleep. The loud ringing of an alarm clock, for example, or a stream of cold water or intense pain – like the pain that brought Leon Nader back to reality.

For a while he had tried to fight against the thing around his neck, which was now pulling him upwards. Even with his eyes shut, he had realised that the pain shooting along his spine would only become more bearable if he gave into the pull at his head. Besides this, the more he struggled, the harder it was to breathe.

Hearing his neck vertebrae crunch, Leon opened his eyes wide. He was sat on the floor completely naked, his legs stretched out, his back against the bed, but if he didn't want his own weight to break his neck, he would have to get up as quickly as possible.

His legs were like rubber. At first he only managed to get to his knees. The pressure around his throat lessened, but the fought-for space quickly disappeared.

Leon looked to the hook on the ceiling, where the previous tenant's chandelier had hung and over which the rope of his noose was being pulled.

The stranger who had come into his bedroom through the secret passageway behind the mirror stood in front of the bureau with an expressionless gaze, pulling at the other end of the noose like a hoist.

Leon doubted that he had the strength to stand, but he had no choice. If he didn't want to suffocate, he had to straighten up.

'Stop,' he croaked, as Natalie's murderer forced him to his feet.

Oh God. What now?

To try to keep his balance, he flailed his arms, which strangely weren't tied. His hands, however, were encased in thick latex gloves. Whenever he tried to grab the rope over his head, the psychopath at the other end pulled even more strongly, making Leon fear that his larynx would burst.

'No,' coughed Leon, choking. 'Please don't.'

He rolled his eyes in panic and noticed a chair next to him. He had thrown it against the mirror earlier, but now it was upright, and within his grasp.

As if wanting to reward him for the discovery, the killer loosened the rope, and Leon hooked the chair towards him with his leg. But as soon as he had, the man mercilessly pulled him upwards once more. And he only stopped once Leon had clambered on to the chair.

'Please, carry on,' the man laughed, fastening the rope to the radiator beneath the window with a complicated-looking knot.

Not just his voice, but his appearance in general seemed familiar to Leon – aside from the fact, of course, that the man had made a great deal of effort to copy Leon's physical appearance.

'Who are you?' Leon croaked, craning his neck a little. He was surprised he could even get a word out. To stop him from freeing the rope from the hook by jumping, the maniac had pulled it so tight that he had to stand on tiptoes if he wanted to avoid losing consciousness.

The man trying to hang him was his age, perhaps a little younger, and apart from a slightly over-large nose and missing left earlobe, there was nothing remarkable about his appearance.

'I have a delivery for you,' he laughed, waving a CD case that he had just pulled from the breast pocket of his overalls.

Then he left the room briefly, returning with a kitchen stool in his hand. His soles squeaked on the wet floor.

He sat down in front of the laptop and put the disc in.

Please, God, make it stop. Don't let it get any worse.

From where he was, Leon could see the right half of the monitor. Every time he moved his head he ran the risk of lacerating his neck, but he still wrenched it to the side when Natalie's face appeared on the screen. Her right eye was shimmering violet, her eyelids were swollen shut, and when she tried to speak her tongue jutted against a cracked front tooth.

Leon couldn't bear to see the pictures that reminded him of his darkest nightmares, and of the fact that he would never see his wife alive again.

But even without the images, the mental torture didn't stop, for there was nothing Leon could do to stop himself from hearing. The psychopath had turned the volume of the video up to the maximum so that Leon didn't miss a single word of Natalie's acoustic goodbye note, which she had dictated for him in a trembling voice:

Leon, I'm so sorry, she began. *I'm a coward, I know. I should be telling you all this to your face. That's what you deserved. But I don't have the strength, so I'm choosing this unusual way. So that, even if it's impersonal, you at least hear it in my own words.*

'Stop the tape!' gasped Leon in the break between her words.

But I'm not sure if I'm going to have enough strength to put this confession in our letterbox. If it turns out I'm too cowardly even for that, then I'll at least leave you a card on the kitchen door.

Leon closed his eyes, then had to open them again at once, feeling like he was about to lose his balance and strangle himself.

Right now, while I'm recording this, you're still sleeping, he heard Natalie say.

I'm going to pack my things in a moment, and hope you won't wake up while I'm doing it. I think you're having nightmares again. Your night terrors have got worse, presumably because you can sense something's wrong. How right you are, my darling. And it's my fault and mine alone.

Leon turned back towards the bureau, in front of which the killer was standing. He had stopped the recording. The frozen image of Natalie suggested that she had recorded it with her mobile in her dark room. Leon could make out the photographic equipment in the background.

'This is very embarrassing,' grinned Natalie's killer all of a sudden. 'But could I use your toilet? It's just that I have diarrhoea.'

As he chuckled, Leon finally recognised who was doing all of this to him. 'I'll leave the entertainment running for you,' said the man who had once pretended to be a courier. Once he had started the video again, he went to the bedroom door.

Feeling faint, Leon had to watch the psychopath leave the room knowing full well that it didn't give him any advantage. He tried to pull himself up on the rope, but he was exhausted from over-exertion and lack of sleep. His arms were too heavy; he would never be able to do it. There was no point contemplating the backrest of the chair; it would tip over as soon as he stepped on it. And he couldn't jump either.

There are no words to apologise for what I've done to you, Natalie continued. *So I'll just come out and say it: I betrayed you. With a man I've fallen for. No, a man I* fell *for, past tense. The two of us never had to speak about my desires, Leon. We both know I have a dark side that's unknown to you. One*

I lived out secretly. At first it was wild, exciting and exotic. At first I thought he was fulfilling my needs. But I was wrong. And now everything, as you can see, has got completely out of control.

She pointed to her injuries and her face contorted into a pain-filled smile.

His name is Siegfried von Boyten. He's the owner of this building, and he's the starting point, the core and the source of all my lies. We never applied for this apartment, my darling. He provided it for me; I had already been with him for a while by then.

Her confession was like a knife to the gut. Leon wondered how much more he could take.

Siegfried approached me in Dr Volwarth's waiting room. He was receiving psychiatric treatment. Just like me.

Natalie swallowed heavily.

Yes, I'm in therapy, and I'm afraid that's far from the only thing I've kept from you. My desires became more and more extreme, more and more bizarre. I was scared of talking to you about it. I was afraid of myself. I was with another doctor originally, but he referred me to Dr Volwarth. Back then we weren't yet married, so he didn't realise I knew you. He helped me a great deal, by the way.

Her expression became bitter.

It's thanks to him that I now know what a bastard my father is. How he destroyed my childhood and why I'm now easy prey for sadists like Siegfried. The man I betrayed you with.

She paused, then added quietly: *The man who made me pregnant.*

'No!' screamed Leon, as loudly as the noose around his neck would allow.

He felt an icy gust of air rush through his body. His legs became numb, he couldn't feel his toes any more, couldn't hold himself up any longer. Pressure forced down on his Adam's apple as he sank, but it was no longer the noose choking him; it was Natalie's confession.

Do you understand now why I can't look you in the eyes? I didn't just betray you. I let you believe that we had lost our child. But it was his baby I aborted. And it looks like now I'm getting the punishment I deserve. Von Boyten is a psychopath, Leon. He beat me, tortured me and raped me.

She held her thumb up to the camera.

This has nothing to do with my fantasies. Von Boyten is a sadist who loves dominating weak people. Tormenting them and watching. He's a perverse voyeur, and assumes other identities to manipulate people. Once he pretended to be a courier to demonstrate to me how powerful he is; he wanted to be close to me while you were standing alongside.

Leon shook his head, disbelieving, uncomprehending. With every movement, the noose cut deeper into his neck, but he didn't care. Nothing had any meaning any more. Not even the fact that he wasn't a twisted murderer after all. Natalie had betrayed him and she was dead. And in a few moments he would share her fate.

I think Siegfried has a spare key to our apartment, and he snoops around when I'm not there. I have no idea how he does it, but he's like one of those ghosts of the Twelve Nights you told me about, in the very worst form. First he poisoned my fish. Then me. And finally us.

Leon looked at the destroyed aquarium and wondered if the water damage had reached Ivana below yet, and if she would fetch help.

He watches me. He knows things I've never told him. About my father. And about your sleep disturbances.

From the tone of Natalie's voice, it sounded like she was coming to the end of what she wanted to say.

I love you, Leon. I tried so often to end things with him, and I accepted your proposal far too quickly because I thought that he would let me go if we were married. But we had already gone too far. He wouldn't take no for an answer. Until today. Now I'm not giving him a choice. I'll go to the police and report him. I've got no idea what I'll do after that, and I don't know when I'll speak to you again. I'm so ashamed, and so scared, but it's what I deserve.

'No,' retorted Leon, pain shooting up his legs. He couldn't stay on his tiptoes for much longer.

No one deserves this.

Everything she said, everything she had done, none of it changed his feelings for her. Not even in the face of the death that had entered their lives because of her betrayal.

Especially not in the face of death.

Under normal circumstances, he would never have been able to forgive her. They would have divorced, broken off all contact, moved to different cities and only heard from each other if a trick of fate had wanted it to be so.

But, and Leon was sure of this, they would never have stopped loving each other.

Don't wait for me, demanded Natalie. If she had seemed surprisingly composed up until this point in the recording, now the dam broke. She looked upwards and jutted out her lower lip, but otherwise made no attempt to stop the flow of her tears.

I'm not worth it. I know that we have no future any more. I've destroyed everything. But if my betrayal was good for anything, it was to show me how much I love you. How much I will always love you.

'How sweet.'

Leon twisted round to the door, and in his shock at the psychopath's words started to teeter. Cold sweat broke out on his forehead. He didn't know whether the man whose name he now knew had been standing in the doorway for a while, or whether he had only just come back.

Natalie's lips formed into one last kiss. Then they contorted, and beneath the tortured grimace Leon was able to recognise an echo of the smile he had fallen in love with years before.

There was a noise, and the monitor went black. Siegfried von Boyten sat down in front of the computer again.

'Why?' rasped Leon.

No reaction. Natalie's murderer brushed his fingers over the keyboard, humming.

Why are you doing this? Why are you destroying our lives?

And why did you just show me that?

Leon watched as von Boyten took the DVD out of the laptop and opened an editing program, then realised that the maniac had not played the recording for his benefit.

He just wanted to make a copy.

Clearly it was the soundtrack that held the sadist's interest, as he now began to edit it. Siegfried made a few, purposeful cuts, shortening the entire audio file to the length of a few seconds. In the end, only a sound file remained, its meaning distorted, with an aim as gruesome as everything else the psychopath had done.

39

Right. Left. And right again.

Regardless of how great the pain is. Regardless of how much blood there is.

Leon had realised what the sadist intended to do, which was why he didn't have any choice. He had to move while there was still time. Before Siegfried von Boyten succeeded in committing the perfect murder.

No! he heard Natalie scream, and knew it was only in his memory. The memory of a dream in which he was in a basement room that looked exactly like this bedroom here.

So the bastard could film the video clip there that he then forced me to watch.

No! screamed Natalie even louder in his thoughts. In his dream (*no, in the third stage!*), he had thought she was afraid of him. Of him falling asleep again and doing something to her. But it was exactly the other way around. He was supposed to wake up and help her. Because as a sleepwalker, he was useless and unable to rescue her.

Von Boyten had gone back into the corridor, so Leon couldn't see what he was doing, but he didn't need to. He could *hear* it.

'Hello, you've reached Natalie and Leon. Please leave your message after the tone.'

He's playing it on to the answerphone machine! Fuck, he's PLAYING IT ON TO MY ANSWER-PHONE MACHINE!

Leon was right. A few seconds later, he heard the compilation of Natalie's last words in that distorted tone typical of recorded messages.

Leon, darling . . . I'm so sorry. There are no words to apologise for what I've done, so I'll just come out and say it: I betrayed you. With a man I've fallen for. He's fulfilling my needs. We have no future any more. I don't know when I'll speak to you again.

'You won't get away with this,' croaked Leon, choking. But he knew he was wrong.

A computer expert would be able to recognise the edits on the soundtrack, but who would even bother to order such an expensive analysis with an obvious suicide? The case was clear-cut: the cheating wife admits her betrayal. Her husband loses his mind. A crime of passion. Then, to end it all, he hangs himself. It was the oldest story in the world.

And to clear up any last doubts, there is even a video of proof. Oh God.

Everyone who saw the recording of Natalie's execution would think it was Leon who had rammed the pen into her neck. After all, even he had fallen for the deception at first. Admittedly Siegfried would have to erase the final seconds after Natalie's murder – the part in which he climbed through the door behind the mirror and into the bedroom – but that was child's play compared to how he had directed their lives for the whole of the last year.

Left. Right.

Keep moving. Just don't make a sound. Even if the pain tears you apart.

Leon was shaking all over. He stopped, so as not to pass out from the pain, while in the hallway Siegfried checked the recording one more time.

By now he had managed to manipulate the time record on the answer machine. According to the digital voice, Natalie's call had been received several days ago.

Long before her death.

Left. Right. Turn again.

Even with the pain, Leon's thoughts wouldn't stop coming.

Damn it, there are even witnesses to incriminate me. I admitted to Sven that I had hit Natalie and filmed myself in the labyrinth.

But at least Sven would confirm his confused mental state.

Left. Right. Left.

Leon couldn't bear the torment for much longer. Neither the physical nor the mental.

How much longer is this going to go on? he screamed in his thoughts, biting his tongue until it bled.

How many video recordings did you fake? How much longer are you going to manipulate me for?

He heard steps from the hallway, saw a shadow and turned towards the bedroom door.

'Right then, now it's your turn—' said von Boyten, stopping short, his sarcastic grin dying away mid-sentence.

Leon was sure that von Boyten would have kicked the chair away from under his feet there and then if he hadn't been so shocked by the sight before him.

Left. Right. And left again.

'What are you doing?' screamed Siegfried, hit by the realisation that his perfect plan wasn't functioning so perfectly any more.

Right. Left again.

No matter how much it hurts.

Leon had lacerated his neck with the rope, and even now he didn't stop moving his head.

Left. Right.

The coarse rope was scraping against his raw flesh

like steel wool. Blood was running down over his chest and stomach, so much that he could even feel it on his scrotum, dropping down in gloopy threads on to the seat of the chair.

'Stop it. Stop that at once.'

Leon had no intention of stopping. Every cut into his flesh was a signal that he was still alive. Better than that: he was creating proof that he had struggled. No forensic in the world could overlook this. No one would assume suicide with these injuries. If there had been more time he would have taken the gloves off too, but wounds on the hands could also be seen as the suicide's attempt to escape after a change of mind. But with the lacerations to his neck, this assumption wasn't possible.

'Fuck. You arsehole.'

Leon started to laugh.

Bound, hung up and bleeding, he was at the pervert's mercy, but he still had the advantage. It was something the sadist just couldn't bear. He had wanted to humiliate, control and feed off his victim's death throes, but Leon was changing the course of events.

'Now I'm really going to hurt you,' screamed von Boyten, lifting his hands above his head in despair. 'Now you're going to know what pain is, you stupid bastard.'

His unremarkable face had transformed into an ugly mask. Spit collected in the corners of his mouth as he shouted. He wandered aimlessly around the room.

Siegfried appeared not to know what to do next, and this made him furious. That and the fact that Leon had lost all his fear of death and was laughing mockingly in von Boyten's face.

Siegfried stopped in front of the chair. His face reddened, the pulse on his neck pumped, and his eyes became dull, losing any hint of human emotion. Leon knew he had only seconds left. Von Boyten was no longer following a plan, apart from the desire to kill him in the most torturous manner possible.

Whatever the murderer wanted to do, Leon knew he couldn't let the psychopath out of his reach. Even in his rage, Siegfried had not made the mistake of getting close to Leon's arms. Von Boyten had stopped for a moment a metre from the chair, but he turned away again, towards the rope tied to the heating pipe. Leon could almost hear his thoughts: was there another position in which he could torture Leon better?

It's now or never.

Just one more step and it would be too late.

'Hey,' yelled Leon, but his voice wasn't strong enough to get through to the crazed killer, which turned out to be a stroke of luck. If Siegfried had turned round, he would have seen the imminent danger. But instead, when Leon clamped his legs around von Boyten's neck it took him completely by surprise.

Leon, who had nothing more to lose, had jumped from the chair with the very last of his energy and was holding the murderer in a stranglehold with his thighs.

Siegfried let out a cry of shock and stumbled backwards, then instinctively tried to rear up and shake the burden from his shoulders – which was his mistake.

If he had kept calm or fallen forwards, Leon's fate would have been sealed. But he was carrying his victim piggyback. The rope lost its tension and began to ride up the hook on the ceiling, eventually looping free.

Siegfried lost his untied boot, stumbled over it and twisted as he fell, taking Leon down with him.

Realising that he could be strangled in a matter of moments, Leon reached up to grasp the rope and was stunned when it didn't stop his fall. Holding the rope, his feet hit the chair, and he fell hard, head first, on to the wet parquet. His last thought was – *The rope came free from the hook* – before the world behind his eyes transformed into a ball of fire.

40

Leon couldn't see anything, couldn't catch his breath, and the pain had reached a new high point. But he was still expecting the torture to get much worse, as soon as von Boyten had struggled to his feet beside him.

For now he was satisfying himself with hefty kicks to Leon's lower body. Protecting his genitals with one hand and holding the other in front of his face, Leon wondered why Siegfried's kicks were so untargeted.

He tried to open his eyes. The world looked blurred, which was no great surprise given the impact the fall must have had on his head.

What is he waiting for?

Von Boyten screamed something that Leon was unable to understand, because the whistling inside his head had reached the volume of an exploding kettle. He tried to prop himself up, and his hands touched a puddle that he hoped wasn't blood.

Siegfried's kicks, meanwhile, were becoming quicker but weaker. And his cries louder.

What is he going to do? What does he want, for me to look him in the eyes as I die?

Leon's vision had improved marginally, so now he was at least able to make out the contours of Siegfried's body. They were lying next to each other as if lovers, on their sides, their faces turned towards each other.

Leon blinked, but the sensation that he was seeing the killer through a pane of glass refused to disappear. Because it *couldn't*.

No more than von Boyten could stop kicking around wildly and making incomprehensible noises.

Unlike Leon, he had tried to brace his fall with his hands. Angel fish, Natalie's favourite, needed a high-sided aquarium, and Siegfried's arms hadn't been long enough to stop a tall, still-standing spike of glass at the front of it from slicing through his throat as he fell into the remains of the aquarium.

But he's still alive. The bastard's still alive.

Leon struggled to his knees. Thick blood was seeping from von Boyten's throat, and he was twitching uncontrollably.

'Hah!' Leon loosened the noose around his neck and sucked air into his lungs, gurgling.

Loud. Despairing. Hysterical.

With both hands he grabbed the dying Siegfried von Boyten by the hair and roared his murdered wife's name again and again. When his voice failed him, he smashed von Boyten's head back on the shards of glass, impaling him even deeper.

He waited until the twitching had stopped, until Siegfried had drawn his last breath.

Then he stood up, the shards of glass cutting his bare feet.

Bloody footprints marked his path across the hallway into the stairwell, and down the steps. It was too late. The working day had come to an end. There were no more workers to be seen.

'Help!' he screamed. Then again, alternating it with Natalie's name. He rang the bell of every apartment door, not waiting to see if anyone opened up, instead stumbling to the exit and out on to the street.

Snow blew into his face.

A couple gave a start at the sight of him, and passers-by gaped in astonishment as he ran naked and covered in blood through the cold, screaming for help.

In front of the supermarket on the corner, he broke down.

No one spoke to him. No one wanted to get too close to a man who was clearly mentally disturbed, but Leon could see a cluster of curious people gathering around. Many had pulled out their mobile phones.

'She's still downstairs,' Leon heard himself scream.

Quickly. I have to tell them before I don't have any strength left.

'Hurry. He's freezing to death,' he heard a woman shout. Cars were beeping. Youths were laughing and taking photos.

'Natalie's downstairs. In the labyrinth.'

They have to look for her. Maybe she can still be saved.

Leon was shaking as though he had just received an electric shock, and then felt a blanket being laid on him. Someone asked what his name was, but that wasn't important, so he just said: 'Push the wardrobe to the side and go into the labyrinth. You'll find Natalie behind the secret door.'

'Yes, we'll do that. But for now you need to come with us.'

Car doors slammed, then everything around him was flashing in blue and white, and the man who was wearing a red high-visibility vest with a white cross grasped him by the shoulders while another grabbed his feet. Leon swayed.

'Don't you understand? He rammed a pen into her neck. The code for the secret door is a-Moll. You have to hurry.'

'Of course. Calm down now,' said the man, belting

him securely to the stretcher in the ambulance. 'Do you know who you are?'

Leon tried to sit up and was pulled back by the restraints. 'It was Siegfried. Siegfried von Boyten.'

'Is that your name?'

'No. His father built the house. He knew the secret world behind the wardrobe.'

'Of course.'

'Noooo!' screamed Leon, shaking at the restraints on his arm.

They don't believe me. Oh God.

'Please, don't waste any time. Natalie might still be alive. You have to look for her.'

'In the secret world behind the wardrobe. Of course.'

He felt something cold on his arm, then a prick, and the ambulance was moving, its siren blaring.

41

The patient hadn't even been on the ward for half an hour, and already he was causing trouble. Sister Susan had *tasted* it, almost as soon as the ambulance opened its doors and the stretcher was pushed out.

She could always taste it when problems rolled into the psychiatric department. She would get this strange sensation in her mouth, as though she was chewing on aluminium foil. It could even be unleashed by patients who at first glance seemed more like victims and not aggressive in the slightest; much like the man who had just activated the alarm in Room 1310.

And at five to eight, of all times.

If he could just have waited another five minutes, Susan would have been on her break. Instead, she had to rush along the corridor on an empty stomach. Not that she had much of an appetite in the evenings anyway.

She took great care not to gain weight, even though she wasn't much bigger than some of the anorexia patients being treated on the ward. The tiny salad and half an egg were part of her evening routine – as was, admittedly, a paranoid schizophrenic with hallucinations, but she would have gladly relinquished the latter.

The patient had been found lying naked in the snow in front of a supermarket, covered in blood and with lacerations on his feet. He had appeared bedraggled, disorientated and dehydrated, but his gaze was alert and steady, his voice clear, and his teeth (teeth, as far as Susan was concerned, were always a sure indication of the state of the soul) showed no signs of alcohol, nicotine or substance abuse.

And yet I could still taste it, she thought, with one hand on her bleeper and the other on her bunch of keys.

Susan unlocked the door and entered the room.

The scene before her was so bizarre that she stood in shock for a moment before pressing the bleeper to call the security team, who were trained especially for situations such as these.

'I can prove it,' screamed the naked man in front of the window. He was standing in a pool of vomit.

'Of course you can,' answered the sister, taking care to keep her distance.

Her words sounded rehearsed rather than genuine, because Susan had indeed rehearsed them and didn't intend them to be genuine, but in the past she had often been able to win time with empty platitudes.

Not this time, though.

Later, in its final report, the inquiry panel would establish that the cleaning woman had been listening to music on an MP3 player, something strictly forbidden during working hours. When her supervisor came by unexpectedly to do a hygiene check, she had hidden the device in the water meter cupboard next to the shower.

But in the moment of crisis it was a mystery to Sister Susan as to how the patient had come into possession of the electronic device. He had ripped open its battery compartment and was holding a bent alkaline battery, which he must have chewed open with his teeth. Although Susan couldn't actually see it, she pictured the viscous battery acid flowing down over the edges like marmalade.

'Everything's going to be OK,' she said, trying to placate him.

'No, nothing's going to be OK,' the man protested. 'Listen to me. I'm not crazy. I tried to throw up to get it out of my stomach, but maybe I've already digested it. Please. You have to take an X-ray. You have to X-ray my body. The proof is inside me!'

He screamed and screamed until, eventually, the security team came in and restrained him.

But they were too late. By the time the doctors

rushed into the room, the patient had long since swallowed the battery.

'So, now you need to push me into the Tube,' he announced triumphantly as he was pressed back on to the bed.

'I tied myself up when I was sleepwalking, down in the labyrinth, do you see? And because Siegfried was just pretending to be me, the handcuff key must still be in my stomach.'

'Sister, inform radiology,' said one of the doctors, shaking his head.

'And prepare for a stomach pumping,' another added. 'We have to get the battery out before it releases too much acid.'

'Fuck the acid,' screamed Leon. 'It's about the key.'

His bed was pushed out of the room.

'You'll find the handcuff keys in my stomach or my bowels, and when you do please—' Leon grabbed the hand of the doctor who was walking to the right-hand side of his bed. He had more hair on his face than on his head and a moustache that couldn't hide his cleft lip.

'Please go to my apartment and push the wardrobe back,' Leon pleaded with him. 'If it won't move, then you can climb into the labyrinth through Frau Helsing's bathroom.'

'Into the labyrinth?' asked the bearded man, introducing himself as Dr Meller.

'That's what I call it, yes. I can draw it for you. At the end of the first shaft there's a fork in the path that leads to a secret door.'

And to my wife's corpse.

Leon closed his eyes in exhaustion as he began to realise that he wouldn't even believe himself. But it was too late anyway. If Natalie hadn't died immediately after the stabbing, there was no chance she was still alive after all this time.

'Do you mean the door with the DANGER sign?' asked Dr Meller abruptly.

Leon opened his eyes wide. 'How do you know about that?'

'The police confirmed your statement.'

Unlike Sister Susan, the doctor seemed to be speaking earnestly. His words didn't sound patronising, but honest.

'You believe me?'

'Yes. A friend of yours, Sven Berger, was worried about you and wanted to check on you. About a quarter of an hour ago he found a man's corpse in your apartment.'

The stretcher came to a halt in front of some swing doors. Leon lifted his head. 'And Natalie?' He tried to sit up. 'What about my wife?'

Has she been found too?

Fear of the truth sealed his throat shut.

The doctor shook his head regretfully.

'I don't know. The police are trying to open a door, I heard, but it's secured with a code.'

'A-Moll,' called Leon. 'Please tell them that the code is: A-H-C-D-E-F-G-A.'

The doctor nodded and a telephone appeared in his right hand. It seemed he was on the line with the police, because he asked if they had heard Leon's last sentence.

'No, he can't be interviewed now, he's swallowed a battery and we need to pump his stomach,' said Dr Meller, trying to end the call. The person at the other end said something, and the doctor looked down at his patient with an expression of shock. Leon's heart stopped.

Have they found her?

'The investigator wants to know what happened to the other tenants,' asked Meller.

Leon's eyes widened. 'Oh my God, did that psychopath do something to them too?'

He thought of old Frau Helsing, who von Boyten surely can't have had anything against.

'No, erm . . .' The doctor wandered out of his line of vision, then appeared again on the other side of the stretcher.

'If I understood correctly, it sounds like no one's there.'

'No one? That's impossible. Ivana never leaves her apartment in the evening.'

'I'm afraid you don't understand.' Leon was pushed through the door into a tubular treatment room. 'According to the police, your neighbours didn't go out. They *moved* out. With all their valuables, cash and papers. All the house doors were open with the keys left in the outside.'

'What? But why?'

Dr Meller shrugged his shoulders cluelessly. 'I don't understand either, Herr Nader. But the police said the whole building looked like it had been evacuated.'

Some months later

Somewhere in the world.
In a town you know.
Maybe even in your neighbourhood . . .

42

Dr Volwarth waited for his colleagues' applause to die down as he entered the conference room of the sleep laboratory.

'Thank you. Thank you very much indeed.'

He fiddled with the stud in his earlobe. Too much attention always embarrassed him.

'It's our joint success. You should be applauding yourselves.'

The group, two women and two men, laughed politely.

Only the chief doctor at the head of the table seemed disgruntled.

'It's a shame that any recognition will take a long time to come,' he interjected.

'You're right, Professor Tareski.' Volwarth's eyes flashed with bitterness. 'But we're not the only ones in the history of medicine to have risked their own well-being and freedom in order to achieve ground-breaking discoveries in the name of science. Just think of our colleagues in the Middle Ages, who were forbidden under threat of the death penalty to open the human body.'

He emphasised this statement with a raised index finger.

'Over thousands of years, doctors and scientists had to steal corpses from cemeteries for dissections, and often paid with their own lives for this desire to research. The Church was afraid that the lies in the Bible would come to light if people realised that Adam wasn't missing the rib Eve was allegedly made from. Back then it was the priests, and today it's other do-gooders who stand in the way of progress.'

The nurse by his side snorted with contempt and stopped stroking the cat on her lap for a short moment.

Ivana Helsing was getting on in years, but she was one of his most reliable helpers when it came to the careful implementation of experiments. And she had also introduced him to the von Boytens, for which Volwarth showed her his gratitude with unconditional loyalty, even if she had a tendency to humanise the test subjects. Over time she had grown so fond of 'darling Leon', as she liked to call him, that in the end she had even pleaded for the experiment to be called off. Today she was happy and content that he had survived, even though Leon had not responded to her subliminal attempts to get him to leave the building. She hadn't developed any fondness for Natalie, on the other hand. Luckily. If you want to break new ground in the field of medicine, you can't be too sensitive. Subjects like Natalie and Leon, in this context, were nothing but animals in a laboratory. Whoever didn't have the emotional strength to take the loss of a chimpanzee had no place in the field of research.

'Anyone who carries out unapproved human testing must be prepared for contempt from the ignorant,' explained Volwarth in a self-congratulatory tone.

It was a vicious circle that his co-researchers knew only too well. Technically speaking, of course, the ethics of their profession required the approval of the test person. But sleep disturbances were anomalies of the subconscious. As soon as the test subject knew he or she was being observed, that changed the very behaviour that was to be investigated. No one slept in a laboratory like they did at home in their own bed. It was precisely for this reason that parasomnias were barely researched and the results gained in traditional sleep laboratories so inadequate. Tests provoking the violent excesses of sleepwalkers were considered unthinkable.

'By letting Leon Nader believe for an entire year that he was living in his own familiar environment, we were able to make groundbreaking discoveries in the field of somnambulism research,' said Volwarth proudly.

Three years of planning. From the selection of the subjects to preparing the laboratory: his deceased patient Albert von Boyten, who he had treated in his clinic until his death, had been the creator of unique architectonic masterpieces, which Volwarth had found to be excellent for his purposes. Distributed all over the globe, von Boyten's buildings had been constructed with secret levels between floors. The genius architect, a war child and Communist, had originally designed them as hiding places for the politically persecuted, but they were also excellently suited to being sleep laboratories. Beyond using them to observe the patients, it was also possible to expose patients to targeted stimulation.

The apartments were connected via secret passage-ways that could be accessed at any time, in order to get test materials in and out while the test subject was either elsewhere in the building or asleep.

The sleep phases which framed Leon's sleepwalking activities were luckily incredibly stable, as is often the case with patients with such disturbances. These created the necessary time windows in which the researchers could painstakingly prepare their experiments, for example copying the edited videos on to Leon's laptop. More complicated was the follow-up stage of the experiment levels in question. For this, Leon's apartment had to be returned to its original state; the wardrobe, for example (which was fixed with an electromagnet), had to be pushed back, the head camera hidden and the laptop turned off. For as soon as Leon awoke, nothing could be permitted to remind him of his nocturnal activities.

The deep-sleep phases were of such intensity that they had been able to undress and dress Leon, move him, and once even lay him in a bathtub.

Volwarth looked over at Ivana. On her lap, Alba was purring and pressing her little head against her mistress's hands so that she would start stroking her again. He couldn't help but remember the stubbornness of the old woman when she had insisted that they use an artificial but convincing fur mock-up instead of a real cat corpse for the experiment in the bathtub.

And yet despite all the personal differences in the team, everything worked wonderfully.

Not for the first time, Volwarth felt proud of himself and his team.

It had demanded a great deal of discipline, concentration and the precise implementation of the experiment procedure, but in the end all their efforts had been rewarded.

'Firstly, we have conclusively proved that intense mental trauma is able to provoke the complicated process of sleepwalking,' pontificated Volwarth.

They all nodded contentedly.

To start with, admittedly, they hadn't known how to actively put Leon into a sleepwalking state, but researching that was part of the experiment, after all. And just like the bacteriologist Fleming's discovery of penicillin, fate had played into their hands here too. Siegfried von Boyten had agreed to provide the house from his father's inheritance on the condition that he himself be allowed to participate in the experiment. Leon, in turn, had only been selected as a test subject because of Natalie. Volwarth's assertion to Leon that the hypnophobia from his childhood was so interesting that he still referred to it today was a lie. In actual fact, he had completely forgotten about Leon, until the day a colleague asked him for advice in a case where a patient was suffering from self-destructive sexual behaviour. When Volwarth encountered the familiar name of Natalie's partner while reading the minutes from her sessions, he instantly saw the potential for his experiments: a sleepwalker and a mentally fragile girlfriend. The perfect conditions to test if and what degree of psychological pressure could unleash sleep disturbances. It had been Volwarth who made contact with Natalie and offered help. Not the other way round.

'We have finally succeeded in proving the phase of sleepwalking to be an independent conscious state in which the patient is not just able to function and react, but also comprehensively communicate,' Volwarth continued.

He directed his colleagues to open the slim file in front of them on the table and look at the photo on the first page. It showed Leon Nader, clothed only in boxer shorts, standing in the corridor of the old laboratory.

'In this picture, our patient was already in the third stage.'

When Leon had woken up in his and Natalie's bed after drinking a bottle of wine alone the night before, he thought he was awake. But, in reality, he was in a highly stable sleepwalking phase that began with Natalie's flight and only ended once he went back in the bedroom and fell asleep again.

'In the subsequent conscious state, Herr Nader was unable to remember the events surrounding his wife's departure. He awoke in an empty bed and thought that she had left as a consequence of weeks of intense marital crisis. While he slept, we closed the wardrobe again and tidied up all the disorder. Given that Natalie had left him a goodbye note on the kitchen door before her abrupt departure, Leon was upset but not incredibly worried about her well-being, and therefore numbed himself with work for the days that followed.'

They had needed to remove the goodbye card in the first sleepwalking phases, of course, to ensure that Leon's mental torment was greater and his sleep-walking state more stable.

Volwarth smiled pensively.

No wonder Leon's friend and business partner was so confused. Sven Berger had experienced his friend in two different stages of consciousness, and according to whether Leon was awake or sleepwalking, the versions that he heard about Natalie's disappearance were completely different. First it was that Natalie was just taking some time out. Then that she had been beaten by him in his sleep. Leon, in turn, was unable to remember in his conscious state either his injuries or the camera, while during his sleepwalking phases he couldn't remember having taken his wedding ring to the jeweller's, giving his parents a cruise or that his friend had picked up the architectural model.

'It is really astounding how much we've learned about the sleepwalking phase,' said Dr Kroeger, who had joined the team two years ago as a neurologist and who was already flicking further forwards in the file.

'Just like when people are dreaming, a sleepwalker, too, remembers specific events from reality. But clearly, and this is the real sensation of our results, not everything. It seems that only intensely emotional events seep into the nocturnal memory.'

Volwarth nodded. This was exactly his hypothesis.

The miscarriage, Natalie's disappearance, the enormous pressure of his work deadline – Leon had been able to remember all of this. Less significant experiences, on the other hand, he hadn't.

But perhaps the most interesting thing, as far as Volwarth was concerned, was the fact that the sleepwalking memory could structure information in building blocks. This had been proven by the (incredibly difficult) staging of the first 'awakening': when Leon thought he woke up wearing latex gloves and the camera on his head, while in reality he was sleepwalking. From the moment he put the camera on his head the first time to his first viewing of the video tapes, fourteen hours passed. But fourteen hours in which Leon hadn't really slept, at least not exclusively. Firstly, with the camera on his head, he had fallen from the sleepwalking phase into an exhausted, almost comatose state, in which the researchers had been able to take the camera off him without any problems. Leon then slept four hours, woke up and worked on his model; a phase that he was unable to remember later when sleepwalking, and this was why he was so astonished when he realised during his phone conversation with Sven how much time had passed.

In order to prepare Leon for the next test, they added a light sedative to his tea. He drank it while conscious, which was why he soon went back to bed with a growing headache. With Leon in this numbed state, they had been easily able to put the gloves on him, as well as the camera on his head. The only thing they forgot was the watch he had been wearing during his last sleepwalking phase and which he'd taken off while awake as he worked. A discrepancy that Leon later noticed, but which luckily had no impact on the continuation of the experiment. Leon thought he was waking up after fourteen hours of sleep, but in reality he had suppressed the conscious phase in between, and his sleep-waking memory latched on – as they had hoped – directly to the point when he had ended his last somnambulistic phase: he got out of bed, looked at the video and discovered the wardrobe.

All the rest is history. They would become world-renowned in the history of medicine!

'The fact that we've been able to prove that a sleepwalking memory exists is phenomenal,' smiled Volwarth. 'And we've also learned that a patient clearly reflects on his state while sleepwalking.'

Volwarth was particularly proud of this result. Many of his colleagues – some of whom were here today – had doubted that it was possible to use external stimuli to penetrate the consciousness of the sleepwalker to the extent that he or she was aware of his situation but without freeing them from it. Yet this had been conclusively proven by the words and numbers Leon had noted on his hand in the experiment room.

'Look at this.' Kroeger held up a photo in which he was handing Leon a mobile phone in his living room. 'Nader was in the third stage here too. During our conversation he seemed absent-minded, as though under the influence of drugs, but he still appeared to take in everything I said to him. He could hardly look me in the eye, but he studied the photos we took of Natalie on the mobile phone in great detail. His speech was a little blurred, but he seemed stable otherwise.'

Volwarth nodded in agreement.

He had experienced at first hand how lasting Leon's imprisonment within the third stage had been.

At first the head camera had not been a planned component of their experiment. They had actually wanted to test with the prescription Volwarth made out to him whether Leon would leave the house during his sleepwalking phase. But by this point, he was already so convinced of his own guilt that he decided to hook himself up again of his own volition. As they hadn't been sure how precise his technical dexterity would be while sleepwalking, they had exchanged the camera he ordered for another, one that was easier to put together and install. In addition, this meant they could upload the manipulated videos on to his computer with the help of the switched USB sticks, without even having to enter the apartment.

Surprised by how adept their patient was, they had then tried out different levels of difficulty to test how strongly Leon was caught in the third stage and what physical and psychological achievements he was capable of during sleepwalking. From simple tasks like looking at pictures on a phone to the discovery of a combination of numbers on the thumbnail – in the course of the experiment, Volwarth had become more and more euphoric about Leon's abilities. He had even been able to solve the a-Moll puzzle.

'Sometimes I think our patient was clearer in the head than our team,' complained Tareski.

Volwarth nodded regretfully. 'I understand your chagrin, Professor, and I promise I'll be more careful next time with the selection of our assistants.'

'You certainly should be. It just wasn't possible to control Siegfried after a while, and he simply played out his own sadistic desires.' Tareski instinctively touched his neck. 'You shouldn't ever trust an amateur again with such an important task as the creation of the trigger footage.'

Volwarth sighed.

In truth they had wanted to find someone more reliable as bait for Natalie, but it had been difficult enough as it was to convince even one daring researcher to take part in their projects. And this time they had been searching for someone with relevant experience in a scene that was too hardcore for even S&M enthusiasts. When von Boyten Jr. unexpectedly offered himself for the task, they were incautious enough to accept due to desperation. It was clear to everyone that Siegfried just wanted to satisfy his own brutal desires, but didn't that make him pre-destined to provoke the kind of psychotic stress in Leon that they so urgently needed for their experiment to succeed?

And so it was von Boyten who offered the apartment to Natalie to reinforce their sexual relationship. It was the catalyst they needed to increase Leon's fear of loss to such an extent that he fell back into his old pattern of consciousness.

'The house belonged to him,' explained Volwarth. 'As you know, he threatened to expose the whole thing if we pulled him out of the experiment. I wish I'd had another option. He was our only weak point.'

They had given von Boyten a certain amount of freedom when it came to the contents of the tapes they played on Leon's laptop. The primary function of these recordings was to examine how defined the I-consciousness of the test individual was in the third stage, similar to the consciousness test carried out with animals to check whether they recognise themselves in the mirror or see their reflections as another creature. At the same time the recordings were intended to help discover to what extent the patient could draw logical conclusions from what he had seen.

The fact that von Boyten had climbed unauthorised into Tareski's apartment and almost strangled him to death with a shoelace had been neither planned nor foreseen. And especially not on a day when Volwarth was delayed, due to a presentation that could not be postponed, and therefore unable to step in.

'Even though you were the affected party, Professor, there was a positive outcome to the attack. The fact that Leon rescued you proved there's a sleepwalking conscience.'

Tareski didn't seem too convinced, but everyone else in the room nodded in agreement.

'And last but not least,' said Volwarth, trying to bring his summary to a conclusion, 'we almost succeeded, as a side benefit, in curing Leon Nader of his hypnophobia.'

The faked video footage had been designed to lure Leon into a labyrinth that seemed to lead down into the darkest passageways of his subconscious.

'For the whole of his life, our patient was afraid of falling asleep because he thought it turned him into a violent monster. The fact that he was able to overpower Siegfried von Boyten in the end meant that he overcame the trauma of his childhood. Now he knows that he doesn't hurt anyone when he sleep-walks, neither his loved ones, like Natalie, nor strangers like Professor Tareski.'

Volwarth smiled modestly and waited until his colleagues had stopped clapping.

'Before I ask you to turn to the last page in the file, I would like to take this opportunity to thank our generous donors. Without the Falconis, it wouldn't have been possible to finance our projects.'

The pot-bellied man of the couple that had inhabited the first floor of the old sleep laboratory smiled smugly, and yet Volwarth knew it was actually the elegant woman by his side who deserved the recognition. She was the wealthy one. For her husband, the experiment had been nothing more than cheap snuff-theatre, and if it was down to him he would have turned off the money tap early on, as soon as he became bored of it.

Volwarth sighed discreetly.

It was a shame that it was necessary to collaborate with such objectionable subjects, but there wasn't much he wouldn't do in the name of science. At least his donors had made an undisputable contribution to the success of the experiment by stopping Natalie's lift on the first floor and coaxing the young woman into their apartment, which was why Leon was so confused when she didn't come out of the lift on the ground floor. But this act and their money had been the Falconis' only noteworthy achievements, and even their financial means hadn't been enough to cover all the expenses. Volwarth had even let Ivana talk him into flogging some of their research recordings to buyers on the internet. It made Volwarth feel sick when he thought about it, but with the money the project swallowed up there'd been no other option. Of course, he was neither able nor willing to lower himself to conversing with such questionable individuals, so he had left it to Ivana to send them the packages containing the tapes.

'I'm very pleased you're with us again today,' said Volwarth to the Falconis, gritting his teeth. Then he asked for the attention of all those present.

'Just like all of you, I regretted the fact that we had to leave our last laboratory in such a hasty manner. But with Leon managing to break free so unexpectedly, we were unfortunately left with no choice.'

Volwarth pulled four security keys, furnished with numbered bands, from his trouser pocket. 'Ladies and gentlemen, these are the keys to your new apartments. As always, you can choose the floor yourselves.'

He beckoned for his colleagues and sponsors to stand up and come closer.

The windowless room in which their meeting was taking place had a low ceiling, and Dr Kroeger had to lower his head as he went to stand beside Volwarth.

'On the last page of your files, you'll find a list with your new identities, as well as a rough overview of the planned series of tests.'

With these words, he pulled a black, opaque curtain from the wall, and a murmur went through the group.

'As I said, it's a shame we're no longer able to use our old space. But here we've been able to find even better conditions. And we'll still be able to act incognito.'

He had begun to whisper, which was silly given that the walls were adequately insulated. Noises could only penetrate into the laboratory space if they really wanted them to.

'Excellent,' said Kroeger in awe.

'Unbelievable,' Ivana agreed.

'Fantastic,' enthused Mr Falconi, for the wrong reasons.

The rest were silent, staring transfixed through the two-way mirror into the bedroom of the couple who were in the process of moving into their new apartment.

43

'It's unbelievable,' said the young man, putting a removal box down next to the bed.

'Isn't it, darling?' The woman, even younger, let herself fall back on to the bed with a suggestive smile. Her boyfriend followed her lead and kissed her full lips.

'I still can't believe we got our dream apartment.'

'Neither can I.'

He pushed his hand beneath her blouse and she giggled.

'It's wonderful,' he said, leaning towards her with a loving look.

'I know, isn't it?'

'I didn't mean the apartment.'

'Then what?'

'It's wonderful that you're smiling again at last.'

He kissed her, then said in a hopeful voice:

'I think everything's going to be OK again here.'

Epilogue

It was impossible to make anything out through the material. Sven had tied the blindfold much too tightly. As soon as Leon took it off he would look like he had just woken up, with tired eyes and sleep creases on his face.

'Where are you taking me?'

He was holding on with both hands to the shoulders of his best friend, who in the last months had become his closest confidant. Numerous doctors had approached him, including prominent personalities, offering to work through the traumatic experiences of his recent past with him, but for obvious reasons Leon didn't want to have anything more to do with psychiatrists for the rest of his life.

'How much longer?' he asked impatiently. It was straining his nerves to stumble along blindly like this. Just a few weeks ago it would have been unthinkable to put himself in someone else's hands like this, but since they had moved into the new apartment he was making advances day by day.

'We're almost there.'

You said that five minutes ago, when we got out of the car.

The path sloped up gradually but steadily. Leon felt the sun on his face and heard music from the radio of a car driving past. His nose was itching, a sure sign the pavement was lined by blooming chestnut trees. The scent of warm asphalt was in the air.

'I hate surprises.'

'Then you'd better avoid your birthday,' replied Sven drily.

Leon thought about what they must look like. Some passers-by stopped their conversations, giggled and made silly comments ('What a lovely couple', 'Have fun, you two'), or whispered behind their backs as soon as they had passed.

Once Sven had led him around two more corners and then straight on for a long stretch, it seemed they had reached their destination, for they came to a halt.

'Finally.'

Leon moved to loosen the tight knot behind his head, but Sven took him by the arm.

'Stop, first I need to tell you something important.'

'What?'

'You won't like my present.'

'Excuse me?'

Leon blinked beneath the blindfold. Even more worrying than Sven's secretive behaviour was the fact that his friend had started to stutter again, albeit barely noticeable.

'They said it's too early, but I'm afraid it might already be too late.'

With these words, Sven pressed something into his hand that felt like a glass of hot water. Leon held it with the tips of his fingers so as not to burn himself.

'What the hell . . .?' He ripped the blindfold from his head and gaped at the object flickering in his hand. 'You're giving me a tea light?'

Sven shook his head. 'No. I'm giving you a vision.'

'Of what?'

'The truth.'

Leon obeyed the order to turn round, and almost let the glass fall.

A sea of lights danced in front of his eyes, fuelled by the numerous candles and tea lights that were arranged on a flight of steps.

'Is this supposed to be a joke?' asked Leon, wishing he had never taken off the blindfold.

The collection of letters, cuddly toys, flowers and pictures – some framed, but mostly wrapped in clear film – looked completely out of place. This was not the side of a street where some accident had taken place. They were not standing at the entrance to the home of some celebrity whose unexpected death was being mourned by their fans. Such a manifestation of collective grief belonged in the evening news and not at the entrance to the building from which Leon had fled, naked, on to the street, a few months ago.

'Why are you doing this to me, Sven?'

Some of the flames were extinguished and many of the flowers had wilted, which was no wonder considering the warm temperatures, but the wreath on the lowest step had been watered just recently. Drops pearled from the fir boughs, and the embroidered sash gleamed like new in the glistening sunlight.

In deepest sorrow.

Leon turned back.

Even his friend's eyes had filled with tears. 'I'm so sorry, Leon. But I think it's time you face up to the truth.'

Sven pointed at a framed photo in which Natalie was laughing directly into the camera. A photocopy with bleached-out edges. Like most of the portraits on the steps, it had been taken from a newspaper. Above it was the attention-grabbing headline:

Natalie Nader –
The Beautiful Victim of a Sadist

'But that doesn't make any sense,' whispered Leon. *It's utterly impossible.*

They had found Natalie in the labyrinth. Without measurable vital functions. Siegfried had punctured her windpipe, torn her oesophagus. Her lungs had filled, at a torturously slow pace, with blood and secretions, every breath had brought her closer to the end. But as she was unconscious, Natalie's breathing had slowed down considerably, and this meant she did not immediately suffocate.

'She survived,' said Leon, throwing his tea light at the ground in anger. The glass shattered. The flame extinguished. 'They brought Natalie back to life!'

Once in the cellar, and once again on the way to the hospital. Even during the emergency operation, the surgeons had needed to fight time and time again against the flat line, but in the end they sent death back to the waiting room.

'She's alive!' screamed Leon, kicking several candles from the first step. Glass shattered, a frame broke.

'I was with her when she woke up!'

For several weeks Natalie had only been able to take in liquid sustenance, and her voice had changed. She didn't talk much, particularly not about what had happened in that building, but when she did, it sounded as though she was choking on something hot. Like the scars on her soul, the ones on her vocal chords weren't visible to the naked eye. Unlike the hollow above her larynx, which changed shape and became lighter when she swallowed.

'What's all this about?' asked Leon, holding in his hand a small crucifix that he had just picked up from the steps. In a rage, he threw it at Sven's feet. 'I had breakfast with her just two hours ago.'

At our place. In our new home.

'It's just a dream,' he heard Sven say, who was standing at the foot of the steps. 'You're stuck in a dream and you need help to get out of it.'

'This is RIDICULOUS!' roared Leon.

Sven stretched his arms out towards him. 'Natalie is dead, you need to accept it. You're not living with her, you're living in a clinic. We have another fifteen minutes, then I need to take you back there.'

'You're lying.'

'If I'm lying, then why are you wearing pyjamas?'

Leon looked down at himself in horror. His legs were encased in thin pyjama bottoms, his feet were bare.

No, no, no!

He began to shake his head and didn't stop, like a child suffering from neglect.

'This isn't true. I'm not in the clinic any more. I live in, in . . .'

Leon looked at Sven helplessly, because he couldn't remember the address. It was a bungalow, without a cellar, without any neighbours.

Without any tunnels.

'Come on, you visited us last week. It's in the centre of town, and we have separate bedrooms because we want to take things slowly!'

And at night, when the doors are closed, the windows bolted and the motion sensors activated, we take turns sleeping.

'You're living in a dream,' repeated Sven. 'And now it's time for you to wake up.'

'Stay away from me.'

'I'm begging you, Leon. Don't fight it any more.'

'No, go away!'

'Leon, listen to me . . .'

Sven stretched his hand back out to him again. It was a blisteringly hot day and the midday sun was burning down, but Leon could feel nothing but cold.

'She's alive,' he cried, shivering and sinking down to the ground. 'Natalie's alive.'

Sven knelt down and grasped his friend's hands. 'I'm here, Leon. Look at me.'

'No.' Leon pulled his legs in towards himself and buried his face.

'LOOK AT ME!' screamed Sven, tearing Leon's hands from his face.

Then he hit him. Leon's cheek burned like fire. He gave Sven a tear-stained, furious look, and that was when it happened.

His friend began to dissolve in front of his eyes like wax on a warm hotplate.

His forehead stretched upwards and his chin became narrower. Cheekbones became defined where previously there had been only fat. At the same time his hair changed colour, becoming darker until it was almost the same shade of brown as his eyes.

'Wake up,' said Sven, who no longer looked like Sven and wasn't stuttering any more either. Instead, he was suddenly talking as though he had choked on something hot.

'WAKE UP!'

There was a crack. Loud and painful. Then Leon felt like he was being dragged into a suction pipe and pulled upwards.

He gave a start, flung his arms up, kicked around, then stamped the quilt to the foot of the bed and opened his eyes.

At first all he could hear was his own breath, then a soft voice whispered his name anxiously: 'Leon?'

He blinked. Warm sunlight, falling through the blinds, caressed his face. He was sweating.

'Can you hear me? Are you OK?'

A woman leaned over him, so closely that the subtle scent of her favourite perfume filled his nose. A mixture of fresh hay and green tea. Over her larynx shimmered a scar that became lighter when she swallowed.

She stroked his cheek, then her smile disappeared and a familiar melancholy was reflected in her eyes.

'I heard you screaming and came across. Is everything OK?'

Leon nodded. 'Yes, everything's fine.'

He sat up and looked at the clock on the night-stand.

He reached up to his neck and touched his scars. Then, once he had gathered his thoughts, he spoke – still a little uncertain, like every morning – 'Don't worry, Natalie. I'm awake.'

Acknowledgements

Early one morning at about half past two, having just finished writing the nineteenth chapter of this book the night before, I woke up my wife Sandra, who was sleeping next to me, and nervously asked her, 'Did you bring the baby back up from the cellar?'

Dazed, she answered, 'Have you gone mad?'

Then I woke up.

It wasn't the first time I'd done strange things in my sleep. I got married while I was asleep, after all.

Seriously, though. One time I started talking when I was wide awake, and then finished the sentence while I was asleep. First part: 'Tomorrow you'll have to remember . . .' Second part: '. . . not to put the pegs into the exhaust.' Something that baffled my wife just as much as my question about the baby which, in my dream, we were unable to save from whatever danger it faced.

I already described 'sleep paralysis' back in *Der Seelenbrecher* (*The Soul Breaker*) – that uncomfortable sensation where the mind thinks it's awake, but sleep is still holding the body captive. I don't suffer from it all that often, maybe once every two years, but when it does happen there's always a man in the room watching me, and there's nothing I can do when he raises his axe. I want to jump up, scream at him, at least try to signal for him to go for my wife, sleeping next to me, and not me – but all in vain.

I'm definitely in good company with this sleeping disorder. More than 20 per cent of the population suffer from similar symptoms. Of course, not all of us walk through the house, look for hidden doors or sleep-drive their cars to kill somebody like Kenneth Parks did; the case described in the book actually happened. But nonetheless many people sit upright, stare with wide eyes, and some of them talk nonsense like me. Others go into the kitchen, get dressed, write letters, have conversations with people who are awake, or even leave the house.

It's not a laughing matter. There's no way to protect yourself when sleepwalking. There's a much larger risk (and it's much more likely) that people will hurt themselves rather than do anything to harm others.

With that said, I want to clear up one thing – this isn't a work of non-fiction. The events occurring in this book are purely fictional, and any resemblance to living or dead people is, of course, unintentional and purely coincidental.

There is, however, a smidgen of truth in this fictional tale, just like there is in any good lie. The statements Dr Volwarth makes during his first conversation with Leon about sleepwalking are accurate. Research about somnambulism really is still in its infancy.

And let's be honest for a second. Are you 100 per cent sure you know what you're doing at night? If not, you could always go and buy a camera. But if you do, make sure you're alone when you watch the recording the next morning ...

Now, before thanking my wonderful team, who all possess the stuff dreams are made of (see the elegant transition I used there?), I'd like to give you, the reader, a virtual handshake. I'll admit it, I would still be writing even if I didn't have you. An author is simply unable to suppress the urge. But it's a lot more fun with you around, and it also means I'm not forced to put a gun to my publisher's head so that he'll publish my book (but you should prepare yourself anyway, Hans-Peter, just in case the circulation dies down at some point).

I could recite the following names in my sleep, either because they've been with me from the very start or because I deal with them on pretty much a daily basis at Droemer Knaur. So, we've got:

Hans-Peter Übleis, Christian Tesch, Kerstin Reitze de la Maza, Theresa Schenkel, Konstanze Treber, Carsten Sommerfeldt, Noomi Rohrbach, Monika Neudeck, Patricia Keßler, Sibylle Dietzel, Iris Haas, Andrea Bauer and Andrea Heiß.

I hope I'll be forgiven for highlighting my editors Carolin Graehl and Regine Weisbrod in particular, as they suffer from an incurable, almost manic urge to improve books, and I always benefit from it. Also, the credit for the title goes to Carolin (much better than what I suggested!), so thank you for that as well.

If you should ever get the idea in your head that you might like to write a book, you're best off looking at your calendar right now and checking when you could go to ground for a good few months without your family, employer or the police sending out search parties. You're also going to have to sort out someone to do all the work in the meantime (appointments, contracts, money transfers and red tape, organising readings and launches, and a great many other things …). In short, you'll be needing someone like Manuela Raschke, but I'm not telling you her name.

You're also going to need someone to make sure you have a publisher in the first place – my literary agent Roman Hocke, who's worth his weight in gold, as well as his loyal co-workers Claudia von Hornstein and Claudia Bachmann from AVA-International, for instance.

Patrick Hocke, Mark Ryan Balthasar and my wife Sandra spent many a sleepless night working on my website, as did Thomas Zorbach and Marcus Meier from vm-people during all those times when I, once again, couldn't figure out the newest Facebook functions. But hey, all the curried sausages and warm beer I got you guys should be more than enough to say thank you, right?

Also, in case you're wondering why I always look so much better in my press photos than in real life, the answer has a name: Sabrina Rabow. My wonderful press agent always watches me like a hawk in public and makes sure I only ever show myself at my best. And my best can take a while to find!

As always, I'd like to thank my father Freimut as well as my brother Clemens and his wife Sabine for all the familial support they've given me. Their surnames are Fitzek as well! Crazy, I know.

And of course I can't leave out my long-term friends, confidants and accomplices: Arno Müller, Thomas Koschwitz, Stephan Schmitter, Christian Meyer, Jochen Trus, the amazing Zsolt Bács (who directed The Child so well and made the impossible possible), Petra Rode, as well as Barbara Herrmann and Karl Raschke, who gave me many a sadistic idea while on the treadmill (to clarify: I run, he stands next to me, whip in hand).

I'd like to thank all the booksellers, librarians and

organisers of readings and literature festivals, without whom my books would have never found their way to you readers.

And I'd like to thank everyone who *didn't* ask me where I got the idea for *The Nightwalker*. I could say it came to me in a dream, but that would be a lie. All I know is that the idea captivated me to the point that I had to tell everyone nearby as soon as it was in my head. One of the first people who wasn't able to cover his ears in time when I told him, while we were having dinner with some friends, was Christian Becker. His production company Ratpack is responsible for some of the biggest German box-office success stories. He was immediately taken by it and commissioned Iván Sáinz Pardo to create a screenplay adaptation. Thank you so much, Iván, for all the inspiration your ideas gave me while I was still in the writing phase, and I'm really eager to see what the transition to film is going to look like, because one thing is certain – if the money does come in (always a bit tricky in Germany, after all), the book and the film will have to be somewhat different. And there's at least one twist in *The Nightwalker* that, in my opinion, is going to be impossible to transfer to the screen.

Speaking of opinions – you can reach me by email at: fitzek@sebastianfitzek.de and at www.facebook. com/sebastianfitzek.de as per usual.

Finally, before I forget, I really want to thank my wife Sandra, who always gives me her whole-hearted support. And who still hasn't told me if she brought the baby back up from the cellar, by the way. I'm going down there now to take a look for myself.

Wishing you dark dreams,
    Sebastian Fitzek
    Berlin, December 2012
    In a (hopefully) conscious state